INDIAN BANKING

INDIAN BANKING

For the Students of BCom, BBA and Management Courses

S. Natarajan
Deputy General Manager (Retd.)
Reserve Bank of India
Department of Banking Supervision
Central Office, Mumbai

Dr. R. Parameswaran
Associate Professor
Department of Commerce
T.S.A.A.S.T. College, Perur
Coimbatore, Tamil Nadu

S. CHAND PUBLISHING

S. Chand And Company Limited
(ISO 9001 Certified Company)

S. Chand And Company Limited

(ISO 9001 Certified Company)

Head Office: D-92, Sector–2, Noida – 201301, U.P. (India), Ph. 91-120-4682700

Registered Office: A-27, 2nd Floor, Mohan Co-operative Industrial Estate, New Delhi – 110 044, Phone: 011-49731800

www.**schandpublishing.com**; e-mail: **info@schandpublishing.com**

Marketing Offices:

Chennai : Ph: 23632120; chennai@schandpublishing.com
Guwahati : Ph: 2738811, 2735640; guwahati@schandpublishing.com
Hyderabad : Ph: 40186018; hyderabad@schandpublishing.com
Jalandhar : Ph: 4645630; jalandhar@schandpublishing.com
Kolkata : Ph: 23357458, 23353914; kolkata@schandpublishing.com
Lucknow : Ph: 4003633; lucknow@schandpublishing.com
Mumbai : Ph: 25000297; mumbai@schandpublishing.com
Patna : Ph: 2260011; patna@schandpublishing.com

First Edition 2001
Subsequent Editions and Reprints 2002, 2003, 2004, 2005, 2007 (Twice), 2010, 2012 (Twice), 2013
Thoroughly Revised Edition 2015; Reprints 2016 (Twice), 2017, 2018, 2019 (Twice), 2020, 2021, 2022, 2023

Reprint 2024

ISBN: 978-81-219-2037-7 **Product Code:** H8INB48BAIN10ENZX15R

PRINTED IN INDIA

By Vikas Publishing House Private Limited, Plot 20/4, Site-IV, Industrial Area Sahibabad, Ghaziabad – 201 010 and Published by S. Chand And Company Limited, A-27, 2nd Floor, Mohan Co-operative Industrial Estate, New Delhi – 110 044.

PREFACE TO THE REVISED EDITION

With the potential to become the largest banking industry in the world, India's banking sector is expanding rapidly. The Indian banks are now utilizing the latest technologies to carry out transactions and communicate with all sections of the business and society. The Indian banking sector consists of public sector, private sector and foreign banks along with regional rural banks and cooperative banks.

The Indian banking industry has emerged to meet out the competitive dynamics of the new Indian and global financial markets and is able to address the issues and challenges of globalization. Banks, the proactive players, by employing information technology are capable of meeting the multifarious requirements of the large and diversified customer base.

The current decade is witnessing the multidimensional approaches of the banking industry through which almost everyone is brought under the bank net. Banking industry in India is dedicated for the development of trade and commerce by supporting their needs at all dimensions. Besides, Indian banking sector has shouldering the social responsibilities of the modern governments, for example, by facilitating LPG subsidy policy of the government and the like. Hence, it is essential to learn about the essence of the fast growing, dynamic and technology blended operations of the banking industry. On this background, the current edition is brought out to ease the understanding of the students about Indian banking.

Many concepts are given with new supporting data, chats and diagrams to enable the readers to capture the essence of the concepts and ideas at a glance.

We hope, this edition will be more useful. It will cater to the needs of commerce and management students in understanding the structure, concepts and operations of the Indian banking sector in the modern economy.

Suggestions for improvement in the contents and quality of this book will be gratefully acknowledged.

S. Natarajan
B-2/66, Snehadhara
Dadabhai Cross Road No.3
Mumbai-400 056
E-mail: SNR_9669@hotmail.com

Dr. R. Parameswaran
Associate Professor in Commerce
T.S.A.A.S.T College
Perur, Coimbatore-641 010

ACKNOWLEDGEMENTS

The authors gratefully acknowledge the valuable efforts, suggestions and clarifications provided by many in bringing out this book to life.

We gratefully acknowledge the valuable guidance and suggestions provided by Shri C.R. Gopalasundaram, Principal, Bankers Training College in bringing out this book.

We are thankful to our teachers, colleagues and friends for their significant support. Our thanks are also due to Dr. Amarchand of University of Madras and Mrs. Alagammal, Principal, Sri Parasakthi College for Women for their encouragement and advice. We owe a special gratitude to friends in the banking industry, particularly the Library Staff of Reserve Bank Staff College and Department of Economic Analysis and Policy (RBI Library), Messrs. L.Ponnudurai (DIT), N.M. Ansari and R.D. Bangar (DRRP) of Reserve Bank of India, P. Krishnamoorthy of Indian Bank and M.V. Ravichandran of Punjab National Bank. We express our grateful thanks to every one who has contributed even in a small way towards successful completion of this book.

We are honoured by the grace and blessings of His Holiness Thavathiru Santhalinga Ramaswamy Adigalar.

Mrs. Indubala Natarajan deserves special thanks for her support and encouragement during the preparation of this book.

We are thankful to the management and the editorial team of S. Chand & Company Pvt. Ltd, New Delhi for all help and support in publication of this book.

S. Natarajan
Dr. R. Parameswaran

CONTENTS

1. INTRODUCTION **1–28**

1.1. Evolution of Financial System 1
1.1.1. Limitations of Barter System 1
1.1.2. Central Role of Banking in the Economy 3
1.2. Evolution of Banking 4
1.2.1. Banking Company 5
1.2.2. Banking 5
1.3. Development of Banking in India 6
1.3.1. Meaning and Definition of Banking 7
1.3.2. Scheduled Banks 8
1.4. Features of Banking 9
1.5. Classification of Banks 9
1.6. Banking Systems 12
1.6.1. Unit Banking 13
1.6.2. Branch Banking 15
1.6.3. Correspondent Banking System 19
1.6.4. Group Banking 19
1.6.5. Chain Banking 20
1.6.6. Pure Banking and Mixed Banking 21
1.6.7. Relationship Banking 22
1.6.8. Narrow Banking 22
1.6.9. Universal Banking 22
1.6.10. Regional Banking 22
1.6.11. Local Area Banks 23
1.6.12. Retail Banking 23
1.6.13. Wholesale Banking 23
1.6.14. Private Banking 23
1.7. Banks and Economic Development 23

2. NATIONALISATION AND PRIVATISATION OF BANKS **29–37**

2.1. Social Control over Banks 29
2.2. Nationalisation of Major Commercial Banks 30
2.3. Reasons for Nationalisation 31
2.3.1. The then Prime Minister, Srimathi Indira Gandhi 31
2.3.2. Prof.Sayers 31
2.3.3. Views given by Others: 31
2.4. Criticisms Against Nationalisation of the Banks 33

2.5. Achievements after Nationalisation 34
2.6. Privatisation of Banks in India 34
2.6.1. Privatization of Commercial Banks 34
2.6.2. Arguments for Privatization 35
2.6.3. Arguments against Privatization 36

3. MONEY MARKET **38–60**

3.1. Definitions of Money Market 38
3.2. Objectives of Money Market 38
3.3. General Features of Money Market 39
3.4. Money Market and Capital Market 39
3.4.1. Differences between Money Market and Capital Market 40
3.5. Characteristics of Developed Money Market 41
3.6. Importance of a Developed Money Market 42
3.7. Constituents of Money Market 42
3.8. Indian Money Market 43
3.8.1. Structure of Indian Money Market 43
3.8.2. Features of Indian Money Market 44
3.8.3. Measures to Strengthen the Indian Money Market 45
3.8.4. Role of RBI in Indian Money Market 46
3.8.5. Money Market Instruments in India 46
3.8.5.1. General Features of Money Market Instruments 46
3.8.5.2. Instruments Traded in Indian Money Market 47
3.9. Discount and Finance House of India (DFHI) 57
3.10. Comparison of London, New York and Indian Money Market 58

4. COMMERCIAL BANKS **61–79**

4.1. General Classification of Banks 61
4.1.1. Scheduled Banks 61
4.1.2. Non-Scheduled Banks 62
4.2. Functions of Commercial Banks 62
4.2.1. Primary Functions of Commercial Banks 62
4.2.2. Secondary Functions of Commercial Banks 67
4.2.3. Fee Based Services of Commercial Banks 69
4.3. Lending to Sensitive Sectors 74
4.4. Balance Sheet of Commercial Banks 75
4.5. Off-Balance Sheet Items 77

5. CREDIT CREATION **80–87**

5.1. Loans Create Deposits 80
5.2. Simple Credit Creation 80
5.3. Multiple Expansion/Creation of Credit 81

5.3.1. The Formula for Credit Creation 82
5.3.2. Creation of Deposit is Essentially an Exchange of Claims 83
5.4. Scope for Multiple Creation of Credit 83
5.5. Credit Contraction 83
5.6. Limitations on Credit Creation 84
5.7. Criticism of the Theory of Credit Creation 86
5.7.1. Answers to These Criticisms 86

6. COMMERCIAL BANKS AND RURAL FINANCING 88–96

6.1. Commercial Banks and Rural Credit 88
6.2. Types of Agricultural Advances 90
6.2.1. Classification on the Basis of Time 90
6.2.2. Classifications on the Basis of Method of Advances 91
6.2.3. Classification on the Basis of Purpose 92
6.2.4. Flow of Credit to the Agricultural Sector 93
6.3. Institutional Setup for Rural Credit 93
6.4. Lending to Priority Sectors by Commercial Banks 94
6.5. DRI Scheme 95

7. CO-OPERATIVE BANKS AND DEVELOPMENT BANKS 97–129

7.1. Co-Operative Banking In India 97
7.1.1. Differences between Co-operative Banks and Commercial Banks 97
7.1.2. Co-operative Banking in India 98
7.1.3. Types of Co-Operative Credit Institutions Based on Structure 99
7.1.3.1. Urban Cooperative Banks 100
7.1.3.2. Rural Co-operatives 101
7.2. Regional Rural Banks 105
7.2.1. Objectives of Regional Rural Banks 106
7.2.2. Capital Structure and Sponsorship 106
7.2.3. Management of Regional Rural Banks 106
7.2.4. Area of Operation 107
7.2.5. Functions of RRBs 107
7.2.6. Consolidation of RRBs 107
7.2.7. Progress and Achievement of RRBs 107
7.3. Development Banks 109
7.3.1. National Bank for Agriculture and Rural Development (NABARD) 110
7.3.1.1. Strategies of NABARD 111
7.3.1.2. Promotional Roles of NABARD 111
7.3.1.3. NABARD and Refinance Facilities 114
7.3.1.4. Criteria for Refinance 115
7.3.2. Industrial Finance Corporation of India (IFCI) 115
7.3.2.1. Services of IFCI 116

7.3.2.2. Targeted Business Segments 117
7.3.2.3. Some Sectors That have Directly Benefited from IFCI Include 118
7.3.2.4. Debenture Trustee 118
7.3.3. Industrial Development of India (IDBI) 118
7.3.3.1. Main functions of IDBI 119
7.3.4. SIDBI - Small Industries Development Bank of India 122
7.3.4.1. Schemes of SIDBI 122
7.3.5. Export Import Bank of India 124
7.3.5.1. Functions of EXIM Bank 125
7.3.5.2. Financing and Services of EXIM Bank 126

8. CENTRAL BANKING 130–137

8.1. Definitions of Central Bank 130
8.2. Nature of Central Banking 131
8.3. Central Banking and Commercial Banking 131
8.4. Functions of the Central Bank 132

9. CENTRAL BANKING AND CREDIT CONTROL 138–150

9.1. Meaning of Credit Control 138
9.2. Advantages and Dangers of the Credit Creation 138
9.2.1. Advantages of Credit Creation 138
9.2.2. Possible Problems of Credit Creation 139
9.3. Methods of Credit Control 139
9.3.1. Quantitative Methods of Credit Control 139
9.3.1.1. Bank Rate Policy 140
9.3.1.2. Open Market Operations 142
9.3.1.3. Variation of Cash Reserve Ratios 143
9.3.1.4. 'Repo' Transactions 145
9.3.2. Qualitative/Selective Methods of Credit Control 145
9.3.2.1. Fixation of Margin Requirements 146
9.3.2.2. Rationing of Credit 146
9.3.2.3. Regulation of Consumer Credit 147
9.3.2.4. Control through Directives 147
9.3.2.5. Moral Suasion 147
9.3.2.6. Publicity 148
9.3.2.7. Direct Action 148
9.4. Monetary Policy of the Central Bank 148
9.4.1. Objectives of Monetary Policy 148
9.4.2. Benefits Monetary Policy 149

10. RESERVE BANK OF INDIA **151–166**

10.1. Objectives for Establishment of RBI 151
10.2. Evolution of the Reserve Bank of India 151
10.3. Management and Administration of Reserve Bank of India 152
10.3.1. Central Board 153
10.3.2. Number of Directors in Central Board 153
10.3.3. Departments of RBI 153
10.4. Functions of Reserve Bank of India 154
10.4.1. Traditional Functions 155
10.4.2. Promotional Functions 161
10.4.3. Supervisory Functions 162
10.5. RBI Balance Sheet 163

11. RESERVE BANK OF INDIA AND CREDIT CONTROL **167–179**

11.1. Methods of Credit Control 167
11.1.1. Quantitative Credit Control by RBI 168
11.1.2. Qualitative/Selective Credit Control by RBI 176

12. RBI- AGRICULTURAL AND INDUSTRIAL FINANCE **180–191**

12.1. Reserve Bank of India and Agricultural Finance 180
12.1.1. Agricultural Credit Department 180
12.1.2. Funds for Agricultural Development 181
12.1.3. Financial Assistance to Co-operative Sector 181
12.1.4. Establishment of Agricultural Credit Board 182
12.1.5. Establishment of NABARD 182
12.1.6. National Agricultural Insurance Scheme 185
12.2. Reserve Bank of India and Industrial Finance 186
12.2.1. Establishment of Institutional Framework for Industrial Finance 186
12.2.2. Transfer of Loan Accounts from One Bank to Another 187
12.2.3. Bridge Loan 187
12.2.4. Prompt Settlement of Bills of Small Scale Industrial Units 187
12.2.5. Role of RBI in Rehabilitation of Sick Industrial Units 187
12.2.6. High Level Committee on Credit to SSI 187
12.2.7. Export Finance 187
12.2.8. Foreign Exchange Benefits 188

13. STATE BANK OF INDIA **192–209**

13.1. Evaluation of State Bank of India 192
13.1.2. Nationalisation of the Imperial Bank 193
13.2. Management of the Bank 194
13.3. Structure and Organisation of the Bank 194

13.4.	Functions of State Bank of India	195
13.5.	Role of SBI in Economic Development	207
14.	**CREDIT CARDS**	**210–218**
14.1.	Meaning and Definition of Credit Card	210
14.2.	Mechanism of Credit Card Operation	211
	14.2.1. Parties involved	211
	14.2.2. Process of Credit Card Operation	211
14.3.	Types of Credit Cards	212
14.4.	Advantages of Credit Cards	213
	14.4.1. Benefits to the Bank	213
	14.4.2. Benefits to the Cardholder	214
	14.4.3. Benefits to the Merchant Establishments	215
14.5.	Limitations of Credit Cards	215
14.6.	Farmers' Credit Card	216
15.	**MERCHANT BANKING**	**219–232**
15.1.	Definition of Merchant Bankers	220
	15.1.1. Definitions of Financial Experts on Merchant Banks	220
15.2.	Reasons for the Growth of Merchant Banking in India	220
15.3.	Objectives of Merchant Banking	220
15.4.	Features of Merchant Bankers	221
15.5.	Difference between Merchant Banking and Commercial Banking	222
15.6.	Types of Merchant Banking Organizations	222
15.7.	Functions of Merchant Bankers	223
15.8.	Merchant Banking in India-SEBI Guidelines on Merchant Banking	230
16.	**FACTORING SERVICE**	**233–243**
16.1.	Factoring: Conceptual Framework	233
16.2.	Definition of Factoring	234
16.3.	Features of Factoring Service	234
16.4.	Mechanism of Factoring	235
16.5.	Factoring –Combination of Services	236
16.6.	Factoring and Bill Discounting	236
16.7.	Types of Factoring	238
	16.7.1. Domestic Factoring	238
	16.7.2. International Factoring	239
16.8.	Benefits of Factoring service	240
	16.8.1. Benefits to the Clients	240
	16.8.2. Benefits to the Banks	241
16.9.	Limitations of Factoring	241
16.10.	Factoring in India	242

17. MUTUAL FUNDS 244–257

17.1. Meaning of Mutual Fund 244
17.2. Concept of Operation of Mutual Funds 244
17.3. Organisation of Mutual Fund 245
17.3.1. Sponsor 246
17.3.2. Mutual Fund Trust 246
17.3.3. Asset Management Company 247
17.3.4. Custodian 247
17.3.5. Transfer Agents 247
17.4. Types of Mutual Fund Schemes 248
17.4.1 Classifications on the Basis of the Structure of the Funds 248
17.4.1.1. Open Ended Schemes 248
17.4.1.2. Close Ended Schemes 249
17.4.1.3. Interval/Hybrid Schemes 250
17.4.2 Classifications on the Basis of Investment Objectives 250
17.4.3 Generic Type Schemes 251
17.4.3.1. General Schemes 251
17.4.3.2. Special Schemes 251
17.5. Regulation of Mutual Funds in India 251
17.5.1. SEBI (Mutual Funds) Regulations-The Rights of Investors under SEBI (MF) Regulations, 1993 252
17.6. Net Asset Value of a Mutual Fund Scheme 253
17.7. Advantages of Mutual Funds 253
17.8. Risks Involved in Mutual Funds 255

18. ACCOUNTS OF NON-RESIDENTS 258–263

18.1. Foreign Exchange Management Act 1999 (FEMA 1999) 258
18.2. Non-Resident Indian (NRI) 258
18.3. Non-Resident Accounts 259
18.3.1. Non-Resident Ordinary Rupee Account (NRO Account) 259
18.3.2. Non-Resident (External) Rupee Account (NRE Account) 260
18.3.3. Foreign Currency Non Resident (Bank) Account – FCNR (B) Account 261
18.4. Foreign Currency Accounts of Residents 262
18.4.1. RFC Accounts 262
18.4.2. Exchange Earners Foreign Currency Accounts (EEFC Accounts) 263

19. CUSTOMER SERVICE AND OMBUDSMAN SCHEME IN BANKING SECTOR 264–277

19.1. Customer Orientation 264
19.2. Basic Aspects of Customer Service 265
19.2.1. Deposit Accounts 266
19.2.2. Remittances Service 267
19.2.3. Collections Service 268

19.2.4. Loans and Advances 269
19.2.5. Discipline and Attitudes 269
19.2.6. Complaints 269
19.2.7. Other Services 270
19.3 Know Your Customer (KYC) Policy 270
19.3.1. Definition of Customer 271
19.3.2. Objectives of Know Your Customer 271
19.3.3. Key Elements of KYC Policy 271
19.3.4. KYC Policy and Customer Education 272
19.3.5. KYC Policy and Introduction of New Technologies – Credit Cards/Debit Cards / Smart Cards/Gift Cards 272
19.3.6. Existing Customer 272
19.3.7. Customer Identification Procedures 273
19.4 Banking Ombudsman Scheme 274
19.4.1. Scope of Complaints 274
19.4.2. Present Scenario 275

20. RECENT TRENDS IN INDIAN BANKING 278–290

20.1. Types of Financing 278
20.1.1. Take-out Financing 278
20.1.2. Revolving Credit Facility 279
20.1.3. Evergreening of Loan 279
20.1.4. Syndicated Loan 279
20.1.5. Bridge Loan 279
20.1.6. Consortium Finance 280
20.1.7. Preferred Financing 280
20.1.8. Guarantee Services / Non-fund Based Business 280
20.2. Repayment Methods 281
20.2.1. Bullet Payment System 281
20.2.2. Balloon Payment System 281
20.3. Venture Capital 281
20.4. Banknet 282
20.5. Deposit Insurance Scheme 282
20.5.1. Coverage 282
20.5.2. Types of Deposits Covered 283
20.6. Gold Deposit Scheme 283
20.6.1. Features. 283
20.7. Core Banking Systems 284
20.8. Bancassurance 284
20.8.1. Factors Influencing Bancassurance 284

20.8.2. Bancassurance in India 285
20.8.3. Benefits of Bancassurance 285
20.9. Payment Systems in India 285

21. BANKING AND TECHNOLOGY 291–313

21.1. Importance of Technology in Banking Industry 292
21.2. Delivery Channels of Banking Sector 293
21.2.1. Branches 293
21.2.2. ATM 293
21.2.3. Phone Banking 296
21.2.4. Kiosks 298
21.2.5. PC Banking through Personal Financial Software 298
21.2.6. PC Banking through Proprietary Software 298
21.2.7. Internet Banking 299
21.2.8. Commercial Online Service Banking 299
21.2.9. Interactive TV 299
21.2.10. Smart Cards and E-Cash 299
21.3. Internet Banking 300
21.3.1. Growth in Internet Banking 300
21.3.2. Types of Internet Banking 300
21.3.3. Services of Internet Banking 301
21.4. E-Banking 301
21.4.1. Meaning of e-banking 301
21.4.2. E-Banking Structure 302
21.4.3. Components of E-Banking 303
21.4.4. E-Banking- Service Requirements 303
21.4.5. E-Banking Services 304
21.4.6. Advantages of E-Banking 304
21.4.7. Limitations of E-Banking 307
21.5. Electronic Banking in India 307
21.5.1. RTGS -Electronic Payment System 307
21.5.2. NEFT -National Electronic Funds Transfer 308
21.5.3. Cheque Truncation 309
21.5.4. NSS- National Settlement System 310
21.5.5. SFMS -Structured Financial Messaging System 310
21.5.6. SWIFT-Receiving Payments from Outside India 310
21.6. Computerisation of Bank Branches 310
21.6.1. Opportunity for Indian Banking Sector in Branch Computerisation 311
21.6.2. Computerisation of Banks in India 311
21.6.3. Present Position of Computerisation of Banks in India 312

ANNEXURE-I 314

Banking Sector Reforms- Second Narasimham Committee Report;
Financial Markets –Reform Measures.

ANNEXURE-II 319

Indian Banks Association

ANNEXURE-III 320

List of Commercial Banks in India

Model Question Papers 322–335

CHAPTER 1

Introduction

1.1 EVOLUTION OF FINANCIAL SYSTEM

Before examining the evolution and importance of banking, we must know the meaning of money. Money cannot originate by order of the Government or by some sort of social agreement by the people and it must always originate in the processes of the free market. Before the coin/currency system, there was barter system. Goods were produced by the people who were familiarize in that production, and their surpluses if any were exchanged for the goods produced by others. Every product had its exchange price in terms of all other products. Thus, their needs were fulfilled with the process of exchange *i.e.*, barter system. It was carried on the basis of mutually beneficial exchanges.

1.1.1 Limitations of Barter System

In barter, there were certain basic limitations:

(*a*) In barter system, existence of market and merchants become difficult and results in many numbers of transactions.

(*b*) Since the scope of exchange is limited in barter system, it affects the production of goods and services.

(*c*) To buy the goods, people have to find a seller who wants exactly what they have available for exchange.

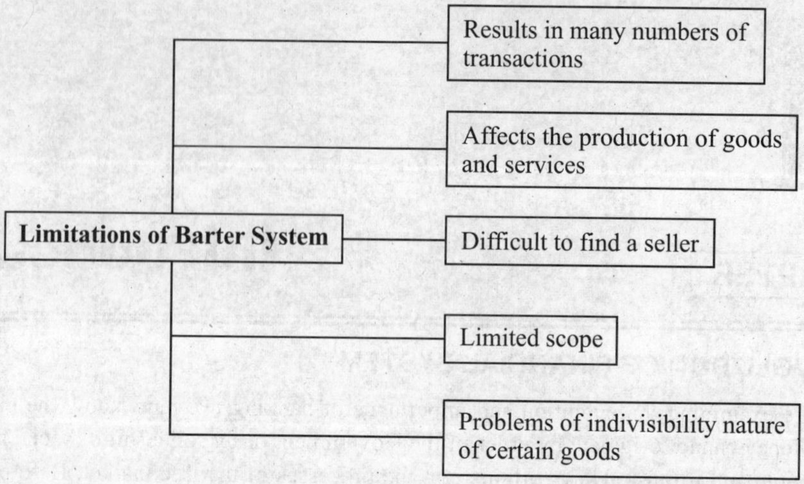

(*d*) The barter system makes it difficult the creation of market where the merchants buy stocks of goods in exchange for value of something in common. Under barter system merchants cannot go on buying all kinds of commodities in anticipation of future sales.

(*e*) The scope of barter system is very limited and hinders the process of exchange. For example, if a meat dealer wanted to buy cloths, he had to find a weaver who wanted to buy meat at the same time. If the weaver had sufficient meat with him already, how was the meat dealer going to buy cloth? He was not sure that he could find a weaver who needed meat. This feature of barter system is called the *double coincidence of wants*.

(*f*) The next problem is due to *indivisibility nature of some goods*. For example a person owns a house would like to sell it and instead, purchase a motor vehicle, household furniture and the like. How can the person get those things under barter system? He could not split his house into different segments and exchange each one for other products. Since the house is *indivisible* and lose all of their value if it gets split in to different segments, we face unsolvable problems. The same would be true of motor cars, machines, and other large-sized products. If houses or motorcars or machines can not easily be bartered, they are not produced in large quantity. The next severe problem with the barter system is that it is difficult to compute *business results*. Business firms must be able to calculate whether they are making or losing income in each of their transactions. But in the barter system, computation of profit or loss would be a very difficult task.

Therefore barter system could not manage modern industrial economies. And to overcome the limitations of barter system the money was invented. Thus, money is the advancement in the history of civilization and in man's economic progress. Money as an element of exchange permits people to overcome all the difficulties of barter system. It should be noted that by the introduction of money the act of sale is separated from the act of purchase. Now to have a better living, man struggles hard to earn money—the medium of exchange. When he earns more to his requirements, he wanted to employ those surplus funds. The flows of money facilitate lending and borrowing transactions in the economy. This obviously encourages economic development and paves the way for the efficient financial system in the economy.

The financial system of an economy includes financial institutions and financial markets. From the following diagram we can easily understand the role of a financial system.

Role of Financial System in the Economy

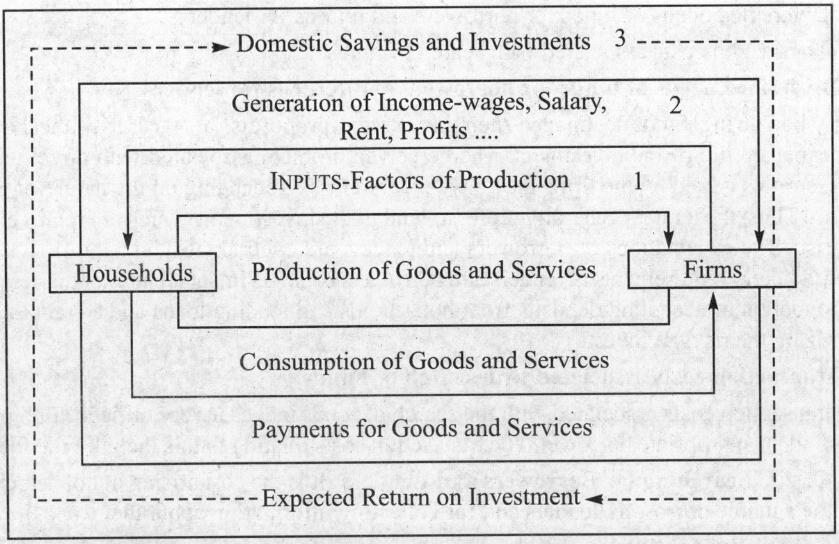

Here, the expected return is a claim for a certain sum of money at some future date.

The important role of the financial system includes the following:

(*i*) Facilitate lending and borrowing

(*ii*) Provides payments mechanism

(*iii*) Enable households to adjust their investment portfolio in financial markets.

1.1.2 Central Role of Banking in the Economy

To facilitate this circular flow of funds, we need financial intermediaries. In all types of economies, both developed and developing, banks play a vital role in their respective financial system. Especially, in developing economies, where the middle income and lower income groups forms majority, the role of banks is inevitable to move the economy to the next stage.

Central Role of Banks as Financial Intermediary

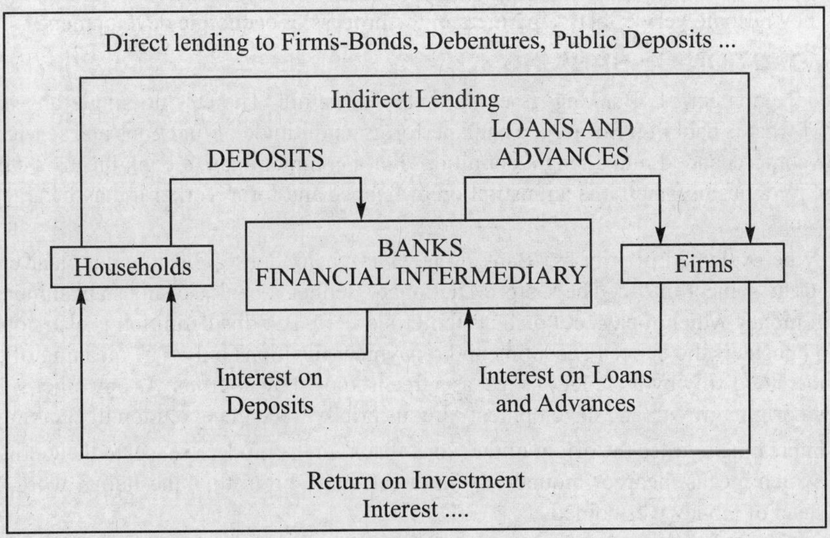

The main reasons for the existence of banks as financial intermediary include the following:

(*a*) Diversified needs of funds for borrowers and returns for lenders.

(*b*) Transaction costs associated with search of funds.

(*a*) Diversified needs of funds for borrowers and returns for lenders:

Firms borrowing funds to finance their investment proposals, aim to repay the borrowing over the expected life of the investment. The perceived problem associated with direct lending is that the securities issued by the firms may have a default risk depending on the nature of business investment. Thus, the lenders generally prefer to lend to the investments which are relatively liquid and low-risk. The expectations of borrowers and lenders are contradictory in nature. To reconcile these contradictory requirements of lenders and borrowers banks as financial intermediaries perform the basic function of accepting deposits from households and lending loans and advances to firms by minimizing the risks to investors.

(*b*) Transaction costs associated with search of Funds

The transaction costs associated with the search of funds makes it very difficult for a potential lender to find an appropriate borrower. The transaction costs relating to this includes the following:

(*i*) **Cost of Searching for Borrowers and Lenders:** It is the cost arising out of searching for the suitable borrowers/lenders and for collecting information about them.

(*ii*) **Cost of Verification:** To avoid risks lenders need to verify the accuracy and authenticity of the information provided by borrowers.

(*iii*) **Monitoring costs:** After the provision of loans, the lenders to avoid the default risk must monitor the activities of the borrowers.

(*iv*) **Cost of Enforcement**: Such costs arise when there is a breach of contract or any default done by the borrower. In such a situation, the lender may have to enforce the terms of the contract agreed upon initially, or to recover the debt in case of default.

All these costs are minimized by the existence of banking institutions and their efficient operations in the economy. Banks as financial intermediaries contribute to risk management by monitoring borrowers to whom credit has been extended. Bankers play very important role in the economic life of the nation. The health of the economy is closely related to the soundness of its banking system. Although banks create no new wealth but their borrowing, lending and related activities facilitate the process of production, distribution, exchange and consumption of wealth. In this way they become very effective partners in the process of economic development.

1.2 EVOLUTION OF BANKING

The development of 'Banking' is evolutionary in nature. There is no single answer to the question of what is banking. Because, a bank performs a multitude of functions and services which cannot be comprehended into a single definition. For a common man, a bank means a storehouse of money, for a businessman it is an institution of finance and for a worker it may be a depository for his savings.

It may be explained in brief as "Banking is what a bank does". But it is not clear enough to understand the subject in full. The Oxford Dictionary defines a bank as "an establishment for the custody of money which it pays out on a customer's order". But this definition is also not enough, because it considers the deposit accepting and repayment functions only. The meaning of the bank can be understood only by its functions just as a tree is known by its fruits. As any other subjects, it has its own origin, growth and development . Let us briefly trace the evolution of Banking.

It is interesting to trace the origin of the word 'bank' in the modern sense, to the German word "Banck" which means, heap or mound or joint stock fund. From this, the Italian word "Banco" meaning heap of money was coined.

Some people have the opinion that the word "bank " is derived from the French words "bancus" or "banque" which means a 'bench'. Initially, the bankers, the Jews in Lombardy, transacted their business on benches in the market place and the bench resembled the banking counter. If a banker failed, his 'banque' (bench) was broken up by the people, hence the word "bankrupt" has come. In simple term, bankrupt means a person who has lost all his money, wealth or financial resources.

Thus, the origin of the word bank can be traced as follows.

Banck – German (Joint stock fund)

↓

Banco – Italian (Heap of money)

↓

Bancus/ – French (Bench/chest a place where valuables are kept)
Banque

↓

Bank – English (common meaning prevalent today *i.e.*, as an institution accepting money as deposit for lending)

In India, the Banking Regulation Act 1949, under which banks are regulated by the Reserve Bank of India, defines a banking company and banking as under:

1.2.1 Banking Company

The Banking Regulation Act, 1949 defines a banking company as a company which transacts the business of banking in India [Section 5(*c*)].

1.2.2 Banking

Section 5(*b*) defines banking as accepting for the purpose of lending or investment of deposits of money from the public, repayable on demand or otherwise and withdrawable by cheque, draft, order or otherwise. Section 49A of the Act prohibits any institution other than a banking company to accept deposit money from public withdrawable by cheque. Students may note that the essence of banking business is the function of accepting deposits from public with the facility of withdrawal of money by cheque. In other words, the combination of the functions of acceptance of public deposits and withdrawal of the money by cheques by any institution cannot be performed without the approval of Reserve Bank.

The origin of modern banks is traced to three important sources. They are,

(*i*) the goldsmiths

(*ii*) the money lenders and

(*iii*) the merchant bankers.

The goldsmith by virtue of dealing in Gold, which is a very valuable item, had facilities for the safe keeping of valuables. He accepted for safe custody the money, another important valuable item, belonging to his customers. The goldsmiths began to lend the money knowing that all the depositors do not withdraw their savings at a time. The money lender lent his surplus funds to the needy and earned the income by way of interest. The merchant bankers were primarily trader and had to oblige his customers by accepting their money for safe custody. He was doing the banking business as a side occupation. Modern banks retain all the characteristics of these three types of institutions/functions.

Banking made its first appearance as a public enterprise in the year 1157 in Italy with the establishment of 'Bank of Venice'. The 'Bank of Barcelona' was started in 1401. The 'Bank of Genoa' in 1407 and the 'Bank of Amsterdam' in 1609. The Lombards who migrated to Europe and England from Italy were responsible for the development of modern banking.

When severe restrictions were imposed on them by the King Charles II, their business was affected at large. The goldsmiths were gradually replaced by private bankers. After the Banking Act was passed in 1833 in England, the growth of joint stock commercial banking was accelerated. Foundations were laid for the growth of modern commercial banking during the 19th century.

1.3 DEVELOPMENT OF BANKING IN INDIA

Banking in India is indeed as old as Himalayas. But, the banking functions became an effective force only after the first decade of 20th century. To understand the history of modern banking in India, one has to refer to the "English Agency Houses" established by the East India Company. These Agency Houses, were basically trading firms and carrying on banking business as part of their main business. Because of this dual functions and lack of their own capital (Agency Houses depend entirely on deposits for their Capital requirements) they failed and vanished from the scene during the third decade of 18th century.

The East India Company laid the foundations for modern banking in the first half of the 19th century with the establishment of the following three banks:

(*i*) Bank of Bengal in 1809
(*ii*) Bank of Bombay in 1840
(*iii*) Bank of Madras in 1843

These banks are also known as "Presidency Banks" and they functioned well as independent units.

During the last part of 19th century and early phase of 20th century, the 'Swadeshi Movement' induced the establishment of a number of banks with Indian Management. For example, Punjab National Bank Ltd in 1895. The Bank of India Ltd in 1906. The Canara Bank Ltd in 1906, The Indian Bank Ltd in 1907, The Bank of Baroda Ltd in 1908, The Central Bank of India Ltd in 1911 and many other banks were established on the same line. But most of the weak banks went bankrupt due to wrong policy decisions taken by the management and due to severe banking crisis during 1913-1918 the period of World War I. However, the stronger and well managed banks like those mentioned above survive the crisis.

In 1920, the "Imperial Bank of India Act" was passed for amalgamating the three Presidency Banks. As such, the 'Imperial Bank of India' was established in 1921. It was given power to hold Government funds and manage the Public debt. The branches of the bank were functioning as clearing houses (Agency for effecting settlement of funds among banks). However, it was not authorised to issue currency.

Even though the need for a Central Bank was felt in the 18th century, it could be materialised only in the 20th century. On the basis of the recommendations of the Banking Enquiry Committee, the Reserve Bank of India Act was passed in 1934. Accordingly the Reserve Bank of India was constituted in 1935 to regulate the issue of Bank notes, securing monetary stability in India and to operate the currency and credit system of the Country to its economic development. Initially, it was constituted as a private shareholders bank with a fully paid up capital of ₹5 Crore. After independence, there was a general attitude towards its nationalisation. Thus, the 'Reserve Bank of India' (Transferred to public ownership) Act was passed in 1948. Accordingly, the entire Share Capital of the bank was acquired by the Central Government from the private shareholders against compensation and it was nationalised on Jan 1, 1949. The total value of compensation paid by Government amounted to ₹5.54 crore or ₹118.63 per share of ₹100 paid up. It is interesting to note that the paid up capital of Reserve Bank continues to remain at ₹5.00 crore even now.

In 1955, the 'State Bank of India Act' was passed. Accordingly the 'Imperial Bank' was nationalised and 'State Bank of India' emerged with the objective of extension of banking facilities on a large scale, specifically in the rural and semi-urban areas and for various other public purposes.

In 1959, the 'State Bank of India' (Subsidiary Banks) Act was passed by which the public sector banking was further extended. The following banks were made the subsidiaries of State Bank of India:

(*i*) The State Bank of Bikaner
(*ii*) The State Bank of Jaipur
(*iii*) The State Bank of Indore
(*iv*) The State Bank of Mysore
(*v*) The State Bank of Patiala
(*vi*) The State Bank of Hyderabad
(*vii*) The State Bank of Saurashtra
(*viii*) The State Bank of Travancore

In 1963, the first two banks were amalgamated under the name of "The State Bank of Bikaner and Jaipur". Then, the seven subsidiaries continued till 2008, when the process of consolidation of SBI began with the merger of subsidiaries. State Bank of Saurashtra merged with SBI in 2008 and State Bank of Indore merged in 2010. Thus, at the end of 2012, in State Bank group there are 5 subsidiaries with State Bank of India.

In 1969, fourteen major Indian commercial banks were nationalised. These banks are Allahabad Bank, Bank of Baroda, Bank of India, Canara Bank, Central Bank of India, Dena Bank, Indian Bank, Indian Overseas Bank, Punjab National Bank, Syndicate Bank, Union Bank of India, United Bank of India, United Commercial Bank and Vijaya Bank. And in 1980 six more banks were nationalised. These banks constitute the public sector banks while the other scheduled banks and non-scheduled banks are in the private sector.

1.3.1 Meaning and Definition of Banking

A bank is an institution which deals in money and credit. Thus bank is an intermediary which handles other people's money both for their advantage and to its own profit. But bank is not merely a trader in money but also an important manufacturer of money. In other words, a bank is a factory of credit.

Let us see the definitions of bank and banking, given by various authorities.

Name of the Expert	*Definitions*
Crowther	Bank is the one that collects money from those who have it to spare or who are saving it out of their income and lends the money so collected to those who require it.
Dr. L. Hart	The banker is the one who in the ordinary course of business honours cheques drawn upon him by persons from and for whom he receives money on current accounts.
Sir Jhon Paget	No person or body corporate otherwise can be a banker who does not, (*i*) Take deposit accounts (*ii*) Take current accounts (*iii*) Issue and pay cheques, and (*iv*) Collect cheques,for his customers.
Sir kinley	A bank is an establishment which makes to individuals such advances of money as may be required and to which individuals entrust money when not required by them for use.
Prof. Sayers	Banks are not merely purveyors of money but also in an important sense, manufacturers of money.

Although the above definitions have described the meaning of bank, none of them precisely defined, 'Banking' incorporating its entire functions. However, an attempt has been made in sec 5(1) (*b* & *c*) of the Banking Regulation Act 1949 to define 'Banking' and 'Banking company'.

According to sec. 5 (1) (*b*), "Banking means accepting for the purpose of lending or investment, of deposits of money from the public, repayable on demand or otherwise and withdrawable by cheques, draft, order or otherwise".

Sec. 5 (1) (*c*) defines banking company as, "any company which transacts the business of banking in India".

1.3.2 Scheduled Banks

The commercial banking structure in India consists of:

- Scheduled Commercial Banks in India
- Non-scheduled Banks in India

Scheduled Banks in India are the banks which have been included in the Second Schedule of Reserve Bank of India (RBI) Act, 1934. RBI in turn includes only those banks in this schedule which satisfy the criteria laid down vide section 42 (6) (*a*) of the Act.

Scheduled banks in India includes, the State Bank of India constituted under the State Bank of India Act, 1955, a subsidiary bank as defined in the State Bank of India (Subsidiary Banks) Act, 1959, a corresponding new bank constituted under section 3 of the Banking Companies (Acquisition and Transfer of Undertakings) Act, 1970, or under section 3 of the Banking Companies (Acquisition and Transfer of Undertakings) Act, 1980, or any other bank being a bank included in the Second Schedule to the Reserve Bank of India Act, 1934, but does not include a co-operative bank.

Categories of Scheduled Commercial Banks:

Commercial Banks refer to both scheduled and non-scheduled commercial banks which are regulated under Banking Regulation Act, 1949.

(*a*) Scheduled Commercial Banks: Scheduled Commercial Banks in India are categorised in five different groups according to their ownership and/or nature of operation. These bank groups are:

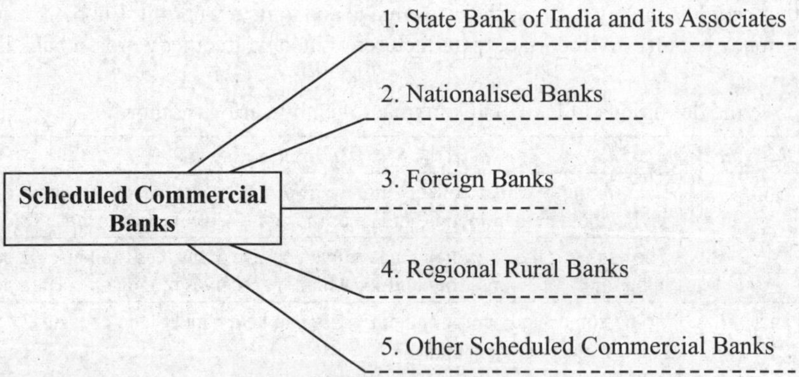

Note: Public sector banks include banks that were in public sector from the starting of their formation and the nationalised banks. Banks in the groups (1) & (2) above are known as public sector banks whereas, other scheduled commercial banks mentioned at group (5) above are known as private sector banks.

(*b*) Non-Scheduled Commercial Banks: Non-scheduled bank in India means "a banking company as defined in clause (*c*) of section 5 of the Banking Regulation Act, 1949, which is not a scheduled bank".

The scheduled banking structure in India can be seen as follows:

Scheduled Banking Structure in India

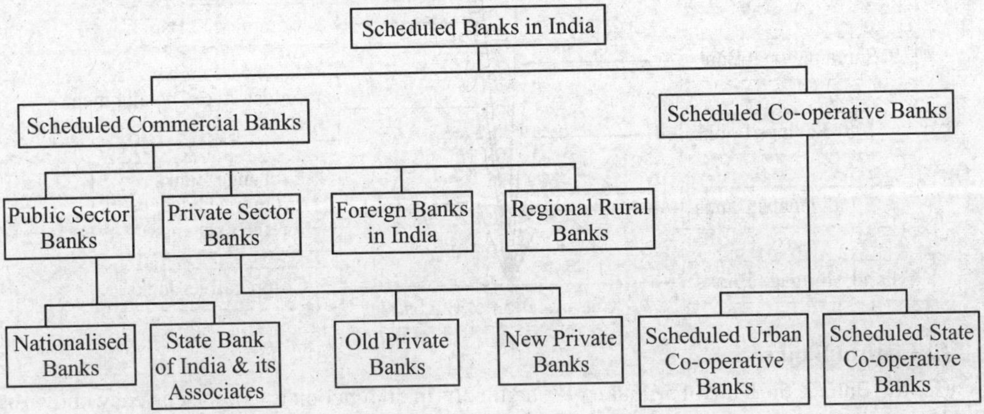

1.4 FEATURES OF BANKING

From the views of the authorities discussed above, we can derive the following basic characteristics of Banking:

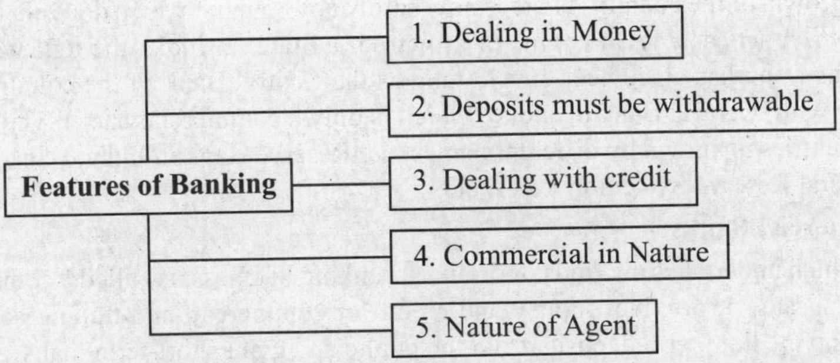

***(i)* Dealing in Money:** The banks accept deposits from the public and advancing them as loans to the needy people. The deposits may be of different types — current, fixed, savings accounts etc. The deposits are accepted on various terms and conditions.

***(ii)* Deposits must be Withdrawable:** The deposits (other than fixed deposits) made by the public can be withdrawable by cheques, draft or otherwise, *i.e.*, the bank issue and pay cheques. The deposits are usually withdrawable on demand.

***(iii)* Dealing with Credit:** The banks are the institutions that can create credit *i.e.*, creation of additional money for lending. Thus, "creation of credit' is the unique feature of banking.

***(iv)* Commercial in Nature:** Since all the banking activities of commercial banks are carried on with the aim of making profit, it is regarded as a commercial institution.

***(v)* Nature of Agent:** Besides the basic functions of accepting deposits and lending money as loans, banks possess the character of an agent because of its various agency services.

1.5 CLASSIFICATION OF BANKS

Today is the Age of specialisation and we can find specialisation in all fields including banking. The banks have specialised in a particular line of finance. Various types of banks have developed to suit the economic development and requirements of the country. The principal banking institutions of a country may be classified into the following types:

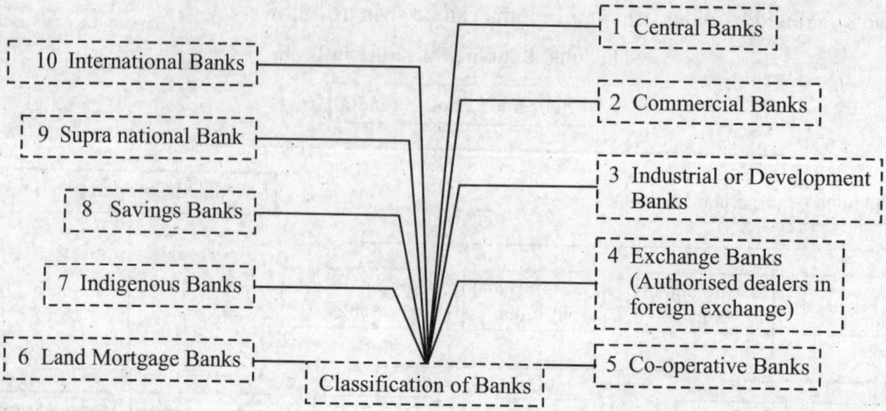

(*i*) Central Banks:

Central Bank is the bank of a Country – a nation. Its main function is to issue currency known as 'Bank Notes'. This bank acts as the leader of the banking system and money market of the country by regulating money and credit. These banks are the bankers to the government, they are bankers' banks and the ultimate custodian of a nations foreign exchange reserves. The aim of the Central Bank is not to earn profit, but to maintain price stability and to strive for economic development with allround growth of the country. There is now hardly any country, which does not have a Central Bank of its own. It acts as a great engine of growth of a State. In India, the RBI was established in 1935 and this Bank has since been functioning as the Central Bank of the country (This is not to be confused with 'Central Bank of India', which is only a commercial bank). The Central Bank of different countries is known by different names like Reserve Bank in India, Bank of England in U.K., and Federal Reserve System in U.S.A etc.

(*ii*) Commercial Banks:

A bank, which undertakes all kinds of ordinary banking business, is called a commercial bank. It is so called because it provides money and credit for commercial and trading activities. They receive short and medium term deposits from the public and grant short-term loans, and advances. They supply working capital to industries and enable them to carry on production and manufacturing activities. They grant loans and advances on the stocks of agricultural commodities, industrial goods etc. They discount internal and foreign bills and thereby finance the International trade. They also perform certain agency services such as collection of cheques, dividends, interest on investments, issue of drafts, letter of credit, Travellers' Cheques, Investment Advisory Services etc.

(*iii*) Industrial Banks or Financial Institutions:

An Industrial Bank is one which specialises by providing loans and fixed capital to industrial concerns by subscribing to share and debenture issued by public companies. They play an important role in the establishment and growth of industries. The block capital required for the acquisition of fixed assets etc., is supplied by investment banks. They provide long-term loans and credits for periods varying between 5 and 15 years for industries to acquire fixed assets. They may serve as catalytic agents in mobilisation of capital in other forms of assistance such as, underwriting, guarantee etc. These banks are nowadays grouped as 'Development Financial Institutions'.

These banks are very popular in Germany and Japan. In India, we have several Industrial Finance Corporations in addition to the "Industrial Development Bank of India".

Both, Development Financial Institutions and Commercial banks, nowadays, finance infrastructural development activities, which include construction of transport facilities, building of power-supply stations etc.

(*iv*) Exchange Banks (Authorised Dealers in Foreign Exchange):

These types of banks are primarily engaged in transactions involving foreign exchange. They deal in foreign bills of exchange import and export of bullion and otherwise participate in the financing of foreign trade. They do a number of incidental services such as opening of letters of credit, issue of foreign currency drafts and Travellers' Cheques and supply of information about foreign customers. They provide credit and loans in foreign currency and also accept deposits in Foreign Currency. They require huge capital and trained staff as it is a risky business. They maintain branches in foreign countries at important trade centres. In the past foreign banks operating in India would deal in foreign exchange and were known as exchange banks. Nowadays, many Indian banks deal in foreign exchange with special authorisation from Reserve Bank of India and known as Authorised Dealers in Foreign Exchange. As per Foreign Exchange Regulation Act, banks dealing in Foreign Exchange related activities require the permission of Reserve Bank of India. This is applicable to both Indian and Foreign Banks.

(*v*) Co-operative Banks:

They are organised on co-operative principles of mutual help and assistance. They grant short-term loans to the agriculturists for purchase of seeds, harvesting and for other cultivation expenses. They accept money on deposit from and make loans to their members at a low rate of interest.(For more details Please see Chapter 7 of this book)

(*vi*) Land-mortgage Banks: (Presently known as Agriculture and Rural Development Banks)

They are agriculture development banks. The Land-mortgage banks supply long-term loans for period upto 15 years for development of land to improve agricultural yields. They grant loan for permanent improvements in agricultural lands. They create negotiable bonds out of real estate like land, buildings etc. They raise funds by floating debentures and by borrowing from the government. The Agriculture Finance Corporation was the first Indian Institution setup finance for development of Agriculture. The National Bank for Agriculture and Rural Development (NABARD) was constituted by the Government to promote rural development.

(*vii*) Indigenous Banks:

The Central Banking Enquiry commission defined an indigenous banker as an individual or firm accepting deposits and dealing in indigenous lending of money to the needy.

They form unorganised part of the banking structure *i.e.*, these are unrecognised operators in receiving deposits and lending money. In India the Marwaris, the Multanis, the Jains, the Sowcars, the Nattukottai chettiars are some of the leading indigenous bankers who charge high rates of interest on their lendings. In rural areas, they still provide substantial finance to agriculturists and small traders.

(*viii*) Savings Banks:

These are institutions which collect the periodical savings of the general public. Their main object is to promote thrift and saving habits among the middle and lower income sections of the society. They have certain restrictions on number of withdrawals in a year to discourage spending. In almost all countries, postal authorities also run savings bank accounts and their working is regulated by the government. The first savings bank was started in Hamburg in 1765. In India, we have postal savings accounts. These days separate savings banks as such are very rare. In India, all commercial banks have savings accounts. The minimum balance which is required to be kept in the accounts differ from banks to banks. The rate of interest payable on the accounts by banks is determined by RBI. Co-operative banks are normally allowed to pay an additional 0.5 percent interest per annum. Interest rate on savings accounts with post offices is determined by Government of India.

(*ix*) Supranational Banks:

Special Banks have been created to deal with certain international financial matters. World Bank is otherwise known as International Bank for Reconstruction and Development (IBRD) which gives long term loans to developing countries for their economic and agricultural development. Asian Development Bank (ADB) is another Supra National Bank which provides finance for the economic development of poor Asian Countries. They generally provide finance at concessional interest rates and for long-term needs. These institutions are the creations of World bodies promoted by various countries or central banks of different countries. The European Central Bank established in June 1998 by countries in the European Union is another example of Supra National Bank.

(*x*) International Banks:

International Banks are those which are operating in different countries. While, the registered office/head office is situated in one country, they operate through their branches in other countries. They specialise in Banking business pertaining to foreign trade like opening of letters of credit, providing short-term finance in foreign currency, issue of performance guarantee, arranging foreign currency credits etc., They are the main traders in International Currencies like US 'dollars', Japanese 'Yen', the new-born European Currency 'Euro' etc., They also perform Currency Risk Management functions for clients. These banks are also known as Multinational Banks since, they operate from many countries. These banks make possible the flow of money/credit from one country to another country. They help grow international trade.

From the above, it can be understood that the classification of banks cannot be rigid. We find that banks are providing finance in more than one field that is why, it is rightly said that they are "Departmental stores of Finance".

1.6 BANKING SYSTEMS

The structure of banking differs from country to country depending upon their economic conditions, political structure and financial system. Banks can be classified on the basis of volume of operations, business pattern and areas of operations. They are termed as systems of banking. The commonly identified systems are as follows:

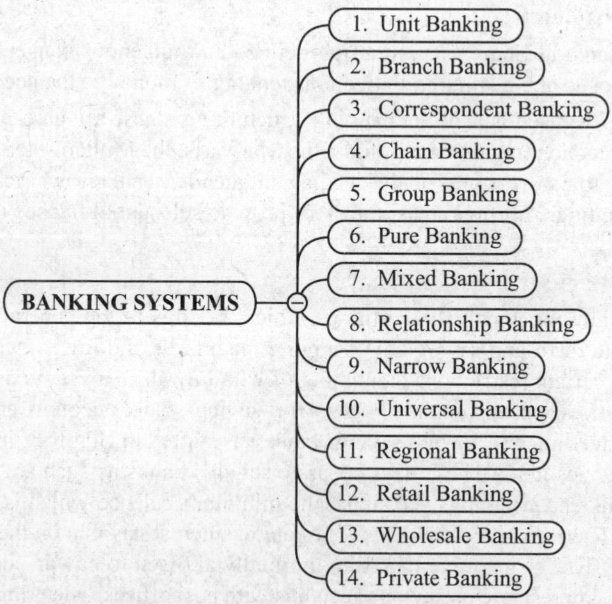

Let us see the concept of these types of banking systems hereunder:

1.6.1 Unit Banking

Unit banking is originated and developed in U.S.A. In this system, small independent banks are functioning in a limited area or in a single town *i.e.*, the business of each bank is confined to a single office, which has no branch at all. It has its own board of directors and stockholders. It is also called as "Localised Banking".

According to Solomon and Whilt, a unit bank is, "a corporation that operates one office and that is not related to other banks through either ownership or control".

The main reason for the development of unit banking in America is said to be the fear of monopoly in banking.

Advantages of unit banking: The unit banking system has the following advantages:

(*i*) Easy Establishment
(*ii*) Easy management and control
(*iii*) Quick-decisions
(*iv*) Local Development
(*v*) Personalised services
(*vi*) No chance for regional disparities
(*vii*) Promotes efficient working
(*viii*) Inefficient banks cannot survive
(*ix*) No chance for monopoly
(*x*) Suitable for the countries aiming at unity in diversity.

Let us discuss these items one by one.

(*i*) Easy Establishment: The unit bank operates on small scale basis. Hence, it requires less capital to promote a unit bank. Besides, the formalities, rules and regulations are comparatively easy with that of branch banking.

(*ii*) Easy management and control: The size and operations of the bank under unit banking system will be small. Therefore, management, supervision and control will be easier.

(*iii*) Quick-decisions: Under unit banking system, the manager can take quick decisions regarding loan sanctioning etc, and he need not wait for the instructions and approval from the head office.

(*iv*) Satisfaction of local needs: Unit banking is the localised banking. The entire operations of the unit bank are confined to a particular area. Therefore, banks have the specialised knowledge of the local problems, their requirements etc. and can serve to fulfil those needs. In this way, local needs are better satisfied than branch banking.

(*v*) Personalised Services: The unit banking gives an opportunity for the bankers to intimately know his customers. The manager has personal knowledge of each of his customers and establishes greater personal contact. This ensures personalised service which is not possible in the case of branch banking where the staff are frequently transferred.

(*vi*) No chance for monopoly: Under unit banking, the size of the bank will be small and limited to a small area. Each bank is independent by itself. Therefore monopolistic trend in banking can not arise.

(*vii*) Promotes efficient working: Too much expansion as in the case of branch banking leads to a reduction in efficient working. The overall control on all branches becomes difficult. It may result in red-tapism, mismanagement and corruption in branches. But it is not so in the case of unit banking since, the size of operation is limited. It ensures efficient working through effective control and supervision.

***(viii)* Inefficient banks can not survive:** Under branch banking system, the running of one branch leads to the running of all other branches. A weak branch cuts into the profit of the concern as a whole. The loss arising from the weak branch will be adjusted against the profits from other branches. This type of adjustment is known as Cross-subsidisation. Hence, the weakness or inefficiency of a branch can be carried forward for years. But, it is not possible in the case of unit banking. In this system efficient banks can only survive *i.e.*, the survival of the fittest.

***(ix)* No chance for Regional Disparities:** Unit banks have no countrywide branches. Hence, the funds collected in one place will not be transferred to other places. The funds collected from the people in an area will be utilised for the benefit and development of that area only. In this way, the unit banking system ensures regional balance and there is no chance for regional disparities.

***(x)* Suitable for the countries aiming at unity in diversity:** Unit banking is more suitable for the countries where there are differences in local laws, languages spoken, habits and customs etc.

Limitations of Unit Banking:

The following are the limitations of the Unit Banking System:

***(i)* No ability to face crisis:** Limited resources, Limited area of operation and non-diversification of investments reduce the ability of unit banks to withstand losses. They cannot face any financial crisis.

***(ii)* No geographical distribution of risks:** Under unit banking system the area of operations of a bank is limited to a particular place only. If there is any business depression in that place, the bank also suffers losses. Because of its localised operations, the unit bank cannot distribute the risks over a wider area.

***(iii)* Variation of interest rates:** There may not be uniformity of interest rates under unit banking. Different banks may charge different rates of interest, because there is no possibility for the transfer of funds to other areas and the availability of funds influence the rates of interest.

***(iv)* Lack of diversification of deposits and assets:** The main factor that affects the survival of a unit bank is its lack of diversification of deposits and assets, loans and advances will be concentrated in the industries located in the area, any difficulty in these industries will automatically affect the bank also.

***(v)* Not able to provide adequate banking facilities:** Because of its restricted areas of operations and limited financial resources, units banks are not able to provide the entire range of banking facilities as provided by branch banking.

***(vi)* Inconvenience in the remittance of funds:** The unit banks have no branches in other place. Therefore, transfer of funds from one place to another becomes costly and inconvenient.

***(vii)* No importance to backward areas:** Unit banking banks may not be started in places where they do not have enough business opportunities because it is unprofitable and uneconomic. But under branch banking, branches can be opened even if it is uneconomical because the losses in one place can be compensated by profits in another place.

***(viii)* Weaker sections may be neglected:** Even in the towns and cities where the unit banks are operating, the weaker sections of the society *i.e.*, poor people may be neglected because of limited resources of the banks.

***(ix)* Influence of local pressures:** The unit banker, being a local man may have to follow local considerations etc. in granting loans and advances. Because of his legitimacy with the local customers, he may be compelled to violate the basic economic principles.

(*x*) Lack of division of labour and specialisation: Generally the size of unit bank is small. So there is not much scope for the introduction of division of labour and specialisation. Because of this, it can not adopt the modern methods of banking. Thus the efficiency of the bank will be affected which in turn affects the profitability of the bank.

(*xi*) Unhealthy Competition: The unit banks are run by different groups of people *i.e.*, the multiplicity of ownership. This may create unhealthy competition among them which will affect the economy adversely.

1.6.2 Branch Banking

The Banking system of England originally offered an example of the branch banking system, where each commercial bank has a network of branches spread throughout the country.

Most of the Indian Banks are falling under this category. They are having large number of branches. All the Public sector banks *i.e.*, nationalised banks and State Bank of India and its subsidiary banks put together have more than 70,000 branches. Banks in India require a licence from Reserve Bank of India under Banking Regulation Act to open a branch as well as to start a bank itself.

Thus branch banking consists of a few big banks with numerous branches spread over wide geographical areas. These branch banks operate under their head offices. Branch banking is also known as "de-localised banking". In India, the State Bank of India has emerged as one of the biggest banks with large number of branches all over the country.

Organisational Structure of Branch Banking:

The organisational Structure of the branch banking in the country is given below:

Head Office
↓
Zonal Offices
↓
Regional Offices
↓
Divisional (District) Offices
↓
Branches

It can be explained in a different way as follows:

Head Office

Zonal Office I or (East)	Zonal Office II or (West)	Zonal Office III or (North)	Zonal Office IV or (South)
↓	↓	↓	↓
Regional offices	Regional offices	Regional offices	Regional offices

Number of Bank Branches in India:

The total number of branches of all scheduled commercial banks including foreign banks operating in India is given below:

Branches of Scheduled Commercial Banks

(As at end-March 2013)

Sr. No.	*Name of the Bank*	*Branches*				
		Rural	*Semi-urban*	*Urban*	*Metro-politan*	*Total*
1	2	3	4	5	6	7
	Scheduled Commercial Banks	26,493	25,009	19,027	18,033	88,562
	Public Sector Banks	24,124	19,554	15,080	13,903	72,661
	Nationalised Banks	17,036	13,539	11,320	10,585	52,480
	State Bank Group	7,088	6,015	3,760	3,318	20,181
	Private Sector Banks	2,361	5,445	3,882	3,881	15,569
	Foreign Banks	8	10	65	249	332

Source: RBI report on Trend and Progress of Banking in India 2012-13.

Advantages of Branch Banking:

The following are the advantages of branch banking:

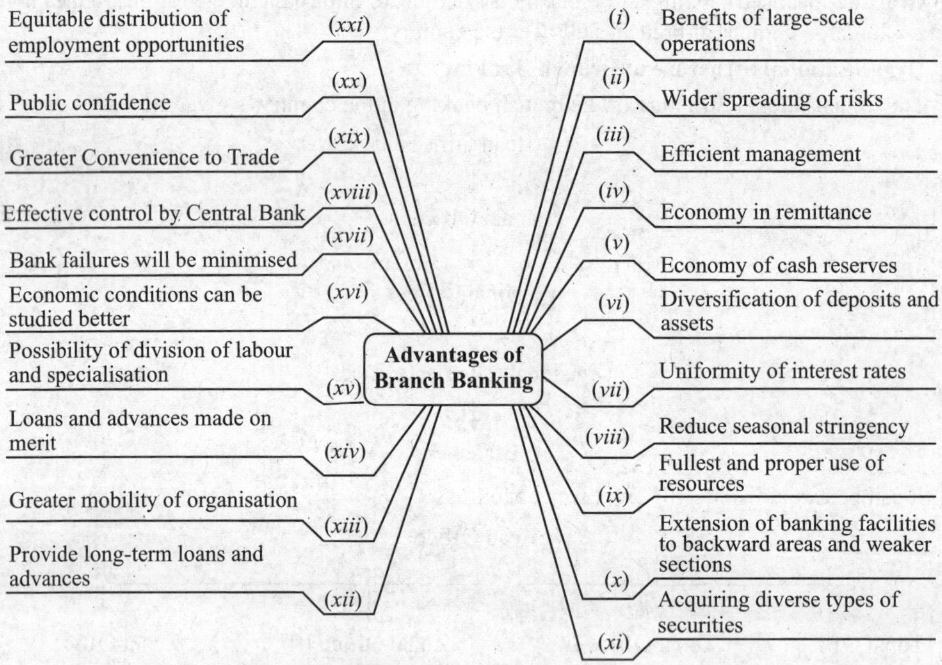

Let us discuss these points one by one.

(*i*) Benefits of large scale operations: A branch bank has all the advantages of large scale operations. It has large resources when compared to a unit bank. It can appoint experts paying high salary and it can use modern mechanical devices in its offices for efficient working.

(*ii*) Wider spreading of risks: A branch bank operates over a wide area with different types of economic development. The losses of branches of one region if any can be set off against the profit of branches in other regions. In this way this risks are distributed geographically. Thus its capacity to withstand times of depression is more than that of unit banks.

***(iii)* Efficient management:** The branch banking system makes for greater efficiency in management. The staff members of a branch bank are more efficient and more experienced when compared to those of a unit bank. The head office arranges transfers of staff from branch to branch. Each staff member has the opportunity to work in various branches, understanding men and matters of different localities. Besides the above, the expertise at head office will be made available to all branches. In this way, the system of branch banking ensures efficient management.

***(iv)* Economy in remittance:** Branch banking has the benefit of economy in remittance of funds. As it has branches in different localities, it need not physically transfer cash from one place to another. It can provide remittance facilities to its customers by mere transfer entries in the books of its branches. It makes the operation easy, quick and cheap.

***(v)* Economy of cash reserves:** Branch banking has the merit of economy of cash reserves. Cash can be transferred from one branch to another whenever necessary. Therefore branch can operate with lower cash balances and they avoid large amount of idle reserves/balances.

***(vi)* Diversification of deposits and assets:** Under branch banking system, there is greater diversification of deposits and assets because of wider geographical coverage. Diversification here means that a bank need not specialise in any particular area or particular industry. Deposits are mobilised from the area where Savings are in plenty and loans are extended in the areas where funds are scarce and interest rates are high.

***(vii)* Uniformity in interest rates:** Branch banking system ensures uniformity in interest rates. Uniformity in banking policies and easy transfer of funds to places where there is demand, results in uniform interest rates.

***(viii)* Reduce seasonal stringency:** In agricultural countries like India, there is greater demand for funds during the seasons of agricultural operations. By a wide network of branches and transfer of funds, branch banking will be in a position to relieve such seasonal scarcity of funds.

***(ix)* Fullest and proper use of resources:** Under branch banking, there is great scope for economic use of funds. The head office analyses the demand for funds in various localities and freely transfers its resources among its branches. At no branch, funds are kept idle. This enables it to earn high profits by employing its funds most economically and profitably.

***(x)* Extension of banking facilities to backward areas and weaker sections:** Under branch banking, the banking facilities are not restricted to profitable localities only but they are extended to the backward areas also. The loss arising from such localities can be compensated by the profits from other developed areas. Besides, because of the availability of resources, the requirements of weaker sections of the society are also satisfied.

***(xi)* Acquiring diverse types of securities:** Branch banking has the advantage of acquiring diverse types of securities from different regions in employing funds. It can invest its funds by lending against securities of agricultural commodities, industrial goods, gold, stock etc. It can choose a variety of securities from different localities. But a unit bank does not have this facility.

***(xii)* Provides long-term loans and advances:** Due to its wider area of operations, they may mobilise large resources which can be used to provide loans and advances on long-term basis which is not possible in case of unit banking.

***(xiii)* Greater mobility of organisation:** The branch banking has the greater mobility of organisation. It can spread its activities to new localities by opening branches with ease.

***(xiv)* Loans and advances made on merit:** Under the system of branch banking loans and advances are made purely on merit and not on other considerations. The branch manager is not influenced by local pressures in granting loans and advances. He can refuse a loan to an undesirable person, without any obligation, fixing the responsibility on the head office. This is not possible in the case of a unit bank.

***(xv)* Possibility of division of labour and specialisation:** Because of the availability of large resources and large scale operations it is possible to adopt division of labour which leads to specialisation. In this way branch banking ensures the overall efficiency of the organisation.

***(xvi)* Economic conditions can be studied better:** Under branch banking, a network of branches spread all over the country. Thus it can have a comprehensive knowledge of the entire economic conditions of the country. It helps the banks to make proper investments.

***(xvii)* Bank failures will be minimised:** In the case of heavy withdrawal of funds in one branch, it can be met by transferring funds from other branches. Thus, bank failures can be avoided.

***(xviii)* Effective control by Central Bank:** Branch banking does not make the control by Central Banking more difficult, as it has to deal only with the Head Offices of Banks, and not with each branch.

***(xix)* Greater convenience to trade:** The traders of one area can get in touch with traders in other parts of the country with ease. If the bank has branches in foreign countries, they can contact the traders in foreign countries also. This helps them to promote their business considerably.

***(xx)* Public confidence:** The large scale operation and the financial viability of branch banking gains public confidence which is the foundation stone for the banking business.

***(xxi)* Equitable distribution of employment opportunities:** A vast network of bank branches at various places offer local employment opportunities and help local people in getting jobs.

Limitations of Branch Banking:

Even though, the branch bank has many advantages as mentioned above, it is not free from criticisms. The following are the limitations of Branch Banking.

(*i*) Difficulty in management and control
(*ii*) Less initiative
(*iii*) Regional disparities
(*iv*) Adjustment of losses
(*v*) Concentration of economic power
(*vi*) Continuance of inefficient branches
(*vii*) Heavy overhead charges
(*viii*) Unhealthy competition
(*ix*) Delayed decision making
(*x*) Local needs may not be satisfied in full
(*xi*) Other defects

We shall explain these items one by one.

***(i)* Difficulty in management and control:** Since the bank has many branches, spread over different places, supervision, management and control becomes more difficult.

***(ii)* Less initiative:** The branches of the bank are not allowed to make their independent decisions. They have to follow the directives of the head office. Besides they have to refer to the matters to the head office for approval. Therefore, the branch managers cannot take initiative.

***(iii)* Regional disparities:** In the case of unit banking system the funds are used for the particular locality alone. It cannot be transferred to other places. But, in the case of branch banking funds collected from backward areas and the villages may be transferred to the places where the profitability is high. This tendency creates regional imbalances in the country.

***(iv)* Adjustment of losses:** In branch banking, the losses of one branch may be adjusted against the profit earned by another branch. This will affect the profitability of the organisation as a whole, as loss making branches will continue to eat into the profits of efficient branches.

***(v)* Concentration of economic power:** Under branch banking system, the financial resources may accumulate in the hands of a few who control big banks with large number of branches. This will cause concentration of economic powers in few big banks. It leads to monopoly.

***(vi)* Continuance of inefficient branches:** Under unit banking system, the inefficient branches cannot survive. But, in the case of branch banking, the inefficient branches may continue to operate because the losses of these branches are compensated by the profits of some other strong branches. In this way, under this system, inefficiency is protected.

***(vii)* Heavy overhead charges:** Establishment of branches in new areas incurs heavy overhead charges. This will affect the operational efficiency of the banks.

***(viii)* Unhealthy Competition:** Under branch banking, many banks may operate their branches in a particular locality where business prospects are very bright. It may create unhealthy competition among various branches of banks.

***(ix)* Delayed decision-making:** In branch banking the manager of a branch cannot take the decision on his own. He has to refer to the matter to the head office seeking permission or approval. This creates red-tapism in the organisation.

***(x)* Local needs may not be satisfied:** As the branch manager is not connected or familiar with local conditions, the local needs may not be attended and satisfied in full.

***(xi)* Other defects:**

(*a*) Preferential treatment may be shown to firms situated near head offices.

(*b*) The lower rates charged in developing regions may be adjusted by charging high rates of interest in developed regions.

(*c*) There are possibilities for mismanagement in branches, like frauds, misappropriation of funds, etc.

As Sayers remarks, "a comparison between unit banking and branch banking is essentially a comparison between small scale and large scale operations". The natural growth is always towards large-scale branch banking. Branch banking has more advantages than unit banking. That is why, it is adopted by most of the countries in the world.

1.6.3 Correspondent Banking System

Correspondent banking system is developed to remove the difficulties in unit banking system. It is the system under which unit banks are linked with bigger banks. The big correspondent banks are linked with still bigger banks in the financial centres. The smaller banks deposit their cash reserve with bigger banks. The bigger banks with whom such deposits are so made are called correspondent banks.

Therefore, correspondent banks are intermediaries through which all unit banks are linked with bigger banks in financial centres. Through correspondent banking, a bank can carryout business transactions in another place where it does not have a branch. This system is very common in international banking transactions. For example, if an Indian bank does not have a branch in Japan, it may find it difficult to carry out Japan-related import/export transactions for its customers. In such a case, the Indian bank may choose a bank in Japan as its correspondent bank to put through all its Japan-related financial transactions. This arrangement avoids the need of opening a branch in another country. Hence, it is cost effective also.

1.6.4 Group Banking

Group Banking is the system in which two or more independently incorporated banks are brought under the control of a holding company. The holding company may or may not be a banking company. Under group banking, the individual banks may be unit banks, or banks operating branches or a combination of the two.

Participating banks retain their own Boards of directors which are responsible to the supervising and regulatory authority and depositors for the proper operation of the bank. That is, each bank in the group has got a separate entity.

This system has developed in United States in 1900. It was popular and extensively developed in 1920's.

Advantages of Group banking:

The following are the advantages of the Group Banking System.

***(i)* Centralised Administration:** The participating banks enjoy the benefits of centralised administration.

***(ii)* Enhancement of operational efficiency:** Because of Group banking system, the operational efficiency of participant banks is enhanced through shared knowledge and experience.

***(iii)* Broader market:** Group Banking offers broader market to the small banks for their excess resources. Thus, their earning capacity and network improved.

***(iv)* Mobility and transfer of resources:** In the case of crisis, the funds are transferred among participating banks. This helps them to face the financial crisis if any, more effectively.

***(v)* Large scale operation:** Group banking paves the way for large scale operation. The member banks can get the economies of large scale operation.

***(vi)* Other Benefits:** The holding company offers the following services to the participating banks.

(*a*) Guidance of experts
(*b*) Auditing
(*c*) Investment counselling
(*d*) Combined Purchase of stationery and office equipments
(*e*) Insurance cover on deposits
(*f*) Advertising and publicity
(*g*) Tax guidance
(*h*) Other advisory services.

Limitations:

The limitations of the Group Banking System are as follows.

***(i)* Lack of effective management and control:** Under Group banking system the control and management is not effective because the control is indirect and more flexible. It cannot offer specialised management.

***(ii)* Inefficiency of member banks protected:** The inefficiency of one participating bank affect the other participating banks.

***(iii)* Less facilities:** This system cannot provide all the facilities offered by branch banking.

***(iv)* Cannot mobilise funds:** Group banking does not have the capacity to mobilise funds as in the case with branch banking Hence, it cannot offer the same economy of operations as are offered by branch banking.

1.6.5 Chain Banking

Chain banking is a system of banking under which a number of separately incorporated banks are brought under the common control by a device other than holding company. This may be:

(*a*) Through some group of persons owning and controlling a number of independent banks.
(*b*) Each bank retains its separate identity.
(*c*) Each one carries out its operations without the intervention of any central organisation.

The main criticism of chain banking is the lack of continuity of existence and diseconomies in its operation.

1.6.6 Pure Banking and Mixed Banking

On the basis of lending operations of the bank, banking is classified into

(*a*) Pure Banking and

(*b*) Mixed Banking

(*a*) Pure Banking: Under pure Banking, the commercial banks give only short term loans to industry, trade and commerce. They specialise in short term finance only. This type of banking is popular in U.K. In U.K., Special institutions like investment houses, finance corporations were established for providing long-term finance. Hence, it is argued that commercial banks should provide only short term loans. It is stressed on the lines of safety and liquidity.

(*b*) Mixed Banking: Mixed banking is that system of banking under which the commercial banks perform the dual function of commercial banking and investment banking *i.e.*, it combines deposit and lending activity with investment banking. Commercial banks usually offer both short-term as well as medium term loans. The German banking system is the best example of mixed banking where banks are permitted besides, lending activity, investment functioning also. In India, Banks are permitted to undertake limited investment activity. In USA commercial or credit banks are not permitted to undertake investment activity. Banks in Switzerland, Denmark, Japan also provide long-term loans.

Advantages:

Mixed Banking has the following advantages:

(*a*) Credit requirements are fully satisfied

(*b*) Banking resources are utilised for industrial development

(*c*) Industries can mobilise greater finance resources through these banks

(*d*) Investment guidance to general public

(*e*) Expert guidance and advice to industries

(*f*) Direct contact with industries

(*g*) Promote rapid industrial development through investment banking.

Limitations:

(*a*) Threat to stability of Banks – The stability of the bank may be affected if the prices of Securities in which banks have invested depreciate.

(*b*) Liquidity of banks may be affected, if the securities are not traded in the market.

(*c*) Possibility of engaging in speculative business.

(*d*) Scope for over lending.

After the Second World War, under developed countries began to show much interest on mixed banking. In recent years, there has been a favourable trend towards mixed banking in India because of the following reasons:

(*a*) Increase in the volume of deposits.

(*b*) Increase in time deposits than demand deposits.

(*c*) RBI initiative to strengthen the banking system.

(*d*) After nationalisation, the Govt. encouraged the public sector banks to grant long-term loans to small scale industries and entrepreneurs. It is made on the grounds of rapid industrialisation in the country.

(*e*) A realisation that overall growth depends upon development of capital market also.

1.6.7 Relationship Banking

It is necessary for every bank to retain its big and good customers. These customers will be a source of regular income for the banks as they will be prompt and regular in repayment of loans & advances. In many cases they may be customers having large deposits with the banks. A bank's profit to a large extent depends upon retaining such honest borrowers and large depositors.

Similarly, it is also necessary to attract new customers who will be a source of income for the bank. Relationship banking refers to the efforts of a bank to promote personal contacts and to keep continuous touch with customers who are very valuable to the bank. In order to retain such profitable accounts with the bank or to attract new accounts, it is necessary for the bank to serve their needs by maintaining a close relationship with such customers. This type of banking activity gains momentum in a highly competitive banking world.

1.6.8 Narrow Banking

A bank engaged in multifarious activities like providing working capital, term loans, doing investment business, consumer loans, housing loans, agricultural loans, advisory services etc. require to maintain group of knowledgeable persons and experts in each field of activity. For lack of proper appraisal of loan documents, verification of important information due to inadequate knowledge, staff or expertise the bank may slip into losing business.

Similarly, having a large number of customers may also result into many defaults in payments and consequently of more bad debts. In order to obviate such pitfalls, a bank may be concentrating only on collection of deposits and lend or invest the money within a particular region or certain chosen activity like investing the funds only in Government Securities. This type of restricted minimum banking activity is referred to 'Narrow Banking'.

1.6.9 Universal Banking

As Narrow Banking refers to restricted and limited banking activity, Universal Banking refers to broad-based and comprehensive banking activities. Under this type of banking, a bank will deal with working capital requirements as well as term loans for developmental activities. They will be dealing with individual customers as well as big corporate customers. They will have expanded lines of business activity combining the functions of traditional deposit taking, modern financial services, selling long term saving products, insurance cover, investment banking, etc. Examples of universal bankers are Citigroup (*i.e.* Citibank), Hongkong and Shanghai Banking Corporation (HSBC). In Europe universal banks are known as "Bancassurance". [All type of financial services and fund-based (loans and advances) activities are undertaken by a bank under Universal Banking.

In India commercial banks like State Bank of India, Indian Overseas Bank and other banks generally provide loans and advances for short-term to meet working capital requirements of borrowing companies. Likewise Developmental Financial Institutions like IDBI, ICICI provide only long term finance for expansion and diversification of business activity. There is now a move to allow banks and Financial Institution to provide both short term and long term finance to corporates under an umbrella system known as universal Banking.

1.6.10 Regional Banking

Small traders, Village artisans, agricultural labourers etc. in rural and semi-urban areas do not get adequate credit facilities from Commercial banks since these banks are generally looking for large borrowers engaged in commercial/business activities. This type of banking leaves the rural areas undeveloped economically. In order to provide adequate and timely credits to small borrowers in rural and semi-urban areas, Central Government set up Regional Banks known as Regional Rural Banks all over India jointly with State Governments and some Commercial Banks. As they are permitted to operate in particular region, it may help develop the regional economy.

1.6.11 Local Area Banks

In some cases, the Regional banks set up by the Governments are not being run profitably for various reasons. Secondly, these banks are not meeting fully the credit requirements of regional borrowers. With a view to bring about a competitive environment and to overcome the deficiencies of Regional banks, Government has permitted establishment of a new type of regional banks in rural and semi-urban centres under private sector known as 'Local Area Banks'. These banks require a low Capital base of ₹5 crore only. The entire share capital has to be mobilised from private sector. They will be permitted to operate only within a region of 2 or 3 districts. Local Area Banks are yet to become operational in India as of June 1999.

1.6.12 Retail Banking

Retail banking is a major form of commercial banking but mainly targeted to consumers rather than corporate clients. It is the method of banks' approach to the customers for sale of their products. The products are consumer-oriented like offering a car loan, home loan facility, financial assistance for purchase of consumer durables etc., Retail banking therefore has large customer-base and hence, large number of transactions with small values.

Retail banks provide various products and services to individuals and small businesses. Traditionally a retail bank provided:

(*a*) Intermediation services and

(*b*) Payments services.

Now in addition to these services, retail banks are providing a much wider range of products/ services including insurance products, pension schemes, stock broking services etc.

It may therefore be cost ineffective in a highly competitive environment. Most of the rural and semi-urban branches of banks, in fact, do retail banking. In the present day situation when lending to corporate clients lead to credit risk and market risk, retail banking may eliminate market risk. It is one of the reasons why many a wholesale bankers like foreign banks also prefer to go for consumer financing albeit for marginally higher net worth individuals.

1.6.13 Wholesale Banking

Wholesale or corporate banking refers to dealing with limited large-sized customers. Instead of maintaining thousands of small accounts and incurring huge transaction costs, under wholesale banking, the banks deal with large customers and keep only large accounts. These are mainly corporate customers. This results into few transactions with large amounts thus resulting into cost reduction and higher fees. Foreign banks in India are mostly concentrating in wholesale banking which is aided by fully computerised banking operations. Growth in this type of banking was aided by increased merchant banking and investment banking activities.

1.6.14 Private Banking

Private or Personal Banking is banking with people – rich individuals instead of banking with corporate clients. Private or Personal Banking attends to the need of individual customers, their preferences and the products or services needed by them. This may include all round personal services like maintaining accounts, loans, foreign currency requirements, investment guidance etc.,. This type of banking is investment and asset management oriented towards individuals and not addressing to the needs of industry and trade.

1.7 BANKS AND ECONOMIC DEVELOPMENT

Today modern banks are very useful for the utilization of the resources of the country. The banks are mobilizing the savings of the people for the investment purposes. If there would be no banks then a great portion of a capital of the country would remain idle. A bank in fact is the backbone of the economic structure and the capital provided by it is like a blood circulation system of the body to the economy. As long as blood is in circulation the organs will remain sound and healthy. If the blood is not supplied to any organ then that part would become paralyzed, so if the finance is not provided to any sector of the economy, say, agricultural sector or industrial sector, it will be greatly affected and will hinder the progress of the economy. Loans and advances extended by banks acts as an incentive to the productive activities and thus ensure higher productivity. The major difficulties in the settlement of overseas payments have been solved and there by the volume of transactions have been increased.

Banks play a very important roll in the economic development of every nation. They have control over a large part of the supply of money in circulation. Through their influence over the volume of bank money, they can influence the nature and character of production in any country.

Economic development is a dynamic and continuous process. Banks are the main stay of the economic progress of a country. Because, the economic development highly depends upon the extent of mobilisation of resources and investment and on the operational efficiency of various segments of the economy. The major roles played by the banks in the development of economy of a country can be summarised as follows:

Economic Development Through Banking System

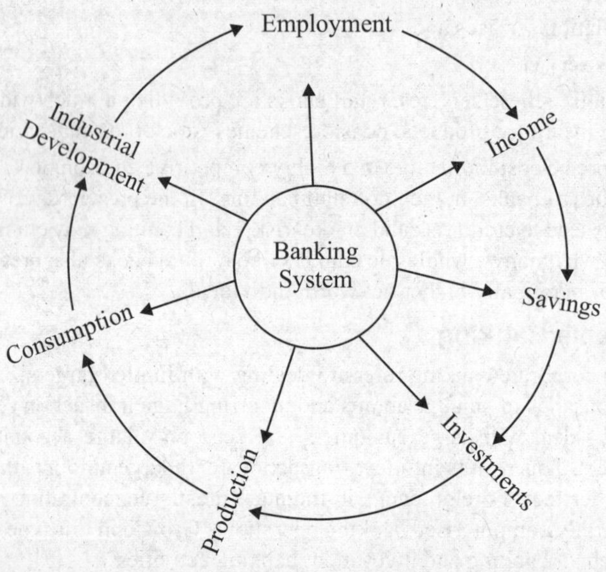

From the above circle of development, one could understand that the banking system functions as a nerve centre of the entire economic system of the country.

Importance of Banking in Economic Development:

In the process of economic development, the significance or contribution of banking system can be summarised as follows:

(*i*) Capital Formation

(*ii*) Creation of money

(*iii*) Strengthen the link between organised and unorganised sectors

(*iv*) Provision of long-term loans

(*v*) Helping agriculture and small scale industries

(*vi*) Entrepreneurial development

(*vii*) Cheque system – Medium of exchange
(*viii*) Regulation of the flow of national savings
(*ix*) Comprehensive infrastructural facilities
(*x*) Maintaining Balance of Trade
(*xi*) Mitigating the effects of trade cycle
(*xii*) Sectoral Priorities
(*xiii*) Catalyst in social change
(*xiv*) Effective implementation of monetary policy
(*xv*) Modernization and Innovations

Let us discuss these items one by one:

(*i*) Capital Formation: The capital formation depends upon savings of various categories of people/organisations. Banks offer facilities for savings and thus encourage the habits of thrift and industry among people. They mobilise the idle and dormant capital of a community and make it available for productive purposes. The banks have designed a variety of novel schemes to attract the prospective customers to save with their banks. Banks can be compared to rivers as they collect the small surplus and scattered savings of the people and make them available for productive purposes in large sums of finance.

(*ii*) Creation of money: Creation of money is the unique feature of commercial banks and is of great economic significance. Banks have become significant by their power to creation of money. Bank money forms a large part of the total quantity of money supply and represents a cheap, efficient and economical means of payment. Banks are described as factories of credit. It results in the economic progress of the country.

(*iii*) Strengthen the link between the organised and unorganised sectors: Indian money market consists of organised and unorganised sectors. Both of them are to be linked for the economic well being of the country. As the nervous system of the economy, the banks link the organised and unorganised sectors for the overall economic development.

(*iv*) Provision of long term loans: The commercial banks in developing and underdeveloped economies invariably give loans and advances for a short period of time. Now they extend it to medium and long term loans to businessmen. Industrial development which is the rock-basis for the economy depends upon the long term loans. As is business enterprises need medium and long term loans for their expansion and diversification banks provide such facilities to the business units.

(*v*) Helping agriculture and small scale industries: The development of a country not only depends upon the industrial development but also on the development of agriculture and small scale and cottage industries. Agriculture contributes a sizable portion (about 25%) to the GDP of our country. Similarly, small scale industries provide large employment opportunities and goods manufactured by this sector are also exported out of India. The banks cater to the financial requirements of these sectors which lead to the economic progress of the country.

(*vi*) Development of Entrepreneurs: Banks have special drives and specific schemes for the development of entrepreneurship. They foster their strength and health. This helps the nation as a whole in various ways including the increase in productivity etc.

(*vii*) Cheque System – Medium of exchange: Banks provide the 'cheque payment system' which is a great convenience and safe method for making payments. Bank cheques settle transactions legally. Payment by cheque economises the time and trouble. Cheques act as a medium of exchange and helps in the promotion of trade and industry. A wrong payment by cheque can also easily be traced, particularly when the cheque is crossed.

***(viii)* Regulation of the flow of national savings:** Banks regulate the flow of national savings into various productive channels, while lending money, they discriminate between a genuine trader and a speculator and they discourage the speculator. Thus banks ensure the diversion of national savings into the productive purposes.

***(ix)* Comprehensive Infrastructural Facilities:** Banks can develop comprehensive infrastructural facilities in the country. It includes the social, educational, fiscal and other aspects, whose development is essential for the economic progress of a nation.

***(x)* Maintaining balance of trade:** Through properly devised banking system the country can promote exports through easy and timely credit facilities to exporters, quickly obtaining money from foreign buyers of goods etc. This may help maintain the balance of trade at favourable position.

***(xi)* Mitigating the effects of trade cycles:** Inflation and deflation are known as trade cycles of the economy. They should be controlled otherwise they will affect the economy of the country. Through effective banking system, the government can control and regulate the circulation of money and thereby mitigate the effects of trade cycles in the economy.

***(xii)* Sectoral priorities:** The mobilised resources can be used for the development of backward areas or a particular sector. This can be effectively done with the efficient banking system. For example, encouraging the flow of credit to Small Scale Industries, artisans and farmers under priority sector is being done very effectively. Such preferential treatment is given on the basis of government policies time to time.

***(xiii)* Catalyst in social change:** Banks are regarded as catalysts in bringing of the desired social change in the community. Through its sectoral priorities and other social development programmes, the desired change can be achieved. In India, banks are required to provide certain percentage of their total loans and advances (presently 40 percent) for the 'priority sector' purposes. This includes loans to weaker sections, Agricultural purposes, Scheduled Caste and Tribes, Small Traders, Labourers etc.

***(xiv)* Effective Implementation of Monetary Policy:** The effective implementation of monetary policy can be done only through properly organised banking system of the country.

Thus the banking system occupies an important position in modern economic organisation not merely because they have financial resources because they have the power to influence the direction in which such resource might be employed. They can discriminate in lending policies. Bankers are regarded as "Public conservator of commercial virtues". A country with a properly developed banking organisation has a secure foundation of industrial and economic progress.

***(xv)* Modernization and Innovations:** Modernization and Innovations are the essential prerequisites for the progress of any economy. They are mostly financed by bank credit in the developed economies. But the entrepreneurs in developing and underdeveloped economies cannot bring about these innovations due to inadequate financial assistance. The banks now days are encouraged to pay special attention to the financing of business modernization and innovations by providing adequate and cheap credit facilities to entrepreneurs.

Role of Banks in Indian Economy:

In India, the commercial banking sector has been the central part in the country's financial system. The sector has performed the key functions of providing liquidity and payment services to the real sector and has accounted for the bulk of the financial intermediation process. Besides institutionalizing savings, the banking sector has contributed to the process of economic development by serving as a major source of credit to households, government, and business and to weaker sectors of the economy like village and small scale industries and agriculture. Over the years, over 30-40% of gross household savings have been in the form of bank deposits and around 60% of the assets of all financial institutions accounted for by commercial banks.

An important landmark in the development of banking sector in recent years has been the initiation if reforms following the recommendations of the first Narasimham Committee on Financial System (please see Appendix for the details of the report of the committee). In reviewing the strengths and weaknesses of these banks, the Committee suggested several measures to transform the Indian banking sector from a highly regulated to a more market oriented system and to enable it to compete effectively in an increasingly globalised environment. Many of the recommendations of the Committee especially those pertaining to interest rate, an institution of prudential norms and transparent accounting norms were in line with banking policy reforms.

REVIEW QUESTIONS

Short Answer Questions

1. Define Banking and Banking Company.
2. What are the scheduled and non-scheduled banks in India?
3. What are the categories of scheduled commercial banks in India?
4. What are the features of banking?
3. Write a short note on the following:
   (*i*) Central Banks
   (*ii*) Commercial Banks
   (*iii*) Industrial or Development Banks
   (*iv*) Exchange Banks (Authorised dealers in foreign exchange)
   (*v*) Co-operative Banks
   (*vi*) Land Mortgage Banks
   (*vii*) Indigenous Banks
   (*viii*) Savings Banks
   (*ix*) Supranational Bank
   (*x*) International Banks
3. Write a short note on the following banking systems:
   1. Unit Banking
   2. Branch Banking
   3. Chain Banking
   4. Group Banking
   5. Pure Banking
   6. Mixed Banking
   7. Relationship Banking
   8. Narrow Banking
   9. Universal Banking
   10. Regional Banking
   11. Retail Banking
   12. Wholesale Banking
   13. Private Banking
4. What is Correspondent Banking system?
5. What is Branch Banking system?
6. What is the difference between Pure banking and Mixed banking?

Essay Type Questions

1. Explain the meaning and general features of banking.
2. Briefly explain the evolution of banking system in India.
3. Explain the different classifications of banks in detail.
4. Describe in detail the banking system.
5. What are the advantages and limitations of unit banking?
6. What are the advantages and limitations of branch banking?
7. What are the advantages and limitations of group banking?
8. Explain the banking structure in India.
9. Explain in detail the role of banks in economic development of the country.
10. Do we really need banking operations? Elucidate your answer.

2 CHAPTER
Nationalisation and Privatisation of Banks in India

After independence, India aimed at a socialistic pattern of society. This goal is expected to be achieved through the effective functioning of joint sector. As such, the two sectors, private and public, were allowed to function independently of each other. The public sector was wholly owned and controlled by the Government. The private sector was regulated through the system of licences, controls and legislative acts etc. The public sector was made to grow by nationalisation of industries and institutions, particularly those which required huge capital outlay like steel and power supply or which provide public utility services like communication services etc.,

2.1 SOCIAL CONTROL OVER BANKS

The banks are the custodians of savings and powerful institutions to provide credit. They mobilise the resources from all the sections of the community by way of deposits and channelise them to industries and others by way of granting loans. In 1955 the Imperial Bank of India was nationalised and SBI was constituted.

It was observed that the commercial banks were directing their advances to the large and medium scale industries and the priority sectors such as agriculture, small-scale industries and exports were neglected. The chairmen and directors of banks were mostly industrialists and many of them were interested in sanctioning large amount of loans and advances to the industries with which they were connected. To overcome these deficiencies found in the working of the banks, the Banking Laws (Amendment) Act was passed in December 1968 and came into force on 1-2-1969. It is known as the scheme of 'social control' over the banks. The then deputy Prime Minister, Mr. Morarji Desai made a statement in the Parliament on the eve of introducing the bill to amend the banking laws Act. He explained that the aim of social control was, "to regulate our social and economic life so as to attain the optimum growth rate for our economy and to prevent at the same time monopolistic trend, concentration of economic power and misdirection of resources".

The following are the main provisions of this amendment,

- Bigger banks had to be managed by whole time chairman possessing special knowledge and practical experience of the working of a banking company or of finance, economics or business administration.
- The majority of directors had to be persons with special knowledge or practical experience in any of the areas such as accountancy, agriculture and rural economy, banking, co-operative, economics, finance, law, small scale industries etc.
- At least two directors had to possess special knowledge and practical experience in respect of agriculture, rural economy and co-operation.
- The banks were also prohibited from making any loans or advances, secured or unsecured to their directors or to any companies in which they have substantial interest.

2.2 NATIONALISATION OF MAJOR COMMERCIAL BANKS

The social control measures outlined above were not considered adequate to achieve the desired social and economic objectives. Therefore, the Government of India, on 19th July 1969 *i.e.*, after five months and eighteen days after the statutory imposition of social control, nationalised fourteen major Indian banks each having deposits of more than ₹ 50 Crore - ₹ 2,741.75 Crore in aggregate as on 31st December 1968. No foreign bank was taken over.

The names of fourteen banks taken over by the Government under the Banking companies (Acquisition & Transfer of Undertakings) Act of 1969 are given below:

Name of the Banks	*Amount of compensation paid by Government (₹ in lakhs)*
1. Central Bank of India Ltd	1750
2. Bank of India Ltd.	1470
3. Punjab National Bank Ltd.	1020
4. The Bank of Baroda Ltd.	840
5. The United Commercial Bank Ltd.	830
6. Canara Bank Ltd.	360
7. United Bank of India Ltd.	420
8. Dena Bank Ltd.	360
9. Syndicate Bank Ltd.	360
10. The Union Bank of India Ltd.	310
11. Allahabad Bank Ltd.	310
12. The Indian Bank Ltd.	230
13. The Bank of Maharashtra Ltd.	230
14. The Indian Overseas Bank Ltd.	250

Nationalisation of Six more Banks: Public sector banking was enlarged on 15th April 1980 with the nationalisation of six more Indian banks, whose demand and time liabilities exceeded ₹ 200 Crore on 14th March 1980. The Six banks were acquired under "The Banking companies (Acquisition and Transfer of undertakings) Act 1980. The names of the banks are given below.

Name of the Banks	*Compensation (₹ in Lakhs)*
1. The Andhra Bank Ltd.	610
2. The Punjab and Sind Bank Ltd.	180
3. The New Bank of India Ltd.	510
4. The Vijaya Bank Ltd.	100
5. The Corporation Bank Ltd.	210
6. The Oriental Bank of Commerce Ltd.	240

Even after nationalisation, the names of the banks were retained. However, the term Ltd was dropped from the names as Central Government has now become the only shareholder of each nationalised bank. The Government as a shareholder will not have 'limited liability' as in the case with shareholders of limited companies or institutions. Hence, the word 'Limited' was dropped. The nationalised banks are subsequently referred as 'Public Sector Banks'.

2.3 REASONS FOR NATIONALISATION

The nationalisation of commercial banks increased the role of public sector banks. Various authorities have advocated many reasons for the nationalisation of major commercial banks. Let us see their views one by one.

2.3.1 The then Prime Minister, Srimathi Indira Gandhi

In her broadcast to the nation on the eve of nationalisation of the fourteen leading Indian banks, she summed up the objectives of the nationalisation as, "The present decision to nationalise major banks is to accelerate the achievements of our objectives. The purpose is to expand bank credit to priority areas which have hitherto been somewhat neglected. It also includes:

(*i*) the removal of control by a few provision of adequate credit facilities to agriculture, small industry and exports

(*ii*) the giving of professional bent to bank management

(*iii*) the encouragement of new classes of entrepreneurs, and the provision of adequate training as well as reasonable terms of service for bank staff.

2.3.2 Prof.Sayers

Prof.Sayers supports the nationalisation and gives his views under the following four issues.

1. Efficiency Issue: According to sayers, nationalisation will increase the efficiency of commercial banks as given below:

(*a*) Deposits will increase because of increasing confidence in public sector bank. Increase in bank resources will lead to economics of scale.

(*b*) The government can appoint experienced personnel to run and manage the banks.

(*c*) Govt. has the country wide administrative net work. Hence, it can make suitable changes in the banking policies according to the prevailing trends in the economy.

(*d*) Nationalised banks can have the main motive of public service.

(*e*) Public sector banks can give preference to priority sectors in advancing loans. Thus, nationalisation promotes efficiency.

2. Monetisation Issue: Commercial banks accumulate deposits from the public. Therefore, they are in a position to bring changes in the supply of money. Such an important power should not be in the private sector. It is the public sector that should have the control over money supply.

3. Integration Issue: Central Banks are established by the Govt. for overall monetary control in the economy and is not aiming at profit. But commercial banks are started mainly to earn profit. Thus, there are contradicting objectives between Central Bank and commercial banks. In this situation, the Central Bank may find it difficult to implement its policies when the commercial banks oppose them. Therefore, in the interest of co-ordination and co-operation between them, commercial banks should be nationalised.

4. Socialisation Issue: When a country aims at socialistic pattern of society, then the role of public sector undertaking should be extended in all spheres of the economy. To start and run the public sector undertaking Govt. requires enormous financial requirements. Private commercial banks may obstruct such policies and may not finance public sector undertakings and above all they may discriminate against them. Therefore, the nationalisation of commercial banks will be necessary if the government wants to establish socialism.

2.3.3 Views given by Others:

1. Preventing concentration of economic power: Initially, a few leading industrial and business houses had close association with commercial banks. The directors of these banks happened to be the same industrialists who established monopoly control on the bank finance. They exploited the bank resources in such a way that the new business units cannot enter in any line of business in competition with these business houses. Nationalisation of banks, thus, prevents the spread of the monopoly enterprise.

2. Social control was not adequate: The 'social control' measures of the government did not work well. Some banks did not follow the regulations given under social control. Thus, the nationalisation was necessitated by the failure of social control.

3. Channel the bank finance to plan - priority sectors: Banks collect savings from the general public. If it is in the hand of private sector, the national interests may be neglected. Besides, in Five-Year Plans, the government gives priority to some specified sectors like agriculture, small-industries etc. Thus, nationalisation of banks ensures the availability of resources to the plan-priority sectors.

4. Greater mobilisation of deposits: The public sector banks open branches in rural areas where the private sector has failed. Because of such rapid branch expansion there is possibility to mobilise rural savings.

5. Help to agriculture: If banks fail to assist the agriculture in many ways, agriculture can not prosper, that too, a country like India where more than 70% of the population depends upon agriculture. Thus, for providing increased finance to agriculture banks have to be nationalised.

6. Balanced Regional development: In a country, certain areas remained backward for lack of financial resource and credit facilities. Private banks neglected the backward areas because of poor business potential and profit opportunities. Nationalisation helps to provide bank finance in such a way as to achieve balanced inter-regional development and remove regional disparities.

7. Greater control by the Reserve Bank: In a developing country like India there is need for exercising strict control over credit created by banks. If banks are under the control of the Govt., it becomes easy for the Central Bank to bring about co-ordinated credit control. This necessitated the nationalisation of banks.

8. Small stake of share holders: The nationalised banks had deposits totalling ₹ 2742 crore at the end of December 1968. But the capital contributed by their shareholders was only ₹ 28.5 Crore, which was just 1 % of deposits. Even if we include the reserves, the amount comes to only 2.4% of the banks deposits with such a small and insignificant stake, it is unjustifiable to allow the private share holders to exercise control over such vital credit machinery with large resources.

9. Greater Stability of banking structure: Nationalised banks are sure to command more confidence with the customers about the safety of their deposits. Besides this, the planned development of nationalised banks will impart greater stability for the banking structure.

10. March Forward towards Socialism: India aims at socialism. This requires the financial institutions to run under the government's control and only through nationalisation, this objective can be effectively achieved.

11. Better service conditions to staff: Nationalisation ensures the staff of banks to enjoy greater job security and higher emoluments. It can provide other benefits as well. In this way the banks can motivate their staff and thereby the operational efficiency of banks will be increased.

12. New schemes: Through nationalised banks, new schemes like village adoption scheme, Lead Bank Scheme can be formulated and implemented. Besides, different types of financial facilities can be extended to persons like Doctors, Engineers, Self-employed persons like artisans *etc.*,

Nationalisation of banks creates great interest among various sections of the public. Many hopes were raised in the middle class and poor people with regard to the financial assistance. The nationalised banks drew up a number of schemes to assist new types of customers and are plans to make each of these banks to adopt a few select districts and concentrate on their intensive development.

2.4 CRITICISMS AGAINST NATIONALISATION OF THE BANKS

The various criticisms against nationalisation of banks can be summarised as follows.

(*i*) Political purpose rather than for Productive purpose: The government has acquired the strength of a giant and there is the danger of using the financial resources for political purposes rather than for productive purpose.

(*ii*) Beginning of state capitalism: Such a drastic step of nationalisation of about 90% of the banking resources is wholly unnecessary, especially if we take into consideration the enormous powers vested in the Reserve Bank of India for controlling banks' resources. It is considered as the beginning of state capitalism and not socialism in India.

(*iii*) Scope for inefficiency: Some are of the opinion that after nationalisation banks will degenerate to the level of agricultural co-operatives, which are known for their inefficiency and corrupt practices. Some fear that the officers who manage these big banks also have to bow down to the politicians in course of time.

(*iv*) India's prestige abroad: The political prestige of India in foreign countries was damaged by this act of nationalisation. Doubts are expressed especially in countries which are rendering large-scale financial assistance to India, about the assurances and promises given by the government with regard to freedom of foreign enterprise in India. This may adversely affect the foreign assistance which India was receiving then.

(*v*) Less attractive customers service: The nationalised banks are sure to join the ranks of other public undertakings which are known for their working to losses. Inefficiency, indecision, corruption, and lack of responsibility are the evils with which the government undertakings are suffering. A government bank may not care to attach importance to the customer service.

(*vi*) Secrecy of customer's accounts: Inspite of the assurances given and provisions made in the Act, businessmen still fear about the maintenance of the secrecy of the customers accounts. As such, they may be forced to withdraw their deposits and go to some bank in the private sector and foreign banks. Thus nationalisation of big Indian banks will divert some of the deposits of Indian banks to the foreign banks which is not at all desirable.

(*vii*) Promises may not materialise: Nationalisation cannot convert the commercial banks overnight into agricultural banks. Similarly, the hopes raised among the poor and middle class people about the bank loans may ultimately prove to be false.

(*viii*) Industry and trade may suffer: Diversion of large sums of finances from the industry and trade to agricultural is sure to starve the large-sized industries and business for finance. We cannot ignore the fact that the big industries and business are providing employment to millions of people and largely contributing to the production of wealth. To starve them for finance simply because they are 'big' will be upsetting the job opportunities and production in these concerns.

(*ix*) Branch Expansion: To argue that nationalisation will help to facilitate branch expansion to rural areas much more rapidly than the private banks cannot be supported by facts. Weather it is private bank or nationalised bank, it has to go by business principles and satisfy itself that the new branch is economically viable. In other words, branch expansion can be achieved by private banks as well, without nationalisation.

(x) Burden of compensation: Nationalisation leads to the payment of heavy compensation to the shareholders. This gives additional financial burden on the government. Moreover, it is also argued that nationalisation will not bring much income to the government.

In spite of these criticisms, we cannot ignore the fact that at present, nationalisation of banks is an accomplished fact. By and large this measure received support from almost all sections of the public. It was welcomed by the middle class people and small industrialists and small traders.

Nationalisation is designed to accelerate the tempo of investment and production to raise the living standards of the people. But it should be noted that nationalisation is not an end in itself - it is a means to the end of increasing the economic prosperity. The success of the measure depends upon the new vigour and dynamism which the nationalised banks can bring about in mobilising the nation's savings and applying them for the rapid economic development to the country.

2.5 ACHIEVEMENTS AFTER NATIONALISATION

To conclude, nationalisation of banks in India did a wonderful job, particularly in the following areas and spheres of activities:

(*i*) Taken banking service to rural and remote areas.

(*ii*) Awaken the rural masses about the need and usefulness of banking service.

(*iii*) Helped enormously speedy transfer of funds from one place to another.

(*iv*) Provided thousands of job opportunities to educated youth.

(*v*) Made credit available to neglected people like agricultural labourer, small traders at reduced interest rate.

(*vi*) Helped to free the rural poor from the clutches of money lenders.

(*vii*) Ensured adequate and timely credit for agricultural activities and farming operations.

(*viii*) Priority sector advances ensured adequate supply of credit to weaker sections of the society like village artisans, labourers, scheduled caste and tribes.

(*ix*) Helped export sector to obtain cheap credit.

(*x*) Ensured even-supply of credit to various industrial activities.

(*xi*) Avoided diversion of funds for harmful activities like speculation in shares, hoarding of essential commodities investment in real estates etc.

(*xii*) Removed concentration of wealth in the hands of few industrialists.

(*xiii*) Ensured use of public money (deposits of public) for social and desirable purposes.

(*xiv*) Removed regional disparities in economic development.

(*xv*) Helped implementation of various welfare measures formulated by Government.

2.6 PRIVATISATION OF BANKS IN INDIA

2.6.1 Privatization of Commercial Banks:

Privatization has become a popular measure for solving the organisational problems of governments by reducing the role of the state and encouraging the growth of the private sector enterprises. However, privatization takes a number of forms and has been approached in various ways during the move away from government control to other forms of ownership in developing countries. In 1969, on 19th July, an event of great political significance took place when the then Government, headed by Smt. Indira Gandhi, nationalized 14 major Indian banks. On 15th April, 1980, six more Private banks were nationalized. Beginning 2nd October, 1975, 196 Regional Rural Banks have been established in the country.

After 31 years, the Government of India, introduced a Bill in the Parliament on 13th December, 2000 providing for reduction in Government equity in the Public Sector Banks from existing "not less than 51%" to 33%. In other words, the 67% of equity would be held by Private Sector and Government equity will be around 33%. This intent was no doubt in continuation of the process of liberalisation of the banking industry that began in the early 1990s. After the deregulation of interest rates, issuing of licences to new private banks, liberalising of branch licensing policy, lending policy, even with recruitment policies of banks, it was natural to progress toward de-nationalisation.

Privatisation is a political process and has important economic and social implications that not only affect enterprise performance, but also social welfare and stability. The social effects have to be considered in any impact assessment, particularly those related to employment, social safety net measures, social privatisation that results from the extension of share ownership to small investors and employees, and the role of public utilities and services in economic and social development. It is therefore important that the framework for evaluating policy developments, including all forms of privatisation, is clearly set in advance.

In the course of banking liberalization, Reserve Bank has so far granted licenses to 9 private sector banks upto March 2003. This apart, many foreign banks are allowed to set up branches / offices in India. Simultaneously banks were encouraged to go for mergers as in the case with Times Bank Ltd with HDFC bank and Bank of Madura Ltd with ICICI Bank Ltd.

The new privatization policy also led to a large-scale reduction in the staff strength PSU banks. We are aware that thousands of bank staff shown the door under 'VRS' policy. However the objective of privatization is to improve the functioning and profitability of Government owned banks. Let us now discuss the merits and demerits of this policy.

2.6.2 Arguments for Privatization:

The following may be the arguments for privatization of banks in India:

(*a*) Public sector ownership has an inherent handicap due to it being extremely diffused. This makes it less amenable to effective control by shareholders, compared to private ownership.

(*b*) Bank nationalisation had given monopoly to the government in the banking industry. As in case of any monopoly situation, the quality of service went down and the people suffered.

(*c*) State ownership of banks reduces competition and breeds inefficiency;

(*d*) There is no evidence to suggest that State ownership lowers the probability of banking crises.

(*e*) Sale of public equity of banks may be particularly lucrative now. Twelve of the 27 PSBs and 19 private sector banks are listed on stock exchanges, and the market has appreciated their recent performance. During the years 2001-02 and 2002-03, all PSBs declared high profits, with some banks reporting 200 to 300 per cent growth in their bottomline! The bullish bond market enabled many banks to book record trading profits in trading in Govt. securities. Additional good cheer was the passage of the new Act, which enable banks to size the assets of defaulting borrowers.

(*f*) A sixth rationale for privatisation is that it enhances efficiency and productivity through proper management and control.

(*g*) The competition, not merely ownership, is the key. And foreign competitors might bring additional benefits take fresh capital as shown in other emerging markets. A foreign owned bank, with large capitalisation, can withstand local disturbances better.

(*h*) The private sector and foreign banks can resist local government pressure to lend to favoured sectors.

(*i*) Frequent recapitalisation of State-owned banks is a huge burden on the Government budget.

(*j*) The relative insensitivity of the public sector banking system to its cost structure, inability to respond quickly to the changing market trends and the greater rigidities in the management decision-making processes because of what may be described as 'non-commercial' considerations.

(*k*) Dr.Jalan, former Governor of RBI has given the following arguments in support of privatization of the banking sector:

(*i*) "Indian legal system provides" full protection to the private interests of the 'public servant' including in the banks and further public sector banks have been afflicted with management by 'non-commercial' considerations. He believes that accountability to the shareholders will make sure that the officers stay on course.

(*ii*) Poor internal control and risk-management systems of the banks; and greater accountability on the part of corporates...".

(*iii*) India should increase its domestic savings and invest them in the services sector to emerge a leader in the world economy. He also quotes W. Arthur Lewis to the effect that the central fact of economic development is that of capital accumulation and that would require an increase in the rate of domestic savings from 4 per cent to 12 per cent. India has failed to accumulate capital despite having secured such an increase in domestic savings because till the 1980s, the state-controlled financial system acted "as deposit-taking agencies and providers of credit and finance for designated and centrally determined purposes...the public sector — instead of being a generator of savings for the community's good — became, over time, a consumer of community's savings".

2.6.3 Arguments against Privatization:

The following are the arguments against privatization of commercial banks in India:

(*a*) One of the Directive Principles is that the Government would strive at redistributive justice in the country. Bank privatization is a step away from this direction.

(*b*) Public sector banks in India have already been exposed to increasing competition. The forces of competition have already pushed Public sector banks to optimise its resources in order to reach technical efficiency. It is felt that conclusions are being drawn on the basis of incomparable units- all of this to favour privatisation and even foreign ownership.

(*c*) Privatisation opens the way for the domination of the economy by foreign capital. Since it is extremely difficult to distinguish in practice between domestic and foreign capital within the private sector when they are operating together in joint ventures, or when a domestic firm can be a front for foreign capital, any expansion in the scope for the private sector necessarily enlarges the sphere of operation of foreign capital as well.

(*d*) Privatization would remove a large chunk of the economy from the purview of public scrutiny and hence from the realm of social accountability. A basic distinction between public and private property consists in the fact that the former, in principle, is socially accountable, and this is enforced through Parliament and its committees. How well this job is done is a separate issue. If it is badly done then that requires reforms in a different sphere. But privatization puts an end to this form of social accountability and hence constitutes in a fundamental sense an abridgement of democracy.

(*e*) Social accountability is not merely intrinsically desirable. It becomes absolutely necessary when enterprises have to fulfill certain social functions going beyond mere profit-making. Privatisation, and even making public enterprises concentrate exclusively on profit-making, effectively does away with these social functions.

(*f*) All privatization involves the selling of state property at "throwaway" prices. This is true the world over. And it has been true in India too as the Comptroller and Auditor-General's report pointed out some time ago. In other words, in privatising enterprises the state is not merely changing the form of its property from enterprises to schools or hospitals or reduced public debt but is transferring gratis some state property to private monopolists. Since state property has been built up through the sacrifices of the common people through tax payments or inflation-induced restraints on consumption, privatisation amounts to an implicit act of plunder, or what Marx called "primitive accumulation of capital": a few are being allowed to filch from many through the courtesy of the state.

(*g*) India has been a planned economy for the last about six decades. But in absence of any effective control over the commercial banks, the economic planning was incomplete and monetary policy targets were difficult to achieve and pursue. With the nationalisation of banks, the government could actually plan and pursue the monetary policy targets and it would be wrong to say that the decision of bank nationalisation was a mistake.

REVIEW QUESTIONS

Short Answer Questions

1. What is meant by Bank Nationalisation?
2. What is Bank privatization?
3. Write a short note on the views of Former Prime Minister Srimathi Indira Gandhi on Bank Nationalisation.
4. Write a short note on the views of Prof.Sayers on Bank Nationalisation.

Essay Type Questions

1. Write an explanatory note on social control over banks.
2. Explain the nationalization of banks in India.
3. Briefly explain the reasons for banks nationalisation in India.
4. Write a note on the criticisms against banks nationalization.
5. Examine the arguments for and against nationalization of commercial banks in India.
6. What are the achievements of banking sector after nationalization?
7. Explain the reasons for bank privatization?
8. What is your opinion on bank privatization? Justify your answer.

CHAPTER 3 Money Market

Money market refers to the activity rather than a place. Money market activities cover the lending and borrowing of short-term funds. The market deals in call and notice deposit, short term bills, promissory notes and government papers, etc. which are drawn for short-periods. These days money market instruments are many, such as Treasury Bills, Commercial Paper, Certificate of Deposits, Commercial Bills, etc.,. However, these securities and instruments should have maturity period of less than one year. It is a segment of the financial market in which financial instruments with high liquidity and very short maturities are traded. It is the market for short terms financial assets that are close substitute for money, facilitates the exchange of money in primary and secondary market.

The money market is designed for making short-term loans where individuals and institutions with temporary surpluses of funds meet borrowers who have temporary cash shortages.

3.1 DEFINITIONS OF MONEY MARKET

According to G. Crowther, "it is the collective name given to the various firms and institutions that deal in the various grades of near money".

According to RBI report, "Money market is the centre for dealings mainly of short-term character, in money assets, it meets short-term requirements of borrowers and provide liquidity or cash to the lenders.

It is the place where short-term surplus investible funds at the disposal of financial and other institutions and individuals are bid by borrowers, again comprising institutions and individuals and also the government itself".

We can define money market as, "the market in which the highly liquid short-term bills are dealt with mainly by government, business concerns and private individuals". Thus, we can say that the money market is a mechanism that deals with the lending and borrowing of short term funds.

3.2 OBJECTIVES OF MONEY MARKET

Money Markets exist to facilitate efficient transfer of short-term funds between holders and borrowers of cash assets. For the lender/investor, it provides a good return on their funds. For the borrower, it enables rapid and relatively inexpensive acquisition of cash to cover short-term liabilities. One of the primary functions of Money Market is to provide focal point for RBI's intervention for influencing liquidity and general levels of interest rates in the economy. RBI being the main constituent in the Money Market aims at ensuring that liquidity and short term interest rates are consistent with the monetary policy objectives.

Money Market ensures that institutions which have surplus funds earn certain returns on the surplus. Otherwise these funds will be idle with the institutions. Similarly, the money market ensures funds for the needy at reasonable interest. This way liquidity position is assured by money market operations. The main objectives of money market are as follows:

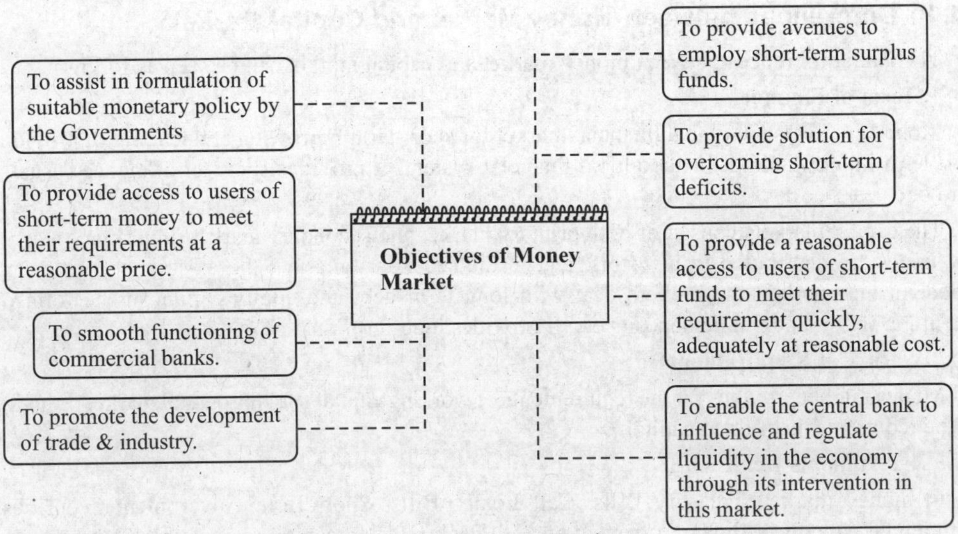

3.3 GENERAL FEATURES OF MONEY MARKET

The following are the common features of money markets:

(*a*) Money market is a market purely for short-terms funds or financial assets called near money.

(*b*) Money market deals with financial assets having a maturity period less than one year only.

(*c*) It is not a single homogeneous market, it comprises of several submarket like call money market, acceptance & bill market.

(*d*) In money market transactions are not conducted in a formal place like stock exchange. There is no fixed place for conduct of operations and the transactions being conducted even over the phone.

(*e*) In money markets, the transactions are taking place only through oral communication, mainly by telephone communications, relevant document and written communication.

(*f*) Transactions are conducted without the help of brokers.

(*g*) The components of money market are the commercial banks, acceptance houses & NBFC (Non-banking financial companies).

(*h*) It is a wholesale market and the volume of funds or financial assets traded in the market are very large.

3.4 MONEY MARKET AND CAPITAL MARKET

Before going to explore the meaning and functions of the money market one should understand the difference between money market and capital market. The capital market is a type of financial market, it includes the stocks and bonds market as well. But in general the capital market is the market for securities where either companies or the government can raise long-term funds. The capital market consists of two markets, the primary market and it is where new issues are distributed to investors, and the secondary market where existing securities are traded.

Where as the money market is the market for short-term borrowing and lending and provides short term liquid funding for the global financial system. The average amount of time that companies borrow money in a money market is about one year or lower. Some of the more common instruments used in the money market are certificates of deposits, bankers' acceptance, repurchase agreements, commercial paper etc.

3.4.1 Differences between Money Market and Capital Market

The main differences between money market and capital market can be seen as follows:

1. Term of Finance:

Money market is the global financial market for short-term borrowing and lending. It provides short term liquid funding for the global financial system. It provides short-term finance (usually up to one year)

The capital markets consist of both primary market and secondary market. In primary market new issues are distributed to investors, and in the secondary market, the existing securities are traded. In this market, the brokers deal with long term debt and equity capital in the form of debenture, shares and public deposits etc. It provides long-term finance.

2. Nature of Requirements:

Money market provides for the requirements of working capital. But the capital market provides for the requirements of fixed capital.

3. Instruments Dealt with:

In money market, Treasury Bills, Call Loans, Bills, Short-Term Government Securities, Commercial paper, Certificate of deposit etc. are dealt with. In capital market shares, debentures and public deposits of industrial concerns, bonds and other long-term securities of Government are dealt with.

4. Assistance:

Money market helps in solving liquidity problems of banks as well as Government. Capital market assists in sourcing out long-term financial needs of industry and Government.

5. Main Participants:

The participants of money market include Central Bank, commercial banks, financial institutions, development financial institutions like IDBI, IFCs, ICICI, UTI, LIC, GIC, foreign banks, mutual funds, co-operative banks etc.

The primary participants in capital market are all companies and large number of investors. The investment banks like IDBI, IFCs, ICICI, SFCs, insurance companies, other financial institutions, etc, are also participating in capital markets.

6. Degree of Risk:

The level of risk is little in the money market. The maturity period of up to one year gives little time for a default to happen, so the risk is minimized.

The risk is high in capital market comparing to money market. The risk varies both in degree and nature in the capital market.

7. Regulating Authorities:

The rate of interest in money market is controlled by the central bank of the country. In India it is controlled by the RBI.

The rates of interest and dividend in capital market depend on the demand and supply of securities and the conditions of stock market. In India, stock market is regulated by SEBI.

Thus, Money Market is a place for short-term lending and borrowing, typically within a year. It deals in short term debt financing and investments. On the other hand, Capital Market refers to stock market, which refers to trading in shares and bonds of companies on recognized stock exchanges. Individual players cannot invest in money market as the value of investments is large, on the other hand, in capital market, anybody can make investments through a broker. Capital/Stock Market is associated with high risk and high return as against Money Market which is more secure. In case of money market, deals are transacted on phone or through electronic systems as against capital market where trading is through recognized stock exchanges. These two markets work together and are possibly interdependent. Some institutions like commercial banks operate in both markets. Basically, money market and capital market are the segments of one market called market of credit.

3.5 CHARACTERISTICS OF DEVELOPED MONEY MARKET

The developed money markets as in the countries of England and U.S.A. have the following characteristics:

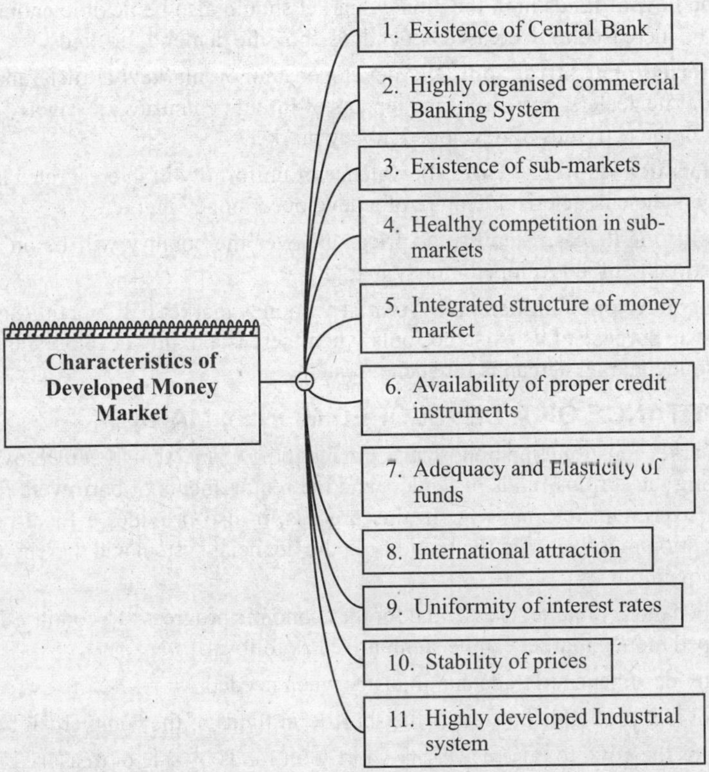

(*i*) Existence of Central Bank: In the developed money market, the role of Central Bank is notable. It controls the entire money market operations by making the availability of funds depending upon the economic cycles. It can be done through its open market operations.

(*ii*) Highly organised Banking System: As they are the main dealers in short-term funds, the commercial banks are considered as nervous system of the money market. Therefore, a well developed money market will have a highly organised and developed commercial banking system.

(*iii*) Existence of sub-markets: In developed money markets the various sub-markets existed and functioning smoothly. That is, the money market will have developed sub-markets such as bill market, call money market, acceptance market, discount market etc. It can be said that the larger the number of sub-markets, the broader and more developed will be the structure of the money market.

(*iv*) Prevalence of healthy competition: In each sub-market there should be a reasonable and healthy competition. That is, in a developed money market, there are a large number of borrowers, lenders and dealers. Then only each market will be active enough to achieve the purpose of its existence.

(*v*) Integration of sub-markets: In the developed money market there will be a perfect integration among various sub-markets of the money market. Their functioning are interdependent.

The funds flow from one sub-market to another and the activities of one sub-market should create effects in the other markets also.

(*vi*) Availability of proper credit instruments: The developed money market should have the necessary credit instruments such as treasury bills, promissory notes, bills of exchange etc. They should be freely available.

(*vii*) Flexibility and adequacy of funds: In a developed money market, there must be ample resources. The flow of funds in to the money market should also be flexible enough, *i.e.*, the flow of funds can be increased or decreased depending upon the demand for funds.

(*viii*) International attraction: The developed money markets attract funds from foreign countries also. The dealers, borrowers and lenders of foreign countries are eagerly coming forward to participate in the activities of developed money market.

(*ix*) Uniformity of interest rates: Prevalence of uniformity in interest rates in different parts of the country is the characteristic feature of a developed money market.

(*x*) Stability of Prices: Stability of prices all over the country will be an outcome of the effective functioning of a developed money market.

(*xi*) Highly developed industrial System: The money market will function smoothly and can achieve the basic purpose of its existence only when there is a highly developed industrial system. Developed money market demands for such a system.

3.6 IMPORTANCE OF A DEVELOPED MONEY MARKET

Money market constitutes an important segment of the financial market by providing an avenue for equilibrating the surplus funds of lenders and the requirements of borrowers for short periods ranging from overnight upto an year. In this process, it also provides a focal point for central bank's intervention in influencing the liquidity in the financial system and thereby transmitting the monetary policy impulses.

A developed money market is essential for the economic progress of a country. The significance of the developed money market can be summarised as follows:

(*a*) It provides finance to trade and industry when needed.

(*b*) It provides profitable out-let for the short-term funds of the commercial banks.

(*c*) It helps the govt. to raise necessary short-term funds by sale of treasury bills.

(*d*) Attracts foreign funds.

(*e*) It helps the Central Bank in the following ways:

- (*i*) Helps to formulate and implement the monetary policy
- (*ii*) Helps to carry out its open market operations on a large scale
- (*iii*) Provides commercial bills to the Central Bank for re-discount
- (*iv*) Helps in the regulation of the movement of funds in the money market.

3.7 CONSTITUENTS OF MONEY MARKET

Money market is the market where money or its equivalent can be traded. Money is synonym of liquidity. Money market consists of financial institutions and dealers in money or credit who wish to generate liquidity. The main participants/various institutions in the money market generally include the following:

1. Central Bank:

It is naturally to be the leader of all banks. It is the bank, which is entrusted with the task of controlling the issue of money & funds to the market and regulates credit facilities provided by various other institutions. Reserve Bank of India is the over all regulator of Indian money market.

2. Commercial Banks:

They play a vital role in the money market. They make advances, discount bills and lend against the promissory notes and the like. They also take help of the market in solving their liquidity problems. They mobilise the savings through acceptance of deposits and lend it to business houses for their short-term working capital requirements. While a portion of these deposits is invested in medium and long-term Government securities and corporate shares and bonds, they provide short-term funds to the Government by investing in the Treasury Bills. They employ the short-term surpluses in various money market instruments.

3. Financial and Investment Institutions:

These institutions (*e.g.* LIC, UTI, GIC, Development Banks, etc.) have been allowed to participate in the call money market as lenders only.

4. Discount Houses:

Discount houses are special institutions for re-discounting the bills of exchange. They usually deal in three kinds of bills.

(*a*) the domestic bills (*b*) the foreign bills and

(*c*) the government treasury bills.

The discount houses borrow huge funds for short periods from the commercial banks and RBI and invest them in discounting bills. But before discounting a trade bill of exchange, the Discount House insists that it should be accepted by an Acceptance House.

5. Acceptance Houses:

Acceptance Houses are institutions which specialise in accepting bills of exchange. Generally they are merchant bankers. They act as second signatories on the bills of exchange. That is they guarantee the bills of a trader whose financial standing is not known, for making the bill negotiable. They maintain correspondents in important towns of various places within and outside the country to collect information about the credit-worthiness and financial position of the customers, who seek the assistance of the Acceptance Houses. For their service, they charge a small amount of commission but ensure great security for the bills discounted by the Discount Houses.

6. Bill Brokers:

The "Bill Brokers" intimately know their customers and act as intermediaries between the sellers and buyers of bill for a small commission. Sometimes, these bill brokers discount bills on their own account.

7. Mutual Funds:

In India Mutual funds also invest their surplus funds in different money market instruments for short periods. They are permitted to participate in the Call Money Market. Money Market Mutual Funds have been set up specifically for the purpose of mobilization of short-term funds for investment in money market instruments.

8. Others: Today on approval RBI the development financial institutions etc., are also actively participate in this market.

3.8 INDIAN MONEY MARKET

In India the money market plays a vital role in the progress of economy. But, it is not well developed when compared with American and London money markets. In this market short-term funds are borrowed and lent among participants permitted by RBI.

3.8.1 Structure of Indian Money Market

Before knowing the instruments traded in the Indian money market let us have a look on its organisational structure.

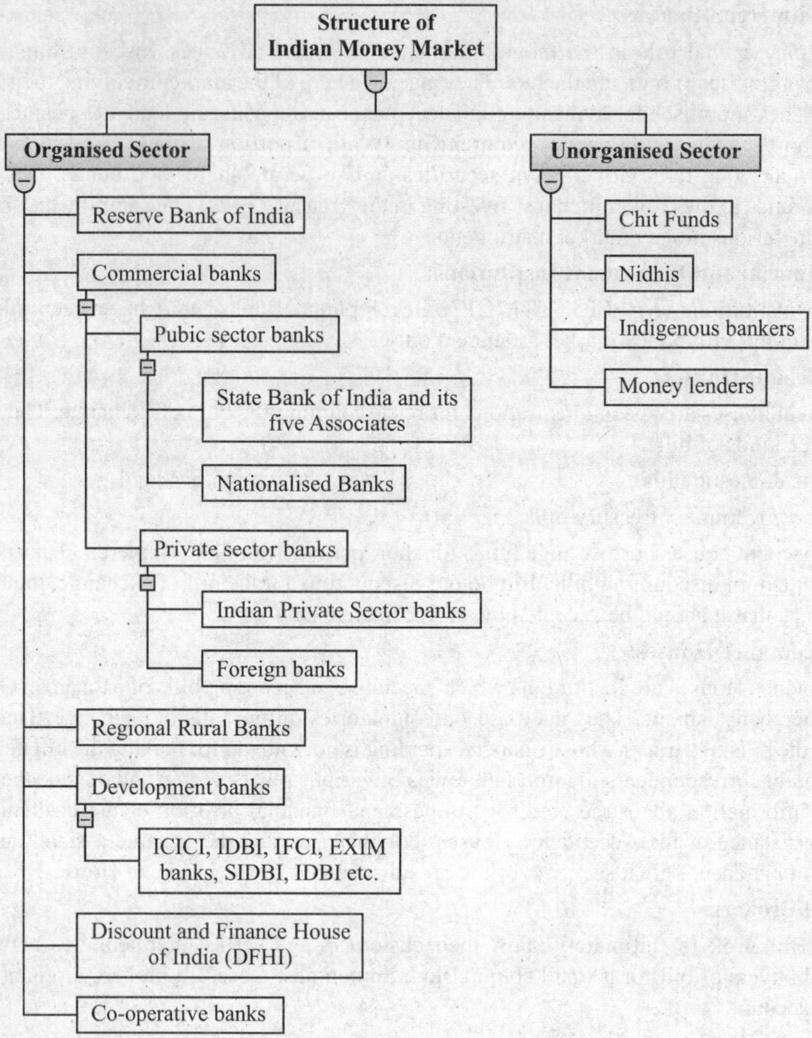

3.8.2 Features of Indian Money Market

The Indian money market till mid-1980s was relatively underdeveloped with few instruments and strict regulations with regard to participants and interest rates. Another issue of concern was that the distribution of liquidity in the market was skewed with a few large lenders and some chronic borrowers. The basic pre-requisite of a deep and liquid market that participants should alternate between borrowing and lending activity (*i.e.*, providing two-way quotes) was also absent.

Indian money market is relatively underdeveloped when compared with developed markets like London and New York money markets. The main features/defects of Indian money market are given below:

1. Lack of Integration:

The Indian money market consists of both organised and unorganised sectors. It is a significant aspect of the Indian money market. The organised money market consists of RBI, all scheduled commercial banks and other recognised financial institutions. However, the unorganised money market includes domestic money lenders, indigenous bankers, chitfunds, etc. The control measures of RBI are very effective in the organised sector. But, it is not so effective in unorganised sector and thus, it remains outside the control of RBI. The organised and unorganised money markets are not well integrated with each other in India.

2. Diversity in Interest Rates:

There are many interest rates prevailing in Indian money market. The interest rates differ from bank to bank from time to time. And in both organized and unorganized markets the interest rates differ. Thus, there are many rates of interest prevailing in Indian money market. These divergent interest rates limit the efficiency of the bank rate policy of the RBI. The immobility of funds from one place to another may also be considered as an important reason for this multiplicity of interest rates.

3. Existence of Unorganized Sector:

The unorganised sector still exists in Indian money market. Indigenous bankers dominate in this sector of the money market. They follow their own rules and practices of finance and banking. They do not make any distinction between short term and long-term finance. They have no coordination with each other and have no link with other banking sectors. They do not follow any sound banking regulations.

4. Absence of an Organised Bill Market:

A well-organized bill market is essential for the smooth working of the credit system of the country. It is also necessary for linking up the various credit agencies effectively with the central bank of the country. In Indian money market, there is no adequate bill market. The commercial bill market and the possibility of discounting bills for short term are not well organized. And this may be due to the reasons such as the commercial transactions are mainly in cash, absence of acceptance houses etc.

5. Inadequacy of Funds in the Money Market:

In Indian money market there is shortage of funds due to inadequate banking facility, less saving habits etc. The increasing demand for funds in the money market exceeds its supply and intensifies the problem of shortage of funds.

6. Seasonal shortage of Money:

The notable feature of the India money market is the seasonal shortage of money and high interest rates due to the increasing demand for funds. That is, the demand for money in Indian money market is of a seasonal nature. India being an agriculture predominant economy, the demand for money is raised from the agricultural operations. During the busy season more agricultural activities takes place leading to a higher demand for money in the money market.

7. Limited Instruments:

In Indian money market the supply of various instruments such as the Treasury Bills, Commercial Bills, Certificate of Deposits, Commercial Papers, etc., is very limited.

8. Other Features:

In addition to the above specific features, the Indian money market has certain other basic defects including restriction of players in the market, undue influence of supply based-sources, inefficient payment systems and lack of transparency.

3.8.3 Measures to Strengthen the Indian Money Market

To strengthen the Indian money market, the government has taken many steps.

1. In pursuance of the recommendations of the Committee to Review the Working of the Monetary System and the Working Group on the Money Market, a number of measures were taken by RBI to widen and deepen the money market through institution building and instrument development.

2. Measures were also initiated to increase the number of participants in the money market.
3. The Discount and Finance House of India Ltd. (DFHI) was set up jointly by the Reserve Bank, public sector banks and financial institutions to deal in short-term money market instruments with the primary objective of imparting improved liquidity to such instruments.
4. While introduction of new instruments, broadening of participants' base and strengthening of institutional infrastructure have been pursued during the 1990s based on the framework provided by the Vaghul Committee.
5. The Narasimham Committee recommended rationalization of the participation of different classes of entities in various segments of money market. Pursuant to these recommendations, RBI has been initiating a number of structural and instrument-specific measures which have further contributed to the growth and sophistication of Indian money market.
6. There are three broad policy objectives that are being followed now for the development of the Indian money market which include
   (*a*) Ensuring stability in short-term interest rates
   (*b*) Minimising default risk
   (*c*) Achieving a balanced development of various segments of money market.

3.8.4 Role of RBI in Indian Money Market

The Reserve Bank of India is regulator of the money market. It plays an important role in the Indian Money Market. It manages the liquidity in the money market by granting refinance facilities to the banks and by stipulating the reserve requirements. Cash Reserve Ratio (CRR) and Statutory Liquidity Requirements (SLR) are the main tools to affect the liquidity with the banks. When the banking system has excess liquidity, Reserve Bank of India raises the Cash Reserve Ratio (CRR) and thus, takes away the surplus liquidity and vice-versa. Statutory Liquidity requirement is raised to divert bank funds mainly to Government and other approved securities and thereby reducing liquidity with banks.

Reserve Bank's operations in the money market aims at the following:

- To ensure that liquidity and short-term interest rates according to levels determined in the monetary policy of the Government.
- To ensure an adequate flow of credit to the productive sector of the economy.
- To bring about order in the foreign exchange market.

The Reserve Bank of India influence liquidity and interest rates through a number of operating instruments – cash reserve requirement (CRR) of banks, conduct of open market operations, repos, change in bank rates and at times, foreign exchange swap operations.

3.8.5 Money Market Instruments in India

Money Market Position:

As already mentioned Money Market refers to all the Institutions which deal in short-term funds, usually up to one year. There is no single meeting place of Money Market like stock market or commodity market. The institutions which have short-term surplus funds and those who require short-term funds (borrowers) get in touch with one another either directly or through agents/brokers over telephone/computer network and exchange funds by writing down cheques/pay orders etc.

3.8.5.1 General Features of Money Market Instruments

Money market securities are highly marketable and are quickly convertible into cash (making them very liquid). They also have the shortest maturities of any debt securities. Money markets are used to invest great amounts of cash safely for short periods. Money market instrument, a debt must meet the following criteria:

(*a*) Money market instruments are un-collateralised short-term (one year or less) debt of an issuer with a high credit standing.

(*b*) Money market instruments easily marketable, readily transferable, and very acceptable to institutional investors.

(*c*) The money market specialises in debt securities that mature in less than one year.

(*d*) Money market securities are very liquid, and considered very safe. As a result, they offer a lower return than other securities.

(*e*) T-bills are short-term government securities that mature in one year or less from their issue date.

(*f*) T-bills are considered to be one of the safest investments, and so do not give a great return.

(*g*) A certificate of deposit is a time deposit with a bank.

(*h*) Certificate of deposits are safe, but the returns are not great, and our money is tied up for the length of the certificate of deposits.

(*i*) Commercial paper is an unsecured, short-term loan issued by a corporation. Returns are higher than T-bills because of the higher default risk.

(*j*) Repurchase agreements (repos) are a form of overnight borrowing backed by government securities.

Money Market ensures that institutions, which have surplus funds, earn certain returns on the surplus. Otherwise these funds will be idle with the institutions. Similarly, the money market ensures funds for the needy at reasonable interest. This way liquidity position is assured by money market operations.

3.8.5.2 Instruments Traded in Indian Money Market

In India RBI regulates the Money Market. Hence the instruments traded and the players in the market require to be approved by RBI. The types of financial instruments traded in the Indian Money Market can be shown in the following chart.

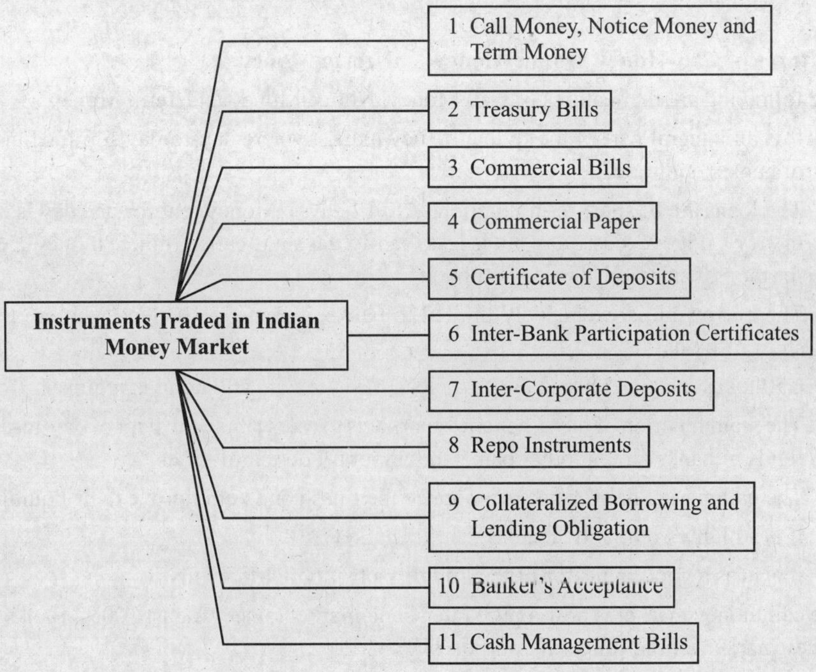

Let us now discuss the various money market instruments in India. In India the Money Market is regulated by RBI. Hence the instruments traded and the players in the market require to be approved by RBI. The instruments currently traded are as follows:

1. Call Money, Notice Money and Term Money:

The call money market is an integral part of the Indian Money Market, where the day-to-day surplus funds (mostly of banks) are traded. The loans are of short-term duration varying from 1 to 14 days. The money that is lent for one day in this market is known as "Call Money", and if it exceeds one day (but less than 15 days) it is referred to as "Notice Money". Term Money refers to Money lent for 15 days or more in the Inter bank Market.

***(a)* Call Money:** Call money is a method of borrowing and lending for one day. This is also called overnight money. The rate of interest used to be decided by RBI earlier. After 1989, the interest rate was deregulated and now the liquidity position (availability of funds) determines the rate of interest. The lender issues a cheque or Pay order on its account maintained with RBI in favour of borrower.

Accordingly, RBI transfers funds by debit to lender's account to the borrower's account. On repayment, the process is reversed through RBI. In times of tight money, situation or liquidity crunch, the call money interest rate goes up even beyond 50 percent per annum. Only permitted organisations like scheduled commercial banks, large co-operative banks, DHFI, Primary dealers, NABARD are permitted to borrow funds through call money market. However, funds can be provided or lent even by other entities like LIC, GIC, large corporates, big mutual funds etc.

***(b)* Notice Money/Short-term Money:** Under Notice Money Market, funds are borrowed and lent for a maximum period of 14 days. Repayment requires a formal notice or demand from the lender. Interest rate is decided by the market forces. The market is similar to call money market explained above.

***(c)* Term Money:** Funds borrowed/lent for 15 days and more up to a maximum period of 1 year.

Features of Call Money, Notice Money and Term Money:

The following are the features of Call Money, Notice Money and Term Money:

(*i*) It is an integral part of the Indian money market where day-to-day surplus funds (mostly of banks) are traded.

(*ii*) The loans are of short-term duration (1 to 14 days). Money lent for one day is called 'call money'; if it exceeds 1 day but is less than 15 days it is called 'notice money'. Money lent for more than 15 days is 'term money'.

(*iii*) The borrowing is exclusively limited to banks & Primary Dealers, who are temporarily short of funds.

(*iv*) Call loans are generally made on a clean basis- *i.e.* no collateral is required.

(*v*) The main function of the call money market is to redistribute the pool of day-to-day surplus funds of banks among other banks in temporary deficit of funds.

(*vi*) The call market helps banks economise their cash and yet improve their liquidity.

(*vii*) It is a highly competitive and sensitive market.

(*viii*) It acts as a good indicator of the liquidity position Participants.

The call money market is now a pure inter-bank market (since August 2005). Banks borrow in this money market for the following purposes:

(*a*) To fill the gaps or temporary mismatches in funds.

(*b*) To meet the CRR & SLR mandatory requirements as stipulated by the RBI.

(*c*) To meet sudden demand for funds arising out of large outflows.

(*d*) Thus call money usually serves the role of equilibrating the short-term liquidity position of banks.

2. Treasury Bills:

The Treasury bills are short-term money market instrument that mature in a year or less than that. The purchase price is less than the face value. At maturity the government pays the Treasury Bill holder the full face value. The Treasury Bills are marketable, affordable and risk free. The security attached to the treasury bills comes at the cost of very low returns. It is the most important money market instrument for the central government. Treasury Bills are short-term promissory notes issued by RBI on behalf of Central Government for raising funds to meet short falls in revenue collections *i.e.*, to meet revenue expenditure. These are issued at discount to face value.

Need for the issue of Treasury Bills: The necessity for issuing treasury bills arises because of the periodic nature of receipts of Government while the Government expenditure is on a continuing basis. Taxes are payable to the Government after quarterly intervals or so, but Government has to meet its expenditure on daily or monthly basis. Thus, to bridge this mis-match between the timings of Government receipts and expenditure, Government borrows money on short-term basis by issuing Treasury Bills.

Maturity Period: RBI auctions these Treasury Bills at regular periodical intervals *i.e.* weekly and fortnightly. These days the types of Treasury Bills depending upon their maturity are auctioned by RBI. These are 91-day,182 day and 364 day Treasury Bills. Any person can invest in Treasury Bills. These are very high liquid and safe instruments. Treasury Bills are approved securities for investment by banks under SLR requirement. Out of the bids received by it, the Reserve Bank of India accepts bids upto the notified amount after determining its cut-off rate.

Amount of Treasury Bills: Treasury bills are available for a minimum amount of ₹ 25,000 and in multiples of ₹ 25,000. Treasury bills are issued at a discount and are redeemed at par. Treasury bills are available for a minimum amount of ₹25,000 and in multiples of ₹ 25,000.

Types of Treasury Bills: Treasury Bills or T-Bills are issued by the Government of India to meet their short-term requirement. T-Bills are issued for 91-day, 182-day and 364-day maturities. T-Bills are issued at a discount to their face value and redeemed at par. The 364-day T-Bills forms part of the government borrowing programme.

There are three types of Treasury Bills.

Type of T-bills	*Day of Auction*	*Day of Payment**
91-day	Wednesday	Following Friday
182-day	Wednesday of non-reporting week	Following Friday
364-day	Wednesday of reporting week	Following Friday

* If the day of payment falls on a holiday, the payment is made on the day after the holiday.

Features of T-Bills auction :

- All T-Bills auctions are Price-based.
- All T-Bills are auctioned on Multiple-Price basis.

Turnover in Government Securities Market (Face Value) (₹ Billion)

*Week / Month**	*Govt. of India Dated Securities*	*State Govt. Securities*	*Treasury Bills*			
			Cash Management Bills	*91 Day*	*182 Day*	*364 Day*
	1	2	3	4	5	6
2012-13						
April	5,335.3	166.7	–	456.5	179.0	167.2
May	5,960.6	143.1	–	358.9	123.0	163.0
June	11,846.3	153.3	–	556.5	191.0	395.1
July	8,753.6	177.5	–	384.0	214.9	308.6
August	7,985.4	223.6	–	681.7	290.9	384.8
WEEK ENDED						
September 7, 2012	2,317.0	42.9	–	125.4	86.4	115.4
September 14,2012	2,745.6	23.7	–	98.4	78.6	61.6
September 21, 2012	2,414.5	34.7	–	78.8	52.6	68.4
September 28, 2012	2,405.5	32.4	–	123.1	51.3	104.9

Source: RBI Publications

Govt. of India: Treasury Bills Outstanding (₹ Billion)

As on September 19, 2014	*Major Holders*			*Total*
	Banks	*Primary Dealers*	*State Govts.*	
	1	2	3	4
14-day	–	–	632.9	636.2
91-day	342.0	340.2	596.8	1,765.4
182-day	261.1	268.7	74.5	775.1
364-day	436.1	454.8	12.0	1,425.3
CMB	–	–	–	–

Source: RBI Publications

3. Commercial Bills:

Banks are discounting Commercial Bills drawn by business entities/organisations. Banks can get such discounted bills rediscounted in Money Market. It is not necessary for banks to rediscount each and every discounted bill. Banks can certify the large number of bills intended to be rediscounted through a single document known as "Derivative Usance Promissory Note" (DUPN). In other words, 'DUPN' is a money market instrument backed by genuine commercial bills. Banks can get the value of DUPN discounted and obtain funds. This way banks can borrow funds without transferring the bills. It is necessary that the original bills in the portfolio of banks should not be drawn for period exceeding 120 days. The maturity of DUPN, however, should not exceed 90 days.

4. Commercial Paper:

Commercial Paper is a short-term money market instrument issued by eligible corporates for raising funds to meet working capital needs. It is used as a source of short-term finance as an alternative to bank finance for working capital. Generally, Corporates prefer to raise funds through this source, when the interest rate on working capital charged by banks is higher than the rate at which funds can be raised through Commercial Paper. It was introduced in 1990. The Commercial Paper is in nature of negotiable usance promissory notes issued at a discount to face value.

The Commercial Paper should have fixed maturity period of not less than 30 days and not more than one year. Corporates having fund-based working capital facility of ₹4 crore or more from banks are only eligible to issue Commercial Papers. Aggregate value of Commercial Papers which can be issued by a corporate is limited to the maximum working capital facility fixed by the banks. They can be issued in denominations of ₹5 lakh or multiples thereof. Investors in Commercial Papers should have a minimum investment of ₹10 lakh and multiples of ₹5 lakh thereafter.

Individuals, banking companies, other corporate bodies registered or incorporated in India and unincorporated bodies, Non-Resident Indians (NRIs) and Foreign Institutional Investors (FIIs) etc. can invest in Commercial Papers. The amount invested by single investor should not be less than ₹5 lakh (face value). However, investment by FIIs would be within the limits set for their investments by Securities and Exchange Board of India – SEBI. The commercial paper issued by companies can be seen in the following Table:

Commercial Paper

Fortnight Ended	*Amount Outstanding (₹ Billion)*	*During the Fortnight*	
		Amount Issued (₹ Billion)	*Rate of Interest (Per cent)*
	1	2	3
Aug. 31, 2014	2,112.0	358.6	8.26 – 12.62
Sep. 15, 2014	2,329.9	685.3	8.26 – 12.00

Source: RBI Publications

Eligibility to issue commercial papers: The Corporates, primary dealers and the All-India Financial Institutions are eligible to issue Commercial Paper. The RBI decides about the eligibility criteria for corporates to raise funds through Commercial Papers on the basis of:

(*i*) Working capital fund limit (₹4 crore or more)

(*ii*) Minimum current ratio (1.33)

(*iii*) Minimum credit rating (P2 of CRISIL or A2 of ICRA etc).

(*iv*) Company has been sanctioned working capital limit by bank/s or All-India financial institution/s.

(*v*) The borrow account of the company is classified as a Standard Asset by the financing bank/s/ institution/s.

Primary Dealers are also recently permitted to issue CPs. Funds raised through CPs should normally be cheaper as compared to bank funds. Hence, corporates raise funds through issue of C.Ps only when the money market interest rates are fairly low.

The aggregate amount of CP from an issuer shall be within the limit as approved by its Board of Directors or the quantum indicated by the Credit Rating Agency for the specified rating, whichever is lower. As regards FIs, they can issue CP within the overall umbrella limit fixed by the RBI *i.e.*, issue of CP together with other instruments viz., term money borrowings, term deposits, certificates of deposit and inter-corporate deposits should not exceed 100 per cent of its net owned funds, as per the latest audited balance sheet.

Mode of Redemption: Initially the investor in CP is required to pay only the discounted value of the CP by means of a crossed account payee cheque to the account of the issuer through IPA. On maturity of CP, (*a*) when the CP is held in physical form, the holder of the CP shall present the instrument for payment to the issuer through the Issuing and Paying Agent. And (*b*) when the CP is held in demat form, the holder of the CP will have to get it redeemed through the depository and receive payment from the Issuing and Paying Agent.

5. Certificate of Deposits:

Certificate of Deposit (CD) is a negotiable money market instrument and issued in dematerialised form or as a Usance Promissory Note against funds deposited at a bank or other eligible financial institution for a specified time period. Guidelines for issue of CDs are presently governed by various directives issued by the Reserve Bank of India (RBI), as amended from time to time. The guidelines for issue of CDs, incorporating all the amendments issued till date, are given below for ready reference.

It is another form of short-term time deposit. The receipt issued for such type of deposit is called Certificate of Deposit. Banks can raise short term funds say for 3 or 6 months at rate of interest different from its normal Time Deposit rate through issue of C.Ds. Interest is paid from the date of purchase till maturity. Banks issue C.Ds to manage liquidity and to raise funds at marginally varying rate of interest as compared to short-term deposit rates. As per RBI regulations CDs can be issued for a minimum maturity of 3 months and a maximum period of 1 year. Minimum investment should be of ₹10 lakh and further investments should be in multiple of ₹5 lakh. These are issued at discount to face value. In India this instrument was first introduced in 1989. Individuals, Corporates, Trusts and any persons can invest in Certificate of Deposits.

Banks issue Certificate of Deposits to manage liquidity and to raise funds at marginally varying rate of interest as compared to short-term deposit rates. Certificate of Deposits are considered as virtually safety instruments as the default risk is almost nil and investors are sure of receiving the invested amount with interest. They are freely transferable by endorsement and delivery, immediately after the date of issue and can be traded in secondary market from the date of issue, unlike conventional deposits.

It is a short-term borrowing more like a bank term deposit account. It is a promissory note issued by a bank in form of a certificate entitling the bearer to receive interest. The certificate bears the maturity date, the fixed rate of interest and the value. It can be issued in any denomination. They are stamped and transferred by endorsement. Its term generally ranges from three months to five years and restricts the holders to withdraw funds on demand. However, on payment of certain penalty the money can be withdrawn on demand.

Eligibility: CDs can be issued by (*i*) scheduled commercial banks {excluding Regional Rural Banks and Local Area Banks}; and (*ii*) select All-India Financial Institutions (FIs) that have been permitted by RBI to raise short-term resources within the umbrella limit fixed by RBI.

Minimum Size of Issue and Denominations: Minimum amount of a CD should be ₹1 lakh, *i.e.*, the minimum deposit that could be accepted from a single subscriber should not be less than ₹1 lakh, and in multiples of ₹ 1 lakh thereafter.

The certificate of deposits issued by the commercial banks in 2014 and be seen from the following table:

Certificates of Deposit Issued by Scheduled Commercial Banks

Item	*2013*	*2014*			
	Jul. 26	*Jun. 13*	*Jun. 27*	*Jul. 27*	*Jul. 25*
	1	2	3	4	5
1 Amount Outstanding (₹ Billion)	3,361.8	3,227.3	3,375.9	3,212.3	3,032.5
1.1 Issued during the fortnight (₹ Billion)	32.4	512.3	448.8	122.0	84.8
2 Rate of Interest (per cent)	7.90–9.85	8.08–9.11	8.48–9.29	8.33–8.96	8.38–9.41

Source: RBI Publications

The returns on Certificate of Deposits are higher than T-Bills because it assumes higher level of risk. While buying Certificate of Deposit, return method should be seen. Returns can be based on Annual Percentage Yield (APY) or Annual Percentage Rate (APR). In APY, interest earned is based on compounded interest calculation. However, in APR method, simple interest calculation is done to generate the return. Accordingly, if the interest is paid annually, equal return is generated by both APY and APR methods. However, if interest is paid more than once in a year, it is beneficial to opt APY over APR.

Resources raised by the Financial Institutions from money market through CPs and CDs can be seen from the following Table:

Resources Raised by Financial Institutions from Money Market

(As at end-March 2013) (Amount in ₹ billion)

Instrument	*EXIM*	*NABARD*	*NHB*	*SIDBI*	*Total*
1	2	3	4	5	6
A. Total	65.2	85.0	11.0	27.3	188.5
(*i*) Term Deposits	6.1	0	0.7	6.7	13.5
(*ii*) Term Money	0	3.1	0	0	3.1
(*iii*) Inter-Corporate Deposits (ICDs)	0	0	0	0	0
(*iv*) Certificate of Deposits (CDs)	6.3	0	0	0	6.3
(*v*) Commercial Paper (CPs)	52.8	81.9	10.3	20.6	165.6
(*vi*) Short-term loans from banks	0	0	38.3	0	38.3
Memo:					
B. Umbrella Limit	85.8	164.1	47.3	64.0	361.1
C. Utilisation of Umbrella limit* (A as percentage of B)	76.0	51.8	23.3	42.6	52.2

*: Resources raised under the Umbrella Limit include A (*i*) through A (v).

Source: RBI Report on Trend and Progress of Banking in India 2012-13

Advantages of Certificate of Deposit:

The main advantages of Certificate of Deposit as a money market instrument include the following:

(*a*) Since one can know the returns from before, the certificates of deposits are considered much safe.

(*b*) One can earn more as compared to depositing money in savings account.

Limitations of Certificate of Deposit:

The following are the general limitations of Certificate of Deposit:

(*a*) As compared to other investments the returns is less.

(*b*) The money is tied up along with the long maturity period of the Certificate of Deposit.

(*c*) Huge penalties are paid if one gets out of it before maturity.

6. Inter-Bank Participation Certificates:

Inter Bank Participation Certificates or simply Participation Certificates are short-term papers issued by scheduled commercial banks to raise funds from other banks against big loan portfolios. When banks are short of liquidity to carry on their immediate operations and need short-term funds, they may approach other banks to share/participate in their lending portfolios. In other words, part of the specified loans and advances of the borrowing bank will be passed on to the lender-bank against cash. This will have the effect of reducing the exposure of borrower-bank on its particular loan portfolio and increase in the portfolio of lender-bank when the participation is without recourse basis. Borrower-banks can have access to the facility only, upto certain percentage (currently 40%) of their standard or performing assets *i.e.*, Loans and Advances which are being serviced without default Participation Certificates can be issued only for a maximum period of 180 days and not less than a 90-day period.

7. Inter-Corporate Deposits:

Inter-corporate Deposits or ICD is another money market instrument for corporates to park their temporary surplus funds with other corporates. What a participation certificate for banks is an inter corporate deposits between corporates. Under ICD, corporates lend temporary funds generally to their own group companies, otherwise the credit risk will be higher. Any corporate can issue the instrument without there being any prescription about minimum size of such lending and borrowings. This market is not well-regulated for want of adequate information.

Inter Corporate Deposits are unsecured loans extended by corporate with excess funds to other corporate bodies. The rates in this market are higher as compared to that of other markets. An ICD is an unsecured loan extended by one corporate to another. This market allows corporates with surplus funds to lend to other corporates. Also the better-rated corporates can borrow from the banking system and lend in this market. As the cost of funds for a corporate is much higher than that for a bank, the rates in this market are higher than those in the other markets. Also, as ICDs are unsecured, the risk inherent is high and the risk premium is also built into the rates.

RBI permits Primary Dealers to accept Inter-Corporate Deposits upto fifty percent of their Net Worth and for a period of not less than 7 days. Primary Dealers cannot lend in the ICD market. Apart from CPs, corporate also have access to another market called the inter corporate deposits (ICD) market.

8. 'Repo' Instruments:

Repo is shortform for 'repurchase agreement'. A repo is a contract between a buyer and a seller of debt securities stating that the seller will repurchase the securities after a certain period of time or after certain conditions have been met. The contract requires that the seller repurchase the securities later for a price higher than what it was originally sold for. This difference between what the buyer paid, and what the seller paid for repurchase, is called the repo rate.

This transaction raises short-term funds to the party selling the securities. It essentially results in cash money form the buyer to the seller at the beginning of the transaction, which will be reversed at the end of the transaction. The underlying securities that are bought and sold are generally government securities. There are no regulations prescribing the minimum or maximum duration for a repo transaction. Hence the minimum period can be even a day while the maximum period is normally 14 days. The repos for a longer-term are also seen in the market. Even though there is no statutory limit for this maximum period, normally it does not exceed 3 months.

Those who deal in government securities use repos as a form of overnight borrowing. A dealer or other holder of government securities (usually T-bills) sells the securities to a lender and agrees to repurchase them at an agreed future date at an agreed price. This short-term maturity and government backing means repos provide lenders with extremely low risk. Repos are popular because they can virtually eliminate credit problems.

There are different types of repos other than standard repos. They are:

- **Reverse Repo** - the complete opposite of a repo, where a dealer buys government securities from an investor and then sells them back on a later date at a higher price.
- **Term Repo** - Term repos are repurchase agreements for periods of 30 to 90 days. They cannot be sold on the open market because they are tailored to the original buyers' and sellers' needs. Overnight repos last only one day. This puts them at the shortest end of the maturity spectrum.

RBI conducts 'Repo' transactions to influence short-term interest level in money market. By Repo operation the RBI transmit interest rate signals to the market. When it announces a fixed rate Repo for certain number of days or period, it conveys its intention to the market about the desirable level of a short-term interest rate. Due to greater level of integration among money market, foreign exchange market and Treasury Bill Market, the Repo transactions ensure stability of short-term rates in all the three markets. At the same time Repo transactions of RBI provide an opportunity to banks to part their surplus funds with a minimum rate of return. We can understand that when RBI conducts 'repos', the short-term interest rate in the money market may not go below the RBI repo rate as if rate of interest is lower in other markets, holders of funds may go for 'Repos' with RBI.

The Government introduced repurchase agreements in order to manage the excess of liquidity in the system. In a situation where there is excess money supply, monetary contraction can be made possible by adopting repo transactions. That is, the Central bank can enter into repo transactions to remove the excess liquidity present in the system. RBI undertakes repos with banks as a part of its monetary management. When RBI enters into repo transactions it sells the securities to banks with an undertaking to buy them back. Thus the liquidity in the system is sucked out for the term of the Repo. RBI can add liquidity to the system by entering into reverse repos with banks and primary dealers against Government securities.

The advantage of a repurchase agreement is that the seller can get needed cash for short-term use without really losing control of their investment portfolio. Because the repurchase agreement specifies the repo rate, the seller may earn a higher return on the repurchased portfolio than with the repo rate. They are usually used for overnight borrowing. Repo/Reverse Repo transactions can be done only between the parties approved by RBI and in RBI approved securities viz. GOI and State Govt Securities, T-Bills, PSU Bonds, FI Bonds, Corporate Bonds etc.

RBI conducts 'Repo' transactions to influence short-term interest level in money market. By Repo operation the RBI transmit interest rate signals to the market. When it announces a fixed rate Repo for certain number of days/period it conveys its intention to the market about the desirable level of a short-term interest rate. Due to greater level of integration among money market, foreign exchange market and Treasury Bill Market, the Repo transactions ensure stability of short term rates in all the three markets. At the same time Repo transactions of RBI provide an opportunity to banks to part their surplus funds with a minimum rate of return. We can understand that when RBI conducts 'repos', the short-term interest rate in the money market may not go below the RBI repo rate as, if rate of interest is lower in other markets, holders of funds may go for 'Repos' with RBI. The RBI also provides liquidity support, *i.e.*, infusion of funds into the market by conducting reverse Repo transactions with Primary Dealers against Government Securities.

9. Collateralized Borrowing and Lending Obligation:

Collateralized Borrowing and Lending Obligation (CBLO), a money market instrument as approved by RBI, is a product developed by CCIL (The Clearing Corporation of India Ltd) for the benefit of the entities who have either been phased out from Inter Bank Call Money Market or have been given restricted participation in terms of ceiling on call borrowing and lending transactions and who do not have access to the call money market.

CBLO is a discounted instrument available in electronic book entry form for the maturity period ranging from one day to ninety days (can be made available up to one year as per RBI guidelines). In order to enable the market participants to borrow and lend funds, CBLO is an obligation by the borrower to return the money borrowed, at a specified future date; An authority to the lender to receive money lent, at a specified future date with an option/privilege to transfer the authority to another person for value received; An underlying charge on securities held in custody for the amount borrowed/lent.

Features of CBLO: It is a money market instrument that enables entities, which have restricted participation in the call money market, to borrow and lend. It has the following features:

(*i*) It is a discounted instrument which can be traded on CBLO Screen.

(*ii*) It is on electronic trading platform with the matching of the bids and yields take place on Best Yield-Time Priority basis.

(*iii*) The maturity ranges generally from 1 day to 90 days and can also be made available up to 1 year.

(*iv*) Central Government Securities including T-Bills are eligible securities that can be used as collateral for CBLO.

10. Banker's Acceptance:

It is a short-term credit investment. It is guaranteed by a bank to make payments. The Banker's Acceptance is traded in the Secondary Market. The banker's acceptance is mostly used to finance exports, imports and other transactions in goods. The banker's acceptance need not be held till the maturity date but the holder has the option to sell it off in the secondary market whenever he finds it suitable.

Although Banker's Acceptance, as they are known, have their origin in trade bills issued by merchants, today they are an important money market instrument. A banker's acceptance is simply a bill of exchange drawn by a person and accepted by a bank. The person drawing the bill must have a good credit rating otherwise the Banker's Acceptance will not be tradable. The drawer promises to make payment of the face value upon a given future date. The most common term for these instruments is 90 days. They can very from 30 days to180 days. The Banker's Acceptance has the advantage of locking the borrower in to a fixed rate over the term of the bill. This can be important if a rise in short-term rates is expected.

11. Cash Management Bills:

The Government of India, in consultation with the Reserve Bank of India, has decided to issue a new short-term instrument, known as Cash Management Bills, to meet the temporary cash flow mismatches of the Government. The Cash Management Bills will be non-standard, discounted instruments issued for maturities less than 91 days.

The Cash Management Bills will have the generic character of Treasury Bills and their sale will be subject to the terms and conditions specified in the General Notification No. F.2 (12)-W&M/97 dated 31st March 1998 issued by Government of India and as amended from time to time.

Features: The Cash Management Bills will have the following features:

(*a*) The tenure, notified amount and date of issue of the proposed Cash Management Bills will depend upon the temporary cash requirement of the Government. However, the tenure of the proposed Bills will be less than 91 days.

(*b*) The proposed Bills will be issued at discount to the face value through auctions, as in the case of the Treasury Bills.

(*c*) The announcement of the auction of the proposed Bills will be made by the Reserve Bank of India through separate Press Release to be issued one day prior to the date of auction.

(*d*) The settlement of the auction will be on T+1 basis.

(*e*) The Non-Competitive Bidding Scheme for Treasury Bills will not be extended to the Cash Management Bills.

(*f*) The proposed Bills will be tradable and qualify for ready forward facility. Investment in the proposed Bills will be reckoned as an eligible investment in Government Securities by banks for SLR purpose under Section 24 of the Banking Regulation Act, 1949.

3.9 DISCOUNT AND FINANCE HOUSE OF INDIA (DFHI)

The DFHI was set up in April 1988 by the Reserve Bank of India to help develop the money market in India. Money market refers to an activity in which financial transactions take place in short term financial assets which are close substitutes for money. The instruments traded in the money market will have maturity period less than a year. Some of such assets are call money (overnight money), notice money (1 to 14 days), inter bank term deposits/loans (15 days and over), commercial bills and treasury bills, certificate of deposits etc.

With a view to impart increased liquidity in the money market instruments the DFHI was set up. It would deal with treasury bills of different maturities and rediscount short-term commercial bills. DHFI operates with emphasis on high turn over of money market assets and provides two way quotes for funds (bid and offer) with a thin spread. DHFI participates both as lender and borrower in the money market since 28th July 1988.

SBI DFHI Ltd: SBI DFHI Ltd came into existence in April 2004 with the amalgamation of 'Discount and Finance House of India (DFHI)', a subsidiary of RBI and 'SBI Gilts Ltd.', a subsidiary of SBI. It is a major participant in the wholesale Debt Market both in the Primary and Secondary Market segment with an outright turnover of Government Securities and Treasury Bills in 2007-08 at ₹54, 919.39 crores and ₹5, 428 crores respectively.

Objectives of DFHI:

The objectives of DFHI include the following:

(*i*) Dealing in Treasury bill

(*ii*) Re-discounting short-term commercial bills

(*iii*) Participating in the Inter-Bank call money, notice money and term deposit market

(*iv*) Dealing in Commercial Papers, Certificates of Deposits and Government Securities

(*v*) Provide liquidity to money market instruments

(*vi*) Provide safe and risk free short term investment avenues to institutions

(*vii*) Facilitate money market transactions of small and medium sized institutions that are not regular participants in the market

(*viii*) Integrate markets at regional centres with the main market at Mumbai, through its network.

Discount and Finance House of India Ltd. provides liquidity in the money market by dealing in the money market instruments, including Treasury Bills. DFHI being an institution promoted by the public sector banks/financial institutions and RBI, enjoys excellent credit rating in the market.

3.10 COMPARISON OF LONDON, NEW YORK AND INDIAN MONEY MARKET

A comparison of London, New York and Indian Money Market is given in the following table:

London Money Market	*New York Money Market*	*Indian Money Morket*
	1. Period of Development	
London money market has enjoyed the supreme position till the beginning of First World War period.	It has come into prominence only during the Second World War period.	It has become popular after independence specifically after nationalisation of banks in 1969.
	2. Nature of Growth	
Highly organised and well developed.	Organised and well developed but next to London Money Market.	Fast catching up woth matured market since 1992.
	3. Control over the Money Market	
The bank of England controls the money market through traditions, Conventions and Persuasion.	The Federal Reserve Banks control the money markets through statutory powers.	RBI has control over the market and regulates liquidity through DHFI, Primary Dealers, Open Market Operations, (OMO) etc.
	4. Weapons used to Control Money Market	
Bank rate and open market operations.	The Federal banks use more direct weapons of credit controls as variation of cash reserve ratios, etc.	CRR, 'Repo' transactions, Moral suasion OMO of Treasury Bills, etc.
	5. Specialised Institutions	
The acceptance houses, Discount Houses, etc., are playing main role in the money market.	It does not have such institutions, Commercial banks perform these functions.	DFHI, Primary Dealers Development Financial Institutions, Money Market Mutual Funds, etc.
	6. Competition among institutions	
The functions of the specialised institutions like discount houses, acceptance houses, Bill brokers, Commercial banks, etc., are all complementary and these Institutions donote compete among themselves for funds.	In this market various institutions function independently and hence compete for funds in the money market. But the competition is healthy.	Healthy competition is gaining ground. RBI determines the players in the market-large number of lenders, including financial institutions, mutual funds, big corporates (through DFHI, etc.). However borrowers and restricted to commercial Bank and fiew institutions like DFHI primary dealers.
	7. System of Banking	
In U.K. branch banking prevails. The banking system is mainly under the control of "Big five" Banks. All banks have their branches in London.	In U.S.A. unit banking is prevailing, since there are numerous banks of small size, they do not have their banks in Washington.	In India branch banking is popular. Even then many private sector banks are small in size.
	8. Number of Central Banks	
In England there is only Central Bank "The Bank of England" for the entire country.	In U.S.A there are 12 "Federal Reserve Banks" for different regions. With Federal Reserve System at the apex level.	In India there is only "RBI" for the entire central banking operations.

	9. Operation of Bill Market	
In U.K. there is a well developed bill market. Commercial banks do not directly discount the bills from customers.	In U.S.A. there is no well developed bill market. Commercial banks directly discount their bills from the customers.	Bill market is not developed in India. Commercial banks discount the bills of the customers but rediscounting of bills are not popular.
	10. Variation of Interest Rates	
There is no big variation in interest rates in the market. It is mainly due to the market aligning its interest rates. Closer to the Central Bank discount rates.	No variation in interest rates. There is close relation between the rates of Federal Banks and market rates.	Since the control of RBI over the money market is not adequate there is no close relation between the RBI rates and the market rates. Hence, there is variation of interest rates in the market. Interest rates are sometimes highly volatile due to few players and lack of depth of the market.
	11. Attraction of Foreign Funds	
Highly developed and attracts the foreign funds.	More attraction of foreign funds.	Underdeveloped due to the restrictions over foreign exchange transactions. Capital account convertibility is required to attract foreign funds.

REVIEW QUESTIONS

Short Answer Questions

1. Define Money Market.
2. What are the objectives of money market in the country?
3. What are the common features of money market?
4. Write a short note on acceptance houses.
5. What is the importance of a developed money market in the economy?
6. Write a short note on the following:
   (*a*) Call money market
   (*b*) Acceptance market
   (*c*) Bill market
   (*d*) Collateral market
7. Give an account on Discount and Finance House of India.
8. Write short notes on the following:
   (*a*) Call Money
   (*b*) Notice Money
   (*c*) Term Money
   (*d*) Treasury bills
   (*e*) Commercial Bills
   (*f*) Commercial Paper
   (*g*) Certificate of Deposit
   (*h*) Inter Bank Participation Certificates
   (*i*) Inter-corporate Deposits

Essay Type Questions

1. Explain the meaning and characteristics of money markets.
2. Differentiate between Money market and capital market.
3. Write an explanatory note on the constituents of Indian money market.
2. Explain the submarkets of the money market.
3. Explain the characteristics of a developed money market.
4. Write a note on the role of Indian money market.
5. Explain the structure of Indian money market.
6. What are the different types of financial instruments traded in the Indian money market?
7. Explain about Repo' Instruments and 'Collateralized Borrowing and Lending Obligation' in detail.
8. Compare Indian money market with other developed money markets.

CHAPTER

4 Commercial Banks

Commercial banks constitute the major portion of the country's credit and banking institutions. In simple term a bank is a dealer in money like a trader in goods. According to Prof. Hart, "a bank is one who in the ordinary course of business receives money which he repays by honouring cheques of persons from whom or on whose account he receives it".

4.1 GENERAL CLASSIFICATION OF BANKS

Commercial Banks in India are organised as joint stock companies and known as banking companies. These banks are primarily classified into:

(*a*) Scheduled banks and

(*b*) Non-scheduled banks.

Scheduled Banks include nationalised banks, State Bank of India and its subsidiaries, Private sector banks and foreign banks. Non-scheduled banks are those which are not included in the 2nd schedule to RBI Act.

4.1.1 Scheduled Banks

The second schedule of the Reserve Bank of India Act contains a list of Banks which are described as "Scheduled Banks". A bank in order to be designated as a scheduled Bank should have a paid up capital and reserves as prescribed by the Act. In terms of Sec. 42 (6) of RBI Act 1934, the required amount is only ₹ 5.00 lakh. However, presently to start a Commercial Bank, the RBI prescribed a minimum capital of ₹ 100 crore and its business must be managed in a manner which, in the opinion of Reserve bank of India, is not detrimental to the interests of its depositors. The Scheduled Banks are also required to maintain with the Reserve Bank of India a deposit in the form Cash Reserve Ratio, based on its demand and time liabilities at prescribed rate.

The scheduled banks enjoy several privileges. An account with a scheduled bank carries a greater assurance of safety and prestige value than an account with a Non-scheduled bank. It is entitled to receive refinance facility as applicable. It may also get currency chest facility. In times of urgent need, it may obtain finance from the Reserve Bank of India to help it tiding over temporary financial difficulties. Further more, the settlement of accounts between scheduled banks is facilitated by the use of the "Bankers' clearing House procedure". On the other hand, scheduled banks have to submit several returns to the Reserve Bank of India and are obliged to comply with the directions received from the Reserve Bank. Some of these returns have to be submitted in each week usually on Friday. The affairs of Scheduled Banks are closely watched and largely controlled by the Reserve Bank of India, in order to safeguard the general health of the Banking industry as a whole.

Nationalised Banks: The Nationalised banks include the fourteen banks nationalised on 19th July 1969 and the 6 banks nationalised on 15th April 1980. They are also scheduled banks. After nationalisation these banks render various types of functions by assuming social responsibilities. Through these banks, the government tries to implement its fiscal policies and various welfare schemes. These banks occupy a pivotal place in the Indian Banking system. They are also called public sector banks. State Bank of India and its subsidiaries are also commercial banks providing services similar to that of nationalised banks.

4.1.2 Non-Scheduled Banks

The commercial banks, not included in the Second Schedule of the R.B.I Act are known as Non-scheduled Banks. They are not entitled to get facilities like refinance and rediscounting of bills, etc. from RBI. They do not get the prestige like Scheduled Banks. They are mainly engaged in lending money, discounting and collecting bills and various agency services. RBI currently does not encourage the opening of non-scheduled banks.

4.2 FUNCTIONS OF COMMERCIAL BANKS

The commercial banks serve as the king pin of the financial system of the country. They render many valuable services. The important functions of the Commercial banks can be explained with the help of the following chart.

FUNCTIONS OF COMMERCIAL BANKS

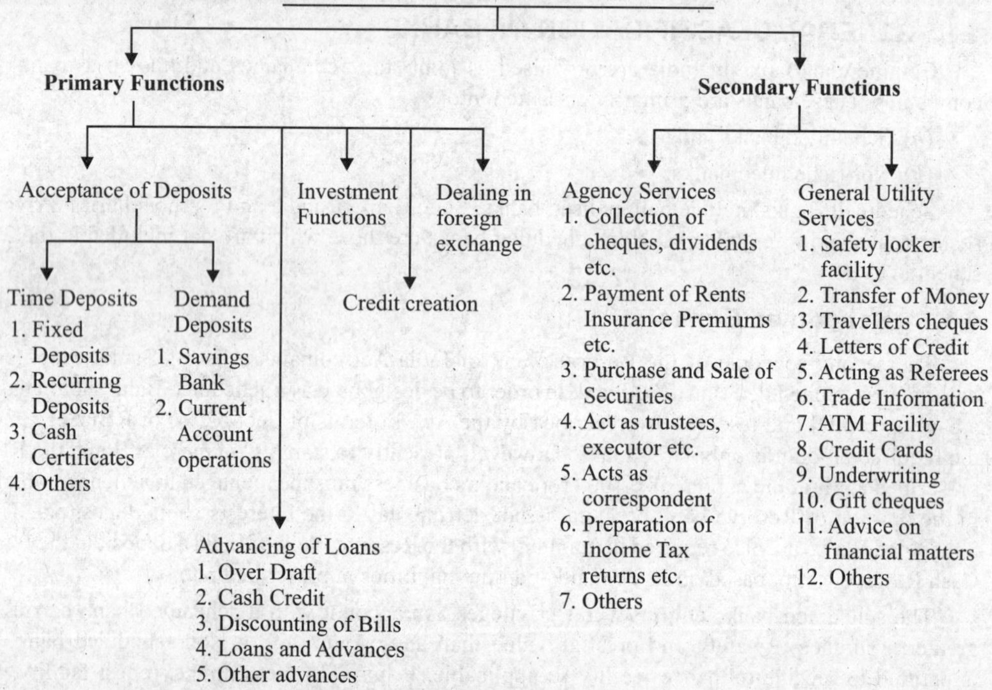

Let us discuss these functions one by one.

4.2.1 Primary Functions of Commercial Banks

The primary functions of the commercial banks include the following:

A. Acceptance of Deposits:

The most important activity of a commercial bank is to mobilize deposits from the public. People who have surplus income and savings find it convenient to deposit the amounts with banks. Depending upon the nature of deposits, funds deposited with bank also earn interest. Thus, deposits with the bank grow along with the interest earned. If the rate of interest is higher, public are motivated to deposit more funds with the bank. There is also safety of funds deposited with the bank.

1. Time Deposits:

These are deposits repayable after a certain fixed period. These deposits are not withdrawable by cheque, draft or by other means. It includes the following:

(*a*) Fixed Deposits: The deposits can be withdrawn only after expiry of certain period say 3 year, 5 year or 10 year. The banker allows a higher rate of interest depending upon the amount and period of time. Previously the rates of interest payable on fixed deposits were determined by Reserve Bank. Presently banks are permitted to offer interest as determined by each bank. However, banks are not permitted to offer different interest rates to different customers for deposits of same maturity period, except in the case of deposits of higher amounts fixed by the banks as per policy norms.

These days the banks accept deposits even for 15 days or one month etc. In times of urgent need for money, the bank allows premature closure of fixed deposits by paying interest at reduced rate. Depositors can also avail of loans against Fixed Deposits. The Fixed Deposit Receipt cannot be transferred to other persons. The rate of interest and other terms and conditions regulating fixed deposits are determined by the Reserve Bank of India for all commercial banks. The Reserve Bank of India keeps on revising the rate of interest from time to time.

(*b*) Recurring Deposits: In recurring deposit, the customer opens an account and deposit a certain sum of money every month. After a certain period, say 1 year or 3 years or 5 years, the accumulated amount along with interest is paid to the customer. It is very helpful to the middle and poor sections of the people. The interest paid on such deposits is generally on cumulative basis. This deposit system is a useful mechanism for regular savers of money.

(*c*) Cash Certificates: Cash certificates are issued to the public for a longer period of time. It attracts the people because its maturity value is in multiples of the sum invested. It is an attractive and high yielding investment for those who can keep the funds for a long time. It is a very useful account for meeting future financial requirements at the occasion of marriage, education of children etc. Cash certificates are generally issued at discount to face value. It means a cash certificate of ₹1,00,000 payable after 10 years can be purchased now, say for ₹20,000/-.

2. Demand Deposits:

These are the deposits which may be withdrawn by the depositor at any time without previous notice. It is withdrawable by cheque/draft. It includes the following:

(*a*) Savings deposits: The savings deposit promotes thrift among people. The savings deposits can only be held by individuals and non-profit institutions. The rate of interest paid on savings deposits is lower than that of time deposits. The savings account holder gets the advantage of liquidity (as in current a/c) and small income in the form of interests. But there are some restrictions on withdrawals. Corporate bodies and business firms are not allowed to open SB Accounts. Presently interest on SB Accounts is determined by RBI. It is 4.5 percent per annum. Co-operative banks are allowed to pay an extra 0.5 percent on its savings bank deposits.

(*b*) Current Account Deposits: These accounts are maintained by the people who need to have a liquid balance. Current account offers high liquidity. No interest is paid on current deposits and there is no restriction on withdrawals from the current account. These accounts are generally in the case of business firms, institutions and co-operative bodies. Nowadays, banks are designing and offering various investment schemes for deposit of money. These schemes vary from bank to bank.

It may be stated that the banks are currently working out with different innovative schemes for deposits. Such deposit accounts offer better interest rate and at the same time withdrawable facility also. These schemes are offered by both foreign and domestic banks. In USA, Current Accounts are known as 'Checking Accounts' as a cheque is equivalent to check in America.

B. Advancing of Loans:

The next important function of a commercial bank is to grant loans and advances. Such loans and advances are given to members of the public and to the business community at a higher rate of interest than allowed by banks on various deposit accounts. The rate of interest charged on loans and advances varies depending upon the purpose, period and the mode of repayment. The difference between the rate of interest allowed on deposits and the rate charged on the Loans is the main source of a bank's income. The commercial banks provide loans and advances in various forms. They are given below:

1. Overdraft:

This facility is given to holders of current accounts only. This is an arrangement with the bankers thereby the customer is allowed to draw money over and above the balance in his/her account. This facility of overdrawing his account is generally pre-arranged with the bank upto certain limit. It is a short-term temporary fund facility from bank and the bank will charge interest over the amount overdrawn. This facility is generally available to business firms and companies.

2. Cash Credit:

Cash credit is an arrangement whereby the bank allows the borrower to draw amounts up to a specified limit. The amount is credited to the account of the customer. The customer can withdraw this amount as and when he requires. Interest is charged on the amount actually withdrawn. Cash Credit is granted as per agreed terms and conditions with the customers.

Cash credit is a form of working capital credit given to the business firms. Under this arrangement, the customer opens an account and the sanctioned amount is credited with that account. The customer can operate that account within the sanctioned limit as and when required. It is made against security of goods, personal security etc. On the basis of operation, the period of credit facility may be extended further. One advantage under this method is that bank charges interest only on the amount utilised and not on total amount sanctioned or credited to the account. Reserve Bank discourages this type of facility to business firms as it imposes on uncertainty on money supply. Hence this method of lending is slowly phased out from banks and replaced by loan accounts. Cash credit system is not in use in developed countries.

3. Discounting of Bills:

Discounting of Bills may be another form of bank credit. Banks provide short-term finance by discounting bills that is, making payment of the amount before the due date of the bills after deducting a certain rate of discount. The party gets the funds without waiting for the date of maturity of the bills. In case any bill is dishonoured on the due date, the bank can recover the amount from the customer.

The bank may purchase inland and foreign bills before these are due for payment by the drawee debtors, at discounted values, i.e., values a little lower than the face values. The Banker's discount is generally the interest on the full amount for the unexpired period of the bill. The banks reserve the right of debiting the accounts of the customers in case the bills are ultimately not paid, i.e., dishonoured. The bill passes to the Banker after endorsement. Discounting of bills by banks provide immediate finance to sellers of goods. This helps them to carry on their business. Banks can discount only genuine commercial bills i.e., those drawn against sale of goods on Credit. Banks will not discount Accommodation Bills.

4. Loans and Advances:

A loan is granted for a specific time period. Generally, commercial banks grant short-term loans. But term loans, that is, loan for more than a year, may also be granted. The borrower may withdraw the entire amount in lump sum or in installments. However, interest is charged on the full amount of loan. Loans are generally granted against the security of certain assets. A loan may be repaid either in lump sum or in installments.

An advance is a credit facility provided by the bank to its customers. It differs from loan in the sense that loans may be granted for longer period, but advances are normally granted for a short period of time. Further the purpose of granting advances is to meet the day to day requirements of business. The rate of interest charged on advances varies from bank to bank. Interest is charged only on the amount withdrawn and not on the sanctioned amount.

It includes both demand and term loans, direct loans and advances given to all type of customers mainly to businessmen and investors against personal security or goods of movable or immovable in nature. The loan amount is paid in cash or by credit to customer account which the customer can draw at any time. The interest is charged for the full amount whether he withdraws the money from his account or not. Short-term loans are granted to meet the working capital requirements where as long-term loans are granted to meet capital expenditure. Previously interest on loan was also regulated by RBI. Currently, banks can determine the rate themselves. Each bank is, however required to fix a minimum rate known as Prime Lending Rate (PLR).

Classification of loans and Advances:

Loans and advances given by bankers can be classified broadly into the following categories :

(*i*) Advances which are given on the personal security of the debtor, and for which no tangible or collateral security is taken; this type of advance is given either when the amount of the advance is very small, or when the borrower is known to the Banker and the Banker has complete confidence in him (Clean Advance).

(*ii*) Advances which are covered by tangible or collateral security. In this section of the study we are concerned with this type of advance and with different types of securities which a Banker may accept for such advances (Secured Advance).

(*iii*) Advances which are given against the personal security of the debtor but for which the Banker also holds in addition the guarantee of one or more sureties. This type of advance is often given by Banker to persons who are not known to them but whose surety is known to the Banker. Bankers also often take the personal guarantee of the Directors of a company to whom they agree to advance a clean or unsecured loan.

(*iv*) Loans are also given against the security of Fixed Deposit receipts.

5. Housing finance:

Nowadays the commercial banks are competing among themselves in providing housing finance facilities to their customers. It is mainly to increase the housing facilities in the country. State Bank of India, Indian Bank, Canara Bank, Punjab National Bank, have formed housing subsidiaries to provide housing finance. The other banks are also providing housing finances to the public. Government of India also encourages banks to provide adequate housing finance. Borrowers of housing finance get tax exemption benefits on interest paid. Further housing finance upto ₹5 lakh is treated as priority sector advances for banks. The limit has been raised to ₹10 lakhs per borrower in cities.

6. Educational Loan Scheme:

A term loan granted to Indian Nationals for pursuing higher education in India or abroad where admission has been secured. The Reserve Bank of India, from August, 1999 introduced a new Educational Loan Scheme for students of full time graduate/post-graduate professional courses in private professional colleges. The loan has to be repaid together with interest within the time period determined by the bank from the date of completion of the course. Today banks provide loan facilities for almost all approved courses and for studying in India and abroad.

Eligible Courses: All courses having employment prospects are eligible.

- Graduation courses/Post graduation courses/Professional courses
- Other courses approved by UGC/Government/AICTE etc

Expenses considered for loan:

- Fees payable to college/school/hostel
- Examination/Library/Laboratory fees
- Purchase of Books/Equipment/Instruments/Uniforms
- Caution Deposit/Building Fund/Refundable Deposit (maximum 10% tution fees for the entire course)
- Travel Expenses/Passage money for studies abroad
- Purchase of computers considered necessary for completion of course
- Cost of a Two-wheeler upto ₹ 50,000/-
- Any other expenses required to complete the course like study tours, project work etc.

Amount of Loan:

- For studies in India, maximum ₹ 10 lacs
- Studies abroad, maximum ₹ 20 lacs

Interest Rates: w.e.f. 29.06.2009 -11.75%. An Interest Rate concession of 0.50% to Girl Student availing Scholar Loans.

This apart, some of the banks have other educational loan schemes against security etc. The schemes may vary among banks. One can check up the details with the banks.

7. Loans against Shares/Securities:

Commercial banks provide loans against the security of shares/debentures of reputed companies. Loans are usually given only upto 50% value (Market Value) of the shares subject to a maximum amount permissible as per RBI directives against dematerialised shares.

8. Loans against Savings Certificates:

Banks are also providing loans up to certain value of savings certificates like National Savings Certificate, Fixed Deposit Receipt, Indira Vikas Patra, etc., The loan may be obtained for personal or business purposes.

9. Consumer Loans & Advances:

One of the important areas for bank financing in recent years is towards purchase of consumer durables like TV sets, Washing Machines, Micro Oven, etc., Banks also provide liberal Car finance. These days banks are competing with one another to lend money for these purposes as default of payment is not high in these areas as the borrowers are usually salaried persons having regular income. Further, bank's interest rate is also higher. Hence, banks improve their profit through such profitable loans.

10. Securitization of Loans:

Banks are recently trying to securitise a part of their part of loan portfolio and sell it to another investor. Under this method, banks will convert their business loans into a security or a document and sell it to some Investment or Fund Manager for cash to enhance their liquidity position. It is a process of transferring credit risk from the banker to the buyer of securitised loans. It involves a cost to the banker but it helps the bank to ensure proper recovery of loan. Accordingly, securitisation is the process of changing an illiquid asset into a liquid asset.

11. Others:

Commercial banks provide other types of advances such as venture capital advances, jewel loans, etc.,.

C. Credit Creation:

Credit creation is one of the primary functions of commercial banks. When a bank sanctions a loan to the customer, it does not give cash to him. But, a deposit account is opened in his name and the amount is credited to his account. He can withdraw the money whenever he needs. Thus, whenever a bank sanctions a loan it creates a deposit. In this way the bank increases the money supply of the economy. Such function is known as credit creation. The detailed discussion on commercial banks and credit creation is given in the following Chapter-5.

4.2.2 Secondary Functions of Commercial Banks

The secondary functions of the banks consist of agency functions and general utility functions.

A. Agency Functions:

Agency functions include the following:

(*i*) Collection of cheques, dividends, Interests:

As an agent the bank collects cheques, drafts, promissory notes, interest, dividends etc. on behalf of its customers and credit the amounts to their accounts. Customers may furnish their bank details to corporates where investment is made in shares, debentures, etc,. As and when dividend, interest, is due, the companies directly send the warrants/cheques to the bank for credit to customer account.

(*ii*) Payment of rent, insurance premiums:

The bank makes the payments such as rent, insurance premiums, subscriptions, on standing instructions until further notice. Till the order is revoked, the bank will continue to make such Payments regularly by debiting the customer's account.

(*iii*) Dealing in foreign exchange:

As an agent the commercial banks purchase and sell foreign exchange as well for customers as per RBI Exchange Control Regulations.

(*iv*) Purchase and sale of securities:

Commercial banks undertake the purchase and sale of different securities such as shares, debentures bonds etc on behalf of their customers. They run a separate 'Portfolio Management Scheme' for their big customers.

(*v*) Act as trustee, executor, attorney, etc.

The banks act as executors of Will, trustees and attorneys. It is safe to appoint a bank as a trustee than to appoint an individual. Acting as attorneys of their customers, they receive payments and sign transfer deeds of the properties of their customers.

(*vi*) Act as correspondent

The commercial banks act as a correspondent of their customers. Small banks even get travel tickets, book vehicles, receive letters etc., on behalf of the customers.

(*vii*) Preparations of Income-Tax returns

They prepare income-tax returns and provide advices on tax matters for their customers. For this purpose, they employ tax experts and make their services available to their customers.

B. General Utility Services:

The General utility services include the following:

(*i*) Safety Locker facility:

Safekeeping of important documents, valuables like jewels are one of the oldest service provided by commercial banks. 'Lockers' are small receptacles which are fitted in steel racks and kept inside strong rooms known as vaults. These lockers are available on half-yearly or annual rental basis. The bank merely provides lockers and the key but the valuables are always under the control of its users. Any customer cannot have access to vault. Only customers of safety lockers after entering into a register his name, account number and time can enter into the vault. Because the vault is holding important valuables of customers in Lockers, it is also known as 'Strong Room'.

(*ii*) Payment Mechanism or Money Transfer:

Transfer of funds is one of the important functions performed by commercial banks. Cheques and credit cards are two important payment mechanism through banks. Despite an increase in financial transactions, banks are managing the transfer of funds process very efficiently. Cheques are also cleared through the banking system. Correspondent banking is another method of transferring funds over long distance, usually from one country to another. Banks, these days employ computers to speed up money transfer and to reduce cost of transferring funds. Electronic Transfer of funds is also known as 'Chequeless banking' where funds are transferred through computers and sophisticated electronic system by using code words. They offer Mail Transfer, Telegraphic Transfer (TT) facility also.

(*iii*) Issue Travellers Cheques:

Banks issue travellers cheques to help carry money safely while travelling within India or abroad. Thus, the customers can travel without fear, theft or loss of money.

(*iv*) Letters of Credit:

Letter of Credit is a payment document provided by the buyer's banker in favour of seller. This document guarantees payment to the seller upon production of document mentioned in the Letter of Credit evidencing despatch of goods to the buyer. The Letter of Credit is an assurance of payment upon fulfilling conditions mentioned in the Letter of Credit.

The letter of credit is an important method of payment in international trade. There are primarily 4 parties to a letter of credit. The buyer or importer, the bank which issues the letter of credit, known as opening bank, the person in whose favour the letter of credit is issued or opened (the seller or exporter, known as 'Beneficiary of Letter of Credit'), and the credit receiving/advising bank. The Letter of Credit is generally advised/sent through the seller's bank, known as Negotiating or Advising bank. This is done because the conditions mentioned in the Letter of Credit are, in the first instance, have to be verified by the Negotiating Bank. It is mostly used in international trade.

(*v*) Acting as Referees:

The banks act as referees and supply information about the business transactions and financial standing of their customers on enquiries made by third parties. This is done on the acceptance of the customers and help to increase the business activity in general. That is, the banks provide reports on the credit worthiness of customers.

(*vi*) Provides Trade Information:

The commercial banks collect information on business and financial conditions etc and make it available to their customers to help plan their strategy. Trade information service is very useful for those customers going for cross-border business. It will help traders to know the exact business conditions, payment rules and buyers' financial status in other countries.

(*vii*) ATM facilities:

The banks, today have ATM facilities. Under this system the customers can withdraw their money easily and quickly and 24 hours a day. This is also known as 'Any Time Money'. Customers under this system can withdraw funds i.e., currency notes with a help of certain magnetic card issued by the bank and similarly deposit cash / cheque for credit to account.

(*viii*) Credit cards:

Banks have introduced credit card system. Credit cards enables a customer to purchase goods and services from certain specified retail and service establishments upto a limit without making immediate payment. In other words, purchases can be made on credit basis on the strength of the credit card. The establishments like Hotels, Shops, Airline Companies, Railways etc., which sell the goods or services on credit forward a monthly or fortnightly statements to the bank. The amount is paid to these establishments by the bank. The bank subsequently collects the dues from the customers by debit to their accounts. Usually, the bank receives certain service charges for every credit card issued. Visa Card, BOB card are some examples of credit cards.

(*ix*) Gift cheques:

The commercial banks offer Gift cheque facilities to the general public. These cheques received a wider acceptance in India. Under this system by paying equivalent amount one can buy gift cheque for presentation on occasions like Wedding, Birthday. Few years back banks were trying to popularise "Gift Cheque " scheme. However it did not turn out to be a successful scheme.

(*xi*) Merchant Banking:

The commercial banks provide valuable services through their merchant banking divisions or through their subsidiaries to the traders. This is the function of underwriting of securities. They underwrite a portion of the Public issue of shares, Debentures and Bonds of Joint Stock Companies. Such underwriting ensures the expected minimum subscription and also convey to the investing public about the quality of the company issuing the securities. Currently, this type of services can be provided only by separate subsidiaries, known as Merchant Bankers as per SEBI regulations.

(*xii*) Advice on financial matters:

The commercial banks also give advice to their customers on financial matters particularly on investment decisions such as expansion, diversification, new ventures, raising of funds etc.

4.2.3 Fee Based Services of Commercial Banks

Fee based services are different from fund based services. In fee based services there is no outflow of funds involved for the banks. The services are being provided on certain charges. The following are the common fee based services provided by commercial banks:

1. Remittance Facilities:

Banks are financial intermediaries. Apart from mobilizing deposits from savers and lending them to needy borrowers, banks help the savers and borrowers to transfer funds from one place to another in a secured way without physically moving the funds. Usually the following methods are adopted by banks for transfer of funds:

(*i*) Mail Transfer

(*ii*) Telegraphic Transfer

(*iii*) Demand Drafts

(*iv*) Pay orders

(*v*) Electronic Funds Transfer

(*i*) Mail Transfer: Under Mail Transfer system, the remitter of funds is required to deposit the amount required to be remitted together with a challan detailing the particulars of remittance. This information will relate to the value of funds to be transferred, the bank account number and address of the receiver of funds, particulars of remitter and purpose of remittance etc. Under this system it is necessary that both the parties to the remittance maintain bank accounts with the same bank, albeit with different branches/places. This method of transfer of funds is called Mail Transfer since the advice of remittance is sent by mail/post by the remitting bank to the branch where the beneficiary has his account. On receipt of remittance information, the receiving branch will credit the account of the beneficiary. Thus it is an intra bank fund transfer.

The banks do not accept large cash (usually restricted to ₹20, 000/-) for remittances. If the required remittance is large, bank will ask the remitter to draw a cheque on his account for the purpose of remitting funds. Bank also charge fees for this type of service. This facility of fund transfer is provided usually to their own customers. Funds can be transferred only between branches of the same bank and not between one bank to another. It is also necessary that both the parties to the transfer maintain account with the same bank. It is however a slow method for transfer of funds as advice regarding remittance is forwarded only through post. The paying branch will credit the account of the beneficiary only on receipt of the advice received from the remitting bank.

***(ii)* Telegraphic Transfer/Telex Transfer:** The method followed for transfer of funds under Telegraphic Transfer/Telex Transfer (TT) is the same as in the case with Mail Transfer. However the advice regarding remittance of funds will be sent by a telegram/telex by the remitting bank to the receiving bank. As such the fund transfer will be quick and fast. Since the advice is sent by telegraphic/telex message, this mode of transfer of funds will be costlier than that of Mail Transfer. However the additional cost will be insignificant if we take into consideration the immediate availability of funds to the beneficiary. This method will be costly mainly for those who remit small amounts of money.

***(iii)* Demand Drafts:** Drafts are basically Bills of Exchange. As in the case of Bill of Exchange, a draft is drawn by one party on another party and made payable to the drawer himself or some one else. Demand Drafts are drafts drawn by a bank on its own branches at different places and made payable to third parties or purchaser of the draft. Supposing you as a student desire to remit certain fees for taking up a competitive examination conducted by the Service Board, usually the Board asks all the candidates to remit the examination fees by demand drafts issued by banks. In such a case, the candidates may pay the requisite sum to a bank along with the prescribed challan detailing the name of the payee, purchaser or remitter, amount, place where it should be remitted etc. The bank on receipt of the amount will issue a draft which has to be sent by the candidates to the Board along with the application. For obtaining money or credit to the account, the payee (in the present case the Board) has to present the draft to the paying bank. Since these drafts are payable immediately on presentation by the payee, they are called demand drafts. The drafts can be crossed "Account Payee" to restrict its transfer. Demand Drafts can be defined as a cheque issued by a bank on its own branches or on other banks under correspondent arrangement.

***(iv)* Pay Order:** Pay Orders are drafts issued by an office/branch of a bank on itself. In other words the issuing branch/office and paying branch/office are one and the same. Pay orders are issued by banks only against receipt of funds first. Suppose, a candidate desires to remit certain examination/admission fees to a particular educational authority. In case both the candidate and the educational authority happen to maintain accounts with the same branch, then the candidate may remit the fees by obtaining a Pay Order instead of a demand draft. If the fees can be paid to any branches of the bank, then a demand draft can be obtained. Thus the main difference between pay order and a demand draft is that whereas a demand draft is issued by a bank on any of its branches, a pay order is issued on itself. In both the cases the bank will issue the instruments only after receipt of funds first.

***(v)* Electronic Funds Transfer:** Normally remittance or transfer of funds between banks gets originated by a paper instrument. For example, under Mail Transfer, the remitter has to fill up necessary challan and give it to the bank along with a cheque or cash for transfer of funds. Under Electronic Funds Transfer the transaction of funds transfer is initiated through an electronic equipment and systems or telephone or computer devices etc.

In India the Reserve Bank of India has introduced Electronic Funds Transfer (EFT) Scheme to assist banks in providing their customers fund transfer facility from one account to another either with the same bank or with different banks.

Under this system a customer desiring to remit certain amount to another place fills in the prescribed EFT application form together with the details like, beneficiary name, bank account number, name of the bank & branch, location of the branch etc. and hands over the form and a cheque drawn on his account. The remitting bank through one of its designated branches for this purpose transmits the details of transfer to the Reserve Bank of India. The Reserve Bank at the transaction originating centres consolidates all such transfer advice and transmits information of transfer to its various centres for advising the concerned banks for providing the requisite credit to the beneficiaries. Thus it acts as an intermediary between the remitting bank and receiving bank and effects the transfer. The banks will charge separately fees on their customers for availing of this facility. However fees charged by banks for transfer of funds under EFT system will be smaller as compared to remittance facilities under MT, TT and Demand Drafts.

This system of funds transfer is available with all the public sector banks and many of the private sector and State Cooperative banks. Fund transfer under EFT is possible from any branch to branch with the same bank or with other banks.

2. Other Fee Based Services: These services can be identified as:

(*a*) Issue of Guarantees

(*b*) Locker Facilities

(*c*) Credit Cards

(*d*) Portfolio Management Services (PMS)

(*e*) Tax Advice

(*f*) Investment Guidance

(*g*) Acting as Agents for selling financial products

(*h*) Sale of Insurance products

(*i*) Project Consultancy

(*j*) Dematerialized (Demat) Accounts

(*k*) Issue of Letters of Credit

(*l*) Custodial Services

(*m*) Arrangement of loans from Overseas Market for customers

(*n*) Other Innovative Services

(*a*) Issue of Guarantees: Issue of guarantees on behalf of customers is one of the important revenue earning services provided by banks. In the course of commercial business the customers may be required to provide with a bank guarantee under different circumstances. Guarantees basically serve the purpose of assuring that the work awarded to a person will be performed/ executed in terms of a contract. If not, the guarantor will step in to pay any compensation stipulated under the contract. This service brings in sizeable income to the banks. The guarantee fees usually depend upon the value and period of guarantees as well as the customer-banker relationship.

(*b*) Locker Facilities: Bankers make available Safety Locker Facilities to customers for keeping their valuables. In return, the bank levies half-yearly or annual charges which may depend upon the size of the lockers. The Lockers may be used to hold valuables like ornaments, jewellery, Share/Bond Certificates and other important documents. These items are held only at the risk of the customers. Banks will not be held liable if the customers misuse the locker facility.

(c) Credit Cards: Banks issue their own as well as Cards of other reputed agencies under arrangement to customers. Banks collect charges for this facility from card holders depending upon the type of card, value limit etc. The fees may be charged on annual basis with certain specified one-time entry fees also.

***(d)* PMS Services:** Under Portfolio Management Services, the banks accept large sums of money from wealthy customers for investment purposes with the permission of Reserve Bank of India. The guidelines governing PMS services are issued by Reserve Bank. Banks are expected to maintain separate accounts for this purpose and they are not permitted to mix up these funds with their own funds. They can not guarantee fixed income to customers under this scheme. Banks are basically expected to utilize the funds for investments and income generated out of such activity will be credited to customers account. Banks are however permitted to levy fees/charges for such services. Funds accepted under the Scheme should normally be for one year or more. Risk related to such investments will be that of the customers and not that of the bank.

***(e)* Tax Advice:** Most of the banks have their own Legal Departments. Although this Department normally engage themselves to protect the interest of the institution from legal disputes, the Department also have experts to provide legal counseling to customers. Such advice may pertain to personal taxation, capital gain tax and other tax issues.

***(f)* Investment Guidance:** These days a number of financial saving products are available for investors. Some of them are money market instruments like, Treasury Bills, Commercial Paper, Certificate of Deposits etc. Some of them are Capital Market instruments like Shares, Bonds, and Government Securities with long term horizon. Banks offer their expertise to customers in choosing the right type of investment depending upon the amount, duration, risk appetite, expected return etc. of customers. Banks charge fees for providing such services. This type of service is different from that of PMS services mentioned above. Under PMS, the banks accepts large sum of money from a customer and utilize the funds for various investment in consultation with the customer and at his own risk. However banks will provide investment advice and guidance for any customers and actual investment decision and employment of funds and maintenance of accounts there to will be done by the customers.

***(g)* Agents for selling Financial Products:** Under arrangement with other agencies engaged in Financial Services, banks sell their products like Credit/Debit Cards, ATM Services etc. to customers. Although the banks may obtain a share of fees from other agencies, banks may also levy certain charges for these additional facilities.

***(h)* Sale of Insurance Products:** Recently, banks in India are permitted to sell insurance products to their customers under arrangement with Insurance Companies. These products may be life insurance policies, accident insurance policies, Pension Policies and other general insurance policies. Banks which have wide net work of branches are expected to earn sizeable income/fees from these services.

***(i)* Project Consultancy Services**: Many first-time entreprenuers need expert advice for crystallizing their investment ideas into workable projects. Unplanned schemes may run into cost escalation and delayed execution. Persons intending to put up small scale industries normally overlook many aspects of the project requirements like environment clearance, legal issues etc. Banks will be in a better position to provide all round advice in such cases for certain fees.

***(j)* Demat Accounts**: Under SEBI guidelines, the issue and transfer of securities of many corporates are now required to be transacted in demat forms. The word "Demat" is an abbreviation for Dematerialized account. Under Demat form, physical securities are converted into electronic form and held in accounts with banks and other institutions permitted to maintain this type of accounts. This helps to avoid loss of securities, facilitate easy method of transfer and avoidance of large quantity of paper work and storage problem. Banks may usually levy a charge for maintaining such accounts although in many cases such service may be provided free of charge.

***(k)* Letters of Credit:** Banks issue Letters of Credits on behalf of their customers particularly in international trade. The issue of Letter of Credit may be a non-fund based service if banks are not providing their own funds to honour the bills drawn under letter of credit. Banks charge fees for issue of letters of credit which may depend upon the value of credit, tenor of credit and customer relationship.

(*l*) Custodial Services: Apart from offering Safety Locker Facility, banks also provide custodial services for holding valuable financial instruments, important legal deeds and documents of customers against payment of periodic fees. It should be remembered that under Locker Facility the banks make available Lockers on rental basis for safe keeping of valuables at customer risk. However under custodial services, the banks accept valuable documents etc. of customers for safe custody, transfer, maintaining of proper accounts relating to it and bank is liable for any wrong doing. Presently Indian Corporates are permitted to raise equity funds from overseas market through issue of Global Depository Receipts (GDRs). The equity share issued against GDR entitlements are held with a bank in India under Custodial Accounts. In this case the bank acting as a Custodian will maintain all records relating to the shares held and transferred under GDR mechanism and the bank will be earning certain fees from the company for this purpose.

(*m*) Arranging Foreign Currency Loans from Overseas Market: Presently Government permits Indian Corporates to raise foreign currency loans from overseas market under certain conditions. Since they may not be well conversant with overseas market and the risk associated with it, the corporate take the assistance of banks for raising the loans at minimum cost. Here the banks will not be providing their own funds but only help the corporate to raise cheap and reliable funds. The banks collect fees like management fees etc. for such services. They may also arrange loan syndication against specific fees. Charges in such cases will relate to the total fund raised, the duration of loan, management of loan accounts and other services expected of the bank under arrangement with the customers.

(*n*) Other Innovative Services: Innovation is one of the catch words in banking services today. Banks tends to innovate new types of services to suit the personal requirements of various customers as well as that of corporate-clients. As such these services will be different from banks to banks. In the established overseas markets, banks may also provide the following specialised services to corporate clients:

(*i*) Factoring Services

(*ii*) Forfaiting Services

(*iii*) Bankers Acceptances etc.

In India Factoring and Forfaiting services are provided by specialized agencies and not by banks. Similarly Bankers Acceptances are not popular in the Indian industry.

Factoring Services: Today the commercial banks provide factoring service to their customers. It is very much helpful in the development of trade and industry as immediate cash flow and administration of debtors' accounts are taken care of by factors. This service is again provided only by a separate subsidiary as per RBI regulations.

It should be noted that the primary functions are the main activities of commercial banks. Performing these functions is obligatory on the part of the commercial banks. But performing the secondary functions is not obligatory on the part of the banks. Generally all commercial banks perform these activities.

Factors are basically institutions financing the receivables of corporates on recourse or non-recourse basis. In other words the accounts receivables are sold outright to factors who arrange to collect the receivables directly from debtors. It is beneficial to the corporates since they are able to realise funds on the bills immediately from the factor. The factor deducts commission or other charges plus interest component from the value of bills before making payment to customers.

Forfaiting Services: It is another method of purchasing the receivables of customers on non-recourse basis. However Forfaiting is more common in international trade while Factoring is a common practice adopted in domestic trade. Under Forfaiting the financing institution purchases long-term bills/instruments on revolving basis upto certain maximum value and period unlike in the case of Factoring where financing is done for a short term. Since Forfaiting is always done under non-recourse basis, the discounted value is higher as compared to the discount under Factoring.

Bankers, Acceptances refer to bills which have been accepted by banks. This acceptance enhances the safety aspect of the bill and becomes a good instrument for value to discount houses. Further bankers acceptances strike a better realisation with lower discount. On behalf of their customers, the banks accept bills drawn by third parties on its customers. This resembles the letter of credit. While banks accept bills, they provide a better security for payment to seller of goods or drawer of bills.

4.3 LENDING TO SENSITIVE SECTORS

Commercial banks' lending to sensitive sectors helps in the development of capital market and real estate. It can be seen from the following Table:

Bank Group-wise Lending to the Sensitive Sectors

(As at end-March) (Amount in ₹ billion)

Sector	*Public Sector Banks*		*Nationalised Banks**		*SBI Group*		*Private Sector Banks*	
	2012-13	*Percentage Variation*	*2012-13*	*Percentage Variation*	*2012-13*	*Percentage Variation*	*2012-13*	*Percentage Variation*
1	2	3	4	5	6	7	8	9
1. Capital Market*	404 (0.9)	5.6	323 (1.0)	–3.9	81 (0.6)	74.4	402 (3.5)	5.7
2. Real Estate*	6,135 (13.7)	16.1	3,843 (12.4)	11.7	2,291 (16.6)	24.3	2,481 (21.7)	21.2
3. Commodities	–	–	–	–	–	–	–	–
Total Advances to Sensitive Sectors	6,539 (14.6)	15.4	4,166 (13.5)	10.3	2,372 (17.2)	25.6	2,883 (25.2)	18.8

Sector	*Old Private Sector Banks*		*New Private Sector Banks*		*Foreign Banks*		*Scheduled Commercial Banks*	
	2012-13	*Percentage Variation*	*2012-13*	*Percentage Variation*	*2012-13*	*Percentage Variation*	*2012-13*	*Percentage Variation*
1	10	11	12	13	14	15	16	17
1. Capital Market#	24 (0.9)	–7.3	378 (4.3)	6.7	69 (2.6)	–17.4	875 (1.5)	3.4
2. Real Estate@	335 (12.4)	13.9	2,146 (24.6)	22.4	716 (27.2)	14.8	9,332 (15.9)	17.3
3. Commodities	–	–	–	–	–	–	–	–
Total Advances to Sensitive Sectors	359 (13.3)	12.1	2,523 (28.9)	19.8	785 (29.8)	11.0	10,206 (17.4)	16.0

– : Nil / Negligible.

: Exposure to capital market is inclusive of both investments and advances.

@ : Exposure to real extate sector is inclusive of both direct and indirect lending.

* : Includes IDBI Bank Ltd.

Note: Figures in parentheses are percentages to total loans and advances of the concerned bank group.

Source: RBI Report on Trend and Progress of Banking in India 2012-13.

4.4 BALANCE SHEET OF COMMERCIAL BANKS

Balance sheet is a statement of assets and liabilities on a given date. In India, banks have to publish their balance sheets according to the proforma given in the schedule to the 'Banking Regulation Act, 1949'. The study of the balance sheet along with its profit and loss account reveals its financial soundness. A customer has to carefully study these statements to choose his banks. The combined balance sheet of all banks in the country reveals certain economic trends. A brief note of a Bank's Balance Sheet is given below:

FORMAT OF BALANCE SHEET AND PROFIT & LOSS ACCOUNT

Balance Sheet of .... (Name of the Banking Company)

(000's omitted)

Balance Sheet as on March 31 (Year)

	Schedule	*As on 31.3. (current year)*	*As on 31.3. (previous year)*
CAPITAL & LIABILITIES			
Capital	1		
Reserves & Surplus	2		
Minorities Interest	2A		
Deposits	3		
Borrowings	4		
Sundry Payables			
Other Liabilities and Provisions	5		
Total			
ASSETS			
Cash and Balances with Reserve Bank of India	6		
Balances with banks and money at call and short notice	7		
Investments	8		
Loans & Advances	9		
Sundry Receivables			
Fixed Assets	10		
Other Assets	11		
Goodwill on Consolidation			
Debit Balance of Profit and Loss A/c			
Total			
Contingent liabilities	12		
Bills for collection			

FORMAT OF PROFIT AND LOSS ACCOUNT OF A BANK

(Name of the Banking Company) .... (Name of the Banking Company)

(000's omitted)

Profit & Loss Account for the year ended March 31 ......

	Schedule	*Year ended 31.3. ___ (current year)*	*Year ended 31.3. ___ (previous year)*
I. Income			
Interest and dividend earned	13		
Share of earnings in Associates			
Other income	14		
Total			
II. Expenditure			
Interest expended	15		
Operating expenses	16		
Provisions and contingencies			
Total			
Consolidated Net profit/(loss) for the year before deducting Minorities' Interest			
Less: Minorities' Interest			
Consolidated profit/(loss) for the year attributable to the group			
Add: Brought forward consolidated profit/(loss) attributable to the group			
III. Appropriations			
Transfer to statutory reserves			
Transfer to other reserves			
Transfer to Government/Proposed dividend			
Balance carried over to consolidated balance sheet			
Total			
Earnings per Share			

The financial statements of a Banking company consists of 16 schedules of which the schedules 1 to 12 are for 'Balance sheet' items and the schedules 13 to 16 are for "Profit and Loss Account" i.e., for Revenue items.

Among the schedules of Balance sheet, schedules 1 to 5 gives Liabilities and the schedules 6 to 11 reveal about Assets. The schedule 12 gives contingent liabilities.

For the ease understanding and comparison, the consolidated balance sheet of Public sector, private sector and foreign banks are given below:

Consolidated Balance Sheet of Scheduled Commercial Banks

(Amount in ₹ billion)

Item	*As at end-March 2012*							
	Public sector banks	*SBI group*	*Nationalised banks**	*Private sector banks*	*Old private sector banks*	*New private sector banks*	*Foreign banks*	*All scheduled commercial banks*
1	2	3	4	5	6	7	8	9
1. Capital	183	12	171	48	13	35	406	637
2. Reserves and Surplus	3,373	1,061	2,312	1,545	266	1,279	531	5,449
3. Deposits	50,020	14,050	35,970	11,746	3,159	8,587	2,771	64,537
3.1 Demand Deposits	3,844	1,197	2,647	1,659	258	1,401	801	6,303
3.2 Savings Bank Deposits	12,140	4,537	7,604	2,729	578	2,152	419	15,289
3.3 Terms Deposits	34,036	8,317	25,719	7,358	2,323	5,035	1,551	42,945
4. Borrowings	4,618	1,588	3,030	2,584	198	2,386	1,199	8,401
5. Other Liabilities and Provisions	2,186	1,002	1,184	855	114	741	929	3,970
Total Liabilities/Assets	60,380	17,712	42,668	16,778	3,750	13,028	5,836	82,994
1. Cash and Balances with RBI	2,800	791	2,009	706	167	538	232	3,737
2. Balances with Banks and Money at Call and Short Notice	1,760	482	1,278	366	71	295	312	2,437
3. Investments	15,041	4,173	10,868	5,260	1,093	4,166	2,005	22,305
3.1 Governments Securities ($a + b$)	12,580	3,513	9,067	3,474	785	2,688	1,376	17,429
(*a*) In India	12,494	3,494	9,000	3,468	785	2,683	1,376	17,338
(*b*) Outside India	85	19	67	5.6	–	5.6	–	91
3.2 Other Approved Securities	10	0.2	9.7	0.2	0.2	0.01	–	10
3.3 Non-Approved Securities	2,451	660	1791	1,786	308	1,478	629	4,866
4. Loans and Advances	38,783	11,520	27,263	9,664	2,301	7,363	2,298	50,746
4.1 Bills Purchased and Discounted	2,307	888	1,419	357	113	244	257	2,922
4.2 Cash Credits, Overdrafts, etc.	16,085	4,958	11,127	2,860	1,120	1,740	1,099	20,044
4.3 Term Loans	20,391	5,674	14,717	6,447	1,068	5,380	942	27,780
5. Fixed Assets	383	74	309	134	27	107	50	567
6. Other Assets	1,613	672	941	649	91	558	939	3,201

Note: Nil/negligible. Components may not add up to their respective totals due to rounding off numbers to ₹ billion.

* : Includes IDBI Bank Ltd.

Source: RBI Publications

Indian banking sector remained broadly public in nature with public sector banks accounting for more than two-thirds of total assets of all scheduled commercial banks, as at end-March 2012.

4.5 OFF-BALANCE SHEET ITEMS

We are aware that banks are engaged in non-fund based activities such as issue of guarantees, acceptance or co-acceptance of bills of exchange, etc. Some of the non-fund based activities result into off-balance sheet exposure. They are off-balance sheet items because they do not create an immediate liability and also such a liability mayor may not arise. However, once such liabilities are brought into the balance sheet, it may tilt the balance of advantage to the bank due to increase in liabilities.

The major off-balance sheet exposures of bank include:

(*a*) Financial guarantees issued
(*b*) Rediscounting of bills with other banks
(*c*) Acceptance of Bills on its owner name
(*d*) Partly paid-up shares and securities transferred in its name
(*e*) Foreign Exchange Forward Contract booked on behalf of customers.

For the understanding of the students, the off-balance sheet exposure of commercial banks in India at the end of March 2009-10 is given in the following Table:

Off-Balance Sheet Exposure of Scheduled Commercial Banks in India

(Amount in ₹ billion)

Item	*Public Sector Banks*		*Nationalised Banks**		*SBI Group*		*Private Sector Banks*	
	2012-13	*Percentage Variation*	*2012-13*	*Percentage Variation*	*2012-13*	*Percentage Variation*	*2012-13*	*Percentage Variation*
1	2	3	4	5	6	7	8	9
1. Forward exchange contract@	19,408 (27.9)	23.0	13,809 (28.2)	24.0	5,599 (27.1)	20.4	18,504 (93.0)	–23.3
2. Guarantees given	5,346 (7.7)	8.4	3,357 (6.9)	11.2	1,989 (9.6)	4.0	2,382 (12.0)	14.5
3. Acceptances, endorsements, etc. #	6,350 (9.1)	7.7	3,254 (6.6)	7.2	3,095 (15.0)	8.3	6,308 (31.7)	285.4
Contingent liabilities	31,104 (44.7)	16.9	20,420 (41.7)	18.8	10,684 (51.7)	13.4	27,194 (136.7)	–2.4

Item	*Old Private Sector Banks*		*New Private Sector Banks*		*Foreign Banks*		*Scheduled Commercial Banks*	
	2012-13	*Percentage Variation*	*2012-13*	*Percentage Variation*	*2012-13*	*Percentage Variation*	*2012-13*	*Percentage Variation*
1	10	11	12	13	14	15	16	17
1. Forward exchange contract@	1,878 (42.2)	1.8	16,625 (107.6)	–25.4	68,868 (1,108.0)	–20.3	106,780 (111.5)	–15.5
2. Guarantees given	252 (5.7)	25.6	2,130 (13.8)	13.3	964 (15.5)	13.2	8,692 (9.1)	10.5
3. Acceptances, endorsements, etc. #	207 (4.7)	55.4	6,101 (39.5)	305.7	4,453 (71.7)	5.6	17,111 (17.9)	45.6
Contingent liabilities	2,338 (52.6)	7.2	24,856 (160.9)	–3.2	74,285 (1,195.1)	–18.8	1,32,583 (138.5)	–9.2

* : Includes IDBI Bank Ltd.

@ : Includes all derivative products (including interest rate swaps) as admissible.

: Includes *inter alia* items like (*a*) Claima against the bank not acknowledged as debt. (*b*) Liability for partly paid investments. (*c*) Bills re-discounted and (*d*) Letters of credit.

Note: Figures in parentheses are percentages to total liabilities of the concerned bank group.

Source: RBI Publications

REVIEW QUESTIONS

Short Answer Questions

1. What is time deposit?
2. What is demand deposit?
3. Differentiate between time and demand deposits.
4. Write a short note on:
   (*a*) Over draft
   (*b*) Cash credit
   (*c*) Mail Transfer
   (*d*) Telegraphic Transfer
   (*e*) Demand Drafts
   (*f*) Pay orders
   (*g*) Electronic Funds Transfer
5. What is discounting of bills by commercial banks?
6. Write short notes on the following:
   (*i*) Factoring Services
   (*ii*) Forfaiting Services
   (*iii*) Bankers Acceptances

Essay Type Questions

1. Write an explanatory note on the functions of commercial banks.
2. Explain the primary and secondary functions of commercial banks.
3. Explain the general utility services provided by the banks.
4. What is the different fee based services offered by the commercial banks in India?

CHAPTER 5

Commercial Banks and Credit Creation

The stability of price level is an essential condition for the economic development. It highly depends upon the demand and supply of money. The supply of money includes the legal tender money and bank money. The legal tender money is issued by the Central Bank or the government of the country in the form of Bank/Currency notes while the bank money is created by the banks. The bank money consists of bank deposits. Cheques drawn on bank deposits act as the legal tender money *i.e.*, with cheques payment obligation can be settled. Thus banks are not merely purveyors of money but also the manufacturers of money.

Bank deposits may be arrived in the following two ways:

(1) Primary deposit and

(2) Derivative deposits.

1. Primary Deposits: It is also known as cash deposit or passive deposit. When customers take actual cash and deposit it with bank, it is known as the primary deposit..

2. Derivative Deposits: It is also called active deposits or creative deposits. Deposits also arise when customers are granted accommodation in the form of loans. These deposits add to the supply of money.

5.1 LOANS CREATE DEPOSITS

When a bank grants a loan to a customer it does not usually pay the amount in cash, instead, it credits his account with the amount of loan. That is, the bank places a deposit at the borrower's disposal and he can freely withdraw the amount as he likes. He can draw cheques against the deposits created in his favour for settling his transactions. Thus cheques against bank deposits become purchasing power in the hands of the public in addition to the legal tender money. But more often, the loan is utilised over a long time gradually and till such time it forms as deposit. Hence the loan which a banker grants to a customer usually large corporates creates additional deposits i.e., by advancing loans, banks create deposits and thus create money. So "Money is said to be created when the banks, through their lending activities, make a net addition to the total supply of money in the economy". Thus, **when a bank credits the account of a person (by granting a loan) without receiving actual cash as deposits, it is said that the bank has created credit.**

The customer may retain the loan amount with the bank as deposits or can issue cheques against this deposit to settle his dues. The receiver of the cheque may deposit it in the same bank in which case his deposits increase while the givers deposit decreases. In case the borrower has account in some other bank the deposit of that bank increases. Hence, we can say that loans create deposits.

5.2 SIMPLE CREDIT CREATION

Credit Creation- Meaning: The process of 'Credit Creation' begins with banks lending money out of primary deposits. As we have seen already, the primary deposits are those deposits which are deposited in banks. As the nature of business, the banks lend the amount of money it accepted as deposits (primary deposits) from its customers. Actually banks cannot lend the entire amount of primary deposits. Because, as per RBI Regulations, the banks have to maintain a certain percentage of primary deposits, in the form of reserves with the RBI. RBI depending upon the prevailing economic conditions alters the percentage of reserves to be kept with it. Accordingly bank can lend the remaining portion of primary deposits. When the banks lend the balance deposit money as loans advances, the process of credit creation starts.

Granting loans and advances- Derivative Deposits

The deposits are raised in the following manner. When a customer goes to his bank for a loan, generally he provides "collateral security". The banker grants a loan and credit to his account with the amount of the loan. The customer is entitled to draw cheques up to the amount of the loan and these cheques can be used to buy goods and to discharge business obligations. In this way, additional money comes into existence and the process is virtually equivalent to the creation of additional supplies of money. It should be noted that primary deposits do not create credit and they go to increase the cash reserve of the bank as actual cash is paid into the bank. But the derived deposits decrease the cash ratio of the bank because those are created without receiving any cash from the customers. Thus, when a loan is granted to a customer a deposit arises. And the bank can lend the amount of deposit thus created based on its experience (for such deposits, there is no need of maintaining reserves with RBI-since it is not obtained as deposits by customers)

Technique of credit creation and Basic Assumptions

The concept of credit creation is based on the following assumptions.

(*i*) The banks, while granting loans, do not give the amount in cash, instead it credits the accounts of the customers with the amount of loan.

(*ii*) The customers do not withdraw the entire amount of loan.

(*iii*) While drawing the money from his account he uses cheque system.

(*iv*) The persons who are receiving the cheques against their claims from others also deposit the money into their respective banks.

(*v*) The accounts are settled with mere book entries.

5.3 MULTIPLE EXPANSION/CREATION OF CREDIT

We can explain the technique of credit creation with the help of an example.

Let us assume as follows:

(*a*) There are number of banks exist and operating in the economy.

(*b*) The banks have to keep 10% of the deposits as cash reserves as per law.

(*c*) The customer Mr X deposits the amount of ₹10,000 into his bank say ABC Bank.

The Balance sheet of ABC Bank appears as follows:

Balance Sheet

Liabilities	₹	*Assets*	₹
Deposits	10,000	Cash and balances	10,000
Total	10,000	Total	10,000

The deposit of ₹10,000/ = is a liability for the bank and the bank has an obligation to repay it on demand. And at the same time, it is an asset to the bank as it can use the deposit to lend/invest to earn income (interest). As we assumed, as per the legal obligation, the bank has to keep 10% of the total deposits as reserve with RBI. Thus, it has a surplus of ₹9,000 for advancing loans.

Now, the banks lend ₹ 9,000 to Mr. Y. Then the position of the balance sheet will be as follows.

Balance Sheet

Liabilities	₹	*Assets*	₹
Deposits	10,000	Cash Reserve with RBI	1,000
			9,000
Total	10,000		10,000

The receiver of the loan Mr. Y has the option to deposit the money with the ABC itself or into his bank say XYZ Bank. Let us assume that, Mr. Y gets the money from ABC bank and deposits it into his bank, XYZ Bank.

XYZ Bank has to keep a reserve of 10% of the deposit and is free to lend the balance. Assume that the bank has purchased the bills from Mr. Z for the balance 90% *i.e.*, ₹8,100. Now the balance sheet of XYZ Bank will be as follows.

Balance Sheet of XYZ Bank

Liabilities	₹	*Assets*	₹
Deposits	9,000	Cash Reserve with RBI	900
		Investments	8,100
Total	9,000		9,000

If we assume that Mr.Z deposits the money ₹8,100 received into his bank, Bank of Mysore.

Here, the Bank of Mysore also has to keep a reserve of 10% of the deposits and can lend the balance. If it lends the balance 90% to a customer "S" then the balance of sheet of Bank of Mysore will be as follows :

Balance Sheet of Bank of Mysore

Liabilities	₹	*Assets*	₹
Deposits	8,100	Cash Reserve with RBI	810
		Advances	7,290
Total	8,100		8,100

If this process is continued till the original deposit of ₹10,000 is fully exhausted(or go on until the last deposit is too small to create any more loan), the total amount of deposits so made will be calculated as follows.

= 10,000 + 9,000 + 8100 + 7,290 + 6561 ......etc.

Then, **Total Amount of Deposits = ₹1,00,000/ =**

Here in this case, the total deposits of all the banks together is increased to ₹1,00,000 *i.e.*, increase by 10 times of the original deposit of cash. This is called multiple expansion of deposits. **This is the process of multiplication of deposits through credit creation.**

5.3.1 The Formula for credit creation

The credit creation depends upon the mandatory percent of cash reserve to the total deposits. Thus, the deposit multiplier is,

$$K = 1/r$$

where

K = Deposit multiplier

r = Ratio of cash reserve to deposits

If the cash reserve ratio is 20% or .2, the deposit multiplier will be,

$$K = 1/r$$
$$= 1/0.2 = 5$$

If the percentage of reserves to the total deposits decrease, the multiplier will increase *i.e.,* higher the cash reserve ratio the lower will be the deposit multiplier and vice versa.

If we assume that the total percentage of cash reserve is 20% and the commercial banks get fresh additional cash of ₹ 100 crore, as a result of government spending, they would be able to create deposits through loans and investments to the extent of ₹ 500 crore. This is calculated as follows :

Credit creation = K × 100 Crores.
= 5 × 100 = ₹500 Crores

Thus, banks are able to create deposits because of the activities of 3 parties.

- The public who are willing to keep its money in the banks as deposits
- The banks, keeping only a fraction of deposits as cash reserves.
- The borrowers from the banks

5.3.2 Creation of Deposit is Essentially an Exchange of Claims

From the above discussion, it can be seen that banks create deposits by granting loans to customers. When a loan is granted and a deposit is created, the liabilities side of the balance sheet of the bank "increases under the head deposits" while the corresponding increase can be found on the assets side of the balance sheet under the head "advances". Banks voluntarily acquire liabilities when they create deposits because they are able to earn more profit on the loans they grant. This process of creation of deposit is essentially an exchange of claims. Because of this capacity to create money, banks are very important institutions for the economy of a country. They create additional purchasing power and there by influence the price level.

5.4 Scope for Multiple Creation of Credit

A single bank cannot create huge deposits. If we take several banks together, there is scope for multiple expansion of bank deposits. They lend many times more than the actual cash held by them and it is possible by mere entries in the books of banks. In this way banks can create credit to a large extent and adds to the total money supply in the country. However the ability of banks to create such additional money supply is curtailed by prescribing higher Cash Reserve Ratio for banks by RBI.

5.5 Credit Contraction

Commercial banks are able to multiply creation of credit, when deposits are made with them. If cash is removed from the banking system, it results in multiple contraction of credit.

Let us trace withdrawal of cash with the help of the following example:

The "Bank B" has a cash reserve of 10,000 at 20% of total deposits of ₹50,000 and ₹40,000 as Investments. Now the position of the bank will be as follows:

Balance Sheet of "Bank B"

Cabital and Liabilities	₹	*Assets*	₹
Deposits	50,000	Cash Reserve with RBI	10,000
		Investments	40,000
Total	50,000		50,000

Let us assume that a depositor withdraws his deposit of ₹ 5,000 permanently from the bank. Now the balance sheet of the bank will be,

Balance Sheet of "Bank B"

Capital and Liabilities	₹	*Assets*	₹
Deposits	45,000	Cash Reserve with RBI	5,000
		Investments	40,000
Total	45,000		45,000

From the balance sheet, it could be seen that the cash reserve is below the legal minimum and it should be ₹9000 *i.e.*, 20% of ₹45,000. There fore the bank must sell ₹4,000 worth of investments. When the bank sells its securities there will be a chain of reaction. The buyer of the security may withdraw ₹4,000 from his bank say Vijaya Bank to pay for it. Then the Vijaya Bank will find its cash reserves fallen by ₹ 4,000. It will therefore sell some of its securities. And so it goes on until all the effects are exhausted. And the original withdrawal of ₹5,000 has produced a chain "Killing off" ₹ 25,000 worth of deposits throughout the whole banking system. The process of contraction of bank deposits is the same as that of credit expansion-but in the opposite direction.

5.6 Limitations on Credit Creation

Bank cannot expand deposits to an unlimited extent by granting loans and advances even though this process of granting loans and advances is profitable to them. Their power to create credit is subject to the following limitations.

(*a*) Total amount of cash in the country
(*b*) Cash reserve ratio
(*c*) Banking habit of people
(*d*) Policy of other banks
(*e*) The availability of good securities
(*f*) Policies of Central Bank
(*g*) Initiative of businessmen
(*h*) Effects of trade cycles
(*i*) Liquidity preference by the people.
(*j*) Leakages

Let us discuss these limitations herein below:

(*i*) The total amount of cash in the country

The banks have power to create deposits depending upon the total supply of cash. The Central Bank of a country has the monopoly power to issue currency notes. The quantity of money in circulation increases with the issue of more currency and vice versa. Hence, the increased money supply or circulation enables the banks to create more credit. If the supply decreases the banks capacity to create credit will be decreased.

(*ii*) Cash Reserve Ratio

The actual cash reserve held by a bank and the cash ratios considered safe in the banking circles, set the limit for creation of credit. Every bank must keep sufficient cash balances to meet the demands of the customers across the counter, and settle the inter - bank indebtness arising out of the clearing house. The need for keeping adequate cash reserves to meet the claims that arise from currency withdrawal sets a limit to the capacity of a bank to create money.

Banks have to maintain the required cash ratios either according to the custom prevailing in the market or as required by law. In India it is decided by the RBI under Reserve Bank of India Act. This is the minimum cash required to be maintained by a bank with RBI. As per Sec. 42 of RBI Act, this ratio can vary from a minimum of 3 percent to a maximum of 15 percent of net demand and time liabilities (deposits) of a bank. Higher the ratio less is the opportunity for credit creation and vice versa. CRR is an instrument of monetary control.

(*iii*) Banking Habit of the People

The banking habit of the people also sets the limit for the capacity of banks to create credit. The volume of employed population, monetary habits etc. determine the amount of cash that the public wishes to hold. The amount of loan given to a customer should again come back to the bank in the form of primary deposits. Then only there can be credit creation. This is possible only when the banking habits among the people are well developed and they keep their money in the banks as deposits and use cheques for the settlement of their claims.

(*iv*) Policy of other banks

The credit creation is possible if all the banks in the industry follow the uniform policy regarding maintenance of cash reserves. If certain banks follow the conservative loan policy and keeping high rate of cash reserves while others are freely lending with minimum cash reserves, the creation of credit will not be upto the extent as determined above *i.e.*, the volume of the credit created will not be upto the extent of the credit multiplier.

(*v*) Availability of good securities

The availability of good securities *i.e.*, the securities acceptable to bank places a limit on credit creation by the banks. While lending, the banks insist upon the securities from the customers. All type of assets are not acceptable to banks as securities. They lend only on liquid assets such as gold, bills, raw materials *etc.*, As Sayers said, the banks do not create credit by lending to everybody "but to those individuals who can offer to the banks the kind of assets which the bank thinks attractive".

(*vi*) Policies of Central Bank

The capacity of credit creation by banks is largely depends upon the policies followed by the Central Bank from time to time. The total supply of cash depends upon the policy of the Central Bank. As the Central Bank can control the supply of cash through various weapons of credit control such as bank rate, open market operations and variation of cash reserves the upper limit of the volume of bank deposits is absolutely determined. Thus, the Central Bank can control the creation of credit by increasing or reducing the total supply of cash in the economy.

(*vii*) Initiative of businessmen

The banks can create credit if only the customers are willing to borrow from them. The capacity of the banks to create credit depends upon the psychology and initiative of businessmen and general market conditions for good business activities.

(*viii*) Effects of trade cycles

The effects of trade cycles also place the limitation on the credit creation *i.e.*, the conditions of inflation and deflation set a limit on the creation. During the period of economic prosperity there will be greater demand for bank loans and therefore they can create greater volume of credit. But in times of recession, there is no prosperity and the business people will hesitate to borrow. Therefore the volume of bank credit will be low.

(*ix*) Liquidity preference by the people

If the general public is highly driven to keep more amount of cash with them, the banks cannot get adequate deposits to create credit and thus the liquidity preference by people place a limitation on the creation of credit.

(x) Leakages

The credit creation by the banks is subject to certain conditions. If there is any leakage in this process the credit creation by the banks will be limited. In credit creation it is expected that the banks lend the entire amount of excess deposits over the minimum statutory reserve. And if there is any down fall in such lending, it will affect the creation of credit to that extent. Likewise it is expected that people who borrow money will deposit the same in their respective banks. If, they do not deposit the loan borrowed, the capacity of the banks to create credit will be limited.

5.7 CRITICISM OF THE THEORY OF CREDIT CREATION

The economists like Edwin Cannon and Walter Leaf have criticised the above theory of multiple creation and concluded that banks cannot lend anything more than the deposits received from the customers. Their arguments may be summarised as under.

(*i*) It is not correct to say that the initiative in the credit creation lies with banks. But, it would be more correct to say that the initiative lies with depositors who deposit their money with bankers. A banker is no more than a middlemen between lender and borrowers.

(*ii*) By granting loans the bank credit the account of the customer with the amount of loan granted to him. But the deposit amount i.e., the loan amount can be withdrawn by the customer at any time. If he withdraws cash from the bank it will reduce the cash reserve of the bank. Thus, it cannot grant loans beyond the cash deposited by customers with it.

(*iii*) The bank can lend only because all the customers do not withdraw their money at one time and consequently there are some funds of the depositors left with it. **Prof. Canon compares the bank with a cloakroom. He supports his argument with the following example.**

Suppose on a rainy day, 100 people come to a music concert with umbrella. They left these 100 umbrellas with the counter clerk of the concert hall. The clerk knows that only 10 members alone require umbrellas from him during an hour. Then he may send out the other 90 umbrellas for the duration of the concert and make some money. Does it mean, that the clerk has created 90 umbrellas ?. Cannan argues obviously no. Similarly the banker when he knows that all the depositors do not withdraw their money at the same time may lend a part of deposits. But, it cannot be said to be creating money, just as the clerk at the counter has not created umbrellas.

5.7.1 Answers to these Criticisms

1. The economists fail to consider the whole banking system

From the point of an individual bank, their argument may have some validity. But the argument loses its force when we take the banking system as a whole where there are number of banks. The banking system can expand the credit in multiplication.

2. Argument of Cloakroom is wrong

They compare the banks with the cloakroom - clerk, but it is a wrong comparison. Because, the clerk does not do business with the articles kept with him, where as the business of a bank is to trade in the money deposited with it.

REVIEW QUESTIONS

Short Answer Questions

1. What is meant by primary deposit?
2. Write a note on derivative deposits.
3. What is credit creation?

4. What is credit contraction?
5. What is the importance of credit creation?

Essay Type Questions

1. Differentiate between primary and derivative deposits.
2. "Loans create deposits" - Explain
3. Explain how banks create credit.
4. Explain the formula for credit creation.
5. Write a detailed note on credit contraction.
6. Differentiate between credit creation and credit contraction of commercial banks.
7. What are the limitations of credit creation?
8. Explain the criticisms on the theory of credit creation. And what are the answers to these criticisms.
9. Explain and illustrate the process of credit creation by commercial banks. What are the limitations of the creation of credit?

CHAPTER 6

Commercial Banks and Rural Financing

India is basically agricultural country although the share of Agriculture in the GDP of our country is falling year by year it can be said that India lives in villages. India's economy till recently was predominantly agricultural. Agriculture is the most important occupation in the country. The problem of poverty and low standard of living cannot be solved unless and until agriculture is placed on a sound footing. One of the basic conditions for improving and developing agriculture is the provision of cheap, efficient and adequate credit facilities to agriculture. Agriculture provides raw materials to the industrial sector. Thus, these two sectors are to be developed for the economic progress of the country. The importance of commercial banks in the process of economic development is much felt by the economists. Thus, rural financing becomes inevitable and it is the catalytic element for the accelerated economic growth of the country.

India has passed through the Green Revolution and the banks have made a departure from their past neglect of agricultural sector. Today, agriculture is becoming a viable commercial activity due to introduction of scientific methods of cultivation, hybrid seeds, fertilizers and pesticides. The incomes of agriculturists in rural areas are increasing. All these changes made the commercial banks to reach rural areas in a big way to mobilise the rural savings and to grant farm credit on a large scale. The state bank of India and the nationalised banks have opened rural branches all over the country. Besides, the banks organised "Lead Banks" in the rural areas to popularise banking habits and for rural development.

6.1 COMMERCIAL BANKS AND RURAL CREDIT

The commercial banks provide rural credit on the following lines.

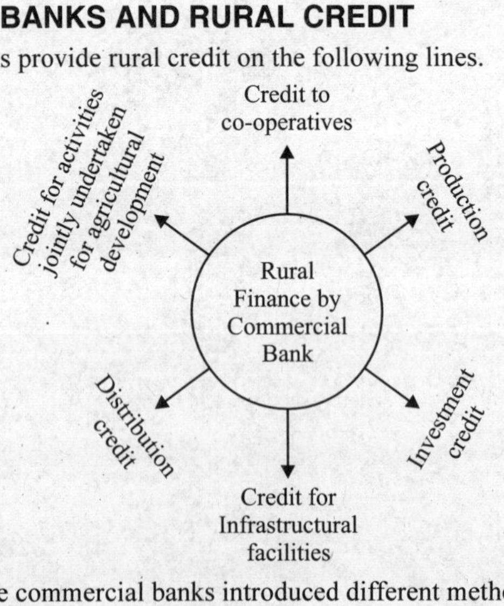

Besides the above, the commercial banks introduced different methods for rural credit. Let us see some of the important methods.

1. Village Adoption Scheme:

Village adoption scheme was introduced in 1973. Under this scheme, a survey of the village proposed to be adopted was first done. The village should satisfy the following criteria.

(*a*) The village should be within a short radius from the branch.

(*b*) It should have assured irrigation.

(*c*) The village should not have been financed by the co-operative sector.

(*d*) The village should have large number of small and medium farmers.

(*e*) The benefits offered by the banks to the villages should be easily accessible.

(*f*) Others

2. Service area approach:

The concept of service area approach was first introduced in April 1989 to bring about an orderly and planned development of villages. Better co-ordination and accountability were the chief advantages envisaged under the concept. Primary objective was to assign specific areas of villages to rural/semi-urban branches and ask the banks to provide adequate credit for productive purposes. This system will help cover all the villages in the country for total development.

Service area approach was a move towards decentralised credit planning which aims at offering the prospect of integration of credit planning with the process of development at the grass root level. All the rural and semi-urban branches have been allotted specific area of operation comprising of 10 to 15 villages for the purpose of rural lending. The basis of allotment of villages to each bank branch is (I) Proximity of villages (II) Contiguity of villages (III) Existing coverage of finance made in the village etc.,

The five distinct stages involved in its implementation are:

(*a*) Identification of Service villages to each bank branch.

(*b*) Survey of the villages for assisting the potential for lending for different economic activities.

(*c*) Preparation of annual credit plans

(*d*) Co-ordination between banks branches and field level development agencies, on an ongoing basis.

(*e*) Monitoring the progress of both individuals benefiting from the schemes and the credit plan as a whole.

Advantages of service area approach: The main aim of service area approach has been effective supervision of rural credit which was earlier suffering from sporadic lending, multiple financing and higher cost of supervision. Villages being compact and functioning of the branch is based on a nonclientele group in a common agro-climatic condition, planning becomes easier and realistic. The branches will also function at minimum transaction costs.

The strengths of service area approach:

(1) Better rapport: Being in constant touch with villagers, the service area branch has been able to create better rapport with people which facilitate tapping of deposits as well as credit dispensation/supervision.

(2) Accomplishment of services: Coverage of all the villages in the country by bank branches for meeting their credit requirements has been accomplished.

(3) Quality lending: The major success of the service area approach has been avoidance of multiple financing. Compactness of the service area only has resulted in better assessment of credit needs of individuals there by leading to quality lending.

(4) Full coverage: Subsequent to introduction of service area approach, banks are able to reach out the neglected group comprising small farmers, landless labourers and belong to the weaker sections of the society. As each of the rural and semi-urban branches of the Banks has been allotted specific number of villages for comprehensive development, the village adoption scheme has been brought under the service area approach.

6.2 TYPES OF AGRICULTURAL ADVANCES

Agricultural Advances provided by the commercial banks can be classified as under:

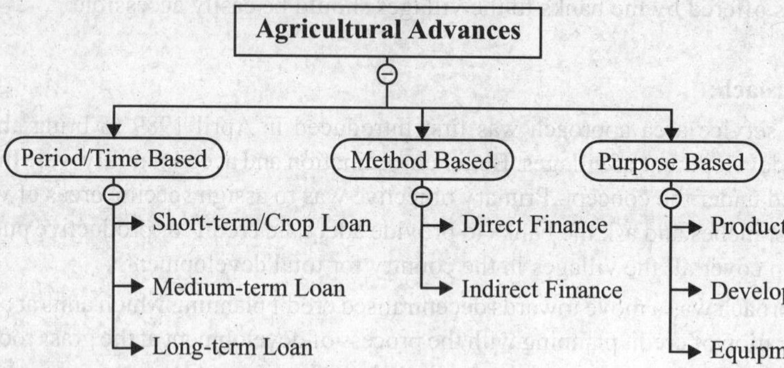

Let us have a brief discussion on these items:

6.2.1 Classification on the Basis of Time

The agricultural advances provided by the commercial banks can be classified on the basis of time or duration as follows:

(*i*) Short-term finance:

Short-term advances, usually for 6 to 18 months may be required by the farmers mainly for:

(*a*) Purchasing manures and fertilizers.

(*b*) Purchasing seeds including hybrid and high yielding varieties.

(*c*) Purchasing pesticides, insecticides and fungicides.

(*d*) Preparing soil for growing of crops or land for irrigation.

(*e*) Energizing existing wells or storage tanks.

(*f*) Purchasing farm implements, say, ploughs, ploughshares, spades, sickles spraying machines, etc.

(*g*) Repairing farm machinery, e.g. tractors.

(*h*) Constructing farm fences to prevent access of stray cattle.

(*i*) Constructing cattle sheds etc.

The inputs are normally required for producing particular crops and the advance should, therefore, be normally adjusted from the sale proceeds of the crop after it is harvested. Similarly, the purchasing of implements and repairs to a well etc. may not cost much and the loan should ordinarily be repaid after a crop or two are harvested and marketed. Certain times, the farmers lose value on their crops due to natural calamities like flood, drought etc., In such cases in consultation with central Government the RBI permits banks to convert short term loan into Medium term loans.

(*ii*) Medium-term finance:

An advance may be required by a farmer of a period of over 18 months but not exceeding, say 3 to 7 years, for any of the following purposes:

(*a*) Sinking of wells and for construction of storage

(*b*) Purchasing of oil — engines, Pump sets or other costly mechanical equipment like power-tillers.

(*c*) Soil conservation by prevention of erosion reclamation of land from rivers or conversion of barren into cultivable land.

(*d*) Purchasing of live stock, say, bullocks or horses, or of animal drawn carts.

(*e*) Drainage of land.

(*f*) Horticulture (gardening)

(*g*) Construction of farmhouses, cattle-sheds and sheds for processing of agricultural produce.

(*h*) Purchase of machinery for crushing sugarcane, manufacturing gur or khandsari.

The medium-term loans are usually repayable by instalments which are conveniently fixed and related generally to harvesting and sale of the produce. As the benefit of the improvement to land or purchasing the machinery may accrue after some time, banks in suitable cases consider the request of borrowers to defer payment of the instalment.

The security in case of medium-term advances is generally by way of hypothecation of machinery and equipment purchased, or mortgage of landed property and/or third party guarantees.

(*iii*) Long-term Finance

Long-term loans are repayable within a period ranging from over 7 years to 15 years. The purpose may be for:

(*a*) Major improvement to land

(*b*) Purchase of expensive and heavy machinery

(*c*) Construction of storage tanks, reclamation and preparation of land.

(*d*) Development of mechanised farming.

(*e*) New Plantations of tea, coffee, coconut, rubber, etc.

(*f*) Construction of warehouses and cold storages.

The repayment of the loan begins normally after a couple of years from the date of the advance. In case of drought or other natural calamity, the period of repayment of the loan may be suitably extended. In case the advance is required for purchasing machinery, the machinery should be hypothecated to the bank. The borrowers additionally execute a legal mortgage (or an equitable mortgage in suitable cases) of the land, and/or furnish suitable guarantees. The long-term loans are repayable by instalments of convenient maturity, say, quarterly, half-yearly, or yearly depending on the number of crops grown on the land and the harvesting seasons.

Banks have also started granting advances on medium/long-term basis to agro-industrial firms or corporations to enable them to purchase power-tillers, Pump-sets, tractors, lorries for transport of agricultural produce etc. These concerns may hire out these items of machinery to the agriculturists or extend them hire-purchase facilities for their purchase.

6.2.2 Classifications on the basis of Method of Advances

The commercial banks provide direct and indirect finance.

1. Direct Finance:

When a loan is given directly to an agriculturist it is classified as direct agricultural advance. Direct Agricultural advances denote advances given by banks directly to farmers for agricultural purposes. Direct finance to agriculture includes the following:

(*i*) Loans to individual farmers [including Self Help Groups (SHGs) or Joint Liability Groups (JLGs), i.e. groups of individual farmers] engaged in Agriculture and Allied Activities, viz., dairy, fishery, animal husbandry, poultry, bee-keeping and sericulture.

(*ii*) Loans to corporates including farmers' producer companies of individual farmers, partnership firms and co-operatives of farmers directly engaged in Agriculture and Allied Activities, viz., dairy, fishery, animal husbandry, poultry, bee-keeping and sericultureup to an aggregate limit of ₹2 crore per borrower.

(*iii*) Loans to small and marginal farmers for purchase of land for agricultural purposes.

(*iv*) Loans to distressed farmers indebted to non-institutional lenders.

(*v*) Bank loans to Primary Agricultural Credit Societies (PACS), Farmers' Service Societies (FSS) and Large-sized Adivasi Multi Purpose Societies (LAMPS) ceded to or managed/controlled by such banks for on lending to farmers for agricultural and allied activities.

2. Indirect Finance:

When a loan is given to an intermediary agency like Farmers service society, Primary Agricultural credits society etc. for on-lending to agriculturists, such finance is classified as indirect agricultural advance. Finance to sugar factories, agro-service centres, customer service units, traders in fertilizers/pesticides, manufacturers of agricultural machinery is also classified as Indirect Agri Advance. Advances granted to state seeds corporations, state Tribal Development corporations, Electricity Boards (for the purpose of energisation of pumpsets) are also indirect advances.

Thus, Indirect finance denotes to finance provided by banks to farmers indirectly, i.e., through other agencies. Important items included under indirect finance to agriculture are as under:

(*i*) If the aggregate loan limit per borrower is more than ₹2 crore in respect of loans to corporates, the entire loan will be treated as indirect finance to agriculture.

(*ii*) Loans upto ₹5 crore to Producer Companies set up exclusively by only small and marginal farmers under Part IXA of Companies Act, 1956 for agricultural and allied activities.

(*iii*) Bank loans to Primary Agricultural Credit Societies (PACS), Farmers' Service Societies (FSS) and Large-sized Adivasi Multi Purpose Societies (LAMPS).

6.2.3 Classification on the basis of Purpose

Agricultural advances are also classified as production finance, Development finance and Equipment finance.

1. Production Finance:

Production finance is given for:

(*a*) Purchase of agricultural inputs e.g.: fertilizers, seeds, pesticides, insecticides, manure etc.

(*b*) Meeting cultivation expenses e.g.: charges for water from neighbouring wells, labour charges, maintenance of oil engines/electric motors, purchase of feed for animals/birds etc.

(*c*) Processing of seeds and crops. e.g.: tea processing.

2. Development Finance:

Development finance is given for:

(*a*) Digging/Deepening of wells

(*b*) Reclamation and development of land, land levelling, contour bunding etc.

(*c*) Construction of farm buildings and structures e.g.: pumpshed, Cattle-shed, tractor-sheds, farm stores etc.

3. Equipment Finance:

The equipment finance is given for

(*a*) Purchasing of Tractors

(*b*) Purchasing of power tillers

(*c*) Purchasing of other farm equipments.

6.2.4 Flow of Credit to the Agricultural Sector

Agriculture credit is one of the major drivers of agricultural production. With the objective of making credit available to farmers, the government has been fixing targets for flow of credit to agriculture by the banking sector every year. The target for 2013-14 was fixed at ₹7,000 billion.

Priority Sector Advances

(Amount in ₹ billion)

As on March 31	*Public Sector Banks*	*Private Sector Banks*	*Foreign Banks*
1	2	3	4
2013	12,822	3,274	849
	(36.2)	(37.5)	(35.1)
2014	16,190	4,645	907
	(39.4)	(43.9)	(35.8)

Notes: 1. Figures in brackets are percentages to ANBC or CE of OBE, whichever is higher, in the respective groups.
2. The data for 2014 is provisional.

Note: ANBC-Adjusted Net Bank Credit CE of OBE-credit equivalent amount of off-balance sheet exposures

Source: RBI Publications

Bank Group-wise Target and Achievement for Agricultural Credit: 2013-14

(Amount in ₹ billion)

Agency	*Target*	*Achievement**
1	2	3
Commercial Banks	4,750	5,090
Cooperative Banks	1,250	1,199
RRBs	1,000	827
Total	7,000	7,116

* : Provisional.

Source: NABARD/Indian Banks Association/PSBs. RBI Publications

Credit to the agriculture sector has been higher than targets in recent years. However, credit by cooperative banks and regional rural banks (RRBs) has been less than their respective targets and it can be seen from the data given in the above Table.

6.3 INSTITUTIONAL SETUP FOR RURAL CREDIT

Prior to our country attaining independence in 1947, rural credit was largely provided by informal agencies such as money lenders and indigenous bankers; to a limited extent co-operative and commercial banks also provided rural credit. Several measures were taken after independence to enhance the flow of institutional credit (i.e, finance from banks/co-operative societies etc.) to the rural areas. The more important of these were the setting up of the State Bank of India in 1955 with a specific direction to open branches in rural areas. The nationalisation of major commercial banks was done in 1969 primarily with a view to ensuring that the large resources commanded by them were used for socio-economic objectives and that they increasingly lend for priority sectors including agriculture.

The establishment of Agricultural Refinance and Development Corporation in 1963 and the setting up of Regional Rural Banks from 1975 onwards was to take care of the credit needs of the weaker sections in rural areas exclusively and formation of the National Bank for Agriculture and Rural Development (NABARD) in 1982. As a result of these and various other steps taken, the rural and semi-urban network of commercial banks (including Regional Rural Banks) underwent expansion.

Rural credit in India is thus provided by a multi-agency system at present. This consists of public sector banks i.e., banks in which majority ownership is with Government of India, regional rural banks and Indian commercial banks in the private sector. Besides, a vast network of village level co-operative credit outlets also forms an integral part of the rural financing structure. The co-operative credit structure in India has two main wings — the long term credit structure and the short term credit structure. Long term credit is provided generally by a two — tier structure. The Land Development Banks, now known as Agriculture and Rural Development Banks which provide long term loans for development of land and agricultural projects. These institutions are generally, precluded from accepting deposits from public. The main source of funds of the Land Development Banks is debentures floated at relatively low rates of interest which are subscribed to by the NABARD.

The short term co-operative credit structure has three tiers. The primary co-operative credit societies operating at the grass root level are channels for flow of funds from the higher level financing agency to the borrower and vice versa, with practically little resources of their own or by means of public deposits. The institutions at the two higher tiers mobilise resources, inter-alia, by way of deposits from general public. Even so the bulk of the short term credit requirements of the co-operative structure are derived from funds provided at low rates by the Reserve Bank of India through NABARD under a system known as General Lines of Credit.

6.4 LENDING TO PRIORITY SECTORS BY COMMERCIAL BANKS

The concept of priority sector was evolved in the late sixties in order to focus attention on the need to ensure adequate credit facilities to certain neglected sectors of the economy particularly in the rural areas where banks had hardly made their presence felt. The involvement of banks in priority sector lending has grown considerably since then along with the extension of the branch network of banks into the rural areas with special emphasis on opening branches in unbanked areas.

Priority sector — Meaning: Priority sector refers to those sectors of the economy which may not get timely and adequate credit in the absence of this special dispensation. Typically, these are small value loans to farmers for agriculture and allied activities, micro and small enterprises, poor people for housing, students for education and other low income groups and weaker sections.

Categories of Priority Sector: Priority Sector includes the following categories:

(*i*) Agriculture

(*ii*) Micro and Small Enterprises

(*iii*) Education

(*iv*) Housing

(*v*) Export Credit

(*vi*) Others

The targets and sub-targets set under priority sector lending for domestic and foreign banks in India are as under:

Targets and Sub-targets for banks under priority sector

Categories	*Domestic commercial banks/Foreign banks with 20 and above branches (As percent of ANBC or Credit Equivalent of Off-Balance Sheet Exposure, whichever is higher)*	*Foreign banks with less than 20 branches (As percent of ANBC or Credit Equivalent of Off-Balance Sheet Exposure, whichever is higher)*
Total Priority Sector	40	32
Total agriculture	18	No specific target.
Advances to Weaker Sections	10	No specific target.

Note: ANBC-Adjusted Net Bank Credit

Source: RBI Publications

The performance of banks in Priority Sector lending as at March 31, 2013 can be seen in the following Table:

Priority Sector Lending by Banks

(As on March 31, 2013) (Amount in ₹ billion)

Item	Public Sector Banks		Private Sector Banks		Foreign Banks	
	Amount Outstanding	Per cent of ANBC/OBE	Amount Outstanding	Per cent of ANBC/OBE	Amount Outstanding	Per cent of ANBC/OBE
1	2	3	4	5	6	7
Total Priority Sector Advances *of which*	12,836	36.3	3,274	37.5	1,033	35.2
Agriculture	5,306	15.0	1,119	12.8	72	2.4
Weaker Sections	3,473	9.8	505	5.7	55	1.9
Micro and Small Enterprises	4,784	13.5	1,417	16.2	283	9.6

Notes: 1. Data are provisional.

2. As on March 31. 2013, priority sector lending targets for domestic scheduled commercial banks/foreign banks with 20 branches or more is set at 40 per cent of Adjusted Net Bank Credit (ANBC) or credit equivalent amount of off-balance sheet exposure (OBE), whichever is higher as on March 31 of the preceding year. The target of 40 per cent for foreign banks with 20 branches or more is to be achieved by March 2018. For foreign banks having less than 20 branches, the target is set at 32 per cent of ANBC or OBE, whichever is higher, as on March 31 of the preceding year.

Source: RBI Publications.

From the above Tables, we can observe there has been an enormous increase in the priority sector advances extended by the public and private sector banks in the recent past.

6.5 DRI SCHEME

Salient features of Differential Rate of Interest (DRI) scheme:

The scheme was introduced in 1972 and is being implemented by all Indian scheduled Commercial Banks.

1. **Objective:** To provide bank finance at a concessional rate of interest of 4 percent p.a. to the weaker sections of the community for engaging in productive and gainful activities so that they could improve their economic conditions.
2. **Area of Operations:** The scheme is being implemented throughout the country.
3. **Target Group/Eligibility Criteria:** The income ceiling for eligibility is annual income of ₹7200/- per family in urban or semi-urban areas and ₹6400/-per family in rural areas.

Size of land holding must not exceed one acre of irrigated land and 2.5 acres of unirrigated land. The land holding criteria is not applicable to SCs/STs. The banks are required to lend under the Scheme, atleast one percent of their aggregate advances as at the end of the previous year. 2/3rd of the total DRI advances must be routed through the banks' rural and semi-urban branches.

4. **Capital Subsidy/Interest:** No capital subsidy is available. Rate of interest to be charged on loans is 4 percent p.a.
5. **Security:** No collateral security/third party guarantee is required. Assets created out of the loan amount would only be hypothecated to the banks.
6. **Repayment:** Not exceeding five years including grace period of two years.
7. **Reservation/Preference:** The banks are required to ensure that at least 40 percent of their DRI advances flow to SC/STs.

Differential Rate of Interest Scheme—Revision of the income limits- 2008:

The scheme known as Differential Rate of Interest Scheme (DRI) is now being implemented by all Scheduled Commercial Banks. Reserve Bank of India on 10th April 2008 has notified that borrowers with annual family income of ₹18000 in rural areas and ₹24000 in urban areas will now be eligible to avail of the facility as against the earlier annual income criteria of ₹6400 in rural areas and ₹7200 in urban areas, fixed by the Government of India in 1986. The other terms and conditions of the DRI scheme remain unchanged. (Source: RBI Circular).

RBI issued a circular that under the DRI scheme, banks provide finance up to ₹15,000/- at a concessional rate of interest of 4 percent per annum to the weaker sections of the community for engaging in productive and gainful activities. In order to ensure that persons belonging to SCs/STs also derive adequate benefit under the Differential Rate of Interest (DRI) scheme, banks have been advised to grant to eligible borrowers belonging to SCs/STs such advances to the extent of not less than 2/5th (40 percent) of total DRI advances(Source: RBI Circular).

REVIEW QUESTIONS

Short Answer Questions

1. Write a short note on the aspects for which the commercial banks provide rural credit in India.
2. What is service area approach of commercial banks?
3. Write a brief note on the strength of service area approach.
4. Write short notes on the purposes for which the commercial banks provide the following types of rural credit:
   (*a*) Short-term loans
   (*b*) Medium-term loans
   (*c*) Long-term loans

Essay Type Questions

1. Briefly explain the role of commercial banks in rural financing in India.
2. What are the different types of agricultural finance provided by the commercial banks?
3. Write a note on the Institutional set up for rural credit in India.
4. Explain the lending policy of commercial banks to primary sectors of India.
5. Briefly explain the performance of Indian commercial banks in primary sector advances.
6. What are direct and indirect financing provided by commercial banks to the rural sector in India?
7. Write a note on DRI Scheme.

CHAPTER 7 Co-Operative Banks and Development Banks

Besides commercial banks, many other types of banks are functioning with the Government support for the development of rural and urban areas, small and medium enterprises, corporate sector and for the promotion of export and import trade in India. This chapter discusses on:

1. Co-operative Banks
2. Regional Rural Banks (RRBs) and
3. Development Banks including NABARD

7.1 CO-OPERATIVE BANKING IN INDIA

In the general sense, the term "co-operation" means, the idea of "living together and working together". Co-operation is a form of business organisation. It is the only system of voluntary organisation suitable for poorer people. In this system, the persons voluntarily associate together as human beings on a basis of equality, for the promotion of their economic interests.

Thus, the co-operative bank can be defined as, "an institution established on the co-operative principles and engaged in the normal banking business of accepting deposits from the public for the purpose of lending and repay it on demand or otherwise"

Cooperative institutions occupy an important position in the Indian financial system. Cooperatives were the first formal institutions developed to provide credit facilities to rural areas of India. Until now, cooperative institutions have been a key instrument of financial service to rural areas. The Urban cooperative banks also have been an important channel of financial service for the middle and low income sections in the semi-urban and urban areas.

Co-operative Banks in India are registered under the Co-operative Societies Act. They are regulated by the RBI. Co-operative Banks are governed by the Banking Regulations Act 1949 and Banking Laws (Co-operative Societies) Act, 1965.

7.1.1. Differences between Co-operative Banks and Commercial Banks

Even though the commercial banks and co-operative banks are similar in nature of business, they differ in many respects. The main differences between them are as follows:

Sl. No.	*FEATURE*	*CO-OPERATIVE BANKS*	*COMMERCIAL BANKS*
1.	**Registration Requirements (India)**	Co-operative banks are required to be registered under the "Co-operative Societies Act", of the concerned state.	Commercial banks are required to be registered under "Banking Regulation Act, 1949".
2.	**Basic Objective**	The basic objective of co-operative banks is to accept deposits from the members and the public for the purpose of providing loans to farmers and small businessmen with service motive.	The main objective of a commercial bank is to accept deposits from public for the purpose of lending to industry and commerce.

3.	**Structure of the system**	Federal structure in nature *i.e.*, at the top level state co-operative banks, at the district level, central co-operative Banks, and at the village level Primary co-operative credit societies.	They are functioning on branch banking system and the branches are located in all areas such as rural, urban etc., The Head Office controls all branches through Zonal Offices.
4.	**Purpose of Credit**	They are generally concentrating on rural credit and provide credit facilities to agricultural and rural activities.	They are mainly concentrating on the credit requirements of trade and industry.
5.	**Funds Available**	Normally Co-operative banks have limited funds available at their disposal for the banking operations.	Commercial banks generally have large volume of funds at their disposal for the banking operations.
6.	**Geographical Territory**	The geographical area of operations of co-operative banks is limited and mostly confined to State. They do not operate at national level or international level.	The geographical area of operations of Commercial banks is very wide and operates in many states in the country. And Some commercial banks have branches in India and abroad.
7.	**Nationalisation of Banks by the Government**	In India co-operative banks are not nationalized by the Government.	In India, the Government has nationalized many commercial banks.
8.	**Voting Rights**	In co-operative banks, members living in a particular area are usually shareholders. one shareholder has one vote.	In joint stock Commercial banks one share one vote system is followed. Shareholder dispersion is very wide and member can be from any part of the country.[Section 12 (2) of B.R. Act however restricts the maximum voting rights of a shareholder to 10 per cent of total votes.
9.	**Interest Rate**	In co-operative banks, the rate of interest for deposits is usually high and for the loan it is lower. This position is in comparison with This position is in comparison with.	When comparing with co-operative banks, the interest rate on loans is high and for the deposits it is generally low.
10.	**Borrowers**	In cooperative Banks the borrowers are usually their members.	In commercial banks the borrowers can be any one including individuals and institutions.

7.1.2. Co-operative Banking in India

In India, the development of cooperative system was originated by the government. It supports all the aspects of development and has made the cooperative institutions in achieving the significant progress in their field. More specifically in banking sector, co-operative institutions have attained a vital place. The co-operative movement in Indian Banking was started with the objective of providing finance to the agriculturists and thus relieving him from the clutches of the village money lenders i.e., to solve the problem of rural indebtedness by supplying credit at low rates of interest. In India, the Co-operative Societies Act was passed in 1904. A new Co-operative Societies Act was passed in 1912.

With the commitment of the government towards cooperatives, RBI supported the development of cooperative institutions in big way. Because of the Reserve Bank's concern and involvement in rural credit specific provisions were made in the Reserve Bank of India Act, 1934 both for the establishment of an Agricultural Credit Department in the bank and for extending refinance facilities to the cooperative credit system. Importance was given for setting up, strengthening and promotion of financially viable state cooperative banks, central cooperative banks, marketing societies and primary agricultural credit societies in each state. From 1942, RBI has started extending credit facilities to the state cooperative banks for seasonal agricultural operations and marketing of crops.

After Independence, rapid and equitable economic development became the central focus of Government's policy. With the beginning of the planning process, cooperatives became an integral part of the Five Year Plans. Rural financial cooperatives were given more importance. The All-India Rural Credit Survey Committee Report, 1954 recommended an integrated approach to cooperative credit and emphasised the need for viable credit cooperative societies by expanding their area of operation, encouraging rural savings and diversifying business. The Committee also recommended for Government participation in the share capital of the cooperatives and in governance and management. The recommendations of the Committee provides for the Government's direct interference in the governance and management of cooperatives. In view of these recommendations, different States brought various schemes for the cooperative movement for organising large-size societies and provision of Government involvement and assistance. Though the movement has completed more than a century, the progress has been slow.

The structure of co-operative credit institutions in India as at the end of March 2013 can be seen in the following diagram:

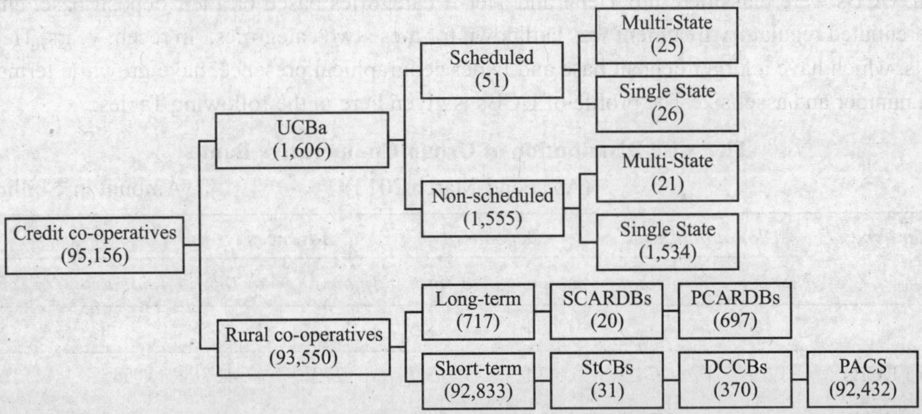

StCBs: State Co-operative Banks; DCCBs: District Central Co-operative Banks; PACS: Primary Agricultural Credit Societies; SCARDBs: State Co-operative Agriculture and Rural Development Banks; PCARDBs: Primary Co-operative Agriculture and Rural Development Banks.

Notes: 1. Figures in parentheses indicate the number of institutions at end-March 2013 for UCBs and at end-March 2012 for rural co-operatives.

2. For rural co-operatives, the number of co-operatives refers to reporting co-operatives.

Source: RBI Publications

7.1.3. Types of Co-Operative Credit Institutions based on Structure

The Co-operative banking structure in India includes the following two main types:

1. Urban Co-operative Banks
2. Rural Co-operatives

Let us discuss these types in turn here under:

7.1.3.1. Urban Cooperative Banks

Urban cooperative banks, also referred to as primary co-operative banks, play an important role in meeting the growing credit needs of urban and semiurban areas of the country. They mobilise savings from the middle and lower income groups and provide credit to small borrowers, including weaker sections of the society. Urban Co-operative banks are small sized cooperatively organized banking units which operate in metropolitan, urban and semi-urban centers to cater mainly to the needs of small borrowers, viz. owners of small scale industrial units, retail traders, professional and salaries classes.

The urban cooperative banks have contributed significantly to the wellbeing of lower income groups of the urban and semi urban population. the urban cooperative credit movement in India, was the first ever attempt at micro credit dispensation in semi urban and urban areas. The UCBs and other cooperative banks were essentially governed by the State Governments under the provisions of their respective State Cooperative Societies Acts. But with the increasing demand for introduction of deposit insurance to cooperative banks, it was felt necessary to bring them under the purview of the Banking Regulation Act, 1949. The urban cooperative banks were, therefore, brought under the purview of Banking Regulation Act, effective from 1 March, 1966. With this, UCBs were subjected to dual command by RBI exercising control over their banking related functions and State Governments exercising supervision over their managerial, administrative and other matters. The area of operation of these banks is usually restricted by its byelaws to a municipal area or a town. UCBs were classified into Tier-I and Tier-II categories based on their deposit base, and a differentiated regulatory treatment was laid down for these two categories. In recent years, Tier-II banks, which have a larger deposit base and wider geographical presence, have grown in terms of both number and asset size The profile of UCBs is given here in the following Tables:

Tier-wise Distribution of Urban Co-operative Banks

(As at end-March 2013) (Amount in ₹ billion)

Tier Type	*No. of banks*		*Deposits*		*Advances*		*Assets*	
	Number	*% to Total*	*Amount*	*% to Total*	*Amount*	*% to Total*	*Amount*	*% to Total*
1	2	3	4	5	6	7	8	9
Tier I UCBs	1.194	74.3	434	15.7	272	15.0	545	16.2
Tier II UCBs	412	25.7	2,335	84.3	1,538	85.0	2,827	83.8
All UCBs	1,606	100.0	2,769	100.0	1,810	100.0	3,372	100.0

Note: Data are provisional.

[2] Tier-I UCBs were defined as UCBs with:

- Deposit base below ₹1 billion operating in a single district.
- Deposit base below ₹1 billion operating in more than one district provided the branches were in contiguous districts, and deposits and advances of branches in one district separately constituted at least 95 per cent of the total deposits and advances, respectively, of the bank.
- Deposit base below ₹1 billion, whose branches were originally in a single district but subsequently became multi-district due to re-organisation of the district.

All other UCBs are defined as Tier-II UCBs.

Source: RBI Publications

Composition of Credit to Priority Sectors by UCBs

(As at end-March 2013) (Amount in ₹ billion)

Sector	*Composition of total priority sector credit*		*Of which, composition of credit to weaker sections*	
	Amount	*Percentage to total*	*Amount*	*Percentage to total*
1	2	3	4	5
1. Agricultural credit	68	3.8	23	1.3
1.1 Direct agricultural credit	25	1.4	7	0.4
1.2 Indirect agricultural credit	43	2.4	16	0.9
2. Small Enterprises	425	23.5	77	4.2
2.1 Direct credit to small enterprises	368	20.3	62	3.4
2.2 Indirect credit to small enterprises	57	3.2	15	9.8
3. Micro Credit	138	7.6	49	2.7
3.1 Loans to SHG/JLG	17	0.9	6	0.3
3.2 Loans to others	121	6.7	43	2.4
4. State-sponsored organisations for SC/ST	1	0.1	0.5	–
5. Education loans	17	0.9	7	0.4
6. Housing loans	195	10.8	68	3.7
7. Loans to SHG/JLG (more than ₹ 50,000)	10	0.5	2	0.1
All priority sectors	853	47.1	225	12.4

– : Negligible.

Notes: 1. Percentages are with respect to total credit of UCBs.

2. Components may not add up to the total due to rounding off.

Source: RBI Publications

The composition of credit to priority sectors by UCBs suggests that small enterprises and the housing sector accounted for over onethird of the total credit of these institutions in 2012-13.

7.1.3.2. Rural Co-operatives

Rural Cooperative Banking plays an important role in meeting the growing credit needs of rural population of India. It provides institutional credit to the agricultural and rural sector. The inadequacy of rural credit engaged the attention of RBI and Government throughout the 1950s and 1960s. One important feature of providing agriculture credit in India has been the existence of a widespread network of rural financial institutions. The rural credit structure consists of many types of financial institutions as large scale branch expansion was undertaken to create a strong institution based in rural area. It has served as an important instrument of credit delivery in rural and agricultural areas. The separate structure of rural Cooperative sector for long-term and short-term loans has enabled these institutions to develop a specialized institution for rural credit delivery. The volume of credit flowing through these institutions has increased. The Rural Co-operative structure has traditionally been bifurcated into two parallel wings, *i.e.*

1. Short-term Rural Co-operatives
2. Long-term Rural Co-operatives

1. Short-term Rural Co-operatives: Since inception, cooperatives have made available institutional credit at affordable cost particularly to the agricultural sector. The Short-term Rural Cooperative Credit Structure (STCCS) provides mainly short term and medium-term production credit besides other financial services. At present, there are nearly 92,432 Primary Agricultural

Credit Societies (PACS), 371 District Central Cooperative Banks (DCCB) with 13,233 branches and 32 State Cooperative Banks (SCB) with 992 branches. On an average, there is one PACS for every 8 villages. These societies have a total membership of more than 120 million rural people making it one of the largest rural financial systems in the world. 60% of population still depends upon the agricultural income.

In India, the structure of commercial banking is based on branch-banking system. But the organisation of Short-term Rural Co-operatives is pyramidal in nature. It has a three-tier structure as given in the following diagram:

Short-term Rural Co-operatives

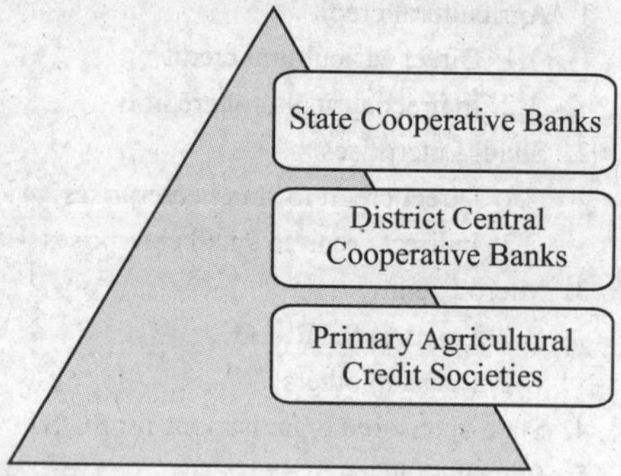

That is, the primary societies are functioning in the various towns and villages, the Central Banks at the district headquarters and the state co-operative banks at the state capitals forming the apex of the system. The Reserve Bank of India assist the co-operative structure by providing concessional finance through NABARD in the form of General Lines of Credit for lending to agricultural activities. Thus, the whole system is integrated with the Banking structure of the country.

Let us discuss about these institutions one by one:

***(i)* The Primary Agricultural Credit Societies:** Basically, a primary society is an association of borrowers and non-borrowers residing in a particular locality and taking interest in the business affairs of one another. As membership is practically open to all inhabitants of a locality, people of different status are brought together into the common organisation. The affairs of those organisation are managed by honorary secretaries and presidents assisted by boards of directors, all these officials being elected from amongst the shareholders on the principle 'of one man, one vote'. Most of the societies are organised and working on the principle of unlimited liability. The society may be started with ten or more persons of a village. Primary Agricultural Credit Societies are established on this basis. Thus, they are the credit institutions at the grass-root level deal directly with individual members or clients.

Primary Agricultural Credit Societies is the foundation of the co-operative credit system on which the superstructure of the short-term co-operative credit system rests. It deals directly with individual farmers, provide short and medium term credit, supply agricultural inputs, distribute consume articles and also arrange for the marketing of products of its members through a c-operative marketing societies. These societies form the basic unit of co-operative credit system in India. These credit societies can extend loans to its members only for the purpose of agriculture connected activities. The success of the co-operative credit movement depends largely on the strength of these village level societies.

***(ii)* Central Co-operative Banks:** A Central Co-operative Bank is a federation of primary societies in a specified area. Where membership of a Central Cooperative Bank (CCB) is restricted to primary societies only, it is known as a 'banking union'. Nowadays, individuals are also admitted as members of almost all CCBs. They are generally situated at the headquarters of district and have on their boards of management, individuals of sufficient effect and business capacity in addition to representatives of primary societies. The CCBs form an important part in the short term structure of co-operative credit institutions.

Operation of the bank: The primary business of CCBs consists of financing primary societies. In some cases, they attract the surplus funds of certain primary societies, to supply the same to others. Thus CCBs act as balancing centers to the primary societies. Again, the deposits of urban areas are made available to the rural areas through the agency of these banks. The deposits with Central Banks have recently grown so great in volume that Central Banks are not able to employ them within the co-operative movement. They do not, as a rule, lend for commercial purposes and therefore are compelled to invest their funds in Government Securities. However, with the growth of other types of co-operative movement these funds may be absorbed by the various types of co-operative societies.

***(iii)* State Co-operative Banks:** At the top of the co-operative banking, there are State Co-operative Banks, organised with the object of attracting deposits from the rich urban classes. These banks are also more suitably equipped to serve as channel between the co-operative movement and the joint stock banks.

The constitution of these banks differs from one another, but generally speaking, their membership comprises of representatives of Central Banks as well as individual shareholders. A logical development of these banks would have been the establishment of all-India Co-operative bank. But there is no such institution, although the Indian State Co-operative Banks Association has been co-ordinating their activities and performing certain services to all these banks. NABARD maintains contact with the State Co-operative Banks. In addition to offering them rediscount facilities, collects and disseminates useful information regarding co-operative movement.

In simple terms, it is a federation of central co-operative bank and acts as a regulator of the co-operative banking structure in the state. Its funds are obtained from share capital, deposits, loans and overdrafts from the Reserve Bank of India. The state cooperative banks lend money to central co-operative banks and primary societies and not directly to the farmers.

Within rural co-operatives, the short-term credit co-operatives occupy a significant position in providing credit to the agriculture sector. The share of short-term credit co-operatives, comprising State Co-operative Banks (StCBs), District Central Co-operative Banks (DCCBs) and Primary Agricultural Credit Societies (PACS), continued to be above 90 per cent of the total assets of the rural co-operative credit institutions at end-March 2012 while the long-term credit co-operatives accounted for the remaining 10 per cent of total assets. It can be seen from the following Table:

A Profile of Rural Co-operatives

(As at end-March 2012) (Amount in ₹ billion)

Item	*Short-term*			*Long-term*	
	StCBs	*DCCBs*	*PACS*	*SCARDBs*	*PCARDBs*
1	2	3	4	5	6
A. Number of Co-operatives	31	370	92,432	20	697
B. Balance Sheet Indicators					
(*i*) Owned Funds (Capital + Reserves)	145	359	160	64	48
(*ii*) Deposits	867	1768	503	11	5
(*iii*) Borrowing	427	505	888	160	135
(*iv*) Loans and Advances	756	1448	912	194	120
(*v*) Total Liabilities/Assets	1,479	2,573	1,605⁺	294	262
C. Financial Performance					
(*i*) Institutions in Profit					
(*a*) Number	28	318	45.433	10	358
(*b*) Amount of Profit	7	17	14	1	2
(*ii*) Institutions in Loss					
(*a*) Number	3	52	36,375	10	338
(*b*) Amount of Loss	2	3	34	3	4
(*iii*) Overall Profit (+)/Loss (–)	5	14	–20	–2	–2

D. Non-performing Assets					
(*i*) Amount	52	154	243++	64	47
(*ii*) As percentage of Loans Outstanding	6.8	9.7	26.8	33.1	38.6
E. Recovery of Loans to Demand Ratio (Per cent)	96	78	73	41.3	47.3

StCBs: State Co-operative Banks; DCCBs: District Central Co-operative Banks; PACS: Primary Agricultural Credit Societies; SCARDBs: State Co-operative Agriculture and Rural Development Banks; PCARDBs: Primary Co-operative Agriculture and Rural Development Banks.

+ : Working capital. ++ : Total overdues

Notes: 1. Data for the year 2011-12 are provisional.

2. Manipur SCARDB is define.

Source: NABARD and NAFSCOB and RBI Publications

Performance of Rural Co-operative Banks in Extension of Agriculture Credit:

Institutional lending to agriculture and allied activities has recorded a significant growth during the last two decades due to the aggressive policy of the government in expanding credit to agriculture. The following figure depicts the growth in agricultural credit distributed by the STCCS:

Performance of STCCS under agricultural Credit

(₹ in crore)

Years	*StCBs*	*DCCBs*	*PACS*
2002-03	35052	52820	33996
2007-08	53314	95974	57642
2008-09	51866	97207	58787
2009-10	59784	104997	74938
2010-11	68481	122795	91304
2011-12	81523	144761	107300

Source: RBI Publications

2. Long-Term Rural Co-operatives:

The long-term rural co-operative provide typically medium and long-term loans for making investments in agriculture, rural industries and, in the recent period, housing. Generally, these co-operatives have two tiers, i.e. State Co-operative Agriculture and Development Banks (SCARBDs) at the state level and Primary Co-operative Agriculture and Rural Development Banks (PCARDBs) at the taluka or tehsil level. PCARDBs are affiliated to the SCARDBs. However, some States have a unitary structure with the state level banks operating through their own branches.

(*i*) State Co-operative Agriculture and Development Banks (SCARBDs):

State Co-operative Agriculture and Development Banks constitute the upper-tier of long term co-operative credit structure. Though long term credit co-operatives have been allowed to access public deposits under certain conditions, such deposits constitute a relatively small proportion of their total liabilities. They are mostly dependent on borrowings for on-lending. The main objective of the Co-operative State Agriculture and Rural Development bank is to finance primary agriculture and rural development banks.

(*ii*) Primary Co-operative Agriculture and Rural Development Banks (PCARDBs):

Primary Co-operative Agriculture and Rural Development Banks is the lowest layer of long term credit co-operatives. It is primarily dependent on the borrowings for their lending business. They provide credit for developmental purposes like minor irrigation, cultivation of plantation crops and for diversified purposes like poultry, dairying and sericulture on schematic basis. They get requisite financial assistance from the Cooperative State Agriculture and Rural Development Bank. In order to widen their scope of lending to compete with other financial agencies, the primary cooperative agriculture and rural development banks have been permitted to finance artisans, craftmen and small scale entrepreneurs.

Cooperatives clearly remain the major source of agricultural credit to small and medium farmers in terms of the number of borrowers and size of individual loans. This can be seen from the following figure:

Agricultural Loans Disbursed during the Year

(₹ in crore)

Agency	2006-07	2007-08	2008-09	2009-10	2010-11	2011-12
Coops.	42,480 (18)	48,258 (19)	46,192 (15)	63,497 (17)	78,121 (17)	87,963 (17)
RRBs	20,435 (9)	25,312 (10)	26,765 (9)	35,217 (9)	44,293 (9)	54,450 (11)
CBs	1,66,485 (73)	1,81,088 (71)	2,28,951 (76)	2,85,800 (74)	3,45,877 (74)	3,68,616 (72)
Total	2,29,400	2,54,658	3,01,908	3,84,514	4,68,291	5,11,029

Figures in brackets indicate percentage share of different agencies to total agricultural credit

Source: RBI Publication

Co-operative Banks are important in the development of Indian economy more specifically in rural areas. The distinctive character of these institutions is providing service at a lower cost and service without exploitation. It has gained its importance by the role assigned to them, the expectations they are supposed to fulfill, their number, and the number of offices they operate. Cooperative banks, though account for a small proportion of the total business undertaken by the banking system in India, have a prominent place in the Indian financial landscape owing to their potential role in furthering financial inclusion as also because of financial inter linkages that these institutions have with the rest of the financial system.

7.2. REGIONAL RURAL BANKS

The rural sector is the back bone of Indian Economy as over 40% of the Gross National Product is coming from this sector. Priority sector credit is one of the strategic inputs for the successful implementation of rural development schemes.

The Government of India had constituted a "Working Group on Rural Banks" headed by Mr. M. Narasimhan on July 1, 1975 to study, in depth, the problem of devising alternative agencies to provide institutional credit to rural people. The committee recommended the establishment of Regional Rural Banks. Regional Rural Banks (RRBs) were created with the objective of combining the good features of cooperatives and commercial banks to provide regionally oriented institutions that could direct credit to the under-privileged sections of the rural population. The Government of India, with certain modification accepted the recommendations of the group and Regional Rural Banks (RRB) were set up under the " Regional Rural Bank ordinance 1975, " promulgated by the President of India on 26th - September 1975, it was subsequently replaced by the " Regional Rural Banks Act, 1976 " on 9th Feb, 1976.

Regional Rural Banks (RRBs) form an integral part of the Indian banking system with focus on service to rural areas. The process of amalgamation of the RRBs was initiated by Government of India in September 2005 in a phased manner. Prior to the process of amalgamation, 196 RRBs sponsored by 27 SCBs and one State Cooperative Bank were operating in the country with a network of 14,484 branches spread over 523 districts as on March 31, 2005. Consequent upon the amalgamation, the number of RRBs declined to 82 operating in 26 States and in one Union Territory covering 619 districts with a network of 15,475 branches as on March 31, 2010. The RRBs have a special place in the multi-agency approach adopted to provide agricultural and rural credit in India. These banks are state-sponsored, regionally-based and rural-oriented.

7.2.1. Objectives of Regional Rural Banks

The RBBs Act has made various provisions regarding the incorporation, regulation and working of RRBs. According to this Act, the RRBs are to be set up mainly with a view to develop rural economy by providing credit facilities for the purpose of development of agriculture, trade, Commerce, industry and other productive activities in the rural areas. Such facility is provided particularly to the small and marginal farmers, agricultural labourers, artisans, and small entrepreneurs and for other related matters.

The objectives of RRBs can be summarised as follows.

(*i*) To provide cheap and liberal credit facilities to small and marginal farmers, agriculture labourers, artisans, small entrepreneurs and other weaker sections.

(*ii*) To save the rural poor from the money lenders.

(*iii*) To act as a catalyst element and thereby accelerate the economic growth in the particular region.

(iv) To cultivate the banking habits among the rural people and mobilise savings for the economic development of rural areas.

(*v*) To increase employment opportunities by encouraging trade and commerce in rural areas.

(*vi*) To encourage entrepreneurship in rural areas.

(*vii*) To cater to the needs of the backward areas which are not covered by the other efforts of the Government.

(*viii*) To develop under developed regions and thereby strive to remove economic disparity between regions.

7.2.2. Capital Structure and Sponsorship

Each RRB is to be sponsored by a scheduled commercial bank mainly by a public sector bank. The RRB is established at the initiative taken by the state and central Government. The sponsoring bank provides assistance to the RRB in several ways such as (i) subscription to its share capital (ii) Provision of managerial assistance (iii) Provision of other staff assistance (iv) funds under Refinance Assistance (v) Investment guidance etc., These were provided on the basis of mutual agreement for the period of first five years of its existence and financial assistance on the terms mutually negotiable. However, the sponsor bank continues to extend all the facilities even beyond 5 years as of now.

The authorised capital of each RRB was fixed at ₹1 crore and the issued capital at ₹25 lakhs. The issued capital would be subscribed by the Central Government, the sponsoring bank and the State Government in the proportions of 50%, 35% and 15% respectively.

The Regional Rural Banks (Amendment) Act 1987, which came in to force on 28th September 1988 has enhanced the authorised capital of RRB to ₹5 crore and paid up share capital to ₹1 crore.

7.2.3. Management of Regional Rural Banks

The general management of each RRB is vested with the Board of Directors. The board consists of 9 directors including a chairman. The chairman is a full-time professional executive, appointed by the Central Government. He is usually a senior officer from the sponsor bank. Of the 9 Directors three are nominated by the Central Government, 2 by State Government and 3 by Sponsoring Bank for the term of five years. RBI and NABARD can also nominate one director each to the Board of RRBs. The central government can increase the number of Board of Directors to a maximum of 15. After the formation of NABARD in July 1982, most aspects relating to the RRBs are looked after by NABARD. The RBI as the Central Banking Authority continues to prescribe various policy objectives and guidelines for the RRBs.

7.2.4. Area of Operation

The Jurisdiction of each RRB is within the specified districts in a state and for its branches certain blocks with in the districts. Generally, the area of operation of the RRB consists of one to five districts with homogenity in agro-climatic conditions. And, a branch office normally covers one to three blocks.

7.2.5. Functions of RRBs

The main functions of RRBs include the following:

1. Mobilization of deposits rural areas by means of various types of deposits
2. Provision of credit in favor of the economically weaker sections of population in the remote rural areas. It is done by providing short-term and medium-term credit for agriculture and long term loans for the land development.
3. Provision of other ancillary banking facilities like remittance of funds and safe keeping of deposits and valuables etc.
4. Setting up and maintenance of godowns and warehouses
5. Undertaking of the supply of agricultural inputs and equipment to farmers.
6. Provision of assistance in the marketing of agricultural and other products through marketing organisations.
7. Encouraging village industries, artisans, carpenters, craftsmen, etc.
8. Reducing the dependence of weaker sections on money-lenders.
9. Identifying a specific and functional gap in the present institutional structure and fulfill the gaps identified.
10. Making backward and tribal areas economically better by opening new branches and extending micro credit facilities and operating the scheme of inclusion.

7.2.6. Consolidation of RRBs

Government of India initiated the process of structural consolidation, in consultation with State Governments and Sponsor Banks, by amalgamating RRBs of the same sponsor bank in the State in September 2005. Prior to the process of amalgamation, 196 RRBs sponsored by 27 SCBs and one State Cooperative Bank were operating in the country with a network of 14,484 branches spread over 523 districts as on March 31, 2005. Consequent upon the amalgamation, the number of RRBs declined to 82 operating in 26 States and in one Union Territory covering 619 districts with a network of 15,475 branches as on March 31, 2010.

7.2.7. Progress and achievement of RRBs

Every RRB has the status of a scheduled commercial bank and has been empowered to mobilise deposits and to grant short and term loans, and operate within its specified area of operation.

Performance of RRBs during 2012-13

The sources of funds of RRBs comprise of owned fund, deposits, borrowings from NABARD, Sponsor Banks and other sources including SIDBI and National Housing Bank.

Owned Funds

The owned funds of RRBs comprising of share capital, share capital deposits received from the shareholders and the reserves stood at ₹19304 crore as on 31 March 2013 as against ₹16462 crore as on 31 March 2012; registering a growth of 17.26%. The increase in owned funds to the tune of ₹2842 crore was mainly on account of accretion to reserves by the profit making RRBs. The share capital and share capital deposits together amounted to ₹6174 crore of total owned fund while the balance amount of ₹13130 crore represented reserves.

Recapitalisation of RRBs

(*a*) The Chakrabarty Committee reviewed the financial position of all RRBs in 2010 and recommended for recapitalisation of 40 out of 82 RRBs for strengthening their CRAR to the level of 9 per cent by 31 March 2012. According to the Committee, the remaining RRBs are in a position to achieve the desired level of CRAR on their own. Accepting the recommendations of the committee, the GOI along with other shareholders decided to recapitalise the RRBs by infusing funds to the extent of ₹2200 Crore. The shareholder wise proportion (GOI/Sponsor Banks/State Governments) is 50:35:15 respectively.

(*b*) As on 31 March 2013, an amount of ₹2015.86 crore has been released to 37 RRBs in 20 States. The released amount includes GoI's contribution of ₹1003.92 crore, State Govt's contribution of ₹303.59 crore and Sponsor bank's contribution of ₹708.35 crore. The recapitalisation is complete in respect of 35 RRBs (5 in Odisha , 3 in MP, 2 in Uttarakhand, 2 in Jharkhand, 2 in Chhatisgarh, 2 in Bihar, 2 in Maharashtra, 3 in West Bengal, 5 in Rajasthan and one each in Assam, Arunachal Pradesh, Nagaland, Tripura, J&K, Karnataka, Tamil Nadu, Gujarat & UT of Puducherry). GoI share ₹7.99 cr. is pending in respect of Manipur Rural Bank. Mizoram State Government has partially released ₹0.50 crore in respect of Mizoram Rural Bank and ₹2.80 crore is pending. Two State Govts. viz. UP(2 RRBs), & J&K (1 RRB) have not released any amount in respect of 3 RRBs operating in their states. Out of 35 fully recapitalised RRBs, 3 RRBs viz. Central Madhya Pradesh GB, Manipur Rural Bank and Mizoram GB have not achieved CRAR of 9 per cent as on 31.3.2013.

Deposits: Deposits of RRBs increased from ₹ 186336 crore to ₹ 211458 crore during the year registering growth rate of 13.48 %. There are Thirty three (33) RRBs having deposits of more than ₹ 3000 crore each.

Loans & Advances: During the year the loans outstanding increased by ₹ 23452 crore to ₹ 139837 crore as on 31 March 2013 registering a growth rate of 20.15% over the previous year.

Loans Issued: Total loans issued by RRBs during the year increased to ₹ 102162 crore from ₹ 82538 crore during the previous year registering a growth of 23.78%.

The purpose-wise Outstanding Advances by RRBs can be seen in the following table.

Purpose-wise Outstanding Advances by RRBs

(Amount in ₹ billion)

Sr. No.	*Purpose/End-March*	*2012*	*2013 P*
1	2	3	4
I.	**Agriculture [(*i*) to (*iii*)]**	**638**	**752**
	Per cent to total loans outstanding	*54.8*	*53.8*
	(*i*) Short-term credit (crop loans)	466	551
	(*ii*) Term loans (for agriculture and allied activities)	172	201
	(*iii*) Indirect advances	–	–

II. Non-agriculture [(*i*) to (*iv*)]	**526**	**645**
Per cent to total loans outstanding	*45.2*	*46.2*
(*i*) Rural artisans, etc.	10	11
(*ii*) Other industries	37	42
(*iii*) Retail trade, etc.	58	62
(*iv*) Other purposes	420	530
Total (I + II)	**1,164**	**1,397**
Memo Item:		
(*a*) Priority sector	955	1,143
(*b*) Non-Priority sector	208	253
Share of priority sector (per cent to total)	82.1	81.8

P : Provisional.
Source: NABARD.

Branch Expansion:

During 2012-13, 947 branches were opened by RRBs taking the cumulative number of branches to 17,856 spread across 635 districts in 26 states and one UT. It is now compulsory for all the new branches to be equipped with Core banking Solution. Sponsor banks are required to extend all necessary help in this regard, including financial assistance, training and back office support. As on March 31, 2013, Core banking Solution was fully implemented in all the 64 RRBs.

Amalgamation of RRBs: A new phase in the amalgamation of RRBs has begun. So far, there have been two broad phases in the amalgamation of RRBs. In the first phase (September 2005-March 2010), RRBs of the same sponsor banks within a State were amalgamated bringing down their number to 82 from 196. In the second and ongoing phase, starting from October 2012, geographically contiguous RRBs within a State under different sponsor banks would be amalgamated to have just one RRB in medium-sized States and two/three RRBs in large States. In the current phase, 31 RRBs have been amalgamated into 13 new RRBs within 9 States to bring down their effective number to 64. These States include Uttar Pradesh, Madhya Pradesh, Uttarakhand, Odisha, Bihar, Karnataka, Rajasthan, Himachal Pradesh and Maharashtra.

7.3. DEVELOPMENT BANKS

Beginning in late 1940s, several financial institutions (Development Finance Institutions (DFIs) were established to provide funds to the large medium and small industry in India. The DFIs provide finance for the establishment of new industrial projects as well as for expansion, diversification, and modernization of existing industrial enterprises. Development Bank is a multi-dimensional development finance institution devoted to improving the social and monetary development of the country. The main functions of a Development Bank:

(*i*) Increase loans and equity investments in the country for its monetary and social development.

(*ii*) Provides technical help for the planning and implementation of development projects and programs and for advisory services.

(*iii*) Promotes and facilitates mobilisation of public and private capital for growth and development.

(*iv*) Responds to requests for assistance in coordinating growth policies and plans of its increasing financial demands in the country.

Reasons for the promotion of Development Banks

Developments were promoted mainly for the following purposes:

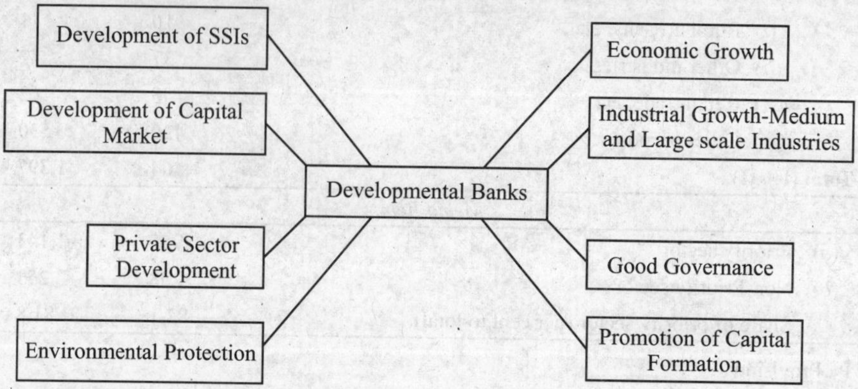

Formation of Development Banks in India:

Development banks were set up in India at various points of time starting from the late 1940s to cater to the medium to long term financing needs of the industry as the capital market in India had not developed sufficiently during the early period. The planned industrialization at the national level encouraged for the organization of Development banks at both all-India level and at state levels. In India the banks can be classified as follows:

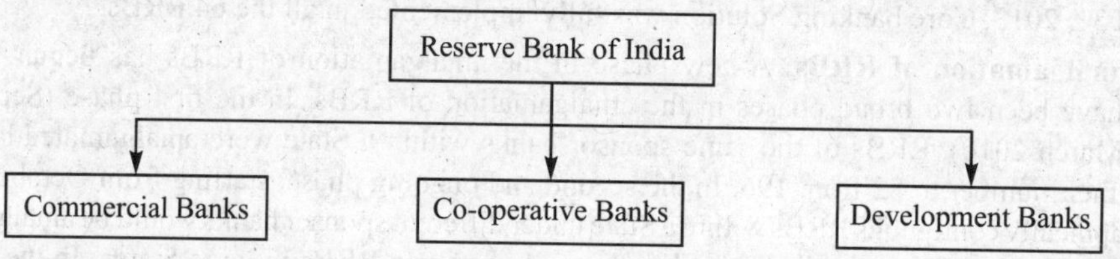

Development Banks were established to finance and nurture the industries. They differ from the other banks in the way that they are mainly involved in the process of lending the money to the required sections. They have some major function like medium and long term loans to the industries, subscription to the share and debenture of the industries and underwriting of the new issues and provide securities to the newly established companies. They have established many subsidiaries all over the country to look after the need for the industrial finance needed for the small and medium scale enterprises and other industrial requirements.

The development banks established in India includes the following:

1. National Bank for Agriculture and Rural Development (NABARD)
2. Industrial Finance Co-operation of India (IFCI)
3. Industrial Development of India (IDBI)
4. Small Industries Development Bank of India (SIDBI)
5. Export-Import Bank of India (EXIM Bank)

Let us see these development banks in detail here under.

7.3.1. National Bank For Agriculture And Rural Development (NABARD)

NABARD is Apex Rural credit institution which plays an active role in implementation of various rural development programmes. The NABARD came into existence in July 1982. It took over the function of providing rural credit from the Reserve Bank of India and also the refinancing and developmental function of Agricultural Refinance and Development Corporation (ARDC). NABARD provides refinance for promoting agricultural activities as well as non-farm sectors particularly programme covered under poverty alleviation.

NABARD's credit functions cover planning, dispensation and monitoring of credit. This activity involves:

(*i*) Framing policy and guidelines for rural financial institutions

(*ii*) Providing credit facilities to issuing organizations

(*iii*) Preparation of potential-linked credit plans annually for all districts for identification of credit potential

(*iv*) Monitoring the flow of ground level rural credit

NABARD plays the key role of a leader in rural credit management. NABARD has to ensure that there is adequate flow of credit for seasonal agricultural operation to maintain agricultural production. Similarly, NABARD has to accelerate the flow of credit for long term investment in agricultural sector. NABARD provides support through formulation of some innovative non-farm schemes, which are very helpful in raising the income level of rural people and bring them above the poverty line. NABARD has two funds to finance agricultural operations. They are:

(*a*) National Rural Credit (Long Term Operation) Fund

(*b*) National Rural Credit (Stabilisation) Fund

The contribution to these funds is received mostly from the Reserve Bank of India. Apart from these funds, NABARD has general lines of credit from the Reserve Bank of India for meeting the credit requirements of seasonal and other than agricultural operations. Some important promotional activities supported by NABARD are discussed below:

7.3.1.1. Strategies of NABARD

For enlarging the scope for catalysing credit flow, NABARD has formulated the following strategies.

(*i*) Involving state level functional and financial-cum-developmental corporations, voluntary agencies, Khadi and village commission under automatic refinance facility as also under group/bulk lendings.

(*ii*) Supporting units jointly with Small Industries Development Bank of India and formulating credit linked area development plans.

(*iii*) Increasing the limits under composite and integrated loans.

(*iv*) Removal of certain constraints under agro-industries and service sector units.

Remember, like a commercial bank, NABARD does not extend direct credit facilities to production units/individual borrowers. A major portion of the money (usually between 70 and 90 percent) lent by commercial, co-operative and regional rural banks for agricultural and other approved activities will be refinanced by NABARD at certain interest rate. It also extends refinance facilities to Land Development Banks. With a capital base of ₹ 2,000 crore provided by the Government of India and Reserve Bank of India, it operates through its head office at Mumbai, 28 regional offices situated in state capitals and 391 district offices at districts.

7.3.1.2. Promotional Roles of NABARD:

NABARD is set up as an apex Development Bank with a mandate for facilitating credit flow for promotion and development of agriculture, small-scale industries, cottage and village industries, handicrafts and other rural crafts. It also has the mandate to support all other allied economic activities in rural areas, promote integrated and sustainable rural development and secure prosperity of rural areas. In discharging its role as a facilitator for rural prosperity NABARD is entrusted with

1. Providing refinance to lending institutions in rural areas
2. Bringing about or promoting institutional development and
3. Evaluating, monitoring and inspecting the client banks.

Besides these pivotal roles, NABARD also performs the following functions:

(*a*) Acts as a coordinator in the operations of rural credit institutions

(*b*) Extends assistance to the government, the Reserve Bank of India and other organizations in matters relating to rural development

(*c*) Offers training and research facilities for banks, cooperatives and organizations working in the field of rural development.

(*d*) Helps the state governments in reaching their targets of providing assistance to eligible institutions in agriculture and rural development

For the promotion of agriculture and rural development, NABARD performs the following roles:

(*a*) Acts as a regulatory authority, supervising, monitoring and guiding cooperative banks and regional rural banks

(*b*) Initiates measures toward institution-building for improving absorptive capacity of the credit delivery system, including monitoring, formulation of rehabilitation schemes, restructuring of credit institutions, training of personnel, etc.

(*c*) Coordinates the rural financing activities of all the institutions engaged in developmental work at the field level and maintains liaison with the government of India, State governments, the Reserve Bank of India and other national level institutions concerned with policy formulation

(*d*) Prepares, on annual basis, rural credit plans for all the districts in the country. These plans form the base for annual credit plans of all rural financial institutions

(*e*) Undertakes monitoring and evaluation of projects refinanced by it

(*f*) Promotes research in the fields of rural banking, agriculture and rural development

Thus the important functions of NABARD can be seen as follows:

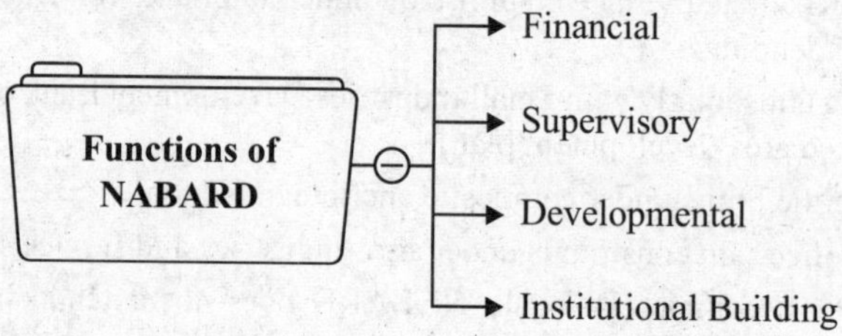

1. Financial and Credit Functions: The credit functions of NABARD cover planning, dispensation and monitoring of credit. And the functions of credit include:

(*i*) Framing policy and guidelines for rural financial institutions

(*ii*) Providing credit facilities to issuing organizations

(*iii*) Preparation of potential-linked credit plans annually for all districts for identification of credit potential

(*iv*) Monitoring the flow of ground level rural credit.

(*v*) Prepares for each district annually a potential linked credit plan which forms the basis for district credit plans.

(*vi*) Participates in finalisation of Annual Action Plan at block, district and state levels.

(*vii*) Monitors implementation of credit plans at above levels.

(*viii*) Provides guidance in evolving the credit discipline to be followed by the credit institutions in financing production, marketing and investment activities of rural farm and non-farm sectors.

(*ix*) Provides refinance facilities to the rural financial institutions.

2. Development and Promotional Functions: Credit is a critical factor in development of agriculture and rural sector as it enables investment in capital formation and technological up gradation. Various initiatives have been taken to strengthen the cooperative credit structure and the regional rural banks, so that adequate and timely credit is made available to the needy In order to reinforce the credit functions and to make credit more productive, NABARD has been undertaking a number of developmental and promotional activities such as:

(*i*) Help cooperative banks and Regional Rural Banks to prepare development actions plans for themselves

(*ii*) Monitor implementation of development action plans of banks and fulfillment of obligations under MoUs

(*iii*) Provide financial assistance to cooperatives and Regional Rural Banks for establishment of technical, monitoring and evaluations cells

(*iv*) Provide financial support for the training institutes of cooperative banks

(*v*) Provide training for senior and middle level executives of commercial banks, Regional Rural Banks and cooperative banks

(*vi*) Create awareness among the borrowers on ethics of repayment through Vikas Volunteer Vahini and Farmer's clubs

(*vii*) Provide financial assistance to cooperative banks for building improved management information system, computerisation of operations and development of human resources.

(*viii*) Nurturing and strengthening of the Rural Financial Institutions (RFIs) like SCBs/ SCARDBs, CCBs, RRBs etc. by various institutional strengthening initiatives.

(*ix*) Fostering the growth of the SHG Bank linkage programme and extending essential support to SHPIs NGOs/VAs/ Development Agencies and client banks.

(*x*) Development and promotional initiatives in farm and non-farm sector.

(*xi*) Extending assistance for Research and Development.

(*xii*) Acting as a catalyst for Agriculture and rural development in rural areas.

3. Supervisory Functions: As an apex bank NABARD involved in refinancing credit needs of major financial institutions in the country engaged in offering financial assistance to agriculture and rural development operations and programmes, NABARD has been sharing with the Reserve Bank of India certain supervisory functions in respect of cooperative banks and Regional Rural Banks (RRBs). It gives special focus on the following (**Source: NABARD publications**):

(*a*) Removal of regional/sectoral imbalances

(*b*) Poverty Alleviation and Employment Generation

(*c*) Development of rural micro-enterprises

(*d*) Strengthening Rural Financial Institutions (RFIs)

(*e*) Encouraging prudential financial standards in RFIs

(*f*) Encouraging capital formation in agriculture

(*g*) Promotion of micro-finance/ development

(*h*) Rural Infrastructure Development

(*i*) Hi-tech and export oriented projects

(*j*) Creating policy environment for flow of rural credit

(*k*) Experimenting with new models, products and innovative practices in rural credit

(*l*) Thrust on rural awareness and financial services

Under these functions, it performs the following:

(*i*) On-site inspection and off-site surveillance of RFIs.

(*a*) Carries out inspection of Regional Rural Banks (RRBs) and cooperative banks (other than urban/primary co-operative banks) under the provisions of Banking Regulation Act, 1949.

(*b*) Carries out inspection of State Co-operative Agriculture and Rural Development Banks (SCARDBs) and apex non-credit co-operative societies on a voluntary basis

(*c*) Carries out portfolio inspections, systems study, besides off-site observation of co-operative banks.

(*ii*) Administering the credit monitoring arrangements in Co-operative banks.

(*iii*) Issue of warning signals to banks showing deterioration in financial position and adverse features.

(*vi*) Taking preventive and revival measures for weak banks

4. Institutional Building: Under institutional building, NABARD provides the following services:

(*i*) Helps cooperative banks and RRBs to prepare development actions plans for themselves

(*ii*) Enter into MoU with state governments and cooperative banks specifying their respective obligations to improve the affairs of the banks in a stipulated timeframe.

(*iii*) Help RRBs and the sponsor banks to enter into MoUs specifying their respective obligations to improve the affairs of the RRBs in a stipulated timeframe

(*iv*) Monitor implementation of development action plans of banks and fulfillment of obligations under MoUs.

(*v*) Provide financial assistance to cooperatives and RRBs for establishment of technical, monitoring and evaluations cells

(*vi*) Provide financial support for the training institutes of cooperative banks

(*vii*) Provide training for senior and middle level executives of commercial banks, RRBs and cooperative banks

(*viii*) Provide financial assistance to cooperative banks for building improved management information system, computerisation of operations, development of human resources, etc.

7.3.1.3. NABARD and Refinance Facilities

The types of refinance facilities provided by NABARD can be seen in the following Table:

Types of Refinance Facilities

Agency	*Credit Facilities*
Commercial Banks	Long-term credit for investment purposes Financing the working capital requirements of weaver's Co-operative Societies (WCS) & State Handloom Development Corporations
Short-term Co-operative Structure (State Co-operative Banks, District Central Co-operative Banks, Primary Agricultural Credit Societies)	Short-term (crop and other loans) Medium-term (conversion) loans Term loans for investment purposes Financing WCS for production and marketing purposes Financing State Handloom Development Corporations for working capital by State Co-operative Banks.

Long-term Co-operative Structure (State Co-operative Agriculture and Rural Development Banks, Primary Co-operative Agriculture and Rural Development Banks)	Term loans for investment purposes Pilot scheme for financing short term loans in the states
Regional Rural Banks (RRBs)	Short-term (crop and other loans) Term loans for investment purposes
State Governments	Long-term loans for equity participation in co-operatives Rural Infrastructure Development Fund (RIDF) loans for infrastructure projects
Non-Governmental Organisations (NGOs)-System Informal Gedit Delivery	Revolving Fund Assitance for various micro-credit delivery innovations and promotional projects under 'Credit and Financial Services Fund' (CFSF) and 'Rural promotion Corpus Fund' (RPCF) respectively

Source : NABARD Publications.

7.3.1.4. Criteria for Refinance:

1. Technical feasibility of the project and adequate response from prospective beneficiaries
2. Financial viability and adequate incremental income to ultimate borrower to repay the loan within a reasonable period
3. Organisational capability to ensure close supervision

The refinance is provided to SCARDBs, SCBs, CBs and RRBs. However, the beneficiaries of the programme are partnership concerns, companies, state-owned corporations or cooperative societies. But, finally the assistance reaches the individuals, who are members of the primary credit institutions.

The refinance is usually 50% to 95% of the project cost. The balance will be met by the banks and the concerned state governments or the Government of India in the case of SCARDBs. With a view to ensure credit flow to certain thrust areas, the quantum of refinance is enhanced to 100% as in the case of special category beneficiaries like SC/ST members and self help groups.

7.3.2. Industrial Finance Corporation Of India (IFCI)

At the time of independence in 1947, India's capital market was relatively under-developed. Although there was significant demand for new capital, there was a dearth of providers. Merchant bankers and underwriting firms were almost non-existent and commercial banks were not equipped to provide long-term industrial finance in any significant manner.

It is against this backdrop that the government established The Industrial Finance Corporation of India (IFCI) on July 1, 1948, as the first Development Financial Institution in the country to cater to the long-term finance needs of the industrial sector. It was established in 1948 under the Industrial Finance Corporation Act, 1948 as a statutory corporation. It was provided access to low-cost funds through the central bank's Statutory Liquidity Ratio (SLR) which in turn enabled it to provide loans and advances to corporate borrowers at concessional rates.

The principal objective of the Corporation is to provide long and medium term funds to the industrial units in the country. Initially, the Corporation was authorised to assist only public limited companies in the private sector and the co-operative societies, which are not able to secure assistance from the banking companies, or from the capital market. In 1960, the IFC Act was amended to widen the scope of its activities and thereby public sector units, private limited companies and partnership concerns were also made eligible for its assistance. The Act was further amended in the years 1970 and 1973 and its scope was further expanded.

By the early 1990s, it was recognized that there was need for greater flexibility to respond to the changing financial system. It was also felt that IFCI should directly access the capital markets for its need of funds. with this objective the constitution of IFCI was changed in 1993 from a statutory corporation to a company under the Indian Companies Act, 1956. According to the IFC (Transfer of Undertaking & Repeal) Act, 1993 the undertaking of IFCI under the former IFC Act, 1948, stood transferred to and vested in the new company called Industrial Finance Corporation of India Ltd. with effect from July 1, 1993. Subsequently, the name of the company was also changed to "IFCI Limited". Today, the IFCI's role extends to the entire industrial spectrum of the country.

7.3.2.1. Services of IFCI

IFCI offers a wide range of products to the target customer segments to satisfy their specific financial needs. The product mix offering varies from one business/industry segment to another. IFCI customizes the product-mix to maximize customer satisfaction. It's domain knowledge and innovativeness make the product-mix a key differentiator for building, enduring and sustaining relationship with the borrowers.

1. General Services:

IFCI offers a wide range of products to the target customer segments to satisfy their specific financial needs. The product range includes following credit products:

(*a*) **Short-term Loans** (upto two years) for different short term requirements including bridge loan, Corporate Loan etc

(*b*) **Medium-term Loans** (more than two years to eight years) for business expansion, technology up-gradation, R&D expenditure, implementing early retirement scheme, Corporate Loan, supplementing working capital and repaying high cost debt

(*c*) **Long-term Loans** (more than eight years to upto 15 years) - Project Finance for new industrial/ infrastructure projects Takeout Finance, acquisition financing (as per extant RBI guidelines / Board approved policy), Corporate Loan, Securitisation of debt

(*d*) **Structured Products:** acquisition finance, pre-IPO investment, IPO finance, promoter funding, etc.

(*e*) **Lease Financing**

(*f*) **Takeover of accounts** from Banks / Financial Institutions / NBFCs

(*g*) **Financing promoters** contribution (private equity participation)/subscription to convertible warrants

(*h*) **Purchase of Standard Assets** and NPAs.

2. Advisory services to corporate sector:

In addition to the above, IFCI ltd provides various advisory services to corporate sector. The advisory services include the following:

1. **Corporate Advisory & Infrastructure Services:** By the time when the Government of India is extending investment avenues in newer sectors and projects, the corporate sector needs advisory services to cope up with the Government policy regulations. IFCI uniquely positioned to fulfill this need. As a catalyst of Industrial growth, IFCI provides the needed advisory services in this regard.
2. **Infrastructure Advisory:** IFCI offers a range of services to the Infrastructure Sector, with specific emphasis on roads, ports, power and urban infrastructure. Total solutions catering to the specific needs of clients, starting from the stage of investment identification to financial closure are provided by IFCI.

3. **Monitoring Agency for Public Issues:** As per the SEBI (Disclosure & Investor Protection) Guidelines, 2000, in case of issues exceeding ₹500 crore, the issuer shall make arrangements for the use of proceeds of the issue to be monitored by one of the financial institutions. IFCI offers its services as Monitoring Agency for the same.
4. **Restructuring Advisory Services:** IFCI provides Advisory Services to corporate and government clients regarding:
   (*a*) Financial restructuring
   (*b*) Operational restructuring
   (*c*) Cost-structure studies and
   (*d*) Process analysis & improvement.
5. **Bid Process Management: IFCI offers a range of services under the Bid Process Management. It includes the following:**
   (*a*) Preparation of Bid Documents (for various modes of Bid process) and Advertisement inviting Expression of Interest (EOI)
   (*b*) Evaluation of Bids and Assisting till the final award of Contract.

7.3.2.2. Targeted Business Segments:

Major Financing Schemes of IFCI included Project Financing and Financial Services mainly to the manufacturing industry along with a diversified industrial portfolio. The targeted business segments of IFCI include the following:

(*a*) Public Sector Undertakings
(*b*) Manufacturing industry
(*c*) Infrastructure projects
  (*i*) Power
  (*ii*) Airports (brownfield)
  (*iii*) Ports
  (*iv*) Hotels
  (*v*) Urban infrastructure projects
(*d*) NBFCs
(*e*) Participation in Private Equity
(*f*) Promoter funding

IFCI has founded and developed prominent institutions like:

(*a*) Management Development Institute (MDI) for management training and development
(*b*) ICRA for credit assessment rating
(*c*) Tourism Finance Corporation of India (TFCI) for promotion of the hotel and tourism industry
(*d*) Institute of Leadership Development (ILD)
(*e*) Rashtriya Gramin Vikas Nidhi (RGVN) for promoting, supporting and developing voluntary agencies engaged in uplifting rural and urban poor in east and northeast India.

IFCI, along with other institutions, has also promoted:

(*a*) Stock Holding Corporation of India Ltd. (SHCIL)
(*b*) Discount and Finance House of India Ltd. (DFHI)
(*c*) National Stock Exchange (NSE)
(*d*) OTCEI

(*e*) Securities Trading Corporation of India (STCI)

(*f*) LIC Housing Finance Ltd.

(*g*) GIC Grih Vitta Ltd., and

(*h*) Bio-tech Consortium Ltd. (BCL)

7.3.2.3. Some sectors that have directly benefited from IFCI include

(*a*) Agro-based industry (textiles, paper, sugar)

(*b*) Service industry (hotels, hospitals)

(*c*) Basic industry (iron & steel, fertilizers, basic chemicals, cement)

(*d*) Capital & intermediate goods industry (electronics, synthetic fibres, synthetic plastics, miscellaneous chemicals) and Infrastructure (power generation, telecom services)

7.3.2.4. Debenture Trustee

IFCI is acting as the Debenture Trustee for debenture issues by the client companies.

Cumulatively, IFCI has sanctioned financial assistance of ₹ 462 billion to 5707 concerns and disbursed ₹ 444 billion since inception. In the process, IFCI has catalysed investments worth ₹ 2,526 billion in the industrial and infrastructure sectors (Source: IFCI website).

7.3.3. Industrial Development Of India (IDBI)

IDBI is one of India's largest commercial Banks. For over 40 years, it has performed a key nation-building role, first as the apex Development Financial Institution (DFI) (July 1, 1964 to September 30, 2004) in the realm of industry and thereafter as a full-service commercial Bank (October 1, 2004 onwards). As a DFI, the former IDBI extended its service to cover an array of services that contributed towards:

(*a*) Balanced geographical spread of industries

(*b*) Development of identified backward areas

(*c*) Emergence of a new spirit of enterprise

(*d*) Evolution of a deep and vibrant capital market

On October 1, 2004, the former IDBI converted into a banking company as "Industrial Development Bank of India Limited" to undertake the entire range of banking activities while continuing to play its basic DFI role. After the merger of the former IDBI Bank with its parent company (IDBI Ltd.) on April 2, 2005 and the subsequent merger of the former United Western Bank Ltd. with IDBI Bank on October 3, 2006, the new generation Bank (IDBI Bank Ltd) with majority Government shareholding today touches the lives of millions of Indians through an array of corporate, retail, SME and Agri products and services.

IDBI Bank Ltd. is a Universal Bank with its operations driven by a cutting edge core Banking IT platform. The Bank offers personalized banking and financial solutions to its clients in the retail and corporate banking arena through its large network of Branches and ATMs, spread across length and breadth of India.

As on March 31, 2014 IDBI Bank has a balance sheet of ₹3, 28,997 crore and business size (deposits plus advances) of ₹4,33,460 crore. As an Universal Bank, IDBI Bank, besides its core banking and project finance domain, has an established presence in associated financial sector businesses like Capital Market, Investment Banking and Mutual Fund Business.(Source: IDBI website).

7.3.3.1. Main functions of IDBI

IDBI is vested with the responsibility of co-coordinating the working of institutions engaged in financing, promoting and developing industries. It has evolved an appropriate mechanism for this purpose. IDBI also undertakes/supports wide-ranging promotional activities including entrepreneurship development programs for new entrepreneurs, provision of consultancy services for small and medium enterprises, upgradation of technology and programs for economic upliftment of the underprivileged.

IDBI's role as a catalyst: IDBI's role as a catalyst to industrial development encompasses a wide spectrum of activities. IDBI can finance all types of industrial concerns covered under the provisions of the IDBI Act. With over three decades of service to the Indian industry, IDBI has grown substantially in terms of size of operations and portfolio.

The main functions of IDBI can be classified in to two categories as follows:

1. Developmental Activities and
2. Banking Services
3. SME Finance Services
4. Infrastructure Finance Services

1. Developmental Activities of IDBI:

The developmental activities of the bank include the following:

(*a*) **Promotional activities:** In fulfillment of its developmental role, the Bank continues to perform a wide range of promotional activities relating to developmental programs for new entrepreneurs, consultancy services for small and medium enterprises and programs designed for accredited voluntary agencies for the economic upliftment of the underprivileged. These include entrepreneurship development, self-employment and wage employment in the industrial sector for the weaker sections of society through voluntary agencies, support to Science and Technology Entrepreneurs' Parks, Energy Conservation, Common Quality Testing Centers for small industries.

(*b*) **Technical Consultancy Organisations:** With a view to making available at a reasonable cost, consultancy and advisory services to entrepreneurs, particularly to new and small entrepreneurs, IDBI, in collaboration with other All-India Financial Institutions, has set up a network of Technical Consultancy Organisations (TCOs) covering the entire country. TCOs offer diversified services to small and medium enterprises in the selection, formulation and appraisal of projects, their implementation and review.

(*c*) **Entrepreneurship Development Institute:** Realising that entrepreneurship development is the key to industrial development, IDBI played a prime role in setting up of the Entrepreneurship Development Institute of India for fostering entrepreneurship in the country. It has also established similar institutes in Bihar, Orissa, Madhya Pradesh and Uttar Pradesh. IDBI also extends financial support to various organisations in conducting studies or surveys of relevance to industrial development.

2. IDBI Bank Ltd –Services

IDBI Bank offers a wide array of products and services to its customers. For different customer groups and needs, there are different types of products and services including Personal Banking, Corporate Banking, SME Finance and Agri Business etc.

(*a*) **IDBI-Personal Banking:** Following are the main services offered under Personal Banking:

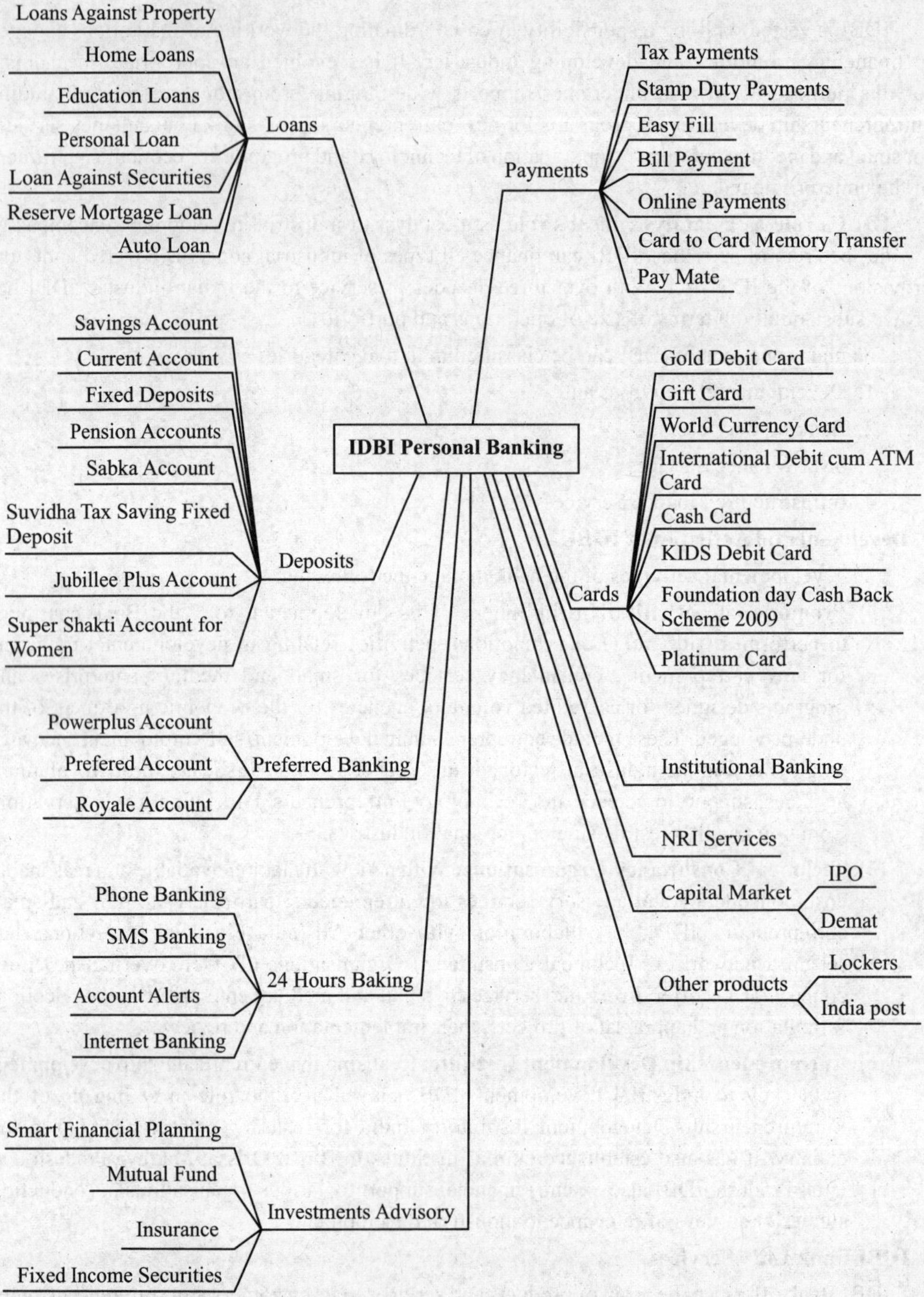

(*b*) **IDBI-Corporate Banking:** Following products and services are offered by IDBI Bank for the corporates:

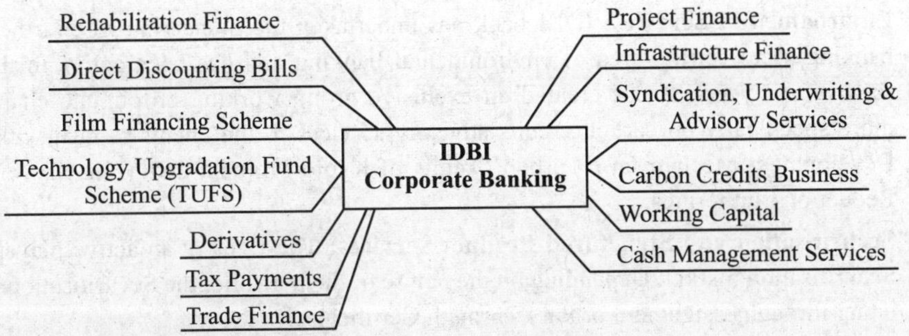

3. IDBI-SME Financing Services

Following SME Finance products are offered by the IDBI Bank:

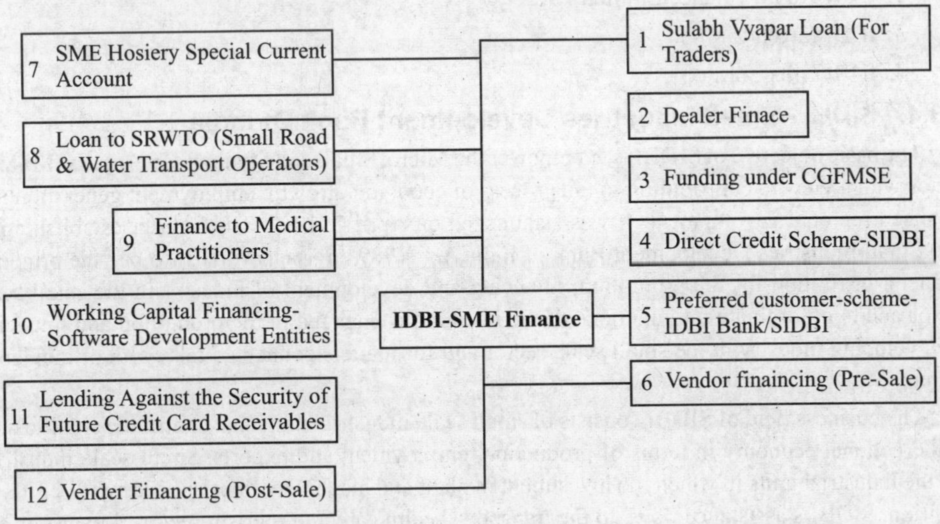

4. IDBI- Infrastructure Financing Services

Services rendered by IDBI Bank under Infrastructure financing cover debt syndication and specialized advisory services to the corporate in the infrastructure and allied sectors. The Bank offers Project Appraisal, Debt Syndication, Corporate advisory services and Securitisation & Structured products as specialized services.

(*a*) **Appraisal:** IDBI Bank has a cutting edge in the appraisal of large infrastructure sector projects. IDBI Bank's appraisals have been used by the corporates, besides availing loan facilities for implementing projects, to finalise their decisions in bidding for new projects, assets acquisition, business plans or disinvestments decisions.

(*b*) **Debt Syndication:** the Bank has been offering its loan syndication services to corporates by arranging financial assistance (both term loan and Working Capital) to their projects and operations.

(*c*) **Corporate Advisory Services:** The range of advisory services offered by IDBI Bank include merchant appraisal of projects, Acquisition / sale of assets, business valuation and pre bid advisory for PPP projects in Road sector. IDBI has been permitted by the SEBI to act as the agent for the IPO monitoring of corporate which come out with public issue of equity shares of issue size higher than ₹ 500 crore.

(*d*) **Environmental Services:** IDBI bank has undertaken the pioneering role in the Indian banking sector in the area of environmental banking and has been active in this area for over 17 years. It has created an exclusive group working on climate change and more specifically on carbon credits advisory services to the clients to deal with Clean Development Mechanism / Carbon Credits of Kyoto Protocol and Voluntary Emission Reductions authorities.

(*e*) **Securitisation and Structured Product Services:** The Bank is an active player in the Securitisation market. Depending on the nature of the portfolio, the Securitisation is done either through assignment or Pass Through Certificates.

Subsidiaries of IDBI Bank Ltd: IBDI Bank has the following subsidiaries:

1. IDBI Capital Market Services Limited
2. IDBI Home Finance Limited
3. IDBI Intech Limited
4. IDBI Gilts Limited

7.3.4. SIDBI - Small Industries Development Bank Of India

The basic objective of SIDBI is to empower the Micro, Small and Medium Enterprises (MSME) sector with a view to contributing to the process of economic growth, employment generation and balanced regional development. It was established on April 2, 1990. The Charter establishing it, The Small Industries Development Bank of India Act, 1989 envisaged SIDBI to be "the principal financial institution for the promotion, financing and development of industry in the small scale sector and to co-ordinate the functions of the institutions engaged in the promotion and financing or developing industry in the small scale sector and for matters connected therewith or incidental thereto.

The business field of SIDBI consists of small scale industrial units that contribute significantly to the national economy in terms of production, employment and exports. Small scale industries are the industrial units in which the investment in plant and machinery does not exceed ₹1 crore. In addition, SIDBI's assistance flows to the transport, health care and tourism sectors and also to the professional and self-employed persons setting up small-sized professional ventures. Its functions include:

(*a*) Refinances loans given to small scale sector by primary lending institutions

(*b*) Discounts and rediscounts bills relating to the transaction of machinery of the small scale sector

(*c*) Extends seed capital through specified agencies

(*d*) Assistance for export of products of small-scale sector

(*e*) Provides services like leasing and factoring

(*f*) Give financial support to purchase raw material and the sales of finished products

(*g*) Provides working capital through single window scheme

(*h*) Undertakes direct financing of SSI units

(*i*) Coordinates of functions of various institutions engaged in finance to SSI and tiny units

7.3.4.1. Schemes of SIDBI

SIDBI offers wide range of assistance comprising financing, extension support and promotional, are made available through appropriate schemes of direct and indirect assistance for the following purposes:

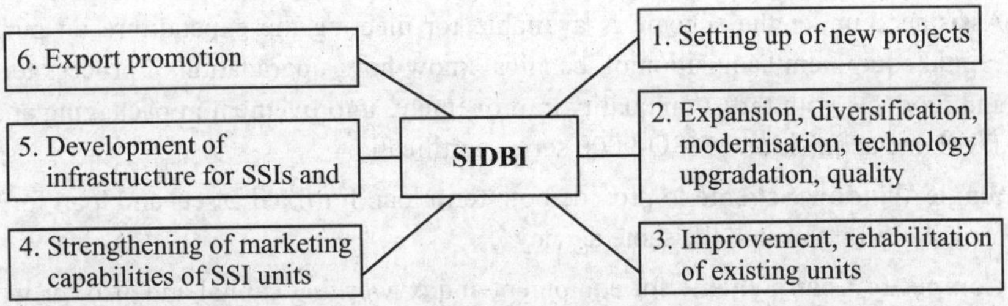

1. Direct Assistance Schemes: SIDBI directly assists SSIs under:

(*a*) Project Finance Scheme

(*b*) Equipment Finance Scheme

(*c*) Marketing Scheme

(*d*) Vendor Development Scheme

(*e*) Infrastructural Development Scheme

(*f*) ISO-9000

(*g*) Technology Development & Modernisation Fund

(*h*) Venture Capital Scheme

(*i*) Assistance for leasing to NBFCs, SFCs, SIDCs and

(*j*) Resource support to institutions involved in the development and financing of small scale sector.

These Schemes are mainly targeted at addressing some of the major problems of SSIs in areas such as high tech project, marketing, infrastructural development, delayed realisation of bills, obsolescence of technology, quality improvement, export financing and venture capital assistance.

2. Indirect Assistance Schemes:

Under its indirect schemes, SIDBI extends refinance of loans to small scale sector by Primary Lending Institutions like SFCs, SIDCs and Banks. At present, such refinance assistance is extended to 892 such institutions and these institutions extend credit through a network of more than 65,000 branches all over the country.

All the Schemes of SIDBI both direct and indirect assistance are in operation in all the States of the country through 39 regional/branch offices of SIDBI.

3. Promotional and Development Activities of SIDBI

SIDBI is actively involved in promoting tiny and small scale industries by means of its promotional and developmental activities through suitable professional agencies for organising Entrepreneurship Development Programmes, Technology Upgradation & Modernisation Programmes, Micro Credit Schemes and assistance under Mahila Vikas Nidhi to bring about economic empowerment of women specially the rural poor by providing them avenues for training and employment opportunities.

4. Main Schemes of SIDBI

The main Schemes available with SIDBI include the following:

(*a*) National Equity Fund Scheme which provides equity support to small entrepreneurs setting up projects in Tiny Sector.

(*b*) Technology Development & Modernisation Fund Scheme: SIDBI has set up Technology Development & Modernisation Fund scheme for direct assistance of small sale industries to encourage existing industrial units in the sector, to modernise their production facilities and adopt improved and updated technology so as to strengthen their export capabilities.

Assistance under the scheme is available for meeting the expenditure on purchase of capital equipment acquisition of technical know-how, upgradation of process technology and products with thrust on quality improvement, improvement in packaging and cost of TQM and acquisition of ISO-9000 series certification.

(*c*) **Single Window Scheme** to provide both term loan for fixed assets and loan for working capital capital through the same agency.

(*d*) **Composite Loan Scheme** for equipment and/or working capital and also for worksheds to artisans, village and cottage industries in Tiny Sector.

(*e*) **Mahila Udyam Nidhi (MUN) Scheme** provides equity support to women entrepreneurs for setting up projects in Tiny Sector.

(*f*) **Scheme for financing activities:** The scheme relating to marketing of SSI products which provides assistance for undertaking various marketing related activities such as marketing research, R&D, product upgradation, participation in trade fairs and exhibitions, advertising branding, establishing distribution networks including show room, retail outlet, wears-housing facility, etc.

(*g*) **Equipment Finance Scheme** for acquisition of machinery/equipment including Diesel Generator Sets which are not related to any specific project.

(*h*) **Venture Capital Scheme** to encourage SSI ventures/sub- contracting units to acquire capital equipment, as also requisite technology for building up of export capabilities/ import substitution including cost of total quality management and acquisition of ISO-9000 certification and for expansion of capacity.

(*i*) **ISO 9000 Scheme** to meet the expenses on consultancy, documentation, audit, certification fee, equipment and calibrating instruments required for obtaining ISO 9000 certification.

(*j*) **Micro Credit Scheme** to meet the requirement of well managed Voluntary Agencies that are in existence for at least 5 years; have a good track record and have established network and experience in small savings-cum-credit programmes with Self Help Groups (SHGs) individuals.

7.3.5. Export Import Bank of India

The Export-Import Bank of India, also known as Exim Bank of India, is the leading export finance institution in the country. The bank was set up in the year 1982 under the Export-Import Bank of India Act 1981. The Government of India launched the Export-Import Bank of India with an aim to augment exports from India and also to combine the country's foreign trade and investment with the overall economic growth. The bank is established with the basic objective of

1. Providing financial assistance to exporters and importers
2. Functioning as the principal financial institution for coordinating the working of institutions engaged in financing export and import of goods and services with a view to promoting the country's international trade

The bank began its operations as a supplier of export credit, but has over the period evolved into an institution that plays a major role in partnering Indian Industries including small and medium enterprises. It is the apex institution for coordinating the working of institutions in India engaged in financing exports and import of goods and services. The evolution of the bank can be seen as follows:

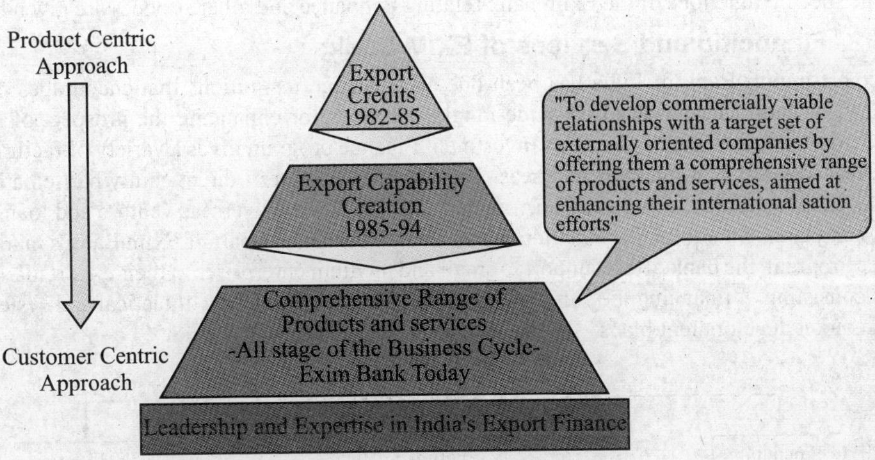

7.3.5.1. Functions of EXIM Bank:

Exim Bank provides the following general functions:

(*a*) Financing of exports and imports of goods and services

(*b*) Financing of exports and imports of machinery and equipment on lease basis

(*c*) Financing of joint ventures in foreign countries

(*d*) Providing loans to Indian parties to enable them to contribute to the share capital of joint ventures in foreign countries;

(*e*) Providing technical, administrative and financial assistance to parties in connection with export and import trade.

In simple, it presence across all stages of business cycle, as given in the following diagram:

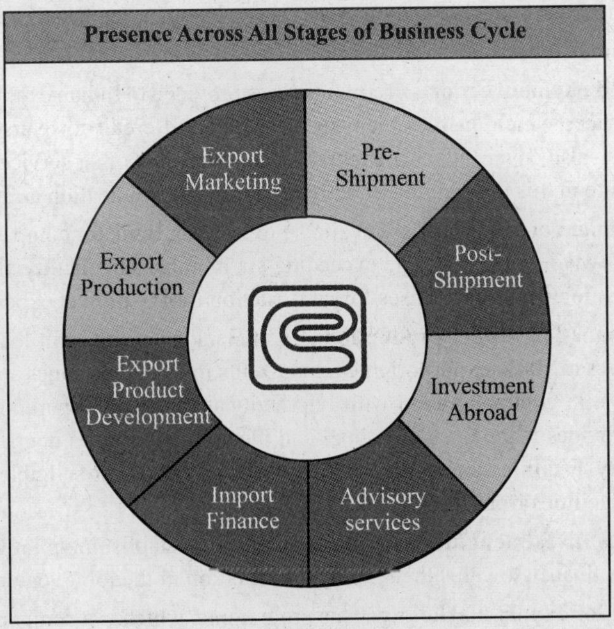

The specific functions of the Exim bank relating to finance and other services are given below:

7.3.5.2. Financing and Services of EXIM Bank:

Export-Import Bank of India has been one of the prime institutions that encourages project exports from India. The bank offers wide-ranging services for enhancing the prospect of Indian project exports. Exim Bank's Overseas Investment Finance program gives a variety of facilities for Indian reserves and acquirements overseas. The facilities consist of direct equity participation by the bank in the overseas venture and non-funded activities by the overseas venture and loan to the Indian companies for equity participation in the venture abroad. As part of Exim Bank's marketing Finance Program, the bank offers support to small and medium enterprises in their export marketing efforts consisting of financing the soft expenditure linking to completion of tactical and systematic export market development plans.

Exim Bank International Trade

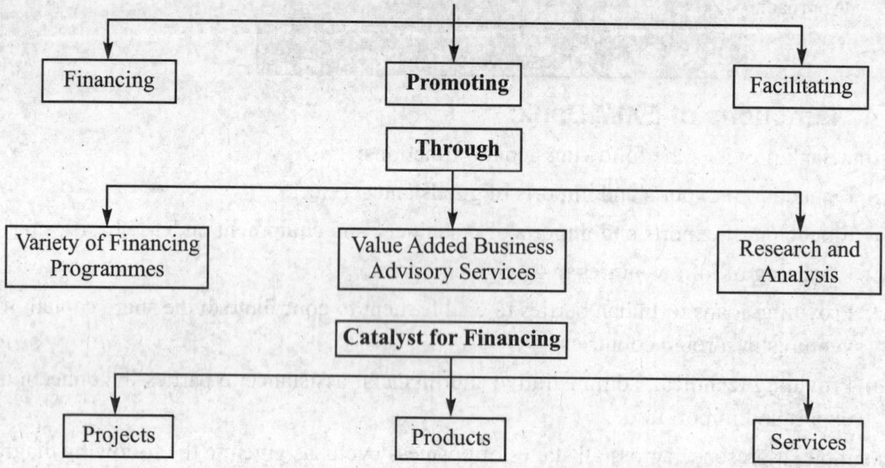

Let us see the main financing and other services offered by the EXIM bank hereunder:

1. Loans to Indian Companies:

(*a*) **Deferred payment exports:** Term finance is provided to Indian exporters of eligible goods and services which enables them to offer deferred credit to overseas buyers. Deferred credit can also cover Indian consultanc, technology and other services. Commercial banks participate in this programme directly or under risk syndication arrangements.

(*b*) **Preshipment credit:** finance is available form Exim Bank for companies executing export contracts involving cycle time exceeding six months. The facility also enables provision of rupee mobilisation expenses for construction/turnky project exporters.

(*c*) **Term loans for export production:** Exim Bank provides term loans/deferred payment guarantees to 100% export.oriented units, units in free trade zones and computer software exporters. In commaboration with International Finance Corporation.Washington, Exim Bank provides loans to enable small and medium enterprises upgrade export production capability. Facilities for deeded exports; Deemed exports are eligible for funded and non-funded facilities from Exim Bank.

(*d*) **Overseas Investment finance:** Indian companies establishing joint ventures overseas are provided finance towards their equity contribution in the joint venture.

(*e*) **Finance for export marketing:** This programme, which is a component of a World Bank loan, helps exporters implement their export market development plans.

2. Loans to Foreign Goverments, Companies and financial Institutions:

(*a*) **Overseas Buyer's Credit:** Credit is directly offered to foreign entities for import of eligible goods and related services, on deferred payment.

(*b*) **Lines of Credit:** Besides foreign goverments, finance is available to foreign finandial institutions and goverment agencies to on-lend in the respective country for import of goods and services from India.

(*c*) **Relending Facility to Banks Overseas:** Relending facility is extended to banks overseas to enable them to provide term finance to their clients world-wide for imports from India.

3. Loans to Commercial Banks in India:

(*a*) **Export Bills Rediscounting:** Commercial Banks in India who are authorised to deal in foreign exchange can rediscount their short term export bills with Exim Banks, for an unexpired usance period of not more than 90 days.

(*b*) **Refinance of Export Credit:** Authorised dealers in foreign exchange can obtain from Exim Bank 100% refinance of de3ferred payment loans extended for export of eligible Indian goods.

4. Guaranteeing of Obligations:

Exim Bank participates with commercial banks in India in the issue of guarantees required by Indian companies for the export contracts and for executions of overseas construction and turnkey projects.

5. Other Services:

In addition to the above functions, Exim bank provides the following services for facilitating the foreign trade in India:

(*a*) Research & Analysis

(*b*) Marketing Advisory Services

(*c*) Export Advisory Services

During the year 2009-10, the Bank extended 22 Lines of Credit (LOCs), aggregating US$ 753.31 mn, covering 20 countries to support export of projects, goods and services from India. 136 LOCs covering 94 countries in Africa, Asia, CIS, Europe and Latin America, with credit commitments aggregating US$ 4.5 billion are currently available for utilisation, while a number of prospective LOCs are at various stages of negotiation. The Bank lays special emphasis on extension of LOCs as it is an effective market entry mechanism especially for Indian exporters. Project export contracts supported by the Bank during the year amounted to ₹ 13,993 crore and the contracts were secured by 13 companies in 12 countries. During the year, 18 corporates were sanctioned funded and non-funded assistance aggregating ₹ 1,054 crore for part financing their overseas investments in 6 countries. Exim Bank has so far provided finance to 259 ventures set up by over 209 companies in 64 countries including Austria, Canada, China, Ireland, Indonesia, Italy, Malaysia, Mauritius, Morocco, Netherlands, Oman, Romania, Singapore, Spain, South Africa, Sri Lanka, UAE, UK and USA. As on March 31, 2010, guarantees on Bank's book were at ₹ 2,274 crore. (Source: Bank Website).

EXIM Bank has laid strong emphasis on enhancing project exports, the funding options for which have been enhanced with introduction of the Buyer's Credit-National Export Insurance Account (BC-NEIA) program. The Bank facilitates two-way technology transfer by financing import of technology into India, and investment abroad by Indian companies for setting up joint ventures, subsidiaries or undertaking overseas acquisitions. To promote hi-tech exports from India, the Bank has a lending programme to finance research and development (R&D) activities of export-oriented companies. During the year ended 31st March, 2013, EXIM Bank sanctioned loans of ₹40,960 crore, while disbursements amounted to ₹40,635 crore. Loan Assets stood at ₹65,563 crore as on March 31, 2013.

EXIM Bank has put in place a Technology and Innovation Enhancement and Infrastructure Development (TIEID) Fund of US$ 500 million exclusively for MSMEs by partnering with Banks/FIs. TIEID seeks to meet long term foreign currency loan requirements of the MSME sector in addition to offering short-term export credit refinance in rupee and foreign currency. The Bank has put in place an Export Marketing Services (EMS) Programme to assist Indian companies in identification of prospective business partners, facilitating placement of final orders and also identification of opportunities for setting up plants or projects or for acquisition of companies overseas. During 2012-13, EXIM Bank became the first ever Indian entity to be included in the Emerging Market Bond Index. The Bank became the first Indian entity to tap the Australian Dollar market and Singapore Dollar market.

REVIEW QUESTIONS

Short Answer Questions

1. Differentiate between commercial banks and Co-operative banks.
2. Write a brief note on Urban Co-operative banking.
3. Explain briefly rural co-operatives for short-term financial assistance.
4. Give an account on Primary Agricultural Credit Societies.
5. Write a note on central co-operative banks.
6. Give a brief note on state co-operative banks.
7. Explain briefly on Primary Co-operative Agriculture and Rural Development Banks.
8. What is nature of RRBs?
9. What are the objectives of RRBs?
10. Write a short note on RRBs.
11. What are the features of RRBs?
12. What are development banks?
13. Give a brief note on the functions of development banks.
14. What are the reasons for the promotion of development banks?
15. What are the objectives of NABARD?
16. Write a brief note on IFCI,
17. What do you know about IDBI?
18. Write a short note on SIDBI.

Essay Type Questions

1. Write a detailed note on the structure of co-operative credit institution in India.
2. Explain in detail about the rural co-operatives in India.
3. Explain about long-term rural co-operatives in detail.
4. Briefly explain the functional structure of RRBs in India.
5. Write a detailed note on the progress and achievements of RRBs in India.
6. What are difficulties faced by RRBs in performing their roles?
7. Explain the measures for the improvement of RRBs in India.
8. Write a note on the reform measures of RRBs.
9. Explain in detail the promotional roles of NABARD in India.
10. Explain the refinance facilities provided by NABARD with the relevant criteria.
11. Explain in detail the various services being rendered by IFCI.
12. Discuss in detail the functions offered by IDBI in India.
13. Explain the various services offerd by SIDBI for the development of SME in India.
14. Give a detailed note on the EXIM Bank relating to its services in import and export trade.

CHAPTER

8 Central Banking

In this chapter the concept of central bank is dealt with. The following Chapter-9-deals with the Central Banking and Credit Control measures in general. The discussion on the Central Bank of India *i.e.*, the RBI is made in Chapter-10.

Today all the countries have a Central Bank, which controls their entire banking system. The first Central Bank was the Swedish Risks Bank established in 1688. The Bank of England was established in 1694 and nationalised in 1946 under Bank of England Act 1946. These banks were established not to provide direct credit to trade and commerce, but to provide money to their governments and they were given special privileges over the issue of notes. In course of time the range of their operations widened and they began to render their governments a variety of services.

In the 19th century many other European countries established their own Central Banks. But the current Central Banking is the idea of 20th century and it took several decades to mature into the present form. The Federal Reserve Bank of USA was established in 1914. An International Conference on Monetary System was held in 1920 at Brussels to consider the currency chaos after the First World War. It recommended that every country having a currency of its own should have Central Bank. Now there is no civilised country which does not possess a Central Bank. In India the Reserve Bank of India Act was passed in 1934 and the Bank began functioning from April 1, 1935

The name 'Central Bank' is given to that bank which is entrusted with the task of controlling the issue of money and regulating all the other banks of the country. Here the task controlling involves the managing of both expansion and contraction of the volume of money in the country.

8.1 DEFINITIONS OF CENTRAL BANK

The Central Bank is defined by various authorities as follows:

Sl.No	*Name of the Expert*	*Definition*
1.	**R.G. Hawtrey**	Central Bank as "the lender of last resort".
2.	**Kisch and Elvin**	The essential function of a Central Bank is the maintenance of the stability of monetary standard.
3.	**Shaw.W.A**	The central bank as "the bank whose main function is control of credit"
4.	**Vera Smith**	"The primary definition of central banking is a system in which a single bank has either a complete or a residuary monopoly in the note issue"
5.	**Sayers R.S.**	"The business of a Central Bank is to control the commercial banks in such a way as to promote the general monetary policy of the state"

The above definitions are not sufficient because they do not provide the entire picture and idea of the Central Bank. Thus, it can be defined as, **"the strategic level, banking and monetary institutions primarily engaging in controlling, and regulating the banking and monetary systems of the country for the progress of the economy".**

8.2 NATURE OF CENTRAL BANKING

The basic nature of Central Banking can be enumerated as follows:

(*a*) The Central Bank does not aim at profits but aims at national welfare.

(*b*) The Central Bank does not compete with the member banks.

(*c*) The Central Bank has special relationship with government and with commercial banks.

(*d*) The Central Bank is generally free from political influence.

(*e*) The Central Bank is the apex body of the banking structure of the country.

(*f*) The Central Bank should have overall control over the financial system.

8.3 CENTRAL BANKING AND COMMERCIAL BANKING

The Central Bank and commercial banks are similar in certain aspects such as dealing in money, creation of credit, dealing in foreign exchange etc., Yet their objectives may be different. But, they are fundamentally different in various respects. Such differences can be summarised as follows:

Central Banking Vs Commercial

Money Market	*Capital Market*
1. Position of the Bank	
It is the apex bank in the banking system of the country	It is part of the banking system.
2. Ownership	
It is Government owned bank.	Commercial banks include public sector banks. Also foreign owned banks.
3. Basic motive	
It aims at economic growth and price stability and has no profit motive.	They aim at maximisation of profit.
4. Dealing with the public	
Cental Bank does not deal directly with the public.	They deal directly with the general public.
5. Competition	
Central Bank does not compete with co-mmercial banks.	Commercial Bank compete among them-selves.
6. Relationship	
The relationship between the Central Bank and commercial banks is unique. The Central Bank has power to exercise control over other banks.	Commercial Banks are functioning at the same level. They cannot exercise control over others except on their subsidiaries.

Central Bank	Commercial Banks
7. Government Transactions	
Central Bank usually acts as Advisor to the Government and also conducts Government transactions.	Public Sector banks partially undertake government transactions. However, other Commercial banks are precluded from such functions.
8. Power of Note Issue	
The Central Bank has the sole authority to issue currency notes.	Commercial Banks cannot issue currency notes
9. Dealing with Foreign Exchange	
Central bank has the responsibility to maintain the stability of foreign exchange rates.	They do not have any such responsibility.
10. Role of Banking	
Central Bank functions as the banker to the government.	They are functioning as the banker to the general public.
11. Basic Functions	
Central Bank acts as the bankers bank, and lender of last resort to the commercial banks.	They do not have such roles and status.
12. Clearing House	
The Central bank acts as National Clearing House for interbank settlements.	The commercial banks do not function as Clearing House. In India SBI conducts clearing operations.
13. Responsibility	
Central Bank is responsible to hold the price line and inflation rate.	comercial Banks donot have responsibility.
14. Supervisory Rule	
Central Bank has supervisory regulatory powers over the entire financial system.	They can supervise and regulate only their own branches.

8.4 FUNCTIONS OF THE CENTRAL BANK

Central Banks differ from country to country in their structure and organisation, in their policies and techniques. But their functions are very similar. The Central Bank renders the following important functions in almost all countries.

1. Issuing of notes and regulating the volume of currency
2. Acts as banker to the government
3. Acts as banker to the banks
4. Acts as custodian of Nation's reserves.
5. Acts as the lender of last resort
6. Functions as National clearing House

7. Acts as controller of credit
8. Publishes economic statistics and other information
9. Development functions.
10. Supervises the activities of financial institutions.

1. Issue of Notes and Regulation of the Volume of Currency

The Central Bank is legally empowered to issue currency notes. The Central Bank is charged with the responsibility of maintaining price stability, inflation level i.e., the domestic value of its money as well as its external value. The supply of money consists of the legal lender money and the bank money.

The Central Bank has the monopoly power of the note issue to regulate the supply of legal tender money. This enables it to impart elasticity to the currency system and to maintain stability in the circulation of money. In Hong Kong the responsibility of issuing currency notes has been entrusted with a private sector bank viz. Hong Kong & Shanghai Banking Corporation (HSBC).

By the function of note issue the central bank achieves the following merits:

(*a*) Enhance the public confidence on the monetary system.

(*b*) Maintaining uniformity in the monetary system throughout the country.

(*c*) Flexibility in the monetary system. By the function of note issue the Central Bank can maintain the circulation of the economy at desired level.

(*d*) Credit creation can be effectively controlled. The sole right of note issue enables the Central Bank to regulate the creation of credit by commercial banks and adjust the supply of money to the demand for it.

(*e*) Maintaining the internal and external value of money.

The Central Bank follows different systems of note issue according to the currency regulations. The different systems of currency are,

(*i*) Fixed fiduciary system.

(*ii*) Minimum fiduciary system

(*iii*) Proportional Reserve system

(*iv*) Foreign exchange Reserve system

(*v*) Minimum Reserve system

Whatever may be the system three basic principles are to be followed. They are (*i*) Uniformity (*ii*) Security and (*iii*) elasticity. The currency issued must be uniform and a single authority must be vested with the power of note issue to achieve uniformity. There must be security for the currency without any dangers of over-issue. Public must have confidence in the currency, which to some extent, depends upon the gold and foreign exchange reserves it holds. At the same time the currency supply must be elastic. The Central Bank must be able to expand or to contract the supply of currency according to the changing needs from time to time.

2. Banker to the Government

The Central Bank acts as the banker, financial agent and advisor to the government. The surplus money of the government is kept with the Central Bank. It lends money to both central and state governments. It helps the government to tide over the time gap between their expenditure and collection of taxes. The Central Bank is usually required to make temporary advances to the government in anticipation of collection of revenues. These advances are known as "ways and means advances" in India and are made for short periods. The Central Bank also undertakes to provide the government with necessary foreign exchange for making payments abroad.

It is necessary that there should be close co-operation between the Central Bank and the government. The government is the ultimate authority for laying down the broad monetary policies of the country and Central Bank is the institution for carrying out of such policies.

The Central Bank as a fiscal agent to the government accepts loans and manages public debts, receives taxes and other payments from the public. The government bonds and treasury bills are issued by the Central Bank on behalf of the government.

As the financial adviser, the Central Bank provides valuable advice to the government on important financial matters like, foreign exchange policy, commercial policy, raising of funds from market, *etc.*,

3. Banker to the banks

The central bank acts as the bankers' bank. As such it performs the following functions:

Custodian of cash reserves of commercial banks: The commercial banks of the country are required to keep a certain percentage of their deposits with the Central Bank. It secures the advantage of centralised cash reserves. In India the Central Bank is authorised to vary these reserve requirements within certain limits. Such cash reserves with the Central Bank have the following advantages:

(*i*) The centralisation of cash reserve is a source of great strength to the banking system of the country as it strengthens the confidence of the public.

(*ii*) Centralised reserves can be used effectively and quickly in times of emergency.

(*iii*) This ensures liquidity and imparts economy in the credit structure of the country.

(*iv*) These reserves promote liquidity of commercial banks as they enable the Central Bank to undertake rediscounting of bills on a more extensive scale for the purpose of meeting the requirements of the money market.

(*v*) The Central Bank can control credit by varying the cash reserves that commercial banks should keep with it.

4. Act as custodian of National reserves

Central Bank is the custodian of nation's gold and foreign exchange reserves. Previously, to some extent, the value of a currency depends upon the gold reserves or foreign exchange reserves held as the backing for the currency. As such, it is the responsibility of the Central Bank to maintain sufficient reserves and to prevent their depletion. The Central Bank manipulates the bank rates and takes other steps to conserve the reserves of gold and foreign exchange. Some Central Banks have absolute powers to control the foreign exchange reserves and to license the various uses to which the foreign exchange is put to use. In modern times, the foreign exchange control has become the essential function of the Central Bank.

5. Acts as Lender of Last Resort

The Central Bank acts as the lender of last resort and as the bank of rediscount. Rediscounting can be defined as conversion of bank credit into Central Bank credit. The commercial banks approach the Central Bank for its financial needs as it is the lender of the last resort or the ultimate source of finance. It lends to the commercial banks by rediscounting the eligible bills. The rediscounting facilities given by the Central Bank impart elasticity and liquidity to the entire credit structure of the country. It helps the commercial banks in a big way to prevent them from bank failures. But its assistance is limited only to the banks which suffer from technical insolvency and not to those unsound and really insolvent banks.

Moreover, a commercial bank is not entitled to financial accommodation simply because it has eligible paper or approved securities. Unless it is conducting its business according to sound banking principles, the Central Bank refuses accommodation. Thus the Central Bank is able to control credit while discharging the function of lender of last resort. The Central Bank is also regarded as performing the function of last resort when it grants accommodation to the government in times of monetary stringency.

6. Functions as National Clearing House

The Central Bank acts as the national clearing house. The maintenance of accounts by all commercial banks with the Central Bank enables it to settle inter-bank indebtedness.

A clearing house is an institution where inter bank claims *i.e.*, where the claims of banks against one another are settled. The net balances or differences called the clearing balances are settled by mere transfers between their respective accounts at the Central Bank. The clearing houses facilitate expeditious and economical settlement of inter-bank claims. The Central Bank acts as a bank of clearance, settlement and transfer and establishes clearing houses in the important cities and towns in the country. They are housed in the premises of the Central Bank administered by it or at their Agent banks.

Clearing houses are established in the important cities and towns of a country by the respective local banks. If the Central Bank has no offices of its own, the clearing houses are housed in the premises of the agents of the Central Bank.

Technique of Clearance: The technique of settling the inter-bank indebtedness is simple. The clearing house operates as follows. The representatives of various member banks of a clearing house meet at the clearing house at a particular time. Every representative delivers to others the cheque and other claims which his bank holds against them. Similarly, he receives from others the claims which they hold against his banks. Cheques dishonoured are returned to the concerned representatives. The amount receivable and payable are added. The net clearing balances of banks are settled by debtor banks by issuing cheques against their accounts with the central bank in favour of creditor banks. Thus the inter-bank claims are settled by mere book entries in the accounts maintained with the central bank. These days the payment system operates more efficiently through computerised operations.

Advantages of Clearing House

Central Banks' function of clearing house provides the following advantages:

(*i*) Clearing houses reduce the cost involved in the collection of cheques and claims.

(*ii*) They avoid the delay in the clearing of cheques.

(*iii*) They ensure convenience and economy in the settlement

(*iv*) They minimise the risk involved in the realisation of cheques.

(*v*) They minimise the necessity of holding large cash balances by commercial banks.

(vi) They can be used as a common platform for the discussion of the problems of member banks.

(vii) They promote co-operation among member banks.

(viii) Central Banks also get information about the liquidity position of commercial banks.

(ix) Clearing houses offer valuable data to know the trends in the operations of commercial banks.

7. Act as the Controller of Credit

The Central Bank functions as the controller of credit in the country. According to De kock, this function is considered as the most important function of the Central Bank. The credit creation by the commercial banks has a direct impact on the economy. If the banks expand the credit limits that leads to inflation and if they unduly contract credit it leads to deflation. Thus, the central bank is empowered to control the credit creation of the commercial banks. The commonly used methods of credit control are,

(a) Bank Rate Policy

(b) Open Market Operations

(c) Variation of cash reserves

(d) Credit rationing

(e) Variation of margin requirements

(f) Regulation of consumer credit

(g) Moral suasion

(h) Direct action

(i) Selective credit control

By adopting these methods, the Central Bank controls both the quantity and quality of credit created by the banks.

8. Publishes Economic Statistics and Other Information

The Central Bank regularly collects and publishes the statistics regarding various economic activities of the government, banking system etc. Further it provides useful information regarding government policies.

9. Development Functions

The Central Bank acts as the catalyst of economic growth of the country. It acts as an agency of economic growth. It renders various developmental functions such as

(i) Provision of credit facilities to agricultural industry and other priority sectors through commercial banks and co-operative banks.

(ii) Expansion of banking facilities in the country

(iii) Maintaining price stability in the country.

(iv) Mitigating the effects of trade cycles by its effective monetary policies etc.

The responsibility of the Central Bank is increasing every day and its functions are expanding. The well-administered central baking functions are necessary for all the countries especially for the developing countries to maintain price stability and economic growth.

However, in India the developmental role of Reserve Bank of India was gradually branched out into separate development financial institutions, such as IDBI and NABARD and investment institutions like UTI over a period of time. This is primarily to allow the Central Bank to concentrate on its core activities like regulating money supply, ensuring price stability and protecting the external value of its currency.

REVIEW QUESTIONS

Short Answer Questions

1. Define central banking.
2. Write a note on the nature on Central Banking.
3. What is meant by monopoly of note issue?
4. What is clearance house?
5. Write a note on lender of last resort.
6. Write a short note on the role of central bank as custodian of national resources.

Essay Type Questions

1. Differentiate between central banking and commercial banking.
2. What are the functions of central bank of a country?
3. What is the importance of clearance house?
4. Explain the roles of central banks as Banker to the Banks and Banker to the Government.

9 CHAPTER Central Banking and Credit Control

In this chapter, the credit control measures of a central bank are discussed in general. The following chapters deal with RBI and its approaches in credit control and the like.

In the modern economy, credit has become an important factor for the development of the country. Thus, it is expected that the commercial bank have to create credit in order to meet the growing needs of trade, industry and other priority sectors. But such creation of credit if not monitored and controlled properly will cause adverse effects in the economy. The advantages and dangers of the credit creation by the commercial banks may be summarised as under:

9.1 MEANING OF CREDIT CONTROL

Credit control implies the following:

(*a*) Restricting the volume of credit created by the commercial banks.

(*b*) Regulating the volume of credit.

(*c*) Directing the credit to the productive purposes, and

(*d*) Introducing measures for strengthening the banking structure.

Objectives of Credit Control: credit controls measures have become essential for the economic well being of the country. The effective credit control measures will bring the following:

(*i*) Stability in the price level

(*ii*) Mitigation of effects of trade cycle both during inflation and deflation periods.

(*iii*) Stability in foreign exchange rates and thereby maintaining the external value of the currency.

(*iv*) Stabilisation of the money market through liquidity control measures

(*v*) Promotion of overall economic development.

(*vi*) National interest is protected.

9.2 ADVANTAGES AND DANGERS OF THE CREDIT CREATION

9.2.1 Advantages of Credit Creation

The credit creation function of commercial banks provides the following advantages:

(*i*) It economises the use of currency

(*ii*) It facilitates growth of large scale enterprise

(*iii*) It stimulates and finances production in anticipation of demand

(*iv*) It permits wealth to be transferred to quarters where more economic use can be made of it.

(*v*) It enables payments to be made at convenient times and so tides over periods of difficulty.

(*vi*) If the creation of credit is properly regulated, it tends to stabilise trade and reduce fluctuations in prices.

9.2.2 Possible Problems of Credit Creation

The over creation of credit suffers from the following problems.

(*i*) An over creation of credit may promote unwise production and expansion, precarious speculation, with danger of over production and serious fluctuations in prices and trade.

(*ii*) It may encourage extravagance

(*iii*) Where a firm is really insolvent, the granting of credit only postpones the event and may intensify the ultimate failure. The temporary concealment of its weakness may push creditors and others into loss.

Credit is thus a sensitive but sharp instrument in modern economies requiring delicate handling. When it crosses the limits of safety, it leads to inflation or deflation. Thus, control and regulation of credit creation by the banks are considered as strategic to monetary, fiscal and general economic policy of the country.

9.3 METHODS OF CREDIT CONTROL

The most important function of the Central Bank is to control credit. The Central Bank uses various methods to control credit. These methods can be classified into the following two broad categories.

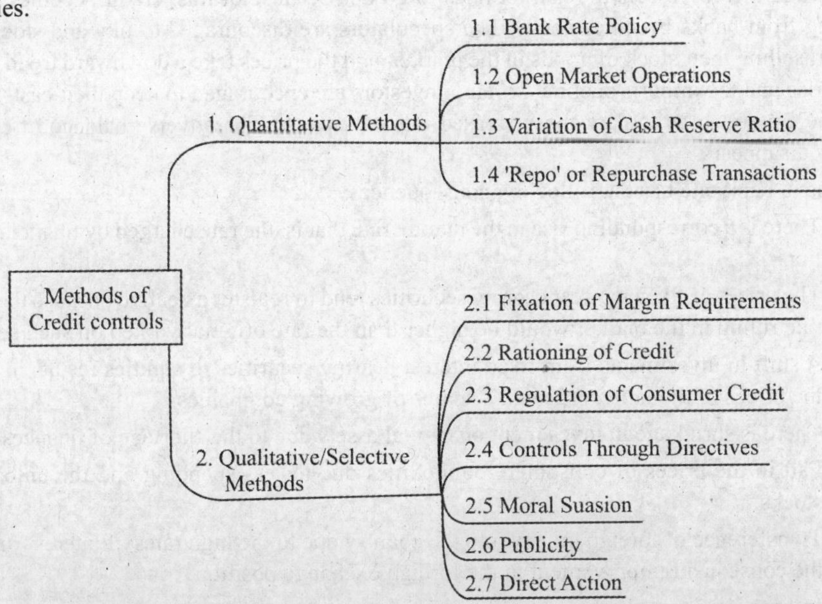

Let us discuss these methods one by one.

9.3.1 Quantitative Methods of Credit Control

The quantitative methods of credit control are the general and traditional methods. They aim at the regulation of the quantity of credit and not its application in various uses. They are expected to control and adjust the total quantity of deposits created by the commercial banks. They relate to the volume in general. These methods are indirect in nature.

The objectives of quantitative methods of credit control are as follows.

(*i*) Controlling the volume of credit in the economy.

(*ii*) Maintaining equilibrium between saving and investment in the economy.

(*iii*) Maintaining the stability in exchange rates.

(*iv*) Correcting disequilibrium in the balance of payments of the country.

(*v*) Removing shortage of money in the money market.

The important methods under this category are:

9.3.1.1 Bank Rate Policy

It is also known as discount rate policy. Bank rate is the rate at which the Central Bank is prepared to rediscount the approved bills or to lend on eligible paper. This weapon can be used independently or along with other weapon. By changing this rate the Central Bank control the volume of credit. The bank rate is raised in times of inflation and is lowered in times of deflation.

A rise in the bank rate is usually preceded by the following events.

(*a*) Over supply of money and rising price level.

(*b*) Great demand for money caused by active trade.

(*c*) Adverse rate of exchange and

(*d*) Unfavourable balance of trade.

In times of adverse balance of payments and rising price level, the Central Bank increases the bank rate and thereby forces the market rates to go up. Because of this, credit becomes dear and borrowing from banks becomes costly. The speculators are discouraged to buy and stock goods. They start selling their stock of goods in the market, and the prices take a downward trend. Exports begin to rise and the imports decline. Foreign investors are encouraged to keep their cash balances within the county so as to earn the increased rate of interest. The adverse balance of payments gradually disappears.

A rise in bank rate has the following consequences:

(*i*) There is a corresponding rise in the market rate that is, the rate charged by financial institution.

(*ii*) The prices of fixed interest bearing securities tend to register a decline because the interest rate ruling in the market would be higher than the rate originally fixed on such securities.

(*iii*) A shift in investments from fixed interest bearing securities to equities results in a rise in the prices of the latter, especially, shares of growing companies.

(*iv*) There is shrinkage in investment on capital assets due to the shortage of finances.

(*v*) Fall in the prices of consumer commodities due to less spending and the unloading of stocks.

(*vi*) Transference of foreign money into the country due to the high rates of interest ruling and the consequent improvement in the foreign exchange position.

(*vii*) Increase in exports.

But in times of falling prices, the Central Bank lowers the bank rate and brings about a fall in the market rates of interest. This will lead to increased volume of trade, investment, production and employment and ultimately leads to the rise in the price level.

Conditions for the Operation of Bank Rate Policy

To use the weapon of bank rate policy some basic requirements are to be fulfilled. The impact of a change in the Bank rate depends upon the following.

(*a*) Existence of close nexus between Bank Rate and market rates, *i.e.*, the extent of the dependence of commercial banks on the Central Bank for funds.

(*b*) The availability of funds to banks from other sources.

(*c*) The extent to which other interest rates are directly influenced by changes in the bank rate. If the other rates of interest in the market do not respond to bank rate changes desired results cannot be realised.

(*d*) The degree of importance attached to a change in the bank rate as an indicator of the monetary policy.

(*e*) There must be an organised short-term funds market in the country.

(*f*) There must be a great measure of elasticity in the economic structure of the country. When prices fall, the various elements in the cost of production like wages must also fall otherwise, the producers incur losses and revival of business activity becomes impossible.

Limitations of Bank Rate Policy

The report of Macmillan committee stated that the bank rate policy is an absolute necessary for the sound management of a monetary system. It is an important weapon of credit control. But, it suffers from the following limitations.

(*i*) The rate of interest in money market may not change according to the changes in the bank rate.

(*ii*) In rigid economic system *i.e.*, planned and regulated economies, the prices and costs may not change as a result of changes in the rate of interest.

(*iii*) The bank rate cannot be the sole regulator of the economic system, and the volume of savings and investments cannot be controlled through the rate of interest alone. The effectiveness of changes in interest rate depends upon the elasticity of demand for capital goods.

(*iv*) The effect of rise in the bank rate in controlling credit for industrial and commercial purpose is limited. If the businessmen take the view that prices will continue to rise, a slight rise in the rate of interest will not discourage them to expand their activity with borrowed money. So long as prices have a tendency to rise and so long as there is business optimism, businessmen would be willing to pay higher interest rates.

(*v*) In ties of depression, a fall in the rate of interest can hardly stimulate economic activity. Because, the businessmen may not be prepared to increase their activity if they fear about the future. Prof. Sayers considers the bank rate as a halting, clumsy and indeed a brutal instrument.

(*vi*) The change in the methods of financing by the business firms reduces the importance of bank rate policy. In recent years the commercial banks have ample liquid resources of their own. The business firms depend more on ploughing back of profits than borrowing from commercial banks.

(*vii*) The conflicting effects of bank rate also reduce the importance of this weapon. When the bank rate is increased the foreign capital may flow into the country, thus making credit control difficult.

(*viii*) Indiscriminate nature of bank rate policy: The bank rate policy does not discriminate the activities into productive and unproductive activities. It affects both the activities on the same footing. This will adversely affect the genuine productive activities with increased rate of interest.

Because of these limitations, the bank rate policy has lost its importance. But during the inflationary situations it can be used with some modifications. But it may not regain its former importance.

9.3.1.2 Open Market Operations

Open market operation refers to buying and selling of eligible securities by the Central Bank in the money market and capital market. The buying and selling of securities by the Central Bank, results in an increase or decrease in the cash resources of the commercial banks. This in turn affects the credit creation of the commercial banks. Open market operations tend immediately to increase or decrease the quantity of money in circulation and the cash resource of Commercial banks.

Objectives of open market operation:

The weapon of open market operation helps in achieving the following objectives.

1. To make the bank rate policy effective and successful.
2. To avoid disturbances in the money market as a result of movement of Government funds or seasonal movements of funds generally.
3. To eliminate the effects of inflow or outflow of gold by import and export under Gold Standard.
4. To support Government credit in connection with the issue of new loans or the conversion of the existing loans.
5. To counteract extreme trends in business situation by buying securities during periods of low economic activity and selling them in periods of high economic activity.
6. To create and maintain conditions of cheap money as an aid to business recovery.
7. To avoid undue fluctuations in the prices of Government securities and to correct undesirable or unjustifiable spreads between the yields of various types of securities.
8. To absorb an excess of liquid funds.
9. To insulate the credit structure from sudden and temporary changes in the balances of payments position.

The most important reason is the decline of discount rate as an instrument of credit control and the consequent need for another and more direct method.

Open market operations became necessary in order to implement the policy of cheap money. These operations have been considerably facilitated as a result of increased volume and variety of Government and other gilt-edged securities traded in markets of most countries.

Method of Operation

If the Central Bank wants to reduce the volume of credit created by the banks, it sells eligible securities in the market. When the banks and the public purchase these securities, they have to make payments to the Central Banks. This results in the movement of cash from Commercial Banks to Central Bank. As a result of this the primary reserves of the banks fall. Hence the capacity of the banks to expand credit will be contracted. In times of inflation the Central Bank sells eligible securities in the open market.

When the Central Bank wants to expand the volume of credit, it starts buying the approved securities from the open market. Now, the Central Bank has to make payments to the commercial banks and the public for the purchases made from them. This results in the movement of cash from the Central Bank to commercial banks. As a result, the cash reserves in the hands of commercial banks will increase. They find themselves in a position to expand credit. This is followed during deflationary situations.

Prerequisites for the success of open market operations:

(*a*) The market for the securities should be well organised, deep, active and broad based.

(*b*) The rate of interest offered on government securities should be competitive.

(*c*) The existence of sufficient number of securities.

(*d*) The willingness of commercial banks to lend.

(*e*) The maintenance of rigid cash reserve ratio by the commercial banks.

(*f*) Willingness of the general public to borrow money from the commercial banks.

(*g*) Commercial banks should not have direct access to accommodation from the Central Bank.

Limitations of open market operations

The following are the main limitations of the open market operations:

(*i*) Quantity of money circulation may not change: It depends upon the close connection that prevails between the operations and the quantity of money in circulation. Quantity of money should at least approximately change according to operations. But in actual practice it may not change in the desired direction due to two factors, such as hoarding and dishoarding of cash and inflow and outflow of capital etc.

(*ii*) Influence of economic and political reasons: It is assumed that the commercial banks increase or decrease their loans and advances in accordance with the changes in their cash reserves. But they may not do so due to monetary, economic and political reasons. Even though there is an increase in their cash reserves, they may not expand the credit for want of credit-worthy borrowers.

(*iii*) Pessimistic approach of Businessmen affects the operations: The demand for bank credit cannot be wholly controlled by commercial banks or by the Central Bank, but it depends upon the actions of the businessmen. The Central Bank may buy securities and increase the cash base of the commercial banks. The commercial banks may be willing to expand credit. But the businessmen may not borrow if they are pessimistic about the future.

(*iv*) Not effective in developing countries: The effectiveness of open market operations depends upon the existence of a broad and active securities market, in short-term as well as long-term securities. But such markets are to be found only in advanced countries. However, the increased volume of treasury bills in many countries is proving helpful for effective open market operations.

(*v*) Dependence of resources of the Central Bank: The Central Bank must be capable of launching operations on the necessary scale, which depends upon its resources. The resources of the Central Bank in turn depend upon its constitution and the policy of its Government.

(*vi*) Lacks immediate effect: The additional cash put into the money market by the Central Bank by purchasing of securities will not come to the commercial banks immediately as deposits. It takes time to reach the commercial banks. Therefore the effect of this weapon may not be immediate due to this time lag.

9.3.1.3 Variation of Cash Reserve Ratios

The weapon of variation of cash reserve ratios has been suggested as a supplement to other methods of credit control because of its efficacy under all conditions. The commercial banks have to keep a minimum cash reserve with the Central Bank. Under this method, the Central Bank has the power to vary the percentage of deposits that must statutorily be kept with it by commercial banks, within certain limits. When the Central Bank wants to reduce credit, it will increase the cash ratio to be kept by the commercial banks. This reduces the capacity of the commercial banks to lend and thus, the credit creation is controlled. When the Central Bank considers increasing the credit, it will lower the cash reserve ratio. Now the commercial banks will nave additional cash which will lead to credit expansion.

In India the Cash Reserve Ratio has become an important tool to control or expand liquidity position with the banking system. When excess liquidity is available with banks the CRR is hiked to impound excess cash. Similarly, this rate is also used to stabilise Exchange Rate of Rupee. When Exchange Rate of Rupee comes under attack from speculators, CRR is raised to arrest the fall in value of Rupee. The CRR is often changed these days. However the rate is drastically reduced in recent times.

Limitations of Variations of Cash Reserve Ratios

The method of variation of reserve ratio suffers from the following limitations.

(*a*) This method may not be successful and effective if the commercial banks have excess cash reserves with them.

(*b*) The success of this method depends upon the customers' willingness to borrow from the banks. If they are not willing to borrow the credit can not be expanded even if the commercial banks have adequate cash reserves with them.

(*c*) This method imposes an increased burden on the credit system. Under this system the commercial banks follow a very cautious activity and many not extend credit facilities even if they have surplus reserves due to the fear that they may be asked to maintain higher cash reserves than before. This results in keeping idle cash reserves. Keeping such idle cash balances leads to higher rate of interest on bank advances and the burden ultimately falls on the borrowers.

(*d*) Discriminatory in effect those banks have to keep a certain percentage of cash reserves with the Central Bank. And the percentage may very depending upon the policy of the Central Bank. This causes serious effects on small banks which find it difficult to maintain additional reserves.

(*e*) This method lacks flexibility. It cannot be well adjusted to meet sectoral requirements or localised situations of reserve stringency or surplus.

(*f*) This method is inexact and creates uncertainty because the commercial banks are always under certain fear of sudden changes in the cash reserves that they have to keep with the Central Bank.

(*g*) The weapon of variation of cash reserves gives a sweeping power to central bank over commercial banks. It is actually a very powerful weapon, but it may cause much suffering if it is not used properly.

(*h*) The variation of cash reserve ratio is a powerful weapon. A slight change in the cash reserve may lead to either multiple expansion or contraction of credit. Thus it is suitable only when it is desired to effect major charges in the reserves of the commercial banks. But when marginal adjustments in the reserves are expected, this method is not suitable.

Variation of Cash Reserve Ratio Vs Open Market Operations

Variation of cash reserves is superior to open market operations in the following respects.

(*a*) The success of open market operations depends upon the existence of a broad and developed capital market and a large supply of Government securities with the Central Bank to conduct such operations on an extensive scale. In countries where open market operations cannot be carried out on an extensive scale due to the absence of these conditions, the variation of cash reserves has an increasing influence on the Central Bank.

(*b*) The large scale sale of securities by the Central Bank as a part of open market operations policy will depress the value of securities and bring loss to the Central Bank. If the values of securities fall, commercial banks also incur loss as their portfolio consists of a large volume of government securities. The variation of cash reserves secures the same results as open market operations but without the loss that may arise in dealing in securities. When commercial banks are asked by the Central Bank to increase the percentage of reserves, they may of course sell securities for maintaining increased case reserve. In order that the sale of Government securities by commercial banks does not depress its price realisation, the central bank may simultaneously buy such securities. It may however be stated that this method may help commercial banks to avoid incurring losses in the sale of securities, it may not serve the objective of the central bank.

(*c*) Another limitation of open market operations is that the cash reserves of commercial banks may be so excessive that Central Bank may not be able to reduce them by selling securities available with it but a change in reserve requirements achieve the result easily with a mere change in the reserve rate.

(*d*) Whenever the Central Bank conducts open market purchase of securities, the volume of earning assets held by the banks in their portfolio are reduced. Variable reserve ratios do not affect the earning assets of banks unless banks sell securities to increase their reserves.

(*e*) The new method of credit control can be adopted to strengthen the Central Banking control under highly liquid monetary conditions or conversely under conditions of severe credit stringency.

It has been suggested that open market operations and variation of cash ratios should be followed as complementary to each other. A judicious combination of both will remedy the defects of each technique when used individually, and produce good results.

9.3.1.4 'Repo' Transactions

'Repo' stands for repurchase. 'Repo' or Repurchase transactions are undertaken by the central bank to influence money market conditions. Under 'Repo' transaction or agreement one party lends money to another for a fixed period against the collateral of securities approved for this purpose. At the end of the fixed period, the borrower will repurchase the securities at the predetermined price.

The difference between the repurchase price and the original sale price will be the cost for the borrower. In other words, instead of a pure or simple borrowing of funds, the borrower parts with securities to the lender with an agreement to repurchase at the end of the fixed period. This parting with the securities will make the cost of borrowing, known as 'Repo Rate' little cheaper than pure borrowing.

'Repo' transactions are conducted in Money market to manipulate short-term interest rate and to manage liquidity levels. 'Repos' are conducted by central banks to absorb or drain liquidity from the system. In case they desire to inject fresh funds in the cash market, they will conduct 'Reverse Repo' transactions. In the reverse repo 'the securities are received first against money paid and returned after receipt of money, at the end of the agreed period. In India, 'Repos' are normally conducted for a period of 3 days. The eligible securities for the purpose are decided by RBI. These securities are usually Government promissory notes, Treasury bills and some public sector bonds.

9.3.2 Qualitative/Selective Methods of Credit Control

The qualitative credit control is also called as selective credit control. It is used as an adjunct to general credit control. In certain situations quantitative credit control may not be helpful. At times it may harm certain sectors of the economy. Because, the quantitative methods control the volume of credit in total, it does not discriminate the credit flow into productive and unproductive purposes. Thus it affects the genuine productive purposes also. But, the selective credit control provides for such discrimination. Under these methods the credit is made available for the productive and priority sectors and restricted to others. This is very much helpful to the developing and under developed economies.

Selective Credit Control: The selective credit control methods control certain types of credit and not all credit. They directly affect the demand for bank credit as also the capacity of the banks to lend. They can be used more effectively without any changes in the prevailing rates of interest.

Objectives of Selective Credit Control:

The following are the main objectives of selective credit control measures:

(*a*) To distinguish between essential and non-essential uses of bank credit.

(*b*) To ensure adequate credit to the desired sectors and curtail the flow of credit to less essential economic activities.

(*c*) To control the consumer credit used for purchase of durable consumer goods.

(*d*) To control a particular sector of the economy without affecting the economy as a whole.

(*e*) To correct the unfavourable balance of payments of the country.

(*f*) To control the inflationary pressures in the particular and important sector of the economy.

(*g*) To control the credit created by other institutions.

Methods of Qualitative/ selective Credit Control

The Central Bank uses the following qualitative methods to control the credit in the economy.

9.3.2.1 Fixation of Margin Requirements

The Central Bank prescribes the margin which banks and other lenders must maintain for the loans granted by them against commodities, stocks and shares. To restrict the speculative dealing in stock exchanges, the Central Bank prescribes the margin requirements for securities dealt with. When the Central Bank prescribes higher margin the borrowers can obtain less amount of credit on his stock. If the margin prescribed is low, the speculators can borrow from bankers buy the commodity, storage and sell only after price rise. To contract credit, the Central Bank raises margins and lowers the margins to expand the credit available.

Objectives of Margin Requirements:

The Central Bank may prescribe margin requirements to achieve the following objectives.

(*i*) To divert investible funds from speculative to productive lines.

(*ii*) To reduce the volume of credit created by commercial banks.

(*iii*) To reduce the prospect of making speculative profits in stock exchanges.

(*iv*) To reduce the risks and uncertainties of joint stock companies by maintaining the stability of stock prices.

9.3.2.2 Rationing of Credit

The Central Bank controls the credit created by the banks through the rationing of credit. Under this method, the Central Bank fixes a maximum limit for loans that a commercial bank can provide to a particular sector or for all purposes. This can be achieved through the following two methods.

(*i*) Variable Portfolio Ceiling: Under this method, the Central Bank fixes a ceiling on the aggregate portfolios of commercial banks above which loans and advances should not be increased. It may even fix a ceiling for specific categories of credit. It may also fix a maximum limit for the loans that the commercial banks can borrow from the Central Bank.

(*ii*) Variable Capital Assets Ratio: Under this method, the Central Bank can fix the minimum ratios which the capital and surplus of banks must bear to the volume of assets or specific categories thereof of the commercial banks. The Central Banks can change such minimum ratio from time to time. Rationing of credit can play a great role in planned economies. It secures diversion of commercial resources into the channels fixed by the public authority in achieving the objectives of planning.

9.3.2.3 Regulation of Consumer Credit

The Central Bank to regulate the consumer credit, fixes the down payments and the period over which the installments are spread. In developed countries, large portion of national income is spent on consumer durable goods such as cars, refrigerators, costly furniture etc. The installment credit for consumer durable goods plays an important part in certain economies. Expansion of such credit affects the developed economies adversely. Many countries have adopted this weapon to control credit allowed to the consumers.

It is essential to regulate consumer expenditure on such durable goods to control inflations. The method of control involves the following steps.

Steps involved in Controlling Consumer Credit

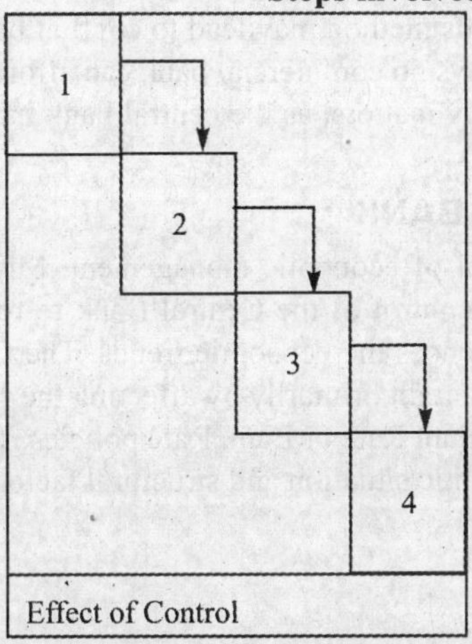

1. The scope of regulation with respect to particular consumer durable goods will have to be defined.
2. Fix the minimum down payment.
3. The length of the period over which instalment payments may be spread will have to be fixed.
4. The maximum cost of instalment purchase exemptions have to be prescribed.

To control inflation a large number of durable goods will be listed for control, the minimum down payments will be raised, the period over which installment payment can be spread will be reduced and finally the maximum exemption costs will be lowered.

9.3.2.4 Control through Directives

The Central Bank issues directives to control the credit created by commercial banks. The directives may be in the form of written orders, warnings or appeals etc. Through such directives the Central Bank aims to achieve the following objectives.

(*i*) To control the lending policies of the commercial banks.

(*ii*) To prevent the flow of bank credit into non-essential lines.

(*iii*) To divert the credit to productive and essential purposes.

(*iv*) To fix maximum credit limits for certain purposes.

The Central Bank issues directives from time to time and the commercial banks abide by them. These directives are issued in supplementing the quantitative methods of credit control.

9.3.2.5 Moral Suasion

Under this method, the Central Bank merely uses its moral influence on the commercial banks. It includes the advice, suggestion request and persuasion with the commercial banks to co-operate with the Central Bank. If the commercial banks do not follow the advice extended by the Central Bank, no penal action is taken against them. The success of this method depends upon the co-operation between the Central Bank and commercial banks and the respect the central bank commands from other banks.

9.3.2.6 Publicity

The Central Banks generally use the method of publicity to control the credit creation of commercial banks. Under this method, the Central Bank gives wide publicity to its credit policy through its bulletins. By this, the Central Bank educates the general public regarding the monetary policy and its objectives. Through such publicity, the commercial banks are guided and change their lending policies accordingly.

9.3.2.7 Direct Action

The method of direct action is the most effective weapon of Central Bank to control credit creation. The Central Bank uses this method to enforce both quantitative and selective credit controls. It is used as a supplement to other methods of credit control. The Central Bank can take action against the banks which contravene its instructions. But this method may lead to conflict between the central bank and commercial banks. However, these days no commercial bank can afford to go against the wishes of the central bank with regard to policy matters, as the central bank has wide powers even to stop banks' operations.

9.4 MONETARY POLICY OF THE CENTRAL BANK

Monetary policy is regarded as an indispensable tool of economic management. Monetary policy refers to the use of official instruments under the control of the Central Bank to regulate the availability, cost and use of money and credit. It influences the economic trends. The Central Bank exercises its influence on the availability and cost of credit primarily by affecting the reserve position of commercial banks and through its official Discount Rate or Bank Rate policies. The efficacy of monetary policy depends on the prevailing economic situation and structural factors like:

(*a*) The proportion of currency in money supply.

(*b*) Size of public debt.

(*c*) Non-monetised sector in the economy.

(*d*) Presence of active sub - markets.

(*e*) The degree of imbalance in the overall supply, demand situation

(*f*) Trends in agricultural and industrial production.

(*g*) General price level and

(*h*) The balance of payment situation.

Since, these factors are constantly changing, the authorities have to adopt the right choice and mix of various techniques depending upon the circumstances. Monetary policy also encompasses institutional changes in the banking and credit structure. In the developing countries, the Central Banks have been called upon to play a positive and energetic role in administering monetary policy to achieve the desired economic goods.

9.4.1 Objectives of Monetary Policy

'Growth with Price stability' is the main theme of Reserve Bank of India with regard to its monetary policy. In modern times, the main objective of monetary policy is the promotion of economic growth of the country with price stability. The Central Bank plays an active and pre eminent role in achieving the objectives of monetary policy. The basic objectives of the monetary policy are as follows.

(*a*) Achieving the optimum level of output
(*b*) Increasing employment opportunities
(*c*) Price stabilisation
(*d*) Maintaining equilibrium in balance of payments
(*e*) Ensure adequate level of liquidity
(*f*) Fullest possible utilisation of available resources
(*g*) Exchange stabilisation.
(*h*) Monetary integration of the country.
(*i*) Directing credit flow according to policy priorities.
(*j*) Assisting in mobilisation of savings in the community
(*k*) Promotion of capital formation and
(*l*) Support the authorities in the allocation of resources,
(*m*) Targetting of reasonable interest rate for growth of industry.

9.4.2 Benefits Monetary Policy

By achieving the above said objectives the Central Bank takes necessary steps to direct the banking and other financial institutions. Through these objectives of the monetary policy various benefits can be obtained. They are:

(*i*) The cyclical fluctuations in output and prices can be eliminated.
(*ii*) The price stability can be ensured.
(*iii*) The economic prosperity can be achieved.
(*iv*) Regional imbalances and disparities can be avoided.
(*v*) The effective monetary policy stimulates production.
(*vi*) It encourages capital formation and mobilises savings.
(*vii*) It promotes business efficiency and thereby its prosperity.
(*viii*) It corrects the disequilibrium in the balance of payments.
(*ix*) It ensures exchange stability
(*x*) Promotes better economic relationship among countries.
(*xi*) Maintaining the stability in price level and thereby maintains the internal value of money.
(*xii*) Effective monetary policy promotes foreign trade.
(*xiii*) The employment opportunities can be expanded at a considerable extent.
(*xiv*) Increases the standard of living of the people by benefiting the consumers through price stability.
(*xv*) It promotes the economic welfare of the country as a whole.

Thus the monetary policy is the main stay of the economic developments of any country. In a planned economy, it plays a crucial role.

REVIEW QUESTIONS

Short Answer Questions

1. What is meant by credit control by commercial banks?
2. What are the objectives of credit control?
3. What is Quantitative/general credit control?
4. What is Qualitative/selective credit control?

5. What is meant by Statutory Liquid Reserve?
6. What is meant by monetary policy?
7. What are the objectives of monetary policy?

Essay Type Questions

1. What is central banking? Why is it called so?
2. Explain the advantages and possible problems of credit creation by commercial banks.
3. Explain the meaning of credit control by central Bank and Why is it important.
4. What is meant by Bank Rate? Explain.
5. Explain the methods of credit control in brief.
6. What are open market operations?
7. What are the quantitative credit control measures of a central bank? Explain.
8. What are the qualitative credit control measures of a central bank? Explain.
9. Explain the monetary policy of the central bank.
10. Explain the important features of monetary policy.

CHAPTER

10 Reserve Bank of India

The attempts to establish a Central Bank in India took a definite shape, when in 1927 a bill was introduced in the Indian Legislative Assembly, to establish a gold standard currency for British India and constitute a Reserve Bank of India. Thereafter various attempts were made and thus the Reserve Bank of India Act was passed in 1934 and the bank began functioning from 1st April 1935. Later it was decided to nationalise the bank and the Reserve Bank of India (transfer to public ownership) Act was passed in September 1948 under which the ownership of the bank was passed into the hands of the Government of India with effect from 1st Jan 1949.

From ensuring stability of interest and exchange rates to providing liquidity and an adequate supply of currency and credit for the real sector; from ensuring bank penetration and safety of depositors' funds to promoting and developing financial institutions and markets, the Reserve Bank plays a crucial role in the economy. RBI decisions touch the daily life of all Indians and help chart the country's current and future economic and financial course.

10.1 OBJECTIVES FOR ESTABLISHMENT OF RBI

The basic objectives for establishment of RBI as the Central Bank of India are as follows:

1. To manage the monetary and credit system of the country.
2. To regulation and supervise of the banking and non-banking financial institutions, including credit information companies.
3. To stabilizes internal and external value of rupee.
4. To ensure balanced and systematic development of banking in the country.
5. To ensure the organized money market in the country.
6. To regulate of money, forex and government securities markets.
7. To make appropriate arrangements for agriculture finance.
8. To make appropriate arrangements for industrial finance.
9. To ensure proper management of public debts.
10. To establish monetary relations with other countries of the world and international financial institutions.
11. To centralise the cash reserves of commercial banks.
12. To maintain balance between the demand and supply of currency in the economy.

10.2 EVOLUTION OF THE RESERVE BANK OF INDIA

The evolution of RBI can easily be traced from the following chart:

Enolution of the Reserve Bank of India

1926: The Royal commission on Indian Currency and Finance recommended creation of a central bank for India.

1927: A bill to give effect to the above recommendation was introduced in the Legislative Assembly, but was later withdrawn due to lack of agreement among various sections of people.

1933: The White Paper on Indian Constitutional Reforms recommended the creation of a Reserve Bank. A fresh bill was introduced in the Legislative Assembly.

1934: The Bill was passed and received the Governor General's assent.

1935: The Reserve bank commenced operations as India's central bank on April 1 as a private shareholder's bank with a paid up capital of rupees five crore (rupees fifty million).

1942: The Reserve bank ceased to be the currency issuing authority of Burma (now Myanmar).

1947: The Reserve bank stopped acting as banker to the Government of Burma.

1948: The Reserve Bank stopped rendering central banking services to Pakistan.

1949: The Government of India nationalised the Reserve Bank under the Reserve Bank (Transfer of Public Ownership) Act, 1948.

Source: RBI Publications

10.3 MANAGEMENT AND ADMINISTRATION OF RESERVE BANK OF INDIA

The Reserve Bank of India is managed by well-structured administrative machinery. The Reserve Bank is wholly owned by the Government of India. The Central Board of Directors manage the Reserve Bank's business. The organisation structure of the RBI can be easily understood with the help of the following chart.

Organisation of Reserve Bank of India

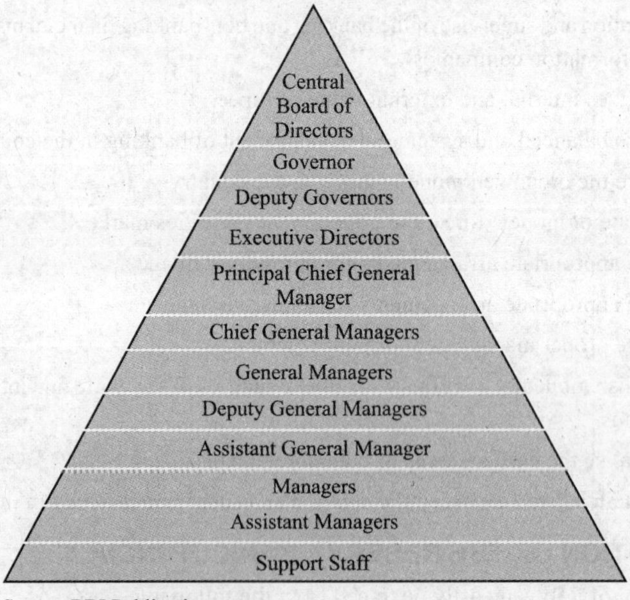

Source: RBI Publications

The management of the RBI is entrusted to the central and local boards.

10.3.1 Central Board

The Reserve Bank's affairs are governed by a central board of directors. The board is appointed by the Government of India in keeping with the Reserve Bank of India Act. The Central Board has primary authority for the management of the Reserve Bank. It delegates specific functions to its committees and sub-committees.

Central Board: Includes the Governor, Deputy Governors and the nominated Directors and a government nominee- Director.

Committee of Central Board: Supervises the current business of the central bank and focuses on current business, including approval of the weekly statement of accounts related to the Issue and Banking Departments.

Board for Financial Supervision: Regulates and supervises commercial banks, Non-Banking Finance Companies (NBFCs), development finance institutions, urban co-operative banks and primary dealers.

Board for Payment and Settlement Systems: Regulates and supervises the payment and settlement systems.

Sub-committees of the Central Board: Includes those on Inspection and Audit; Staff; and Building. Focus of each subcommittee is on specific areas of operations.

Local Boards: In Chennai, Kolkata, Mumbai and New Delhi, representing the country's four regions. Local board members, appointed by the Central Government for four-year terms, represent regional and economic interests and the interests of co-operative and indigenous banks.

10.3.2 Number of Directors in Central Board

The number of directors working in Central Board is as follows:

1. Official Directors

(*a*) 1 Governor

(*b*) 4 Deputy Governors, at a maximum

2. Non-Official Directors

(*a*) 4 directors—nominated by the Central Government to represent each local board

(*b*) 10 directors nominated by the Central Government with expertise in various segments of the economy

(*c*) 1 representative of the Central Government

10.3.3 Departments of RBI

The various departments of RBI are given below:

1. Department of Information Technology
2. Department of Economic Analysis and Policy
3. Department of Statistical Analysis and Computer Services
4. Monetary Policy Department
5. Premises Department
6. Secretary's Department
7. Press Relations Division
8. Exchange Control Department
9. Rural Planning and Credit Department
10. Financial Institutions Division

11. Department of Banking Supervision
12. Department of Banking Operations and Development
13. Department of Financial Companies
14. Department of Non-Banking Supervision
15. Department of Administration and Personnel Management
16. Human Resources Development Department
17. Deposit Insurance and Credit Guarantee Corporation
18. Inspection Department
19. Urban Banks Department
20. Department of Currency Management
21. Department of External Investments and Operations
22. Department of Expenditure and Budgetory Control
23. Department of Government and Bank Accounts
24. Internal Debt Management Cell
25. Industrial and Export Credit Department
26. Legal Department

10.4 FUNCTIONS OF RESERVE BANK OF INDIA

The following are the important functions of RBI. They can be explained with the help of the following chart.

FUNCTIONS OF RESERVE BANK OF INDIA

A. Traditional Functions

1. Monopoly of Note Issue
2. Banker to the Government
3. Agent and adviser to the Government
4. Banker to the Banks
5. Acts as the clearing House of the country
6. Lender of last resort
7. Controller of credit and forex
8. Custodian of foreign exchange reserves
9. Maintaining the external value of domestic currency
10. Ensures the internal value of currency
11. Publishers the Economics Statistics and other Information
12. Fights against economic crisis and ensures economic and price stability in the country.

B. Promotional Functions

1. Promotional of banking habit and expansion of banking systems
2. Provides refinance for export promotion
3. Expansion of facilities for the provision of agricultural credit through NABARD
4. Extension of facilities for the Small Scale Industries
5. Helping the co-operative sector
6. Prescription of minimum statutory requirements
7. Innovations in banking business.

C. Supervisory Functions

1. Granting licence to banks
2. Inspect and make enquiry or determine position in respect of matters under various sections of RBI and Banking Regulation Act
3. Implementation of Deposit Insurance Scheme
4. Periodical review of the work of commercial banks
5. Giving directives to commercial banks
6. Control the non-banking finance corporations
7. Ensuring the health of financial system through on-site and off-site verifications.

Let us discuss the important functions one by one in detail.

10.4.1 Traditional Functions

The RBI functions on the traditional lines regarding the following activities.

1. Monopoly of Note Issue:

In terms of section 22 of the Reserve Bank of India Act, the RBI has been given the statutory function of note issue on a monopoly basis. The note issue in India was originally based upon "Proportional Reserve System". When it became difficult to maintain the reserve proportionately, it was replaced by "Minimum Reserve System".

The Government of India issues rupee coins in the denomination of ₹1, 2, and 5 to public. These coins are required to be circulated to public only through Reserve Bank under section 38 of the RBI Act. The RBI presently issues notes of denominations ₹10 and above. RBI manages circulation of money through currency chests. Originally, RBI issued currency notes of ₹2 and above. However, due to higher cost of printing small denomination notes these denominations are now coinised and issued by Government. The Reserve Bank estimates the demand for bank notes on the basis of the growth rate of the economy, the replacement demand and reserve requirements by using statistical models.

Denominations of coins and notes in circulation:

- Coins in circulations: 25 paise, 50 paise, 1, 2, 5, and 10 Rupee

- Notes in circulation: ₹ 5, 10, 20, 50, 100, 500 and 1000

Bank notes are legal tender at any place in India for payment without limit.

Currency Chests: Currency Chests are receptacles in which stocks of issuable and new notes are stored along with rupee coins. Currency Chests are repositories run by RBI, SBI, subsidiaries of SBI, public sector banks, Government Treasuries and Sub treasuries. Currency Chests help in expansion and contraction of currency in the country. The advantages for a bank having currency chest are:

(*a*) The bank can draw funds whenever it is required for its use and deposit funds when found surplus.

(*b*) Exchange old and mutilated notes for new notes and coins.

(*c*) Enjoy remittance facilities.

(*d*) Cash remitted to currency chests by banks can be taken into account for maintenance of CRR.

To facilitate the distribution of notes and rupee coins, the Reserve Bank has authorised selected branches of banks to establish currency chests. These are actually storehouses where bank notes and rupee coins are stocked on behalf of the Reserve Bank. At present, there are over 4422 currency chests. The currency chest branches are expected to distribute notes and rupee coins to other bank branches in their area of operation.

2. Banker to the Government:

The RBI acts as banker to the Government under section 20 of RBI Act. Section 21 provides that Government should entrust its money remittance, exchange and banking transactions in India to RBI. Under section 21A RBI has to conduct similar transactions for State Governments also. RBI earns no income by conducting those functions but earns commissions for managing the Governments public debt. Where RBI has no branch, SBI or its subsidiaries are appointed as agents and subagents under section 45 of the RBI Act. Agency Banks receive commission on all transactions conducted on turnover basis.

Under the administrative arrangements, the Central Government is required to maintain a minimum cash balance with the Reserve Bank. Currently, this amount is ₹10 crore on a daily basis and ₹100 crore on Fridays, as also at the end of March and July.

Under a scheme introduced in 1976, every ministry and department of the Central Government has been allotted a specific public sector bank for handling its transactions. Hence, the Reserve Bank does not handle government's day-to-day transactions as before, except where it has been nominated as banker to a particular ministry or department.

All the State Governments are required to maintain a minimum balance with the Reserve Bank, which varies from state to state depending on the relative size of the state budget and economic activity. To tide over temporary mismatches in the cash flow of receipts and payments, the Reserve Bank provides Ways and Means Advances to the State Governments.

Ways and Means Advances: "Ways and Means Advances" (WMA) is not a commercial bank credit. It is a system under which the RBI provides credit to Central and State Governments for meeting temporary shortfall in government revenues as compared to the monthly expenditures. In other words, this facility is provided to meet temporary mismatches between revenue collections and revenue expenditures of governments. The maximum volume and period of such advances are governed by agreements between RBI and the concerned government. To the State Governments, this facility is extended under three categories known as (1) Normal WMA (2) Special WMA and (3) as an overdraft facility.

In brief, as a banker to the Government the RBI renders the following functions.

(*a*) Collects taxes and makes payments on behalf of the Government.

(*b*) Accepts deposits from the Government.

(*c*) Collects cheques and drafts deposited in the Government accounts.

(*d*) Provides short-term loans to the Government.

(*e*) Provides foreign exchange resources to the Government.

(*f*) Keeps the accounts of various Government departments.

(*g*) Maintains currency chests in treasuries at some importance places for the convenience of the government.

(*h*) Advises governments on their borrowing programmes.

(*i*) Maintains and operates Central Government's IMF accounts.

3. Agent and Adviser of the Government:

The RBI acts as the financial agent and adviser to the Government. It renders the following functions.

(*a*) As an agent to the Government, it accepts loans and manages public debts on behalf of the Government.

(*b*) It issues Government bonds, treasury bills etc.

(*c*) Acts as the financial adviser to the Government in all important economic and financial matters.

4. Banker to the Banks:

The RBI acts as banker to all scheduled banks. Commercial banks including foreign banks, co-operative banks and RRBs are eligible to be included in the second schedule of RBI Act subject to fulfilling conditions laid down under sec 42 (6) of RBI Act. RBI has powers to delete a bank from the second schedule if the bank concerned fails to fulfil the laid down conditions such as erosion in paid up capital below the prescribed limits and the banks' activities became detrimental to the interest of depositors, etc.,

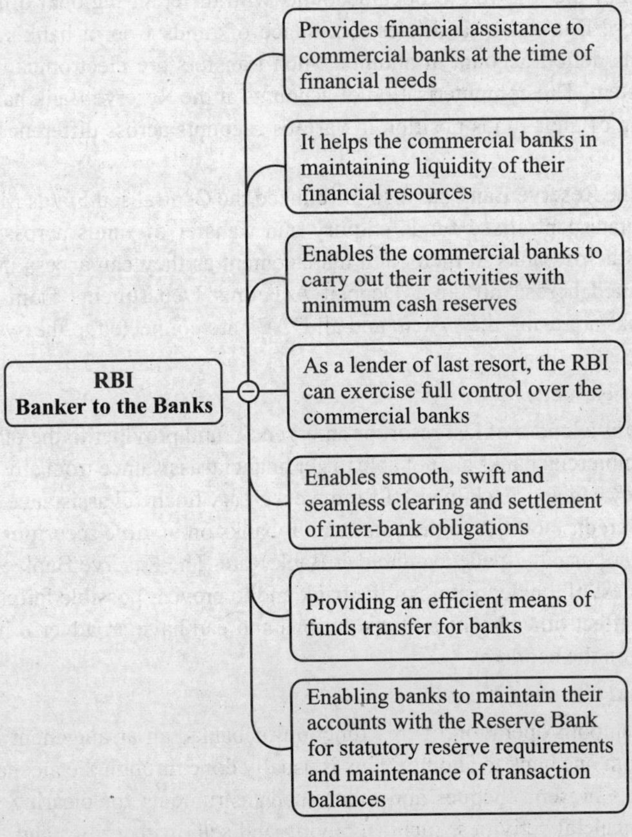

All banks in India, should keep certain percentage of their demand and time liabilities as reserves with the RBI. This is known as Cash Reserve Ratio or CRR. They also maintain Current Account with RBI for various banking transactions. This centralization of reserves and accounts enables the RBI to achieve the following:

(*a*) Regulation of money supply credit.

(*b*) Acts as custodian of cash reserves of commercial banks.

(*c*) Strengthen the banking system of the country.

(*d*) Exercises effective control over banks in Liquidity Management.

(*e*) Ensures timely financial assistance to the Banks in difficulties.

(*f*) Gives directions to the Banks in their lending policies in the public interest.

(*g*) Ensures elasticity in the credit structure of the country.

(*h*) Quick transfer of funds between member banks.

To fulfill the function as banker to the banks, the Reserve Bank opens current accounts of banks with itself, enabling these banks to maintain cash reserves as well as to carry out inter-bank transactions through these accounts. Inter-bank accounts can also be settled by transfer of money through electronic fund transfer system, such as, the Real Time Gross Settlement System (RTGS).

The Reserve Bank continuously monitors operations of these accounts to ensure that defaults do not take place. Among other provisions, the Reserve Bank stipulates minimum balances to be maintained by banks in these accounts. Since banks need to settle funds with each other at various places in India, they are allowed to open accounts with different regional offices of the Reserve Bank. The Reserve Bank also facilitates remittance of funds from a bank's surplus account at one location to its deficit account at another. Such transfers are electronically routed through a computerised system. The computerisation of accounts at the Reserve Bank has greatly facilitated banks' monitoring of their funds position in various accounts across different locations on a real-time basis.

In addition, the Reserve Bank has also introduced the Centralised Funds Management System (CFMS) to facilitate centralised funds enquiry and transfer of funds across Deposit Accounts Department. This helps banks in their fund management as they can access information on their balances maintained across different Deposit Accounts Departments from a single location. Currently, 75 banks are using the system and all DADs are connected to the system. (*Source*: RBI Publications).

5. Lender of Last Resort:

The RBI acts as a lender of last resort or emergency fund provider to the other member banks. As such, if the commercial banks are not able to get financial assistance from any other sources, then as a last resort, they can approach the RBI for the necessary financial assistance. In such situations, the RBI provides credit facilities to the commercial banks on eligible securities including genuine trade bills which are usually made available at Bank Rate. The Reserve Bank extends this facility to protect the interest of the depositors of the bank and to prevent possible failure of a bank, which in turn may also affect other banks and institutions and can have an adverse impact on financial stability and thus on the economy.

6. Acts as National Clearing House:

To facilitate smooth operation of this function of banks, an arrangement has to be made to transfer money from one bank to another. This is usually done through the mechanism of a clearing house where banks present cheques and other such instruments for clearing. Many banks also engage in other financial activities, such as, buying and selling securities and foreign currencies. Here too, they need to exchange funds between themselves. In order to facilitate a smooth inter-bank transfer of funds, or to make payments and to receive funds on their behalf, banks need a common banker.

RBI acts as the clearing house for settlement of banking transactions. This function of clearing house enables the other banks to settle their inter bank claims easily. Further it facilitates the settlement economically. Where the RBI has no offices of its own, the function of clearing house is carried out in the premises of the State Bank of India. The entire clearing house operations carried on by RBI are computerised.

The retail payments system in India comprising of paper based and electronic systems, handle large volume of transactions. These relate to various customer segments spread across the country. The cheque clearing is the dominant retail payment system in India. The model rules and regulations are prescribed by RBI and are adopted by the clearing houses spread across the country.

In order to meet the above objectives, in India, the Reserve Bank provides banks with the facility of opening accounts with itself. This is the 'Banker to Banks' function of the Reserve Bank, which is delivered through the Deposit Accounts Department at the Regional offices. The Department of Government and Bank Accounts oversees this function and formulates policy and issues operational instructions to Deposit Accounts Department.

7. Acts as the Controller of Credit:

The RBI controls the credit creation by commercial banks. For this, the RBI uses both quantitative and qualitative methods. The important methods used by RBI are,

(*a*) Bank Rate Policy
(*b*) Open Market Operation
(*c*) Variation of Cash Reserve Ratio
(*d*) Fixing Margin Requirements
(*e*) Moral Suasion
(*f*) Issue of Directives
(*g*) Direct Action

By controlling credit, the RBI achieves the following:

(*i*) Maintains the desired level of circulation of money in the economy.
(*ii*) Maintains the stability in the price level prevailing in the economy.
(*iii*) Controls the effects of trade cycles.
(*iv*) Controls the fluctuations in the foreign exchange rate.
(*v*) Channelise credit to the productive sectors of the economy.

8. Custodian of Foreign Exchange Reserves:

The RBI acts as the custodian of foreign exchange reserves. Adequate reserves may help maintain foreign exchange rates. In order to minimise the undue fluctuations in the rates it may buy and sell foreign currencies depending upon the situations. The Reserve Bank, as the custodian of the country's foreign exchange reserves, is vested with the responsibility of managing their investment. The legal provisions governing management of foreign exchange reserves are laid down in the Reserve Bank of India Act, 1934.

Its purchase and sale of foreign currencies from the market is done like commercial banks. However the objective of the RBI will not be profit booking. It may buy the foreign currency to build up adequate reserves or to arrest unwarranted rise in the value of rupee which may be due to sudden inflow of foreign currencies into India. It may also buy and sell foreign currencies in international market to switch the portfolio of investments denominated in different international currencies depending upon circumstances and needs.

The basic parameters of the Reserve Bank's policies for foreign exchange reserves management are safety, liquidity and returns. Within this framework, the Reserve Bank focuses on:

(*a*) Maintaining market's confidence in monetary and exchange rate policies.
(*b*) Enhancing the Reserve Bank's intervention capacity to stabilise foreign exchange markets.
(*c*) Limiting external vulnerability by maintaining foreign currency liquidity to absorb shocks during times of crisis, including national disasters or emergencies.

(*d*) Providing confidence to the markets that external obligations can always be met, thus reducing the costs at which foreign exchange resources are available to market participants.

(*e*) Adding to the comfort of market participants by demonstrating the backing of domestic currency by external assets.

9. Exchange Control:

When a country faces Balance of Payment of problems usually when its foreign exchange payments exceed foreign exchange receipts – it controls the whole gamut of forex (foreign exchange) transactions and regulates payment system for its advantage. Keeping in view the changed environment, the Foreign Exchange Management Act (FEMA) was enacted in 1999 to replace FERA with effect from June 1, 2000.

FEMA aimed at consolidating and amending the laws relating to foreign exchange with the objective of facilitating external trade and payments and for promoting the orderly development and maintenance of foreign exchange markets in India. Emphasising the shift in focus, the Reserve Bank in due course also amended (since January 31, 2004) the name of its department dealing with the foreign exchange transactions to Foreign Exchange Department from Exchange Control Department.

The Reserve Bank supervises the foreign exchange market in India. It supervises and regulates it through the provisions of the Foreign Exchange Management Act, 1999. Like other markets, the foreign exchange market has also evolved over time, and the Reserve Bank has been modulating its approach towards its function of supervising the market.

Issues licenses: The Reserve Bank issues licences to banks and other institutions to act as Authorised Dealers in the foreign exchange market. In keeping with the move towards liberalisation, the Reserve Bank has undertaken substantial elimination of licensing, quantitative restrictions and other regulatory and discretionary controls.

The Reserve Bank's exchange rate policy focuses on ensuring orderly conditions in the foreign exchange market. For the purpose, it closely monitors the developments in the financial markets at home and abroad. When necessary, it intervenes in the market by buying or selling foreign currencies. The market operations are undertaken either directly or through public sector banks.

10. Maintaining the Value of Currency:

The RBI, by its operation of credit control and price stability, maintains the internal value of domestic currency and ensures its stability.

11. External Value of Rupee:

In terms of preamble to RBI Act, the Bank is also required to maintain external, value of the Rupee. It however depends upon many factors like inflation levels, interest rates Balance of payments situation etc., ruling in different countries on which RBI does not have control. Earlier, till 1993 the RBI uses to prescribe the Exchange Rate of Rupee. The external value of rupee is now determined by market forces. RBI by virtue of its position as the Central Bank of the country and custodian of large forex reserves can influence the level of External Value in the short run.

12. Publishes the Economic Statistics and other Information:

The RBI collects statistics on economic and financial matters. It publishes periodically an analytical account of the operations of joint stock and co-operative banks. It presents the genuine financial position of the government and companies. The publications like the report on currency and finance, the report on the trend and progress of banking in India, the review of co-operative movement present a critical account and a balanced review of banking developments commercial, economic and financial conditions of the country.

13. Fights against Economic Crisis:

The RBI aims at economic stability in the country. Whenever there is a danger to the economic stability, it takes immediate measures to put the economy on proper course by effective policy changes and implementation thereof.

10.4.2 Promotional Functions

These are non-monetary functions. They include the following

1. Promotion of Banking Habits:

The RBI institutionalise saving through the promotion of banking habit and expansion of the banking system territorially and functionally. Accordingly RBI has set up Deposit Insurance Corporation in 1962, Unit Trust of India in 1964, the IDBI in 1964, the Agricultural Refinance Corporation in 1963, Industrial Reconstruction Corporation of India in 1972, NABARD in 1982 and the National Housing Bank in 1988 etc. It has helped to bring into existence several industrial finance corporations such as Industrial Finance Corporation of India, Industrial credit and Investment Corporation of India for industrialisation of the country. Similarly sector specific corporations took care of development in their respective spheres of activity.

2. Provides Refinance for Export Promotion:

The RBI takes the initiative for widening facilities for the provision of finance for foreign trade particularly of exports. The Export Credit and Guarantee Corporation (ECGC) and Exim Banks render useful functions on this line. To encourage exports the RBI is providing refinance facilities for export credit given by commercial banks. Further the rate of interest on export credits continues to be prescribed by RBI at a lower rate. The ECGC provides an insurance cover on Export receivables. EXIM Bank extends long term finance to project exporters and foreign currency credit for promotion of Indian exports. Students should know that many of these institutions were part of Reserve Bank earlier although they are currently functioning as separate financial institutions.

In recent years, with the liberalisation of real and financial sectors of the economy, interest rates on export credit have been rationalised within the overall monetary and credit policy framework. In order to provide adequate credit to exporters on a priority basis, the Reserve Bank has also prescribed a minimum proportion of banks' adjusted net bank credit to be lent to exporters by foreign banks.

3. Facilities for Agriculture:

Given the predominantly agrarian character of the Indian economy, the Reserve Bank's role has been to ensure timely and adequate credit to the agricultural sector at affordable cost. The scope and extent of priority sectors have undergone several changes since the formalisation of description of the priority sectors in 1972. The guidelines on lending to priority sector were revised with effect from April 30, 2007.

The guiding principle of the revised guidelines on lending to priority sector has been to ensure adequate flow of bank credit to those sectors of the society/economy that impact large segments of the population and weaker sections, and to the sectors which are employment-intensive, such as, agriculture and small enterprises. The broad categories of advances under priority sector now include agriculture, micro and small enterprises sector, microcredit, education and housing.

The RBI extends indirect financial facilities to agriculture regularly. Through NABARD it provides short-term and long term financial facilities to agriculture and allied activities. It established NABARD for the overall administration of agricultural and rural credit. Indian agriculture would have starved of a cheap credit but for the institutionalisation of rural credit by RBI.

The Reserve Bank was extending financial assistance to the rural sector mainly through contributions to the National Rural Credit Funds being operated by NABARD. It, however, extends cheap indirect financial assistance to the agricultural sector by providing large sums of money through General Line of Credit to NABARD.

Special Agricultural Credit Plan With a view to augmenting the flow of credit to agriculture, Special Agricultural Credit Plan (SACP) was instituted and has been in operation for quite some time now. Under the SACP, banks are required to fix self-set targets showing an increase of about 30 per cent over previous year's disbursements on yearly basis (April – March). The public sector banks have been formulating SACP since 1994. The scheme has been extended to Private Sector banks as well from the year 2005-06.

4. Facilities to Small Scale Industries:

The RBI takes active steps to increase the supply of credit to small industries. It gives directives to the commercial banks regarding the extension of credit facilities to small scale industries. It encourages commercial banks to provide guarantee services to SSI sector. Banks advances to SSI sector are classified under priority sector advances. SSI sector contributes to a very great extent to employment opportunities and for Indian Exports. Keeping this in view, RBI has directed commercial banks to open specialised SSI bank branches to provide adequate financial and technical assistance to SSI branches. Meeting the needs of small scale units, financial needs are one of the prime concerns of RBI.

With the enactment of the Micro, Small and Medium Enterprises Development (MSMED) Act, 2006, the services sector has also been included in the definition of micro, small and medium enterprises, apart from extending the scope to medium enterprises. The Act sought to modify the definition of micro, small and medium enterprises engaged in manufacturing or production and providing or rendering of services. Some of the major measures by RBI/GOI to improve the credit flow to the MSE sector are as under:

(*a*) Collateral Free Loans

(*b*) Credit Guarantee Scheme for Small Industries by SIDBI

(*c*) Specialised MSE Branch in every District

(*d*) Formulation of "Banking Code for MSE Customers

(*e*) Working Group on Rehabilitation/Nursing of Potentially Viable Sick SME Units

5. Helps Co-operative Sector:

RBI extends indirect financing to State co-operative banks thereby connects the co-operative sector with the main banking system of the country. The finance is mostly is routed through NABARD. This way the financial needs of agricultural sector are taken care of by RBI.

6. Prescription of Minimum Statutory Requirements for Banks:

The RBI prescribes the minimum statutory requirements such as, paid up capital, reserves, cash reserves, liquid assets etc. RBI prescribes reserves requirements both under Banking Regulation Act and RBI Act to ensure different objectives. For example, SLR prescription is done to ensure liquidity position of the bank. CRR prescription is done to have effective monetary control and money supply. Statutory Reserves Appropriation is done to ensure sound banking system etc., It also asks banks to set aside provisions against possible bad loans. With these functions, it exercises control over the monetary and banking systems of the country to ensure growth, price stability and sound banking practices.

10.4.3 Supervisory Functions

The Reserve Bank of India performs the following supervisory functions. By these functions it controls and administers the entire financial and banking systems of the country.

1. Granting Licence to Banks:

The RBI grants licence to the banks, which like to commence their business in India. Licences are also required to open new branches or closure of branches. With this power RBI can ensure avoidance of unnecessary competitions among banks in particular location evenly growth of banks in different regions, adequate banking facility to various regions etc. This power also help RBI to weed out undesirable people from starting banking business.

2. Function of Inspection and Enquiry:

RBI inspects and makes enquiry in respect of various matters covered under Banking Regulations Act and RBI Act. The inspection of commercial banks and financial institutions are conducted in terms of the provisions contained in Banking Regulation Act. These refer to their banking operations like loans and advances, deposits, investment functions and other banking services. Under such inspection RBI ensures that the banks & financial institutions carry on their operations in a prudential manner, without taking undue risk but aiming at profit maximisation within the existing rules and regulations. This type of inspection is carried on periodically once a year or two covering all branches of banks.

Banks are obliged to take remedial measures on the lapses/deficiencies pointed out during inspection. In addition RBI also calls for periodical information concerning certain assets and liabilities of the banks to verify that the banks continue to remain in good health. This type of inspection/verification is known as off-site inspection. The RBI team visiting bank offices to conduct verification of books and records is known as on-site inspection. RBI inspects banks under RBI Act only when there is a threat to close down a bank for mismanagement and there is a need to verify the fulfilment of conditions for the status of 'scheduled bank'. RBI presently conducts inspection of commercial banks, Development Financial Institutions like IDBI, NABARD etc., Urban co-operative banks and non-banking financial companies like Lease Financing Companies, Loan Companies.

3. Implementing the Deposit Insurance Scheme:

RBI Implements the Deposit Insurance Scheme for the benefit of bank depositors. This supervisory function has improved the standard of banking in India due to this confidence building exercise. Under this system, deposits up to ₹1.00 lakh with the bank branch are guaranteed for payment. Deposits with the banking system alone are covered under the scheme. For this purpose banking system include accounts maintained with commercial banks, co-operative banks and RRBs. Fixed Deposits with other financial institutions like IDBI etc., and those with financial companies are not covered under the scheme.

4. Periodical Review of the Working of the Commercial Banks:

The RBI periodically reviews the work done by commercial banks. It takes suitable steps to enhance the efficiency of the banks and make various policy changes and implement programmes for the well being of the nation and for improving the banking system as a whole.

5. Controls the Non-Banking Financial Corporations:

RBI issues necessary directions to the Non-Banking financial corporations and conducts inspections through which it exercises control over such institutions. Deposit taking NBFCs require permission from RBI for their operations.

10.5 RBI BALANCE SHEET

RBI prepares its Balance Sheet as on 30th June every year and requires transmitting copies thereof to Government of India in terms of Sec. 53 of RBI Act.

Two Segments:

RBI historically prepares its balance sheet under two segments of activities as required under RBI Act. One category pertains to its Notes/Currency issue functions and the other relating to its banking activities. The Note issue function is carried out by its Issue Department, hence separate items of Assets and Liabilities are prepared for this department. We can observe from the balance sheet given at the end of this chapter that the entire liabilities of Issue Department consist only of total notes/currency issued by RBI. The other segment *viz*. Banking Department part of balance sheet covers its other banking activities like loans and advances to Government ,scheduled banks, financial institutions, deposits from scheduled banks, etc.

The Financial Statements of RBI as at 30th June 2013, are given below:

Reserve Bank of India
Balance Sheet as at 30th June 2013
Issue Department (₹ thousands)

2011-12	*Liabilities*	*2012-13*	*2011-12*	*Assets*	*2012-13*
	Notes hold in the			Gold Coin and Bolian:	
80,169	Banking Department	80,169	760,006,797	(*a*) Hold in India	674,316,432
11,034,645,327	Notes in Circulation	12,016,157,427	–	(*b*) Hold outside India	–
			10,261,966,851	Foreign Securities	11,329,100,584
11,034,734,496	Total Notes Issued	12,016,237,596	11,022,063,648	Total	12,003,417,016
			2,206,548	Rupee Coin	2,956,280
			10,464,300	Government of India Rupee Securities	10,464,300
			–	Internal Bills of Exchange and other Commercial Paper	–
11,034,734,496	Total Liabilities	12,016,237,596	11,034,734,496	Total Assets	12,016,237,596

Banking Department (₹ thousands)

2011-12	*Liabilities*	*2012-13*	*2011-12*	*Assets*	*2012-13*
50,000	Capital paid-up	50,000	80,169	Notes	80,169
65,000,000	Reserve Fund	65,000,000	418	Rupee Coin	296
210,000	National Industrial Credit (Long Term Operations) Fund	220,000	125	Small Coin	63
1,950,000	National Housing Credit (Long Term Operations) Fund	1,960,000	–	Bills Purchased and Discounted :	–
			–	(*a*) Internal	–
			–	(*b*) External	–
				(*c*) Government Treasury Bills	
	Deposits				
	(*a*) **Government**		**3,640,273,093**	**Balances Hold Abroad**	**3,395,014,736**
1,004,903	(*i*) Central Government	1,002,895			
424,570	(*ii*) State Government	424,847			
	(*b*) **Banks**		**6,305,897,052**	**Investments**	**7,276,101,007**
3,419,536,741	(*i*) Scheduled Commercial Banks	3,391,427,816			

33,242,701	(*ii*) Scheduled State Co-operative Banks	32,038,844		**Loans and Advances to:**	
53,643,644	(*iii*) Other Scheduled Co-operative Banks	55,210,206	–	(*i*) Central Government	146,510,000
916,213	(*iv*) Non-scheduled State Co-operative Banks	2,241,459	7,307,400	(*ii*) State Government	21,449,487
92,870,015	(*v*) Other Banks	90,595,353			
				Loans and Advances to:	
122,045,831	(*c*) **Others**	**165,973,592**	167,962,800	(*i*) Scheduled Commercial Banks	187,170,300
			300,000	(*ii*) Scheduled State Co-operative Banks	–
			1,290,000	(*iii*) Other scheduled Co-operative Banks	1,650,000
270,361	**Bills Payable**	**1,873,179**	–	(*iv*) Non-scheduled State Co-operative Banks	–
			–	(*v*) NABARD	–
			28,902,408	(*vi*) Others	8,236,648
			–	**Loans, Advances and investments from National Industrial Credit (Long Term Operations) Fund:**	–
			–	(*a*) **Loans and Advances to:**	–
7,263,548,128	**Other Liabilities**	8,082,655,793	–	(*i*) Industrial Development bank of India	–
			–	(*ii*) Export Import Bank of India	–
			–	(*iii*) Industrial Investment Bank of India Ltd.	–
			–	(*iv*) Others	–
			–	(*b*) **Investments in bonds/ debentures Issued by:**	–
			–	(*i*) Industrial Development Bank of India	–
				(*ii*) Export Import Bank of India	
			–	(*iii*) Industrial Investment Bank of India Ltd.	–
			–	(*iv*) Others	–
				Loans, Advances and investments from National Housing Credit (Long Term Operations) Fund:	
				(*a*) Loans and Advances to National Housing Bank	
				(*b*) Investments in bonds / debentures Issued by National Housing Bank	
			902,599,552	Other Assets	854,531,276
11,054,712,107	Total Liabilities	11,890,873,984	11,054,712,107	Total Assets	11,890,873,984

Source: RBI Publications

Profit and Loss Account for the Year ended 30th June 2013 (₹ thousands)

2011-12	Income		2012-13
261,508,821	Interest, Discount, Exchange, Commission etc.		455,635,749
261,508,821	Total		455,635,749
	Expenditure		
587,780	Interest		25,725
29,934,972	Establishment		58,595,877
29,802	Director's and Local Board Member's Fees and Expanses		30,613
528,245	Remittance of Treasure		640,702
33,508,790	Agency Charges		28,066,536
27,037,058	Security Printing (Cheque, Note forms etc.)		28,724,406
257,177	Printing and Stationary		228,203
804,859	Postage and Telecommunication Charges		818,627
1,022,927	Rent, Taxes, Insurances, Lighting etc.		1,503,660
26,794	Auditor's Fees and Expenses		30,139
27,879	Law Charges		36,316
2,424,716	Depreciation and Repairs to Bank's Property		2,390,152
5,177,822	Miscellaneous Expenses		4,404,794
101,368,821	Total		125,495,750
160,140,000	Available Balance		330,140,000
	Loss: Contribution To:		
	National Industrial Credit (Long Term Operations) Fund	10,000	
	National Rural Credit (Long Term Operations) Fund*	10,000	
	National Rural Credit (Stabilisation) Fund*	10,000	
	National Housing Credit (Long Term Operations) Fund	10,000	
40,000			40,000
160,100,000	Surplus Payable to the Central Government		330,100,000

1. After making the usual or necessary provisions in terms of section 47 of the Reserve Bank of India Act, 1934 amounting to ₹ 287,940,115 thousands (2011-12 - ₹ 270,254,405 thousands).
2. These funds are maintained by the National Bank for Agriculture and Rural Development (NABARD).

Source: RBI Publications

REVIEW QUESTIONS

Short Answer Questions

1. Write a short note on RBI.
2. Write a brief note on the following:
   (*a*) RBI - Lender of last resort.
   (*b*) RBI - Custodian of foreign exchange reserves.
   (*c*) RBI - Monopoly of Note issue.
4. Write a short note on RBI's role on National Clearing House.

Essay Type Questions

1. Explain briefly the organizational structure of RBI.
2. Briefly explain the promotional functions of RBI.
3. Explain the role of RBI as agent and adviser of the Government.
4. Write a detailed note on the supervisory roles of RBI.
5. Explain in detail the various functions RBI.

CHAPTER 11

Reserve Bank of India and Credit Control

Reserve Bank of India has its objectives the maintenance of internal and external value of our currency and also the promotion of economic growth with reasonable price stability. It has to formulate suitable credit policies for achieving these objectives. The major function in this regard is the formulation and administration of the credit policy.

In recent years, the objectives of monetary policy in India has two folds:

(*a*) It has to facilitate the flow of adequate volume of bank credit to industry, agriculture & trade, and provide selective encouragement to the priority sectors for overall growth.

(*b*) To keep inflationary pressures under check, it has to restrain credit expansion and also ensure that credit is not diverted to undesirable purposes.

Controlled Expansion: As the Central Monetary authority, the Reserve Bank's main function is to ensure the availability of credit to the extent, that is appropriate to sustain the tempo of development and promote the maintenance of internal price stability. This policy of RBI is termed as "controlled expansion".

RBI has recognised the needs for expansion of credit and money supply for the rapid development and diversification of the economy. At the same time it was equally aware that an excessive expansion of money and credit could be clearly inflationary and would ultimately endanger the financial stability of the economy. The unlimited credit creation by the commercial banks poses a serious threat for maintenance of internal and external value of rupee and thereby to the national economy. Hence, it should be controlled and regulated at desired levels.

11.1 METHODS OF CREDIT CONTROL

As the custodian of cash reserves of the commercial banks, the RBI plays an important role in the control of credit created by the banks. For this, the RBI is vested with wide powers under RBI Act and Banking Regulation Act. The important methods adopted by RBI can be classified as under:

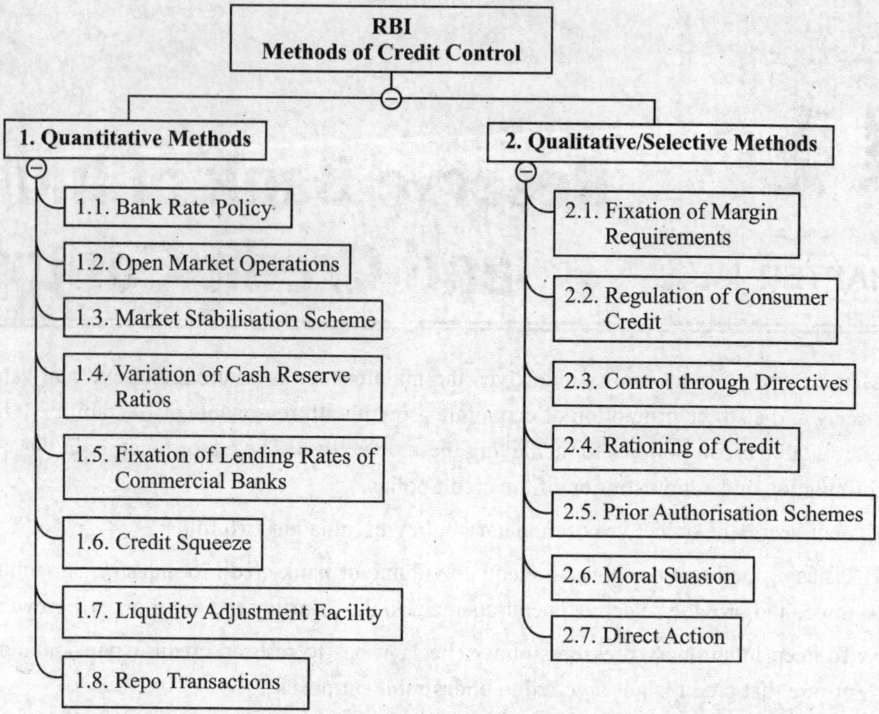

Let us discuss these methods here under:

11.1.1 Quantitative Credit Control by RBI

These methods are called traditional methods because they have been in use for decades. Through these methods, the credit creation is controlled by changing the cash reserves of commercial banks.

The methods of Bank Rate Policy, open market operations and variation of Cash Reserve Ratios are designed to effect the lendable resources of commercial banks either directly affecting their reserve base or by making the cost of funds cheaper or dearer to them. The important methods of this nature or explained herein below:

1. Bank Rate Policy:

According to the Reserve Bank of India Act, the Bank Rate is defined as " the standard rate at which the RBI is prepared to buy or rediscount bills of exchange or other commercial papers eligible for purchase under the provisions of the Act ".Thus, the bank rate is the rate of interest at which RBI rediscounts the first-class bills in the hands of commercial banks to provide them with liquidity in case of need. However, presently RBI does not accept any bills for re-discounting. This function is being done by separate financial institutions like DHFI created for similar purposes.

Bank Rate: It is the rate at which the Reserve Bank is ready to buy or rediscount bills of exchange or other commercial papers. It also signals the medium-term stance of monetary policy. Whenever the RBI provides refinance or other financial assistance to Commercial Banks, the rate of interest on such assistance is determined with reference to Bank Rate. The RBI also charges interest with reference to Bank Rate on 'ways and means' advances to governments. When Reserve Bank wants a reduction in general lending rates of Commercial Banks, it will signify its intention by reducing Bank Rate and vice versa. The rate is changed depending upon immediate monetary policy objectives.

Reserve Bank of India controls credit by affecting quantity and cost of credit money through its bank rate policy. But this method of credit control would be effective only when there is organized money market and commercial banks depend on reserve bank for their credit. Reserve Bank adopts Cheap Monetary Policy or Dear Monetary Policy according to the economic conditions of the country. RBI decreases bank rate to increase the quantity of the credit. This is called Cheap monetary policy. Decrease in bank rate decreases cost of credit *i.e.,* decrease in interest rate. As a result of this quantity of credit will increase. Under dear monetary policy, RBI increases bank rate to decrease quantity of credit in the country. Increase in bank rate increases cost of credit *i.e.,* increase the interest rate and this will in turn result in decrease in quantity or volume of the credit.

In simple terms, if the RBI wants to increase the liquidity and money supply in the market, it will decrease the bank rate and if it wants to reduce the liquidity and money supply in the system, it will increase the bank rate. It can be seen from the following table the movement of key policy rates as per RBI norms:

Ratios and Rates (Per cent)

Item/Week Ended	*2013*	*2014*				
	Sep. 27	*Aug. 29*	*Sep. 5*	*Sep. 12*	*Sep. 19*	*Sep. 26*
	1	2	3	4	5	6
Ratios						
Cash Reserve Ratios	4.00	4.00	4.00	4.00	4.00	4.00
Statutory Liquidity Ratio	23.00	22.00	22.00	22.00	22.00	2200
Cash-Deposit Ratio	–	–	4.70	–	4.76	–
Credit-Deposit Ratio	–	–	75.51	–	75.82	–
Incremental Credit-Deposit Ratio	–	–	34.37	–	38.01	–
Investment-Deposit Ratio	–	–	29.88	–	29.32	–
Incremental Investment-Deposit Ratio	–	–	50.80	–	41.00	–
Rates						
Policy Repo Rate	7.50	8.00	8.00	8.00	8.00	8.00
Reverse Repo Rate	6.50	7.00	7.00	7.00	7.00	7.00
Marginal Standing Facility (MSF) Rate	9.50	9.00	9.00	9.00	9.00	9.00
Bank Rate	9.50	9.00	9.00	9.00	9.00	9.00
Base Rate	9.80/10.25	10.00/10.25	10.00/10.25	10.00/10.25	10.00/10.25	10.00/10.25
Term Deposit Rate > 1 Year	8.00/9.00	8.00/9.05	8.00/9.05	8.00/9.05	8.00/9.05	8.00/9.05
Savings Deposit Rate	4.00	4.00	4.00	4.00	4.00	4.00
Call Money Rate (Weighted Average)	9.46	8.01	7.48	7.82	7.93	7.85
91-Day Treasury Bill (Primary) Yield	9.69	8.60	8.60	8.60	8.60	8.52
182-Day Treasury Bill (Primary) Yield	9.47	8.68	–	8.71	–	8.66
364-Day Treasury Bill (Primary) Yield	–	–	8.66	–	8.66	–
10-Year Government Securities Yield	8.71	8.57	8.54	8.51	8.47	8.45
RBI Reference Rate and Forward Premia						
INR-USS Spot Rate (₹ Per Foreign Currency)	61.81	60.47	60.44	60.84	60.81	61.57
INR-Euro Spot Rate (₹ Per Foreign Currency)	83.42	79.86	78.20	78.64	78.47	78.45
Forward Premia of US$ 1-month	10.97	9.82	8.44	8.38	9.47	8.38
3-month	9.93	8.47	8.54	8.51	8.49	8.32
6-month	9.04	8.43	8.54	8.45	8.42	8.22

Source: RBI Publications

Reasons for the Ineffectiveness of Bank Rate Policy in India:

The bank rate policy as an instrument of monetary control was not successful in India for a long time. The main factors responsible for this are, (*i*) Inherent inflexibility involved in the use of this instrument

(*ii*) The dominance of the Public Sector whose investment requirements are cost inelastic.

(*iii*) The higher rate of inflation experienced in the economy.

(*iv*) Restricted availability of refinance facilities to banks.

(*v*) As the government expenditure increase, the tax burden also increases. Under heavy taxation, the businessmen feel that the interest rate is a minor factor. And the decrease in the importance of interest rate has led to the decline in the importance of bank rate.

Even though the bank rate policy has not been effective in India, the Reserve Bank has been using it more and more as a weapon to control deflationary pressure in the economy. During the last few years, the bank rate has been reduced several times to combat the deflationary pressures in the economy. It can be seen form the above table that the rate was constantly at 6 percent for from 2004-09. And as of 5 May, 2011 the bank rate was 6%.

The effectiveness of this instrument can be improved by restructured monetary system. Particularly necessary steps are to be taken to develop an active money market in the economy. Further if banks' recourse to Reserve Bank accommodation rises, the RBI will be in a better position to influence banks' operation through Bank Rate Policy.

2. Open Market Operations:

Open market operations are outright sales/purchases of government securities, in addition to Liquidity Adjustment Facility, as a tool to determine the level of liquidity over the medium term. These operations are conducted by the RBI mainly with a view to manage short-term liquidity in the market. These operations directly or indirectly affect the reserves of the commercial banks and thereby the extent of credit creation is controlled.

Section 17 (8) of the Reserve Bank of India Act confers legal powers on the Reserve bank to use this instrument of monetary policy. Under this section the Reserve Bank is authorised to purchase and sell the securities of the Central or State Government of any maturity and the security of a local authority specified by the central government on the recommendation of its Central Board. However, at present the Reserve Bank deals only in the securities issued by the central government and not in those of State Governments and local authorities. It may be noted that in terms of section 33 of the Reserve Bank of India Act, securities issued by the State Governments or local bodies are not eligible to be used as reserve assets against note issue.

The Government securities market in India is narrow and is dominated by financial institutions especially by commercial banks. The Reserve Bank of India occupies a pivotal position in the market. It is continuously in the market, selling government securities of different maturities on tap; it stands ready to buy them in switch operations. The Reserve Bank of India does not ordinarily purchase securities against cash. There are no dealers in the market who are engaged in continuous sale and purchase of securities on their own account. Incidentally, it may be noted that the Reserve Bank effects purchases and sales from time to time out of the surplus funds of IDBI, EXIM Bank, and NABARD under special arrangement. The market, however, is served by stock brokers who act as intermediaries between prospective buyers and sellers of government securities. The Reserve Bank also enlists the services of brokers, if necessary.

The role of open market operation as an instrument of credit control will assume importance in the restructured monetary system. With the interest rate offered on government securities becoming truly competitive, a broad enough securities market may emerge for the Reserve Bank to use open market operations as an instrument of credit control. It will sell the securities in open market to drain out excess liquidity from the financial system and thereby contraction of credit. When it buys securities it injects additional funds into the market and consequently credit expansion may take place. "Repos" and "Reverse Repos" transactions may be considered a supplementary operation to these systems.

Open Market Operations in the form of outright purchase/sale of Government securities are an important tool of the Reserve Bank's monetary management. The Bank carries out such operations in the secondary market on the electronic Negotiated Dealing System – Order Matching (NDS-OM) platform by placing bids and/or taking the offers for securities. All the secondary market transactions in Government Securities are settled through Clearing Corporation of India Limited (CCIL). The entire settlement is under Delivery versus Payment mode. The netted funds settlement is carried out through members' Current Account maintained at the Reserve Bank and through Designated Settlement Bank for those members who do not maintain current account with the Reserve Bank.

Open market operations are used as supporting instrument of bank rate. This method is used to influence the flow of credit Sale and purchase of Government securities influence the cash reserve ratio with the commercial banks and hence these operations control their credit creation power. These operations will have both anti-inflationary and anti-deflationary effects. When the economy is faced with the inflationary pressures, the central bank would like the commercial banks to contract the supply of credit. To achieve this objective the RBI would sell the Government securities to the commercial banks. The banks would transfer a part of their cash reserve to the central bank towards the payment for these securities. Consequently the cash reserve with the commercial banks will be reduced. It would lead to a contraction in the credit creation power of the commercial banks.

Similarly, open market operations can also be used as anti-deflationary measures. In this situation, the central bank will purchase securities from the commercial banks. In the process the cash reserves with the commercial banks will increase and they would be enabled to create more credit. The open market operations in India are limited by Reserve Bank. The bank has used this policy only to make successful government debt policy and to maintain price stability of Government securities. It is used to fulfil seasonal credit requirements of commercial banks.

3. Market Stabilisation Scheme

The Market Stabilisation Scheme (MSS) was introduced in April 2004 under which Government of India dated securities/treasury bills could be issued to absorb surplus structural/durable liquidity created by the Reserve Bank's foreign exchange operations. MSS operations are a sterilisation tool used for offsetting the liquidity impact created by intervention in the foreign exchange markets. The dated securities/treasury bills are the same as those issued for normal market borrowings for avoiding segmentation of the market.

The issuances under MSS are matched by an equivalent cash balance held by the Government in a separate identifiable cash account maintained and operated by the Reserve Bank. These securities are also traded in the secondary market. By design, the MSS has the flexibility of not only absorbing liquidity but also of injecting liquidity, if required, through unwinding as well as buy-back of securities issued under the MSS.

4. Variation of Reserve Ratios

Reserve Ratio means that The Reserve Bank requires banks to maintain a certain amount of cash in reserve as a percentage of their deposits to ensure that banks have sufficient cash to cover customer withdrawals. RBI adjust this ratio on occasion, as an instrument of monetary policy, depending on prevailing conditions. Its centralised and computerised system allows for efficient and accurate monitoring of the balances maintained by banks with the Reserve Bank.

The Reserve Bank traditionally relied on direct instruments of monetary control such as Cash Reserve Ratio (CRR) and Statutory Liquidity Ratio (SLR). Under this requirement, certain percentage of Deposit liabilities of banks is impounded in cash form with RBI and/or to be maintained in liquid assets like government securities. The reserve requirements were originally evolved as a means for safeguarding the interests of depositors. Later it was developed as an instrument of credit control. The variation in the reserve requirements has the effect of increasing or decreasing the funds available with commercial banks for lending. In India, the reserve requirements are of two types. They are,

(*a*) The Cash Reserve Ratio, and

(*b*) The Statutory Liquidity Ratio

Cash Reserve Ratio indicates the quantum of cash that banks are required to keep with the Reserve Bank as a proportion of their net demand and time liabilities. SLR prescribes the amount of money that banks must invest in securities issued by the government. That is, commercial banks are required to maintain a certain portion of their Net Demand and Time Liabilities in the form of cash with the Reserve Bank, called Cash Reserve Ratio (CRR) and in the form of investment in unencumbered approved securities, called Statutory Liquidity Ratio (SLR). The Reserve Bank also monitors compliance with these requirements by banks in their day-to-day operations.

(*a*) Cash Reserve Ratio: Under the provisions of the RBI Act, the Scheduled and non-scheduled banks were required to maintain a minimum amount of cash reserve with the Reserve Bank. The reserve is made out of demand and time liabilities at certain percentage fixed by the RBI. Section 42 (1) of the Act empowers the RBI to stipulate, by giving notification in the Gazette, the percentage of reserve, on the total net demand and time liabilities to be maintained by every banking company with RBI. In terms of Section 18 of RBI Act non-scheduled banks can maintain the cash reserve either with them or with RBI in cash.

The cash Reserve Ratio is required to be maintained in cash with RBI, in addition to the percentage to be maintained under the Statutory Liquidity Ratio. It was observed that the credit control instruments in the hands of RBI have been used to maintain the economic growth with controlled inflation and as a sharp knife to curb inflation. RBI has used this flexibility to ensure that institutional finances for productive purposes are not lacking.

The CRR is being gradually reduced after initiating banking sector reforms from 1994-95. The rate was 10.5 percent as on April 1999. It stands reduced to 10.0 percent from May 1999 and from November 1999 it stands further reduced to 9.0 per cent. Ever since financial sector reforms and market determined exchange for Rupee the RBI uses this instrument to influence liquidity in money market and thereby exchange rate fluctuations. In the recent past, when the exchange rate of rupee came under attack from bank speculators, it increased the CRR thereby impounding excess liquidity in the market. This policy helped RBI to maintain stable rate in short term.

During the financial year 2012-13, growth has slowed markedly, even as inflation remained above the Reserve Bank's comfort level. Monetary Policy has responded to this evolving growth-inflation dynamics through calibrated easing. After lowering the cash reserve ratio (CRR) by 125 basis points (bps) during Q4 of 2011-12, the Reserve Bank frontloaded a reduction in its repo rate by 50 bps in April 2012. Even as elevated inflation and the twin deficits have severely restricted the space for further easing of the policy rate since April 2012, subsequent measures were directed towards ensuring adequate liquidity to facilitate a turnaround in credit deployment to productive sectors for supporting growth. As part of liquidity management measures, the CRR was reduced in two stages by a further 50 bps in a pre-emptive manner to ease monetary and liquidity conditions. Also, the statutory liquidity ratio (SLR) of scheduled commercial banks (SCBs) was reduced to improve the credit conditions facing the private sector. It can be observed From the following Tables

Ratios and Rates (Per cent)

Item/Week Ended	2013				2014	
	Jan. 11	Dec. 13	Dec. 20	Dec. 27	Jan. 3	Jan. 10
	1	2	3	4	5	6
Ratios						
Cash Reserve Ratios	4.25	4.00	4.00	4.00	4.00	4.00
Statutory Liquidity Ratio	23.00	23.00	23.00	23.00	23.00	23.00
Cash-Deposit Ratio	5.17	5.16	–	4.95	–	–
Credit-Deposit Ratio	77.12	75.77	–	76.73	–	–
Incremental Credit-Deposit Ratio	68.46	56.98	–	65.94	–	–
Investment-Deposit Ratio	30.28	29.71	–	29.52	–	–
Incremental Investment-Deposit Ratio	38.44	29.60	–	27.79	–	–
Rates						
Policy Repo Rate	8.00	7.75	7.75	7.75	7.75	7.75
Reverse Repo Rate	7.00	6.75	6.75	6.75	6.75	6.75
Marginal Standing Facility (MSF) Rate	9.00	8.75	8.75	8.75	8.75	8.75
Bank Rate	9.00	8.75	8.75	8.75	8.75	8.75
Base Rate	9.75/10.50	10.00/10.25	10.00/10.25	10.00/10.25	10.00/10.25	10.00/10.25
Term Deposit Rate > 1 Year	8.50/9.00	8.00/9.05	8.00/9.05	8.00/9.05	8.00/9.05	8.00/9.05
Savings Deposit Rate	4.00	4.00	4.00	4.00	4.00	4.00
Call Money Rate (Weighted Average)	8.00	7.63	8.64	8.72	8.19	8.25
91-Day Treasury Bill (Primary) Yield	8.06	8.77	8.65	8.69	8.73	8.73
182-Day Treasury Bill (Primary) Yield	–	–	8.84	–	8.77	–
364-Day Treasury Bill (Primary) Yield	7.85	8.85	–	8.84	–	8.74
10-Year Government Securities Yield	7.82	8.91	8.80	8.94	8.82	8.75
RBI Reference Rate and Forward Premia						
INR-USS Spot Rate (₹ Per Foreign Currency)	54.54	62.13	62.24	62.06	62.41	61.94
INR-Euro Spot Rate (₹ Per Foreign Currency)	72.29	85.41	84.88	85.27	85.20	84.31
Forward Premia of US$ 1-month	7.37	9.08	9.25	9.28	8.46	9.30
3-month	7.04	9.01	8.74	8.64	8.40	8.52
6-month	6.60	8.72	8.42	8.60	8.20	8.14

Source: RBI Publications

Movements in Key Policy Variables (Per cent)

Effective since	Reverse Repo Rate	Repo Rate	Cash Reserve Ratio*	Statutory Liquidity Ratio*
1	2	3	4	5
May 3, 2011	6.25 (+ 0.50)	7.25 (+ 0.50)	6.00	24
June 16,2011	6.50 (+ 0.25)	7.50 (+ 0.25)	6.00	24
July 26, 2011	7.00 (+ 0.50)	8.00 (+ 0.50)	6.00	24
September 16,2011	7.25 (+ 0.25)	8.25 (+ 0.25)	6.00	24

October 25, 2011	7.50 (+ 0.25)	8.50 (+ 0.25)	6.00	24
January 28, 2012	7.50	8.50	5.50 (– 0.50)	24
February 13, 2012	7.50	8.50	5.50	24
March 10, 2012	7.50	8.50	4.75 (– 0.75)	24
April 17, 2012	7.00 (– 0.50)	8.00 (– 0.50)	4.75	24
June 18, 2012	7.00	8.00	4.75	24
August 11, 2012	7.00	8.00	4.75	23 (– 100)
September 22, 2012	7.00	8.00	4.50 (– 0.25)	23
November 3, 2012	7.00	8.00	4.50 (– 0.25)	23

Figures in parentheses indicate changes in policy rates/ratios.
* : Per cent of Net Demand and Time Liabilities.

***(b)* Statutory Liquidity Ratio:** The share of net demand and time liabilities that banks must maintain in safe and liquid assets, such as, government securities, cash and gold.

Objectives of SLR: The main objectives of SLR are as follows:

(*a*) To assure solvency of Commercial banks by compelling them to hold low risk assets up to the stipulated extent.

(*b*) To create or support a market for government securities in the economy which do not have a developed capital market and

(*c*) To allocate resources to government for augmenting the resources of the Public sector.

Banks like Regional Rural Banks may hold entire SLR requirements in the form of cash with the sponsor banks.

Under Sec 24 of the Banking Regulation Act 1949, RBI is empowered to stipulate the liquid assets every banking company is required to hold against their demand and time liabilities in addition to cash reserve requirement. Accordingly the banks both scheduled and non-scheduled have to maintain liquid assets in cash, gold or unencumbered approved securities amounting to not less than 25% of their net demand and time liabilities in India. This requirement of 25% can be increased by the RBI from time to time by a notification in the official Gazette. But the ratio so prescribed cannot exceed 40% (In the first half of 1986-87 the ratio was 37%). However, Regional Rural Banks, non-scheduled Banks and co-operative Banks are allowed to maintain statutory Liquidity Ratio at 25% only. Further, all banks are required to maintain this reserve only at 25% in respect of N.R.E accounts. Frome the above Table, it could be observed that the prescribed SLR on Commercial Banks in April 2009 stands at 24 percent of net demand and time liabilities (NDTL) of each bank. The NDTL is worked out twice in a month on reporting Fridays. The value of SLR securities for Balance Sheet purposes is determined not with reference to cost of their acquisition but, with reference to their market quotations.

Banks are required to submit position in regard to SLR to the Reserve Bank as on alternate Fridays every month, before the 20th of succeeding month. But the Reserve Bank can call for daily position in such form as it may prescribe. The movement of SLR can be seen in the Tables given in the previous point.

Effects of Statutory Liquidity Ratio:

The main purpose of prescribing SLR is to ensure the liquidity position of banks in meeting the withdrawal requirements of depositors. Since these funds are mostly invested in Government Securities they are considered to be highly liquid and also no risk of loss of value *i.e.,* they can be encashed at quick notice or immediately. One of the effects of SLR is to raise or lower the liquidity requirements of banks thus affecting their capacity to lend. In order to discourage the banks from contravening the liquidity provisions, the RBI may not allow the defaulting banks access to further refinance and may charge additional interest on their borrowings from it.

It is to be noted that stepping up SLR and CRR have the same effects, viz, they reduce the capacity of commercial banks to expand credit to business and industry and they are anti-inflationary.

4. Fixation of Lending Rates of Commercial Banks-BASE RATE:

The RBI controls the credit created by the commercial banks by fixing the lending rates of the banks. When the lending rates are fixed at higher level, the credit becomes costlier and it may lead to contraction of credit. Similarly when the rates are lowered, it may result into expansion of credit.

Besides controlling the rates of interest on the advances made by the banks, the RBI places certain restrictions on the grant of advances against term deposits. These relate to the quantum of advance that can be granted and the rate of interest to be charged. As such banks usually grant only up to 75% of deposit value by way of advance. However after introduction of banking sector reforms in October, 1994, RBI has allowed the banks to fix their own lending rates. The Reserve Bank no longer decides the lending rates of Commercial Banks from 1996. Each bank is however, required to fix a minimum lending rate known as Prime Lending Rate (PLR). All loans and advances of each bank is a mark-up over PLR *i.e.*, the bank will charge PLR plus 1 to 3 percent depending upon the customer risk and security offered for loan.

New System: RBI issued notification to the banks to change the old Prime Lending Rate (BPLR) and switch over to the Base Rate method. In order to make the credit market more transparent and ensure that banks pass on the lower cost of fund automatically to existing customers, RBI replaced the existing system of prime lending rate (PLR) to a new **Base Rate, which will be fixed on the basis of cost of funds.**

The Reserve Bank gave banks another six months till June 30 to adopt the new method for computing **base rate** — below which lenders are not allowed to extend loans. "Banks are permitted to change the benchmark and methodology used in the computation of **Base Rate** for a further period of six months, *i.e.* upto June 30, 2011," the RBI said in a notification. Earlier, banks were given time till December 31 to adopt the new method for computing base rate. Last April, the RBI had directed all the banks to switch to the base rate system with effect from July 1, from the then prevailing Benchmark Prime Lending Rates (BPLR) system. The minimum lending rate, or base rate, is intended to bring about more transparency in banks' lending operations.

In the existing system, banks are free to fix their PLRs. Most of the variable rate loans, like home loan and some of the term loans are pegged against PLR. This means, if the PLR is not changed, the loan rates remain the same.

Banks have taken advantage of existing PLR system at the cost of their borrowers. When interest rates increase, banks hike their PLRs immediately, leading to rise in the home loan rates. But, when interest rates fall, they don't reduce PLRs Because of this, the existing customers are not benefited by the lowering of the interest rates. However, banks pass on the benefit to new customers by increasing the discount against PLRs.

Under the new system, home loans and other variable loans will be pegged against a base rate. As the new base rate is fixed on the basis of cost of funds, any change in the interest rate will reflect in the base rate. And therefore, it will be automatically passed on to the existing customers also. At the same time, RBI has clearly said that the base rate will be minimum rate for all commercial loans and banks will not be permitted to resort to any rate below it. The circular said, base Rate shall include all those elements of lending rates that are common across all categories of borrowers.

5. Credit Squeeze:

When the bank rate policy has not been successful in controlling the expansion of credit, the method of credit squeeze is useful. Under this method, the maximum amount of bank credit is fixed at a certain limit. And, the maximum limit for commercial banks borrowing from the RBI is also fixed. The banks are not allowed to expand the credit beyond these limits. These limits may be fixed in general for all credits or may be sector-specific like for steel industry, textile industry, etc. But it should be noted that a general credit squeeze may make the trade and industry suffer even for legitimate purposes. Reserve Bank rarely applies credit squeeze of this nature these days.

6. Liquidity Adjustment Facility (LAF):

In the late 1990s, the Reserve Bank restructured its operating framework for monetary policy to rely more on indirect instruments such as Open Market Operations.. In addition, in the early 2000s, the Reserve Bank instituted Liquidity Adjustment Facility (LAF) to manage day-to-day liquidity in the banking system. These facilities enable injection or absorption of liquidity that is consistent with the prevailing monetary policy stance. The repo rate (at which liquidity is injected) and reverse repo rate (at which liquidity is absorbed) under the LAF have emerged as the main instruments for the Reserve Bank's interest rate signalling in the Indian economy. The armour of instruments with the Reserve Bank to manage liquidity was strengthened in April 2004 with the Market Stabilisation Scheme (MSS). The MSS was specifically introduced to manage excess liquidity arising out of huge capital flows coming to India from abroad.

7. Repo/Reverse Repo Rate:

These rates under the Liquidity Adjustment Facility (LAF) determine the corridor for short-term money market interest rates. In turn, this is expected to trigger movement in other segments of the financial market and the real economy.

The liquidity management operations are aimed at modulating liquidity conditions such that the overnight rates in the money market remains within the informal corridor set by the repo and reverse repo rates for the liquidity adjustment facility (LAF) operations. In a repo transaction, the Reserve Bank infuses liquidity into the system by taking securities as collateral, while in a reverse repo transaction it absorbs liquidity from the system with the Reserve Bank providing securities to the counter parties.

11.1.2 Qualitative/Selective Credit Control by RBI

The selective or qualitative credit control is intended to ensure an adequate credit flow to the desired sectors and preventing excessive credit for less essential economic activities. The RBI issues directives under section 21 of the Banking Regulation Act 1949, to regulate the flow of banks' credit against the security of selected commodities. It is usually applied to control the credit provided by the banks against certain essential commodities which may otherwise lead to traders using the credit facilities for hoarding and black marketing and thereby permitting spiralling prices of these commodities. The selective credit control measures by RBI are resorted to commodities like, wheat, sugar, oilseeds.

Methods of Selective Credit Control: The RBI adopts a number of credit control methods from time to time. The important methods are given here under.

1. Fixation of Margin Requirements on Secured Loans:

Here the term "margin" refers to that a portion of the loan amount which cannot be borrowed from bank. In other words, the margin money is required to be brought in by the borrower from his own sources. This much percentage of money will not be lent by banks. The RBI lowers the margin to expand the credit and raises margin to contract or control the credit for stock market operations.

This system was introduced in 1956. The RBI has been prescribing minimum margin for advances against commodities under selective credit control. To begin with there was a single margin for each commodity. Subsequently, separate margins have been stipulated on the basis of level of stocks, type of borrower, variety of commodity, nature of credit instrument and documents, regions, stocks earmarked for free sale or otherwise and public & private sectors.

The RBI made use of the weapon of regulation of margin requirements to check bank advances against food grains *i.e.*, cereals and pulses, selected oil seeds indigenously grown and oil thereof vanaspati and all imported oil seeds and vegetable oils, raw cotton, jute, sugar, gur and Khandsari, etc. The changes in the minimum margin requirements were effected mainly to discourage speculative hoarding tendencies and to check the rising prices of agricultural commodities.

2. Regulation of Consumer Credit:

The credit facilities provided by the banks to purchase durable consumer goods like cars, refrigerators, T.V., furniture, etc. is called as consumer credit. If consumer credit is expanded, it leads to the increase in production of consumer goods in the country. Such increased sale of consumer goods will affect savings of people and capital formation in the economy. Hence, RBI may control the consumer credit extended by the commercial banks. These days RBI does not use such credit control measure as increased consumption lead to more economic activity.

3. Control through Directives:

The Reserve Bank of India (Amendment) Act and the Banking Regulation Act has empowered the RBI to issue directives to a particular bank or to the banks in general in regard to the following:

(*i*) The purpose for which advances may or may not be made.

(*ii*) The maximum amount of advances that can be granted to any individual, firm or company.

(*iii*) The margins to be maintained on secured loans

(*iv*) The rate of interest to be charged, etc.

For example,

(*a*) Banks are not allowed to provide finance for speculative purposes in stock market operations or to deal in real estate business.

(*b*) No banks can make advances to a single borrower company beyond the fixed percent of its paid-up capital and reserves.

(*c*) Reserve Bank prescribes margin on advances made by banks against the security of Commodities covered under selective credit control measures like sugar.

(*d*) Advances made under DRI scheme should be only at interest rate prescribed by RBI *i.e.*, 4 percent per annum.

The RBI has used this weapon for many times to bring down the prices of agricultural commodities. The directives are issued by the RBI as supplement to the traditional weapons of control like the bank rate policy, open market operations.

4. Rationing of Credit:

This method is used to control the scheduled banks borrowings from the RBI. The RBI shows differential treatment in giving financial help to its member banks according to the purpose for which the credit is used. This is done by framing different eligibility rules for various kinds of paper, as well as offering differential rates of rediscount on different kinds of bills offered for rediscount. The RBI prescribed a lower rate of interest on advances to sectors like export trade, small scale industries and agriculture. Higher rate of interest was fixed for general loans.

5. Credit Authorisation Scheme:

Under this Scheme, the commercial banks have to obtain the RBI's prior approval for sanctioning any fresh credit of ₹1 crore or more to any single party in the private sector and for sanctioning any fresh credit of ₹5 crore or more to any single concern in the public sector. This measure was intended to ensure a uniform approach by all banks in regard to assessment and appraisal of large credits. The scheme has however, been discontinued from November 1988. Presently no authorisation is required from RBI for commercial banks sanctioning credit limit for normal business operations.

Originally this system was adopted to ensure that borrowers actually need that much credit facility and to find out the purposes for which it was required. It was also ensured that credit facility was not diverted for other than stated purposes.

6. Moral Suasion:

In addition to the methods of credit control as given above, the RBI has been exercising moral suasion on banks. Moral suasion is a means of strengthening mutual confidence and understanding between the monetary authority and the banks as well as financial institutions and, therefore, is an essential instrument of monetary regulation.

Either by holding meetings or by circular letters the RBI is persuading the banks to follow a particular line of action. In certain times a mere statement or speech by a top executive of RBI does this function. Following are the few examples for such line of action given to banks.

(*i*) To refrain from lending for speculative purposes.

(*ii*) To reduce the level of advances against certain commodities without prejudice to their assistance to industry.

(*iii*) To increase their investment in government securities.

(*iv*) To invest their liquid funds in the shares of State Electricity Boards, Land Development Banks, Industrial Finance Corporations.

(*v*) To achieve the target set in regard to lending to priority sectors. The nationalisation of the leading banks has enhanced the scope of this weapon in credit control.

(*vi*) To maintain exchange rate stability, mostly to arrest falling rate of rupee.

7. Direct Action:

When the moral suasion proves ineffective the RBI may have to use direct action on banks. The RBI is empowered to take certain penal actions against banks which do not follow the line of policy dictated by it. The banks in default will be made to suffer by way of the following:

(*i*) Levying penal interest rates on the defaulting banks.

(*ii*) Cancelling the licences of such banks (extreme step)

(*iii*) Refusing to grant refinance facilities to such banks

(*iv*) Putting lending restrictions on the banks.

(*v*) Not permitting opening of new branches for the banks.

(*vi*) Not allowing participation in money market, etc.

This method is essentially a corrective measure which may bring about some psychological pressure on the commercial banks to follow the RBI instructions.

Limitations of Selective credit controls in India:

The selective credit control suffers from the following limitations.

(*a*) The Banks find it difficult to ensure that the loans granted to businessmen are used for the purposes for which they are intended.

(*b*) Money once spent does not vanish into thin air. It will be re-spent again and again, depending on the size of the multiplier and extent of leakages. Though the banks can ensure that the credit granted by them is made use of in the first instance for purposes approved by them, they cannot have any control over the purposes for which the resulting additional purchasing power is spent. Thus, the purchasing power that has originated from the credit granted for a particular purpose may work its way into unwanted lines when it is spent over and over again.

(*c*) Selective credit control has the serious limitation that it can control only a small part of investment, on such lucrative and soon – get – rich commodities in as much as substantial volume of investments may be financed sources other than bank credit *e.g.,* unaccounted money. Further investment is largely financed by capital issues, undistributed profits, borrowing from non-banking institutions. Banking policy therefore can only have a very limited effect.

Directives are issued to banks only. Other providers of funds may not follow these directives.

Thus it should be noted that the **selective credit control is not competitive and alternative to the quantitative measures. They are complementary to the general traditional methods.** The credit control can be made more effectively by the comprehensive approach *i.e.*, including both quantitative and qualitative measures.

REVIEW QUESTIONS

Short Answer Questions:

1. Write a brief note on the credit policy of RBI.
2. Write a short note on the following in relation to credit control by RBI:
   (*a*) Bank Rate Policy
   (*b*) Open Market Operations
   (*c*) Variation of Cash Reserve Ratios
   (*d*) Credit Squeeze
   (*e*) 'Repo' Transactions
   (*f*) Liquidity Adjustment Facility
3. Explain briefly the following in relation to credit control by RBI:
   (*a*) Fixation of Margin Requirements
   (*b*) Regulation of Consumer Credit
   (*c*) Rationing of Credit
   (*d*) Prior Authorization Schemes
   (*e*) Moral Suasion

Essay Type Questions

1. Explain the methods of credit control followed by RBI.
2. What are the reasons for the ineffectiveness of Bank rate Policy in India?
3. Explain SLR and what are the effects of SLR.
4. What are the quantitative credit control measures of RBI? Explain.
5. What are the qualitative credit control measures of RBI? Explain.
6. Explain the meaning and importance of variation of cash reserve ratio of RBI.
7. What are open market operations of RBI? Explain.

12 CHAPTER RBI-Agricultural and Industrial Finance

In India, the Reserve Bank contributes to a great extent in the economic development in various ways. It assumes special responsibility in the development of agriculture and industry. The RBI concentrates more on these two vital sectors of the economy. RBI does not presently provide these finances directly.

12.1 RESERVE BANK OF INDIA AND AGRICULTURAL FINANCE

Agricultural development is regarded as a prerequisite of economic development of the country. The Reserve Bank of India realises the following basic contributions of the Agricultural sector in the overall economic development.

(*i*) Product contribution - making available food and raw material.

(*ii*) Market contribution - providing the market for producer goods and consumer goods produced in the non - agricultural sector.

(*iii*) Factor contribution - making available labour and capital to non – agricultural sector

(*iv*) Foreign exchange contribution.

Being the largest industry in the country agriculture is the source of livelihood for over 70% of population in the country. On recognising the fact that Agriculture is the foundation on which the entire super structure of the growth of industrial and other sectors of the economy has to stand, the RBI developed the agricultural sector in the following ways:

12.1.1 Agricultural Credit Department

According to section 54 of the RBI Act, it is required to set up a separate Agricultural credit department. With the formation of NABARD in 1982, all the activities of this Department have been transferred to NABARD. However, the Rural Planning and Credit Department in the Reserve Bank deals with the following agriculture related matters.

(*i*) To study and identify all issues relating to Agricultural credit for policy formulations.

(*ii*) To provide necessary advice to the Central and state Governments, NABARD, Commercial Banks and Co-operative Banks, in the area of Agricultural Credit and priority sector credit.

(*iii*) To co-ordinate with NABARD the activities of the banking sector relating to agricultural promotion.

(*iv*) To prepare suitable plans to improve agricultural development in the country.

(*v*) To help in the establishment of nationwide warehouse facilities for processing and market of agriculture produce etc.

(*vi*) To implement and monitor special rural schemes announced by Government of India for poverty alleviation and employment generation like IRDP schemes.

(*vii*) To monitor and guide successful operation of Lead Bank Schemes.

(*viii*) To prescribe policy measures for the operations of Regional Rural Banks.

(*ix*) To formulate policy for successful conduct of Banking ombudsman Scheme

(*x*) To assist in the formation of local area banks.

12.1.2 Funds for Agricultural Development

On the recommendations of the Rural Credit Survey Committee, the RBI Act was amended in 1955. As per the provisions of the new Act, the RBI has established two kinds of funds for the agricultural development. They are:

(*i*) National Agricultural Credit (Long term operations) Funds, and

(*ii*) National Agricultural Credit (stabilization) Fund.

The National Agricultural Credit (Long term Operation) Fund was started with an initial contribution of ₹10 crore. And, every year the RBI out of its profit has to contribute certain sum to this fund. It is used for the following purposes.

(*a*) providing loans and advances to state governments for subscribing to the share capital of co-operative credit institutions

(*b*) providing medium term loans to co-operative banks

(*c*) providing long term loans to central co-operative land development banks

(*d*) for purchasing the debentures of land development banks

The National Agricultural Credit (Stabilisation) Fund is started with the initial contribution of ₹1 crore. And every year the RBI has to contribute out of its profits certain sum to this Fund. This fund is used to provide loans to state co-operative banks to convert the short term loans (extended to rural farmers) into medium term loans during the period of natural calamities such as floods, famine *etc.*, Upon setting up the NABARD the operations on these funds were transferred to NABARD. However RBI continued to contribute very liberally to both the funds.

After the announcement of Banking Sector Reforms in 1993-94, Reserve Bank stopped contributing large sums to these funds. RBI now contributes only a token of ₹1 crore to each of these two funds. NABARD however transfers large sums out of its own profit. Further, with the establishment of NABARD, these Funds are redesignated as National Rural Credit Fund instead of Agricultural Credit Fund as advances are provided out of these Funds by NABARD for various rural developmental activities.

12.1.3 Financial Assistance to co-operative sector

The RBI does not provide agriculture finance directly to the farmers. It provides such financial facilities through NABARD which in turn provides financial assistance to the state co-operative banks so as to enable them providing credit to rural farmers.

(*i*). Short term loans to State co-operative banks: The short term loans are provided to the co-operative banks for financing seasonal agricultural operations and marketing of agricultural operations and marketing of agricultural produce at a concessional rate. It also helps the marketing societies in the form of providing working capital for purchasing, stocking and distribution of fertilisers, seeds, pesticides *etc.*, RBI makes available liberal finance to NABARD at concessional rate of interest for this purpose. The finance is provided through a General Line of Credit to NABARD.

(*ii*).Medium Term Credit to Co-operative banks: With part of RBI funds, NABARD extends medium term loans for the period up to 5 years to the state co-operative banks for financing for land improvements, land reclamation, purchase of machinery, construction of small irrigation works, dairy farming *etc.*,

If natural calamities such as earthquake, floods, fire, and famine occur, the farmers who availed short term loans from the co-operative banks cannot repay their loans in time. Under such circumstances, the RBI permits converting short term loans into medium term loans. These loans are sanctioned at concessional rates.

12.1.4 Establishment of Agricultural Credit Board

In order to co-ordinate the activities of co-operative credit institutions and policies and the functions of RBI, the RBI established a permanent consultative committee in 1951. On the recommendations of the "Rural Credit Survey Committee" it was reorganised in 1956. In 1965 the committee was renamed as "Rural Co-operative Credit Consultative Committee"

Again, in 1970 it was reorganised and renamed as "Agricultural Credit Board". The Governor of the RBI used to be the Chairman of this Board. The Board supervised and co-ordinated the activities of the RBI and other agencies and ensured the adequate and timely farm credit.

12.1.5 Establishment of NABARD

The Reserve Bank of India, in consultation with the Government of India, set up a Committee to Review Arrangement for Institutional Credit for Agriculture and Rural Development (CRAFICARD) in 1979 under the chairmanship of Shri.B. Shivraman. The CRAFICARD recommended that the NABARD be set-up. The objective was that such a national bank would be able to give undivided attention to the problems of providing production and investment credit to different rural sectors like agriculture, small scale and cottage industries and allied activities in an integrated manner. Based on this recommendation, the Government of India had set-up NABARD in July 1982.

Ever since NABARD began functioning, the different functions of the Reserve Bank of India relating to agricultural finance are now performed by NABARD. The entire refinancing work for rural credit has now been transferred to NABARD. The Agricultural Refinance and Development Corporation (ARDC) has been merged with the NABARD. The National Agricultural Credit (long-term Corporation) Fund and National Agricultural Credit (Stabilisation) Fund have been transferred to NABARD. These funds are now called National Rural Credit (Long-term Operations) Fund and National Rural credit (Stabilisation) Funds. Central and State Governments also contribute to the funds. The main function of NABARD are discussed below:

NABARD provides refinance to State Co-operative Banks, Regional Rural Banks, State Land Development Banks, State Government and commercial banks as indicated below:

NABARD Credit Functions

NABARD provides different types of refinance to the following eligible institutions:

1. Short-term Credit: Eligible Institutions

(*a*) State Co-operative Banks(SCBs)

(*b*) Regional Rural Banks (RRBs)

(*c*) Other financial institutions approved by RBI

Purposes of Short-term Credit: The purposes include the following:

(*a*) Seasonal agricultural operations and marketing of crops

(*b*) Marketing & distribution of inputs like fertilizers, pesticides, etc.

(*c*) Any other activity connected with rural/agricultural sector.

(*d*) Bonafide commercial trade transactions.

(*e*) Production & Marketing activities of (*i*) Artisans, (*ii*) Small-scale Industries, (*iii*)Village & Cottage Industries, (*iv*) Handicrafts, (*v*) Sericulture, (*vi*) Handlooms *etc.*

Period : Upto 15 months.

2. Medium-term Credit: Eligible Institutions:

(*a*) State-Co-operative Banks (SCBs)

(*b*) State Land Development Banks (SLDBs)

(*c*) Regional Rural Banks (RRBs)

(*d*) Other financial institutions approved by RBI.

Purposes of Medium-term Credit: Any investment connected with agriculture and rural sector requiring MT credit assistance.

Period: Between 18 months and 7 years.

3. Long-term Credit: Eligible Institutions:

(*a*) State Land Development Banks (SLDBs)

(*b*) Regional Rural Banks (RRBs)

(*c*) Commercial Banks (CBs)

(*d*) State Co-operative Banks (SCBs)

(*e*) Other financial institutions approved by RBI.

Purposes of Long-term Credit

(*a*) Refinance for investment in agriculture and allied activities such as minor irrigation, land development, soil conservation, dairy, sheep, poultry, piggery, farm mechanization, plantation/horticulture, forestry, fishery, storage and market yards, agricultural aviation, biogas and other alternative sources of energy, sericulture, apiculture, animals and animal driven carts, agro-processing, agroservices centres, compost plants, modern abattoirs, pumpsets, energisation etc.

(*b*) Refinance for artisans/small-scale industries/tiny sector industries, village & cottage industries, handicrafts, etc. (Non-farm Sector).

(*c*) Loans to State Governments for share capital contribution to co-operative institutions.

(*d*) Investment in share capital/securities of institutions concerned with agriculture and rural development.

Period: Available upto a maximum of 25 years.

4. Conversion & Rescheduling facilities

NABARD provides refinance to eligible institutions Normally for SCBs and RRBs for conversion and rescheduling of loans under conditions of drought, famine or other natural calamities, millitary operations, enemy action etc. Similar facilities are also available in respect of loans made to artisans, small-scale industries.

Period: Generally not exceeding a period of 7 years.

5. Financing cottage/villages/small scale industries, *etc.*,

All such industries located in 'rural areas' will be eligible for refinance from NABARD.

6. Refinance Facilities

NABARD provides refinance for various purposes like minor irrigation,land development, farm mechanisation, plantation / horticulture poultry / sheep / piggery, fisheries, dairy development, storage and marketing yields, forestry, gobar-gas plants, non-farm sector, IRDP, etc. About 80-82 percent of disbursements are made for farm sector. Loans provided to small and marginal farmers and other weaker sections of the society enjoy major share of refinance support from NABARD, nearly 80 percent of the refinance disbursed for the purposes which are relevant for rural households. NABARD also encourages scheduled castes/tribes corporations to formulate special action plan outside. IRDP Scheme for SC/ST beneficiaries for which refinance is given under Action Plans.

7. Assistance to Co-operative Banks in SFDA and MFAL

Small Farmers Development Agency (SFDA) and Marginal Farmers and Agricultural Labourers (MFAL):- To bridge the gap between the small and big farmers, which is likely to be widened in the course of induced development, the All India Rural Credit Review Committee recommended the setting up two agencies, namely, the SFDA and the MFAL, in 1970-71.

The SFDA assists small farmers in the matter of irrigation facilities, land improvement, technical know-how with a view to changing the farms into progressively prosperous and viable units. Those holding between 1.25 and 2.5 acres of wet lands or 2.5 and 5 acres of garden lands are described as small farmers. Marginal farmers are those having 1.25 acres of wet lands or 2.5 acres of garden lands. Agricultural labourers comprise those having a homestead and earning 50 percent or more of their income from agricultural labour wages.

The scheme aims at enabling these farmers to maximise production on their small holdings and to take up subsidiary occupations like poultry and sheep breeding which generate additional income. Credit will be channelised through co-operative institutions at the apex and at the primary levels. The scheme also envisages the development of co-operative marketing by linking up cultivation credit with marketing.

The NABARD used to help the co-operative banks in the project of MFAL and SFDA. By this assistance it fulfils the credit needs of economically weak farmers.

8. Reform measures for Regional Rural Banks

The Regional Rural Banks have come a long way since their inception in 1975 and have now become an integral part of the rural financial system. As a part of financial sector reforms, the RBI along with government of India and NABARD initiated various measures since 1994 for improving the performance and operations of Regional Rural Banks. The noteworthy measures among them are : Removal of the condition relating to 100 percent of lendings to 'target group' ; Providing investment avenues like bonds, share, units of Mutual Funds; Permission to undertake fee-based services like guarantee issuance, locker-room facility, issue of drafts etc.

9. Promotion of Warehouse Facilities

The RBI subscribed to the share capital of Central and State Warehousing Corporations. This enables the corporations to establish warehouses at various places of the country. The farmers can avail loan facilities from the banks against warehouse receipts.

10. Other Facilities to Agriculture

Besides the above specific facilities, the RBI assists the Government of India and NABARD in the formulation and implementation of various schemes meant for agriculture and rural development. Such schemes include the following:

(*a*) Intensive agricultural district programme
(*b*) Intensive agricultural area programme
(*c*) High yielding varieties programme
(*d*) Integrated rural development programme
(*e*) community development programme
(*f*) Drought prone area programme
(*g*) Integrated dry land agriculture development programme *etc.*,

12.1.6 National Agricultural Insurance Scheme

Government of India in July 1999 introduced an Agricultural Insurance Scheme. Farmers availing of seasonal agricultural operations, loans from financial institutions/banks will be covered under the scheme compulsorily. Under the scheme risk insurance will be provided by the Government to cover farmers yield losses arising on their crops due to non-preventable risks like:

(*i*) Natural fire and lightening

(*ii*) Storm, cyclone etc.

(*iii*) Flood, landslide

(*iv*) Drought, dry spells and

(*v*) Pest/diseases etc.

The scheme covers crops like sugarcane, potato, cotton and even pulses. The scheme will be implemented through General Insurance Corporation of India (GIC) in co-ordination with commercial banks, co-operative banks and regional rural banks. This scheme is known as "Rashtriya Krishi Bima Yojana" in Hindi.

The significance of agriculture in India arises also from the fact that the development of agriculture is an essential condition for the development of the national economy. The planned programme for agriculture in India is of recent origin. Because of the vital role played by RBI and subsequently by NABARD, the following benefits are obtained:

(*i*) There is a steady increase in the area under cultivation

(*ii*) There is a steady rise in average yield per hectare, or rise in agricultural productivity and

(*iii*) As a result of an increase in the area as well as increase in yield per hectare, total production of all crops recorded a rising trend.

The following tables show the details of advances extended to agriculture by the banking sector in India:

Outstanding Agricultural Advances

(Amount in Rupees crore)

A on the last Reporting Friday of March	*Public Sector Banks* Amount Outstanding	Percent of Net Bank Credit	*Private Sector Banks* Amount Outstanding	Percent of Net Bank Credit
1	2	3	4	5
2003	70,501	14.5	9,924	10.9
2004	84,435	15.1	14,730	12.7
2005	1,09,917	15.3	21,636	12.3
2006	1,55,220	15.3	36,712	13.6
2007	2,02,614	15.4	52,034	12.7
2008	2,49,397	17.5	58,567	15.4
2009*	2,98,211	17.2	76,062	15.9

* · Data are provisional.

Note: The target to advances to agriculture was 18.0 percent of net bank credit for the domestic banks. The target has been linked to ANBC or credit equivalent of OBE, whichever is higher, with effect from April 30, 2007.

Targets and Actual Disbursement to Agriculture by Banks

(Amount in Rupees crore)

Agency	2004-05		2005-06		2006-07		2007-08		2008-09	
	Target	Disbursement	Target	Disbursement	Target	Disbursement	Target	Disbursement	Target	Disbursement
1	2	3	4	5	6	7	8	9	10	11
Commercial Banks	57,000	81,461	87,200	1,25,477	1,19,000	1,66,486	1,50,000	1,81,088	1,95,000	2,23,663
Co-operative Banks	39,000	31, 231	38,600	39,786	41,000	42,480	52,000	48,258	55,000	36,762
RRBs	8,500	12,404	15,200	15,223	15,000	20,435	23,000	25,312	30,000	26,724
Other Agencies*	-	193	-	-	-	-	-	-	-	-
Total	1,04,500	1,25,309	1,41,000	1,80,486	1,75,000	2,29,401	2,25,000	2,54,658	2,80,000	2,87,149

* : Co-operative societies, State Financial Corporations, Agricultural Development Finance Corporation.

Source: NABARD.

12.2 RESERVE BANK OF INDIA AND INDUSTRIAL FINANCE

The Reserve Bank does not provide direct finance for industrial activity. The financing of industrial activity is done by financial institutions and banks. The Reserve Bank however provided refinance and financial assistance to certain financial institutions and to commercial banks' industrial lendings. Presently, RBI provides refinance only towards export credit made by banks. The Reserve Bank of India, however plays a vital role in the field of industrial finance. The economic development in modern times has come to be associated with industrialisation. The industrial growth largely depends upon the availability of financial facilities. The money market, mainly for short term finance provides working capital to industry and commerce whereas the capital market primarily for long term finance provides block or fixed capital to business. These two markets are collectively called market of credit. The RBI has associated with the Government of India for the establishment of specialised financial institutions as an integral part of the capital market. The commercial banks were neither willing nor competent to provide long term loans to Indian Industries as bulk of their funds were in the form of short term or demand deposits. Thus, RBI realised the need for setting up financial institutions which can specialise in offering long term financial assistance to industry.

12.2.1 Establishment of Institutional Framework for Industrial Finance

The RBI has played an active role in the field of Industrial Finance. Its most notable contribution has been in establishing a broad institutional frame work to cater to the medium and long-term needs of finance to industrial sector. Some of the institutions in this category for the establishment of which the RBI was responsible are as follows.

(*a*) Industrial Finance Corporation

(*b*) Industrial Development Bank of India

(*c*) State Finance Corporations

(*d*) National Industrial Development Corporation

(*e*) State Industrial Development and Investment Corporation

(*f*) National Small Industries Corporation

(*g*) Unit Trust of India

(*h*) Industrial Reconstruction Corporation of India

(*i*) Industrial Refinance Corporation of India

(*j*) Credit Guarantee Scheme through Export Credit Guarantee Corporation, Export Import Bank of India *i.e.*, EXIM Bank.

12.2.2 Transfer of Loan Accounts from one Bank to Another

The RBI had laid down certain procedural guidelines/safeguards relating to the transfer of loan accounts by borrowers from one bank to another. These were issued in June,1977 in pursuance of the recommendations contained in the reports of the Committee on Transfer of Loan Accounts appointed by the Bank.

12.2.3 Bridge Loan

Companies approach banks for provision of bridge loans so as to expedite on going capital work, pending disbursal of financial assistance from All India Financial Institutions or against expected equity issues. In November 1975, banks were advised that bridge loans could be granted to companies without prior authorization of RBI, against the committed financial assistance form the All India Financial Institutions. However, subsequent to the submission of the Report of the Committee to review the working of the Credit Authorisation Scheme (Marathe Committee)in March 1985, it was made compulsory for banks to take prior authorization from RBI before granting bridge loans.

12.2.4 Prompt Settlement of Bills of Small Scale Industrial Units

With a view to ensuring prompt settlement of dues of small scale industrial units as also encouraging bills culture, banks have been advised to ensure with effect from Jan. 1,1998, that the corporate borrowers finance their domestic credit purchases from small scale industrial units, atleast to the extent of 25 percent by way off acceptance of bills drawn on them by the suppliers. Banks have been advised to monitor compliance with this requirement through the information system designed by them and charge penal interest in cases of non-compliance.

12.2.5 Role of RBI in Rehabilitation of Sick Industrial Units

The RBI co-ordinates the efforts of banks, financial institutions and government agencies in the rehabilitation of such units. A single window concept for lending has been introduced and made mandatory by the bank in respect of fresh disbursement under working capital as also for disbursement of rehabilitation term loan and subsequent disbursement of working capital under the sanctioned credit limits to facilitate easy and quick disbursal of funds to sick/ weak industrial units at a single source.

12.2.6 High Level Committee on Credit to SSI

The one-man committee on SSI headed by Shri S.L.Kapur, appointed by RBI to review the credit delivery system to SSIs and suggest measures for its improvement. The Committee has made in all 126 recommendations covering wide range of areas pertaining to financing of SSI sector. The RBI examined these recommendations and advised banks to take necessary steps for immediate implementation. The more important among these are:

(*i*) Delegation of more powers to branch managers to grant adhoc limits.

(*ii*) Simplification of application forms

(*iii*) Freedom to banks to decide their own norms for assessment of credit requirements

(*iv*) Opening of more specialised SSI branches

(*v*) Enhancement in the limit for composite loans to ₹5 lakhs

(*vi*) Strengthening the recovery mechanism.

12.2.7 Export Finance

One of the important areas of industrial finance is Export Credit Export finance is a preferred finance for the Central Bank and the country because this sector earns valuable foreign exchange. Hence the RBI continues to prescribe a preferential rate of interest on export finance. Not only a reduced rate of interest but also exporters avail of a number of benefits against their exports like tax exemption, facility to maintain foreign currency accounts, *etc.*, The RBI also provides refinance facility to commercial banks against their outstanding export credit. The RBI itself does not extend any credit facility to exporters but provide indirect incentives and benefits like cheap credit, adequate credit, refinance facilities, foreign exchange accounts, *etc.*, As per RBI guidelines commercial banks have to extend export credit facilities to all genuine exporters. It is normally granted on the strength of Letter of credit received from overseas buyers.

Types of Credit: The credit is granted under two stages.

(*a*) **Preshipment Credit**: Before shipment of goods – for the purposes of procurement of raw materials, purchasing them and arranging for the transportation of goods. This type of facility is known as Preshipment finance or packing credit. It is normally extended for a maximum period of 180 days at concessional rate. The credit can be availed of by exporters either in India Rupee or in foreign currency. However, repayment for foreign currency credit should be made in foreign currency out of export sale.

(*b*) **Post-Shipment Credit:** This credit is extended by banks after shipment of goods. It is in the form of discounting or purchasing the bills drawn by the exporters on overseas buyers. When a customer avails of Preshipment Credit, automatically post shipment credit will be utilised to repay the earlier credit. Under post-shipment credit, the RBI prescribes a lower rate of interest for earliest period of export realisations – usually within 90 days of shipment. All export sales should be realised as per RBI guidelines, within 180 days of shipment. The rate of interest on post-shipment credit increases as the period of realisation becomes longer. It is because the RBI desires to encourage those exporters who will bring in foreign exchange at the earliest.

(*c*) **Priority Sector:** Foreign banks' advances to export sector are considered as priority sector advances. Banks are directed not to reject any export credit proposal unless such decision is taken at higher levels in the bank. The preferential lower rate of interest is charged on export credit. The Reserve Bank, many a times, changes the rate depending upon general level of interest rate and export performance.

12.2.8 Foreign Exchange Benefits

The RBI allows exporters to retain a part of (usually 50 percent)the foreign exchange earned by exporters in our account known as EEFC A/c. (Exchange Earner's Foreign Currency Account). It allows commercial banks to sell foreign exchange to exporters for various business purposes including for foreign tours.

In these ways the RBI renders valuable services in the promotion of industries and commerce in India. The following Tables give a clear picture of it.

RESERVE BANK OF INDIA AND INDUSTRIAL FINANCE

(Rupees crore)

Year	*Long-term finance oustanding*								*Short-term finance oustanding*			
	IDBI	*SIDBI*	*EXIM Bank*	*IIBI*	*NHB*	*IFCI*	*SFCs*	*ICICI*	*IDBI*	*SIDBI*	*SFCs*	*DFHI*
1	2	3	4	5	6	7	8	9	10	11	12	13
1971	60	-	-	0	-	2	2	0	0	-	1	-
1972	118	-	-	0	-	2	4	0	0	-	0	-
1973	135	-	-	0	-	0	4	0	0	-	0	-
1974	204	-	-	0	-	0	5	0	0	-	0	-
1975	320	-	-	0	-	0	9	0	11	-	0	-

1976	385	-	-	0	-	0	12	0	0	-	0	-
1977	517	-	-	0	-	0	3	0	0	-	0	-
1978	614	-	-	0	-	0	1	0	0	-	0	-
1979	868	-	-	0	-	0	0	0	0	-	0	-
1980	1097	-	-	0	-	0	5	0	0	-	0	-
1981	1303	-	-	0	-	0	5	0	23	-	0	-
1982	1520	-	25	0	-	0	3	0	0	-	0	-
1983	1828	-	70	0	-	0	11	0	0	-	0	-
1984	2065	-	125	0	-	3	8	0	141	-	0	-
1985	2341	-	180	0	-	0	4	2	188	-	0	-
1986	2595	-	260	10	-	0	11	3	138	-	0	-
1987	2885	-	345	25	-	0	20	15	88	-	0	-
1988	3199	-	435	45	-	0	30	10	38	-	0	-
1989	3531	-	530	70	50	0	58	0	262	0	0	878
1990	3822	-	625	95	75	30	53	0	262	0	0	981
1991	3705	400	745	130	125	44	35	0	0	0	0	849
1992	3577	840	877	170	175	0	66	0	0	0	0	630
1993	3422	840	877	170	175	0	93	0	0	0	143*	0
1994	3244	1172	877	170	175	0	32	0	360	0	0	0
1995	3033	1380	877	170	175	0	49	0	280	0	0	0
1996	2809	1604	877	170	175	0	0	200	0	0	0	0
1997	2563	1730	852	170	175	0	0	0	120	0	0	0
1998	2266	2004	607	170	875	0	48	0	40	0	0	0
1999	2000	2004	752	170	875	0	25	0	0	0	0	0
2000	1740	2004	697	170	875	0	43	0	0	0	0	0
2001	1440	2004	617	160	875	0	80	0	0	0	0	0
2002	0	0	0	0	175	0	93	0	0	0	0	0
2003	0	0	0	0	175	0	89	0	0	0	0	0
2004	0	0	0	0	175	0	40	0	0	0	0	0
2005P	0	0	0	0	50	0	0	0	0	0	0	0

P : Provisional.

* : Under Section 17(4)(a) of the Reserve bank of India Act, 1934.

Note: Data relate to end-March for long-term finance and last Friday of March for short-term finance. Also see notes on Tables.

Source: RBI Publications.

INDUSTRIAL REFINANCE BY RESERVE BANK OF INDIA

(Rupees crore)

Year	*Long-term finance oustanding*					*Short-term finance oustanding*					
	IDBI	*SIDBI*	*EXIM Bank*	*IIBI*	*NHB*	*IFCI*	*SFCs*	*ICICI*	*IDBI*	*SIDBI*	*DFHI*
1	2	3	4	5	6	7	8	9	10	11	12
1971	60	-	-	0	-	2	3	0	0	-	-
1972	118	-	-	0	-	2	4	0	0	-	-
1973	135	-	-	0	-	0	4	0	0	-	-
1974	204	-	-	0	-	0	5	0	0	-	-

1975	320	-	-	0	-	0	9	0	11	-	-
1976	385	-	-	0	-	0	12	0	0	-	-
1977	517	-	-	0	-	0	3	0	0	-	-
1978	614	-	-	0	-	0	1	0	0	-	-
1979	868	-	-	0	-	0	0	0	0	-	-
1980	1097	-	-	0	-	0	5	0	0	-	-
1981	1303	-	-	0	-	0	5	0	23	-	-
1982	1520	-	25	0	-	0	3	0	0	-	-
1983	1828	-	70	0	-	0	11	0	0	-	-
1984	2065	-	125	0	-	3	8	0	141	-	-
1985	2341	-	180	0	-	0	4	2	188	-	-
1986	2595	-	260	10	-	0	11	3	138	-	-
1987	2885	-	345	25	-	0	20	15	88	-	-
1988	3199	-	435	45	-	0	30	10	38	-	-
1989	3531	-	530	70	50	0	58	0	262	0	878
1990	3822	-	625	95	75	30	53	0	400	0	981
1991	3705	400	745	130	125	44	35	0	0	0	849
1992	3577	840	877	170	175	0	66	0	0	0	630
1993	3422	840	877	170	175	0	236	0	0	0	0
1994	3244	1172	877	170	175	0	32	0	360	0	0
1995	3033	1380	877	170	175	0	49	0	280	0	0
1996	2809	1604	877	170	175	0	0	200	0	0	0
1997	2563	1730	852	170	175	0	0	0	120	0	0
1998	2266	2004	607	170	875	0	48	0	40	0	0
1999	2000	2004	752	170	875	0	25	0	0	0	0
2000	1740	2004	697	170	875	0	43	0	0	0	0
2001	1440	11454	617	160	875	0	80	0	0	2956	0
2002	0	10252	-	-	175	0	93	-	0	2908	0
2003	0	8361	-	-	175	0	89	-	0	4367	0
2004	-	8549	-	-	175	0	40	-	-	1515	0
2005	-	8523	-	-	50	0	0	-	-	2339	0
2006	-	11295	-	-	-	0	0	-	-	2595	0
2007	-	12461	-	-	50	0	0	-	-	3570	0
2008	-	11489	-	-	50	0	0	-	-	8737	0
2009	-	14786	-	-	0	0	0	-	-	16100	0

Note:
1. Data for 2009 are Provisional.
2. Data for short-term finance outstanding by SFCs for 1993 are as per Under Section 17(4)(a) of the Reserve Bank of India Act, 1934.
3. For EXIM BANK, outstanding have been converted into Tier 1 bonds of Government of India since 2002-03.
4. Pursuant to the Industrial Development Bank (Transfer of undertaking and repeal) Act 2003, IDBI Act was replaced on October 1, 2004 and IDBI was converted into bank w.e.f. that date.
5. ICICI was merged with ICICI Bank Ltd. effective March 30, 2002.
6. IIBI is in the process of voluntary winding up.
7. Data relate to end-March for Long term finance and last Friday of March for Short term finance.

Source: RBI Publications

REVIEW QUESTIONS

1. What are the basic contributions of agricultural sector to the economy?
2. Explain the role of Agricultural Credit department of RBI.
3. What is the indirect financial assistance provided by RBI through NABARD to agricultural sector?
4. Explain the role of RBI in agricultural finance in India.
5. Explain the role of RBI in industrial finance in India.
6. Write a note on Agricultural Insurance Scheme.

CHAPTER 13

State Bank of India

In this chapter we shall discuss about State Bank of India and its special place in the banking scene.

13.1 EVALUATION OF STATE BANK OF INDIA

The State Bank of India is a statutory institution like the RBI and is governed by the SBI Act 1955. The evaluation of the State Bank of India can be divided into four periods. Such classification is given below:

Evaluation of SBI

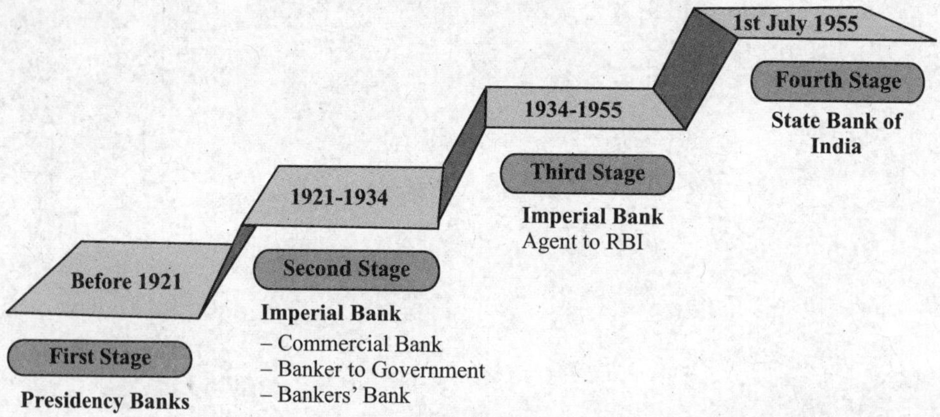

Before 1921, there were three Presidency Banks of Bombay, Calcutta and Madras. In 1921, by the amalgamation of these three banks the Imperial Bank was established. It was governed by the Imperial Bank of India Act of 1920. The Imperial Bank was mainly a commercial bank owned by private shareholders. But it was simultaneously performing some of the functions of Central Bank such as the banker to the government, bankers' bank and national clearing house. But it was not given the powers to issue notes or to engage in foreign business.

The Imperial Bank was functioning on this line till 1934 when a separate Central Bank *i.e.*, RBI was established. Then the Imperial Bank of India Act was amended by the Imperial Bank (Amendment) Act of 1934. Besides its regular functions, the Imperial Bank acted as the agent of the Reserve Bank of India in all places where the later had no branches of its own. Besides enjoying great prestige on that account, it was coming into possession of large sums of Government Funds, on which no interest had to be paid.

13.1.2 Nationalisation of the Imperial Bank

Proposals for the nationalisatión of the Imperial Bank were under consideration ever since the attainment of independence in 1947. It was nationalised in 1955 according to the recommendations of Rural Credit Survey Committee. The committee recommended that the government should establish a strong government owned commercial bank, which would undertake rapid expansion of banking facilities in rural areas. For this purpose, it suggested the government to nationalise the Imperial Bank and other state associated banks.

The basic reasons for the nationalisation of the Imperial Bank are given below:

(1) **Already functioning as a semi-government bank:** The Imperial Bank from its establishment in 1920, had enjoyed a number of privileges and was functioning as a semi-government bank. It was established under a separate Act of Parliament, the Imperial Bank of India Act. It acted as the agent of Reserve Bank of India in the places where the RBI did not have its branches. Hence, it was considered more appropriate to nationalise the Imperial Bank.

(2) **Transfer of profits to the government:** The Imperial Bank earned huge profits because of the public confidence on it and because of its association with the government, large amount of government funds are kept with it. Thus, the government considered that it was necessary to transfer the profits arising out of government funds to the government account.

(3) **Promotion of agriculture and rural development:** After the Second World War, the agricultural prices had gone up, and the rural areas were not covered by the banking operations. Hence, in order to increase the agricultural produce there was a need to extend credit facilities to the rural areas. To promote agriculture in all respects, the government considered that it was necessary to nationalise the Imperial Bank.

(4) **Implementation of the monetary policy of the government:** Finally, the government required strong commercial base for the implementation of its monetary policy and five year plans. It also became the root cause for the nationalisation of the Imperial Bank.

Accordingly, an act was passed in Parliament in May 1955 and the State Bank of India was constituted on 1 July 1955. More than a quarter of the resources of the Indian banking system thus passed under the direct control of the Government. Later, the State Bank of India (Subsidiary Banks) Act was passed in 1959, enabling the State Bank of India to take over eight former State-associated banks as its subsidiaries (later named Associates).

SBI has seven associate banks:

1. State Bank of Bikaner & Jaipur
2. State Bank of Hyderabad
3. State Bank of Mysore
4. State Bank of Patiala
5. State Bank of Travancore
6. State Bank of Saurashtra - merged with SBI in 2008.
7. State Bank of Indore - merged with SBI in 2010.

Initially SBI had only seven associate banks constituting the State Bank Group. All the seven associate banks use the same logo of a blue keyhole and all the associates use the "State Bank of" name, followed by the regional headquarters' name. In 1951, when the First Five Year Plan was launched, the development of rural India was given the highest priority. For this purpose, the government of India integrated these seven banks into the State Bank of India system to expand service to attain its basic objective of rural development.

There has been a proposal to merge all the associate banks into SBI to create a "mega bank" and restructuring their operations for the development of the country. The first step towards this direction was made on 13 August 2008 by merging State Bank of Saurashtra with SBI. It reduced the number of state banks from seven to six.

Thereafter, on 19 June 2009 the SBI Board approved the merger of its subsidiary, State Bank of Indore, with itself. SBI holds 98.3% in State Bank of Indore. The acquisition of State Bank of Indore added 470 branches to SBI's existing network of 12,448 and over 21,000 ATMs. Total assets of SBI and the State Bank of Indore stood at ₹ 998,119 crore as on March 2009. The process of merging of State Bank of Indore was completed by April 2010, and the SBI Indore Branches started functioning as SBI branches on 26 August 2010.

Note: Now, in State Bank group there are 5 subsidiaries with State Bank of India.

13.2 Management of the Bank

The head office of the SBI is located in Mumbai. And the Bank has local offices at Calcutta, Mumbai, Chennai, New Delhi, Lucknow, Ahmedabad, Hyderabad, Patna, Bhopal, Bhubaneswar, Chandigarh, Guwahati and Bangalore.

The bank is administered by a central board of directors. The Chairman, vice-chairman and Managing Director shall hold office for such terms not exceeding five years, as the central government may fix when appointing them and shall be eligible for reappointment. The directors elected by the shareholders and nominated by the central government will hold office for four years and are eligible for re-election or renomination. Other nominated directors will hold office during the pleasure of the authority appointing them. At each place where the State Bank has a local head office, there is a local board consisting of the members of the Central Board residing in that area and not more than 8 directors, of which one will be elected by shareholders whose names appear in the branch register concerned, 6 will be nominated by the central government and the remaining one will be filled by the secretary and treasurer. Further, there can be local committees where there are no head offices. No person who is a member of the central or state legislature can be a director of the bank. The local boards will be required to exercise all powers and perform all functions of the bank in relation to the specified business that may be carried on under the provisions of sections 32 and 33 of the Act. With a view to enabling the local boards to cater much more effectively and expeditiously to the banking requirement of their respective regions, their powers and authority have been enhanced.

13.3 Structure and Organisation of the Bank

The SBI took over the assets and liabilities of the Imperial Bank. The bank had an authorised capital of ₹ 200 crore which is divided into shares of ₹ 100 each and an issued capital of ₹ 56.25 crore. The shares of the Imperial Bank were transferred to RBI and the shareholders were paid a compensation of ₹ 1765 for each fully paid shares and ₹ 431 for each partly paid shares. It was paid in cash upto ₹ 10,000 and beyond this amount, the compensation was paid in 3 ½ % government bonds repayable in 1965. The shareholders were also given the option of taking up the shares in the SBI in lieu of the compensation at the rate of ₹ 350 per share of the paid-up value of ₹ 100.

It should be noted, that the nationalisation of the State Bank does not involve the transfer of the entire share capital to the government. The shares are as a matter of fact held by the RBI. Further, there is a provision for ordinary shareholders to hold share capital upto 45%. That is, only the controlling interest is held by the RBI.

The number of branches of SBI group can be seen from the following Table:

Number of Branches of SBI and its Associates - 2013

SBI and its Associates	*Number of branches as on March 31, 2013*				
	Rural	*Semi-urban*	*Urban*	*Metropolitan*	*Grand Total*
	(1)	(2)	(3)	(4)	(5)
State Bank of Bikaner and Jaipur	365	296	192	186	1039
State Bank of Hyderabad	434	488	319	299	1540
State Bank of India	5589	4153	2601	2357	14700
State Bank of Mysore	245	173	159	203	780
State Bank of Patiala	376	296	275	176	1123
State Bank of Travancore	79	609	214	98	1000
Total	**7088**	**6015**	**3760**	**3319**	**20182**

Source: RBI Publications

13.4 FUNCTIONS OF STATE BANK OF INDIA

The functions of SBI can be grouped under two categories *viz.*, the Central Banking functions and ordinary banking functions.

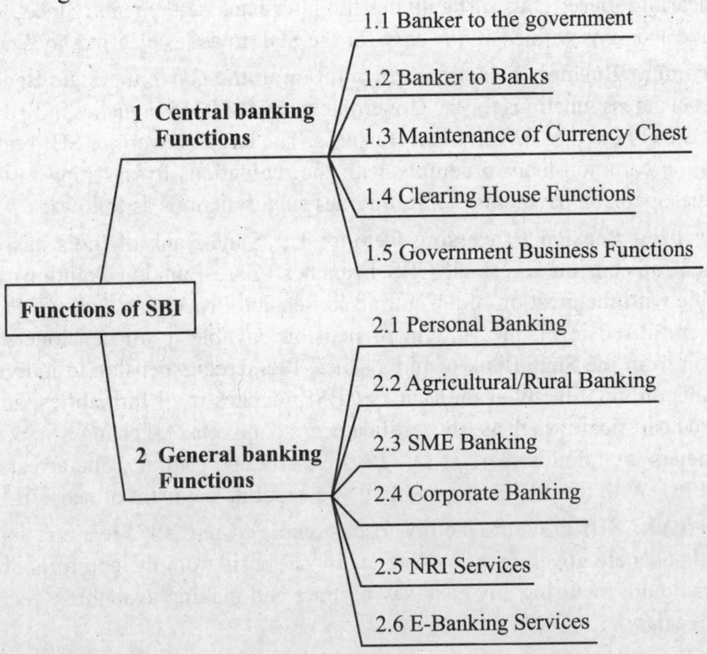

A. Central Banking Functions:

The SBI acts as agent of the RBI at the places where the RBI has no branch. Accordingly, it renders the following functions.

(*a*) Banker to the government
(*b*) Banker to banks in a limited way
(*c*) Maintenance of currency chest
(*d*) Acts as clearing house
(*e*) Renders Government Business Functions

(1) Banker to the Government: The SBI functions as the banker to the central and state governments. It receives and pays money on behalf of the governments. Especially it renders the following functions as directed by the RBI in this regard.

(*a*) collection of charges on behalf of the government *e.g.*, collection of tax and other payments

(*b*) grants loans and advances to the governments

(*c*) provides advises to the government regarding economic conditions, etc.,

(2) Banker's Bank: Commercial banks have accounts with SBI. When the banks face financial shortage, the SBI provides assistance to them as it is considered a big brother in the banking industry. It discounts the bills of the other commercial banks. Due to the functions on this line the SBI is considered in a limited sense as the bankers bank.

(3) Currency Chest: The RBI maintains currency chests at its own offices. But RBI Offices are situated only in big cities. SBI, buy its wide network of branches operate in urban as well as rural areas. RBI therefore, in such places keeps money at currency chests with SBI. Whenever needs arise, the currency is withdrawn from these chests under proper accounting and reporting to RBI. Presently RBI entrust currency chest to other Public Sector banks and a few private sector banks also.

(4) Acts as Clearing House: In all the places, where RBI has no branch, the SBI renders the functions of clearing house. Thus, it facilitates the inter bank settlements. Since, all the banks in such places have accounts with SBI, it is easy for the SBI, to act as clearing house.

(5) Government Business Functions: In addition to the above the State Bank of India also renders various business functions for the Government. Out of 9315 branches of SBI in India, about 7000 branches are conducting Government Business. The large network of SBI branches provides easy access to the common man to comply with the regulations by assisting in the payment of Government dues, pension payments etc. It provides such functions as follows:

(***a***) **Centralized Pension Processing Center:** The State Bank of India has centralised the payment of pension across all CBS Branches (Core Banking Solution). This has been possible with the creation of a Centralised Pension Processing Cell (CPPC) to calculate, at a centralised level, the amount of pension payable to all pensioners drawing their pension from the State Bank of India. The CPPC credits pension to individual customer accounts online directly at the Bank's CBS branches if all formalities, and obtention of required certificates such as life certificate, are complete. All changes in pension payment parameters including arrears of DA etc are also done centrally and arrears calculated by the CPPC. With this SBI assures timely and accurate payment of pension.

(***b***) **SBI e-TAX:** SBI provides facility to customers to pay all direct and indirect taxes of central and state governments online on 24 × 7 basis from the comforts of their office or home without incurring any cost, saving time and making available e-receipt for the tax paid instantly.

SBI e-Freight: It is the electronic Payment of Railway Freight Scheme. It has been devised for corporates regularly transporting goods (raw material/finished goods) through the Railways and making payment of Railway freight.

Government Accounts: Government business transactions are handled by SBI branches. The Government Accounts Department (GAD) supervises the handling of government business undertaken by SBI branches as sub-agent of Reserve Bank of India. It is a co-ordinating agency between the branches dealing in Central Government transactions and Reserve Bank of India Central Accounts Section (CAS), Nagpur, on the one hand and Accounting Authorities of Department of Central Government on the other.

All authorised dealing/receiving branches of SBI report their Central Government transactions on a daily basis to their respective focal/nodal/link branches who consolidate and report to GAD, Navi Mumbai. The main function of GAD is to settle Central Government transactions reported by nodal/focal/link branches with RBI, CAS, Nagpur.

Public Provident Fund: SBI provides the facility of the PPF Scheme introduced by Central Government in 1968. The Scheme enables the members of the public to make contributions to the Fund and obtain Income Tax rebate under the relevant provisions of the Income Tax.

Senior Citizens Savings Scheme: Government of India has decided to operate the scheme through all branches of Public Sector Banks which are operating PPF Scheme, 1968. As such SBI provides the facility of Senior Citizens Savings Scheme to assist senior citizens of India.

B. General Banking Functions:

Besides the above specialised functions, the SBI renders the following functions general functions:

1. Personal Banking: SBI offers a wide range of services in the Personal Banking Segment. They can be seen in the following diagram:

SBI Personal Banking

SBI Personal Banking Functions

Deposit Schemes

1. Current Account
2. Savings bank Account
3. Term Deposits
4. Recurring deposits
5. Special Term deposit
6. Multi Option deposit Scheme
7. Demat Account
8. Savings Plus Account
9. Basic banking - no frills account
10. Premium savings account

Personal Finance

1. Housing Loan
2. Property Loan
3. Car Loan
4. Educational Loan
5. Personal Loan
6. Loan to Pensioners
7. Credit Khazana
8. Loan Against Shares/Debentures
9. Loan for employee stock option scheme
10. Festival Loans
11. Tribal-Plus Scheme

Personal Banking Services

1. ATM services
2. Internet banking
3. Mobile Banking
4. Online trading
5. SBI vishwa yatra foreign travel card
6. Pay roll cards
7. Gift cards
8. Gift cheques
9. Internet banking
10. Foreign inward remittance
11. Safe deposit locker

Salary Administration Service

1. Corporate Salary Package
2. Defence Salary Package
3. Para Military Salary Package
4. State Government Salary Package
5. Railway Salary Package Special Package for Insurance Commission Agents and Broking Clients Account

(*a*) **Deposit schemes:** SBI offers deposit schemes that suit all the needs of the individuals. The Multi Option Deposit Scheme is a term deposit which is not fixed at all and comes with a unique break-up facility which provides the depositor full liquidity as well as benefits of higher rates of returns, through their savings bank account. Alternately, the depositor can keep that deposit intact by availing an overdraft facility, to meet his/her occasional temporary funds requirements. Under Recurring Deposit Account people can save a little every month to build up the desired corpus to meet their future requirement of funds. SBI deposit schemes are designed with flexibility to suit the personal requirements of the public. SBI offers 24 hour banking facility through its Internet Banking/widest network of ATMs.

(*b*) **Personal Finance:** SBI offers different types of schemes under Personal Finance to satisfy the varying needs of the public. It offers the schemes including housing loan, property loan, car loan, educational loan, personal loan, loan to pensioners, credit khazana (offers housing loan customers concessions in interest rates and margins when they subsequently avail of any of other loans such as car loans, etc.), loan against shares and debentures, loan for employee stock option scheme, festival loans and tribal-plus scheme, with attractive rates of interest.

(*c*) **Personal Banking Services:** SBI offers a wide range of services in the personal banking segment including SBI vishwa yatra foreign travel card, pay roll cards, ATM services, gift cards, gift cheques, internet banking, foreign inward remittance, safety locker facility, online trading, mobile banking, etc.

(*d*) **Salary Administration Services:** SBI provides a convenient way of salary administration across a large number of centers through its core power and its corporate internet banking. Such salary administration services include, corporate salary package, defence salary package, Para military salary package, State government salary package, Railway salary package and the special package for insurance commission agents and broking clients' account.

This facility reduces the employers' paperwork and the cost of salary administration. And there is no charges for uploading of salaries for the employers. The employees also benefited by receiving instant credit of salaries.

2. SBI and Agriculture and Rural Banking

One of the basic objectives with which the SBI established is to provide banking facilities to rural areas. The Rural Credit Survey Committee envisaged a dominant part for the State Bank in rural finance. SBI provides to the needs of agriculturists and landless agricultural labourers through a network of 8750 rural and semi-urban branches. Apart from the branches, there are 428 Agricultural Development Branches which also fulfills the needs of agriculturists. SBI and its subsidiaries are the leaders in agro finance in the country with a portfolio of ₹ 64,000 crs in agro advances covering around 80 lac accounts.

SBI branches covers a whole range of agricultural activities like crop production, horticulture, plantation crops, farm mechanization, land development and reclamation, digging of wells, tube wells and irrigation projects, forestry, construction of cold storages and godowns, processing of agri-products, finance to agri-input dealers, allied activities like dairy, fisheries, poultry, sheep-goat, piggery and rearing of silk worms.

To give special focus to agriculture lending SBI has also appointed agro specialists in various disciplines to handle projects and guide farmers in their agricultural ventures. Advances are given to borrowers for very small activities covering poorest of the poor to hitech activities involving large fund outlays.

Now SBI setting up Agricultural Commercial Branches which will handle high value agro financing involving large investments. It envisages lending through corporate partnerships and other large enterprises for commodity financing, investment credit, other high value agriculture segments like horticulture, floriculture & food processing etc. It also focuses on Agra related SME including setting up of Rice and Dhal mills, seed processing industry, food processing industry, large and small scale dairy units, etc.

Considering that agriculture would continue to be significant driver of Indian economy, with the possibilities of rapid growth in emerging areas like contract farming, agro-processing and agro-export zones, etc., a separate Agri Business Unit with a distinct organizational structure has been set up in the SBI in 2004. It has following objectives:

(*a*) Providing focused attention on the banking requirements of the agriculture segment

(*b*) Achieving 18% target under agricultural advances as required under priority sector norms

(*c*) Focus on micro finance and SHG opportunities (now part of non-farm sector in Rural Business)

(*d*) Focus on Key Corporate and Institutional relationships in agriculture, emerging opportunities, and special initiatives, as may be necessary

(*e*) Focus on product development and management

(*f*) Reduce NPA levels in Agriculture

(*g*) Make agriculture a commercial proposition

Agri Business Unit has the following four departments:

1. Agri Business, Planning, Monitoring and Market Intelligence
2. Corporate and Institutional Relationship.
3. Product Development and Marketing.
4. RRBs & Lead Bank Department.

SBI also has an effective marketing and recovery team in each region with responsibilities for marketing and building relationships with dealers of agri-products, organizing promotional events and for loan sanction, processing, monitoring and recovery.

SBI Provides the following specific services under Agriculture and Rural banking services:

(*a*) Agricultural Gold Loans

(*b*) Kisan Credit Card

(*c*) Produce Marketing Loan

(*d*) Kisan Gold Card Scheme

(*e*) Setting Up of Agri-Clinic & Agri Business Centres

(*f*) Land Purchase Scheme

(*g*) Tractor Loans

(*h*) Financing Power Tillers

(*i*) Financing for combine harvesters

(*j*) Scheme for financing farm machinery – Where Tangible Assets Are Created

(*k*) Dairy Plus Scheme for financing dairy units

(*l*) Broiler Plus

(*m*) Gramin Bhandaran Yojna - Capital Investment Subsidy Scheme For Construction/ Renovation of Rural Godowns

(*n*) Scheme for financing private cold storage/private ware houses for on lending to farmers

(*o*) Scheme For Financing Seed Processors

(*p*) Mortgage loan to seed processing units

(*q*) Capital investment subsidy scheme for commercial production units of organic inputs under national project on organic farming

(*r*) Arthiyas Plus Scheme - To finance commission agents against their receivables of farmers.

(*s*) Minor Irrigation Schemes

(*t*) Finance to horiculture

(*u*) Scheme for financing Micro Finance Institutions and Non-Government Organisations (NGOs).

(*v*) Sanjeevani - To assist the farmers, who are regular in their repayments for repairs/ maintenance of tractor and for purchase of additional implements.

(*w*) Krishi Kalyan- farmers easy empowered loan- To provide timely and adequate credit to farmers to meet production and consumption expenses and the like.

(*x*) Financing for organic farming

(*y*) Lead Bank Scheme

(*z*) Micro Credit- for assisting Self-Help Groups.

The details of agricultural advances by SBI can be seen from the following:

Distribution of Outstanding Advances of State Bank and its Associates to Agriculture - 2013

(No. of Accounts in Million and Amount in ₹ Billion)

Bank group/Bank	*As on the last reporting Friday of March*					
	Total Agricultural Advances		*Direct Agricultural Advances*		*Indirect Agricultural Advances*	
	Number of Accounts	Amount Outstanding	Number of Accounts	Amount Outstanding	Number of Accounts	Amount Outstanding
	(1)	(2)	(3)	(4)	(5)	(6)
A. SBI and its Associates	**15.25**	**1728**	**15.12**	**1507**	**0.13**	**221**
State Bank of India	11.22	1248	11.10	1086	0.12	163
State Bank of Bikaner & Jaipur	0.76	92	0.76	83	0.00	9
State Bank of Hyderabad	1.46	145	1.45	111	0.01	34
State Bank of Mysore	0.41	64	0.41	58	0.00	6
State Bank of Patiala	0.35	76	0.35	70	0.00	6
State Bank of Travancore	1.05	103	1.04	100	0.00	3

Source: RBI Publications

SBI and RRBs: The Regional Rural Banks (RRBs) were established with a view to developing the rural economy by providing, for the purpose of development of agriculture, trade, commerce, industry and other productive activities in the rural areas, credit and other facilities, particularly to small and marginal farmers, agricultural labourers, artisans and small entrepreneurs, and for matters connected therewith and incidental thereto.

3. State Bank of India and Small Scale Industries (MSME):

Micro, Small and Medium Enterprises (MSME) sector has emerged as a highly vibrant and dynamic sector of the Indian economy over the last five decades. MSMEs not only play crucial role in providing large employment opportunities at comparatively lower capital cost than large industries but also help in industrialization of rural & backward areas, thereby, reducing regional imbalances, assuring more equitable distribution of national income and wealth. MSMEs are complementary to large industries as ancillary units and this sector contributes enormously to the socio-economic development of the country.

The Government of India has enacted the Micro, Small and Medium Enterprises Development (MSMED) Act, 2006 in terms of which the definition of micro, small and medium enterprises is as under:

Micro, Small and Medium Enterprises

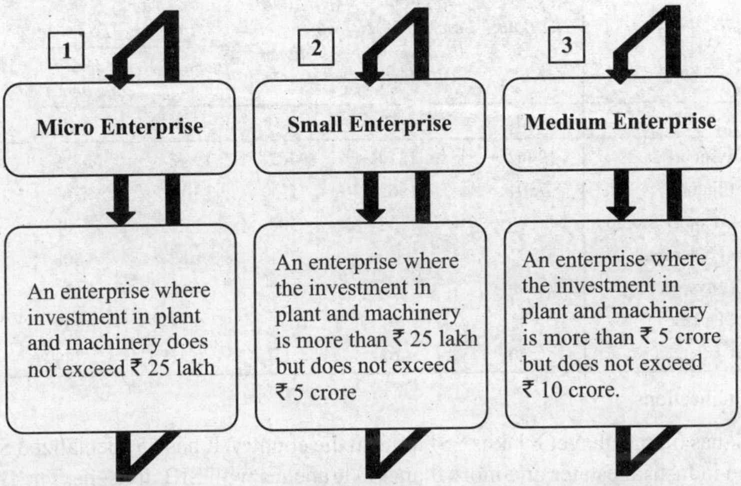

In case of the above enterprises, investment in plant and machinery is the original cost excluding land and building and the items specified by the Ministry of Small Scale Industries.

Micro, Small and Medium Enterprises (MSME) contribute nearly 8 percent of the country's GDP, 45 percent of the manufacturing output and 40 percent of the exports. They provide the largest share of employment after agriculture. They are the nurseries for entrepreneurship and innovation. They are widely dispersed across the country and produce a diverse range of products and services to meet the needs of the local markets, the global market and the national and international value chains.

Development of small scale industry and small business is another important aim of the State Bank of India and its associates.

The SBI offers assistance to all these types of units. The SBI has reoriented its policies and adapt flexible approach to serve this important sector of the economy. In 1956 the bank initiated a 'Pilot Scheme' for the provision of co-ordinated finance to small industries. In the light of its experience the scheme was extended to all the branches with effect from 1.1.1959. The scheme has been simplified from time to time to overcome various practical difficulties and make it more broad-based with the objective of helping small units in all possible ways.

State Bank of India has reported around 19 per cent (₹ 24,982 crore) growth in priority sector advances in the first nine months of the financial year 2008-09. The bank, in a statement, said its priority sector advances portfolio as on December 31, 2008, stood at ₹ 1,57,282 crore. SME advances (₹ 11,482 crore) accounted for 46 per cent of the incremental priority sector advances, with the balance being accounted for by agriculture, small business finance, and educational & housing loans. As on December 31, 2008, SME advances (₹ 85,521 crore) accounted for 54 per cent of the priority sector advances. The bank said that it has surpassed the stipulated target (40% of Adjusted Net Bank Credit) as on March 31, 2008 (source: The Hindu Business Line Jan 21, 2009).

Distribution of Outstanding Advances of SBI and its Associates to Priority Sectors - 2013

(No. of Accounts in Million and Amount in ₹ Billion)

Bank group/Bank	*As on the last reporting Friday of March*					
	Adjusted Net Bank Credit (ANBC)	*Total Off-Balance Sheet Exposures (OBE)*	*ANBC/OBE whichever is higher*	*Total Priority Sector Advances (PSA)*		*% of PSA to ANBC/OBE (Target 40%)*
				Number of Accounts	*Amount Outstanding*	
	(1)	(2)	(3)	(4)	(5)	(6) = (5)/(3)*100
A. SBI and its Associates	**10462**	**2310**	**10462**	**19.48**	**3899**	**37.26**
State Bank of India	7591	1962	7591	14.16	2765	36.42
State Bank of Bikaner & Jaipur	500	32	500	1.00	208	41.61
State Bank of Hyderabad	771	–	771	1.82	308	40.01
State Bank of Mysore	399	56	399	0.57	135	33.82
State Bank of Patiala	641	197	641	0.52	239	37.21
State Bank of Travancore	560	62	560	1.41	244	43.50

Source: RBI Publications

The Bank has financed over 8 lakhs SSI units in the country. It has 55 specialized SSI branches, 99 branches in industrial estates and more than 400 branches with SIB divisons. The Bank finances for Small Business activities which are of special significance to a large number of people as many of these activities can be started with relatively lower investment and with no special skills on the part of the entrepreneurs.

SBI Assistance to Small Units: The SBI helps the small units in the following ways:

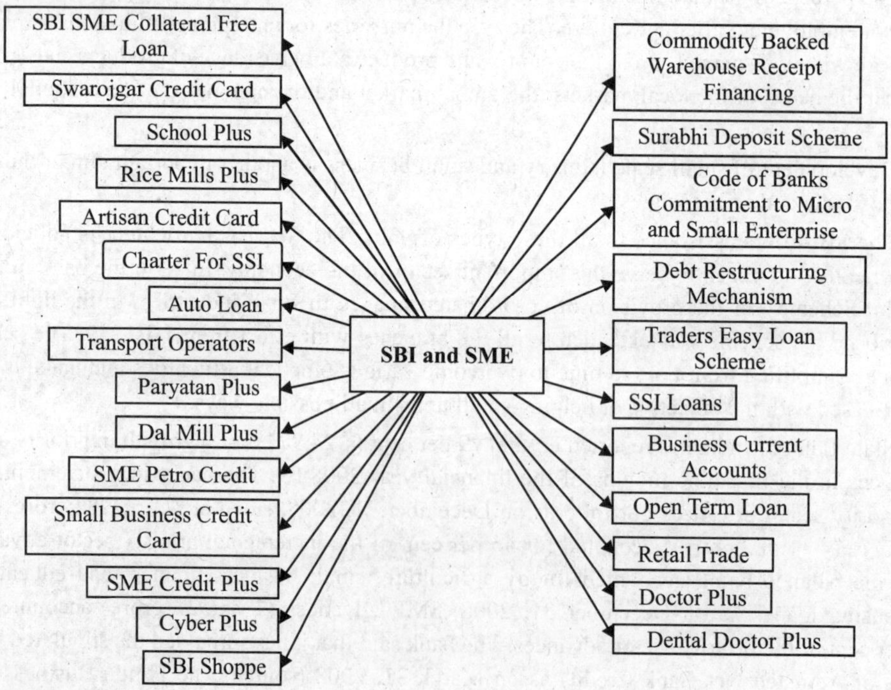

Source: SBI Publications

Commodity backed warehouse receipt financing: It is provided to finance traders or owners of goods against warehouse receipts of warehouses managed by Central and State Warehousing Corporations by way of demand loan or cash credit.

Code of banks commitment to micro and small enterprise: This is a voluntary code, reflecting the bank's positive commitment to its micro and small enterprise (MSE) customers to provide easy, speedy and transparent access to banking services in their day-to-day operations and in times of financial difficulty. This code is not only a charter of rights of the MSE but also enshrines his obligations vis-à-vis his bank.

Traders easy loan scheme: This scheme is launched by SBI to provide hassle free loan to traders. Any businessman/ entrepreneur/ professional and self-employed person can avail this loan. Loan under the scheme can be availed to meet normal business requirements and is sanctioned against equitable mortgage of property. Any residential or commercial property in the name of unit/ proprietor/partner or their close relatives is acceptable. Agriculture property or property outside urban limits is not accepted.

Others: In addition to the above SBI offers various other facilities under SME segment including Business current accounts, Open term loan, Retail trade, Doctor plus, Dental doctor plus, SBI Shoppe (to purchase of new/old shops/establishments/offices, modernization/expansion of establishments/shops, etc. and to purchase of furniture/fixtures, electrical fittings and other accessories required for shops/showrooms/offices), Cyber plus (to set up internet/cyber cafes especially at rural and semi-urban centers with potential for such a facility), SME credit plus, Small business credit card, SME Petro credit, Dal mill plus, Transport operators, Auto loan, Artisan credit card, Rice mills plus, School plus, Swarojgar credit card (to provide service to Individuals or group of individuals engaged in any viable micro-enterprise. Self Help Groups can also be provided with the facilities) and SBI SME collateral free loan.

SBI provides the following specific facilities to SMEs:

1. Provides term loan facility for acquiring fixed assets like purchase of land, construction of building, purchase of machinery/equipment, modernization/technology up-gradation activities.
2. Provides working capital loan for funding required level of current assets, employment of labour, power & fuel charges, other pre-operative and tangible expenses to enable the units to carry on its operations at the expected levels uninterruptedly.
3. Working capital loan is provided in terms of cash credit, bill discounting, Letter of Credit, Bank Guarantee, Pre-shipment and post shipment finance, working capital demand loan, etc.
4. SBI SME Collateral Free Loan: SBI provides Collateral Free Loan to Micro and Small Enterprises engaged in manufacturing and service sector. The purpose of the loan is to meet the working capital needs (Fund Based+ Non Fund Based) of such enterprises.

The details of lending during 2013 can be seen in the following Table:

Distribution of Outstanding Advances of SBI and its Associates to Micro and Small Enterprises, Education, Housing and to Weaker Sections under Priority Sector - 2013

(No. of Accounts in Million and Amount in ₹ Billion)

SBI and its Associates	*As on the last reporting Friday of March*							
	Credit to Micro and Small Enterprises (Direct + Indirect)		*Educational Loans*		*Housing Loans*		*Loans to Weaker Sections under Priority Sector*	
	Number of Accounts	*Amount Outstanding*	*Number of Accounts*	*Amount Outstanding*	*Number of Accounts*	*Amount Outstanding*	*Number of Accounts*	*Amount Outstanding*
	(1)	(2)	(3)	(4)	(5)	(6)	(7)	(8)
	1.74	**1110**	**0.81**	**175**	**1.67**	**876**	**13.30**	**1133**
State Bank of India	1.13	735	0.59	126	1.23	656	9.77	770
State Bank of Bikaner & Jaipur	0.15	81	0.02	6	0.07	29	0.78	77
State Bank of Hyderabad	0.16	86	0.05	11	0.14	66	1.17	81
State Bank of Mysore	0.08	38	0.03	6	0.05	28	0.37	54
State Bank of Patiala	0.09	113	0.01	3	0.07	37	0.35	59
State Bank of Travancore	0.13	57	0.11	24	0.13	60	0.85	91

Source: RBI Publications

4. Corporate Banking:

SBI provides financial products and services of a wide range for large, medium and small customers both domestic and international. Its powerful corporate banking formation deploys multiple channels to deliver integrated solutions for all financial challenges faced by the corporate universe. The Corporate Banking Group and the National Banking Group are the primary delivery channels for corporate banking products.

The Corporate Banking Group consists of dedicated Strategic Business Units that cater exclusively to specific client groups or specialize in particular product clusters. Foremost among these specialized groups are the Corporate Accounts Group (CAG), focusing on the prime corporate and institutional clients of the country's biggest business centers. The others are the Project Finance unit and the Leasing unit. The National Banking Group also delivers the entire spectrum of corporate banking products to other corporate clients, on a nationwide platform.

The SBI offers an exhaustive range of financial products and services that answers any business or market circumstance, backed by an expertise in customizing the product to meet the most sensitive specificities of each client and each business context. It provides the following specific facilities to SMEs.

(*a*) **Term Loans**: It is provided to support capital expenditures for setting up new ventures as also for expansion, renovation, etc.

(*b*) **Deferred Payment Guarantees:** It is provided to support purchase of capital equipment.

(*c*) **Corporate Loans:** It is provided for a variety of business related purposes to corporates.

(d) Export Credit: It is provided to both Corporates and Non Corporates for the purpose of promoting export business.

(e) Working Capital Financing: This assistance extended both as Fund based and Non-Fund based facilities to Corporates, Partnership firms and Proprietary concerns. It is extended to all segments of industries and services sector such as IT. Working capital finance to small industrial units for maintaining the current assets namely raw materials, consumable stores & spares, stock-in-process, finished goods and trade credit receivables are provided by the bank as follows:

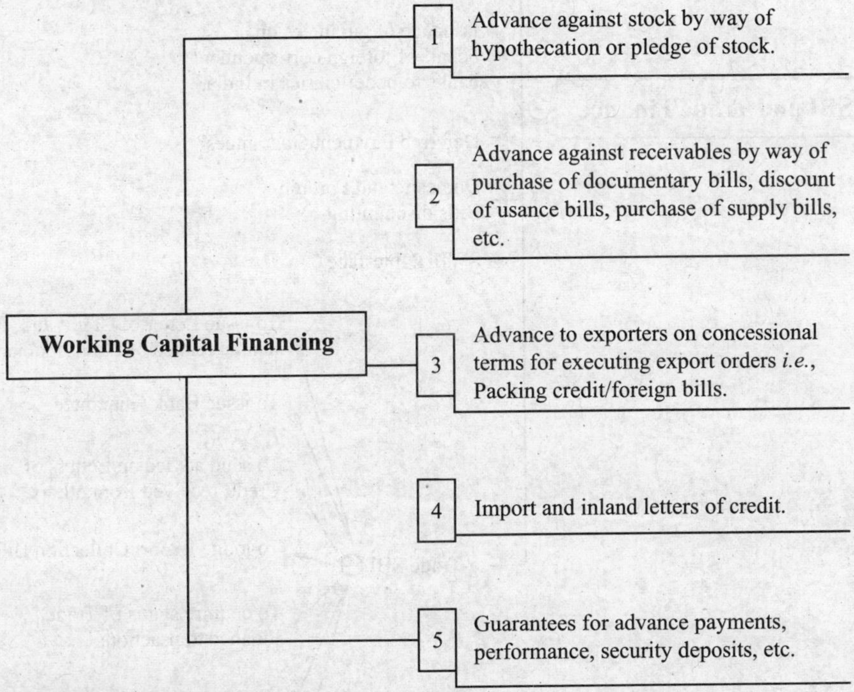

(f) Corporate Accounts Group (CAG): CAG is Strategic Business Unit of SBI, set up exclusively to cater to the specialised banking needs of top corporate clients of the country. It was the direct outcome of SBI's structural reorganisation in the light of Deregulation, Globalisation & Liberalisation of the Banking Industry. Created in the year 1995, CAG's" mission is to:

(a) Focus on top corporate clients

(b) Establish itself as the most professional outfit of its kind in the country

(c) Render world class and cost effective financial services

(d) Evolve new products on a sustained basis-customised to the changing needs of the corporates

(g) Trade Finances: SBI offers the following facilities of trade finances:

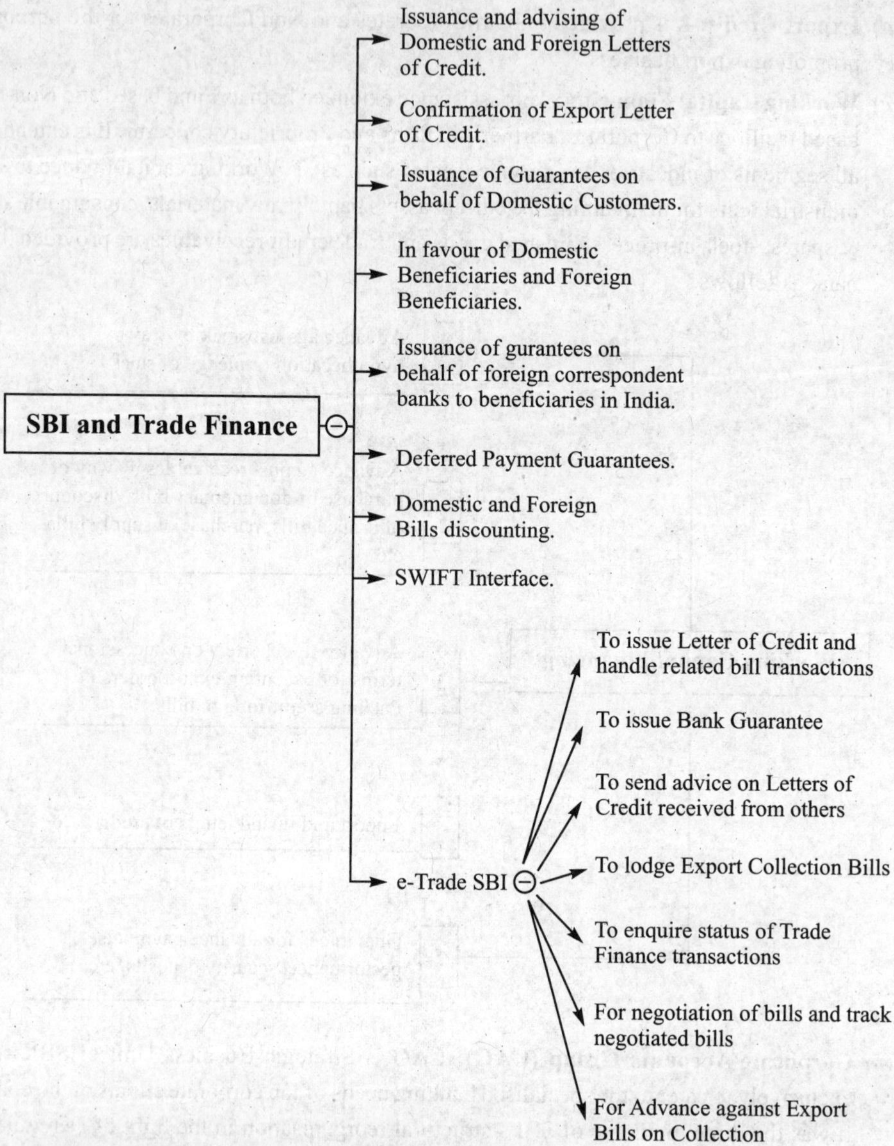

(*h*) **Treasury & Forex Products:** SBI being the largest Forex and money market player in the country, it offers an array of treasury and forex products at very competitive rates.

5. NRI Services:

SBI offers the following types of deposit accounts to NRIs.

(*a*) NRE Rupee Accounts.

(*b*) Savings Bank

(*c*) Current Accounts.

(*d*) Term Deposits (Interest Paid out Quarterly).

(*e*) Special Term deposits (Interest compounded Quarterly).

(*f*) Non-Resident (Ordinary) Account.

(*g*) NRO A/cs - Rupee Accounts for crediting income in India.

(*h*) Foreign Currency Non Resident Accounts.

(*i*) FCNR(B) Premium Account.

(*j*) Fixed Deposits in Pound Sterling, US Dollar Euro Canadian Dollar and Australian Dollar

(*k*) Resident Foreign Currency Accounts.

6. SBI and E-services:

SBI offers the following e- services for the efficient service delivery:

RTGS/NEFT: Bank offers Real Time Gross Settlement System (RTGS) & National Electronic Fund Transfer system (NEFT) which enables an efficient, secure, economical and reliable system of transfer of funds from bank to bank as well as from remitter's account in a particular bank to the beneficiary's account in another bank across the country.

SBI Vishwa Yatra Foreign Travel Card: It a prepaid plastic card issued in association with VISA International, is presently available in three different currencies - US Dollars, Euro and GBP. It is a safer method of carrying funds in a safe, convenient and cost effective way on customer visit abroad. It takes away the hassles of going around Money changers and loosing valuable foreign currency by way of high exchange margins.

SBI and its associates offers other e-services including ATM Services, Internet Banking, E-Rail, EFT, E-Pay, Magnetic Ink Character Recognition (MICR) and Foreign inward remittance.

13.5 ROLE OF SBI IN ECONOMIC DEVELOPMENT

Financial stability is the main factor for accelerating the development of any country. Commercial banks are playing an important role in the economic development of a country. If the banking system in a country is effective, it will confirm the economic prosperity.

In a fast growing economy like India, the economic development is determined by the factors like the industrial development, modernization of agriculture, organization of internal trade and expansion of foreign trade, etc. From the discussions made in the preceding sections of this chapter, we can understood the commitment of SBI and its associates in the developing process of the country.

They play a vital role in the economic development by ensuring:

(1) Mobilising Saving for Capital Formation

(2) Extending banking services to all and there by reducing the transaction costs.

(3) Financing industries- corporate and micro, small & medium enterprises

(4) Rural and agriculture finance

(5) Supporting domestic and international trade

(6) Help the weaker sections of the society

(7) Financial Inclusions

(8) Consumer credits and personal loans

(9) Financing employment generating activities

(10) Help the Central bank-RBI, in achieving the objectives of monetary policy.

The occupation wise distribution of credit by state bank and its associates can be seen in the following Table and Figure:

Outstanding Credit of State Bank of India and its Associates According to Occupation - 2012

Occupation	*State Bank of India & its Associates*	
	No. of Accounts	*Credit Limit*
	(1)	(2)
I. Agricultre	**12880806**	**1588.11**
1. Direct Finance	12715603	1421.92
2. Indirect Finance	165203	166.20
II. Industry	**630363**	**7391.74**
III. Transport Operators	**127272**	**215.65**
IV. Professional and Other Services	**182155**	**544.12**
1. Professional Services	10926	11.93
2. Tourism, Hotel & Restaurants	22844	132.39
3. Recreation services	6463	14.06
4. IT and Telecommunications	2468	26.94
5. Others	139454	358.81
V. Personal Loans	**9895674**	**3339.48**
1. Housing	2243611	1760.16
2. Consumer Durables	98089	4.34
3. Vehicles	1077192	343.00
4. Education	803494	234.45
5. Personal Credit Cards		
6. Others	5673288	997.53
VI. Trade	**1258804**	**2287.53**
1. Wholesale Trade	80598	1718.22
2. Retail Trade	1178206	569.31
VII. Finance	**30400**	**512.78**
VIII. All Others	**113700**	**26.34**
Total Bank Credit	**25119174**	**15905.76**

Source: RBI Publications

Occupation-Wise Distribution of Credit by Stat Bank and its Associates - 2012

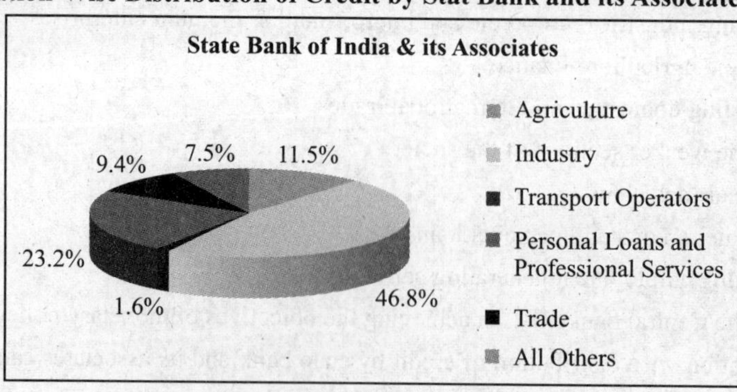

Source: RBI Publications

Thus, SBI and its associates being the bank for everyone offer services to all sections of the society and all sectors of the economy, contribute in the economic development of the country at a large extent.

REVIEW QUESTIONS

1. Write a note on the evolution of SBI.
2. What are the subsidiaries of SBI?
3. Explain the functions old SBI in detail.
4. Discuss in detail the central banking functions of SBI.
5. Write a detailed note on Agriculture and Rural banking functions of SBI.
6. Explain the functions of SBI towards Small and medium scale industry.
7. Write a note on SBI role on Corporate banking
8. What are the NRI services offered by SBI?
9. Write a note on E banking services of SBI.
10. Explain the role of SBI in the economic development of the country.

14

CHAPTER

Credit Cards

A barometer of the maturity of an economy with a few exceptions is the stage of development reached by its payment systems. Cash in the form of notes and coins makes up just one form of payment system. The development in banking brought about a second phase in payment system, through paper instruments namely cheques and credit transfers.

14.1 MEANING AND DEFINITION OF CREDIT CARD

The requirement for greater flexibility and convenience and development of technology has given rise to electronic payments and this is where plastic cards have been provided with. A credit card is basically a plastic card with a magnetic strip invented with the intention to simplify the complicated banking process for an individual in case he/she is short of cash, be it something casual like shopping or something severe like an emergency situation. Various banks and private financial organizations have now started providing credit card facility to their clients to offer them better and simpler financial solutions to their problems.

During 1914, a number of oil companies in United States issued the first credit card to their customers for the purchase of gasoline, oil and accessories at the companies' stations. Thereafter, local departmental stores, air travel companies and railway companies also started issuing credit cards.

In 1950, the Diners' club Inc, was the first company to issue an all purpose card. The Franklin National Bank of New York was, in 1951, the first bank in the United States to adopt a credit card plan. Around 1958, the American Express Company and two large banks, the Bank of America and Chase Manhattan entered the credit card field. Some of these companies introduced their cards into United Kingdom, and in 1966 Barclays Bank was the first British Bank to introduce credit cards, known as 'Barclays Cards'. In 1972 "Access" cards were introduced by Lloyds Bank. Credit Cards by Indian Banks is a recent history.

Definition:

The Credit Card can be defined as "a small plastic card that allows its holder to buy goods and services on credit and to pay at fixed intervals through the card issuing agency".

The dictionary meaning of credit card is "A card which can be used to obtain cash, goods or services up to a stipulated credit limit. The supplier is later paid by the credit card company which in due course is reimbursed by the credit card holder who will be charged interest at the end of the credit period if money is still owing".

This means that using a credit card is effectively like taking-out a loan. That loan must be repaid to the credit card company (the lender) within the credit cycle agreed upon. If the money is not repaid within this time an interest charge is applied to the remaining balance.

14.2 MECHANISM OF CREDIT CARD OPERATION:

The mechanism of operation of the credit card can be explained with the help of the following diagram.

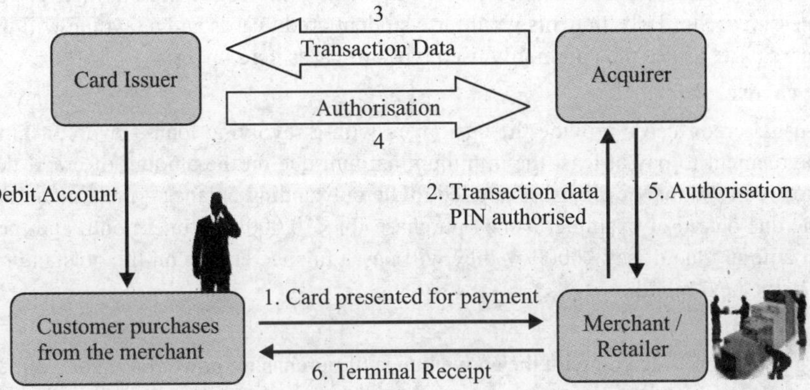

Note: 1. Acquirer credits funds to merchant's nominated bank account

2. Card Issue/customer bank sends monthly statement of transactions to the customer.

14.2.1 Parties involved:

For the completion of these transactions, a number of parties are involved in the process which may be either directly involved or can act as facilitator. They are:

1. Card holder
2. Card issuing agency
3. The merchant
4. The acquiring bank.

Note: 1. To take any payment via a card, the merchants need a relationship with a card transaction ACQUIRER who acquires the transaction from the merchants and passes them onto the various card issuing companies, or card schemes, globally.

2. The correct way to process transactions is by opening a separate internet acquiring account via the merchant's normal acquirer if they provide this, or by going to an intermediary called a PSP (Payment Service Provider).

14.2.2 Process of Credit Card Operation:

The process of credit card operation involves the following steps:

(1) The credit card holder makes purchases by credit card.

(2) Merchant swipes or key enters credit card and purchase information and submits the transaction to the acquirer (acquiring bank)

(3) The acquirer (if acquirer service is not available then PSP is engaged for this purpose), in turn, verifies the credit card number of the holder and the transaction type. And makes some basic checks to ensure that the card has not been reported stolen, that the card has not been cancelled and that the customer is still within their credit limit.

(4) Issuer sends Authorisation to Acquirer.

(5) If approved by issuer, acquirer credits the merchant account and submits the transaction for settlement. That is, Acquirer funds merchant account.

(6) The checking and verification is done in seconds. And the final receipt is given to customer.

(7) The Card Issuer debits the customer's account.

Later, the Issuer posts the transaction to the cardholder's account and sends monthly statement to cardholder. Cardholder receives monthly statement and pays issuer.

14.3 TYPES OF CREDIT CARDS:

There are many types of credit cards which are used by different types of customers and account holders. Mostly business personnel use credit cards which are convenient in their use and which suit businessmen. Similarly students would use student credit cards and a layman will use general purpose cards. Let us see the commonly used types of cards here under:

1. Credit cards:

The usual credit cards provide the customers with a revolving loan—or credit limit—based on their agreement to pay at least the minimum amount due on the amount of credit they use by the payment date. A finance charge is applied to the outstanding balance—the amount they do not pay by the due date. For example, if they purchase for ₹10,000/= in one month and they pay the minimum amount due of say ₹6000/=, they will pay a finance charge on the outstanding balance of ₹4000/= the next month.

2. Charge Card:

Charge cards provide you with the convenience of purchasing power based on your agreement to pay the full amount of the charges due each month, so there is no finance charge. A small usually plastic card provided by an organisation with which one may buy goods from various shops, etc. The full amount owed must then be paid on demand. In credit cards, the card holders get credit or loan for payment of periodical bills when sufficient balance is not available in their accounts. In a charge card such credit facility is not available. The periodical bill amount should be paid off by charging it to customers' account. A fee is also payable by the card holder to the card issuing institution.

3. General-purpose credit cards:

General-purpose credit cards are credit cards that can be used to pay for just about anything and any where the customer purchased as well as to get cash advances. Another advantage of using this type of card is that it combines many different types of expenses in a single bill, making payment easier.

4. Single or limited-purpose credit cards:

Single or limited-purpose credit cards can be used only in a specific store or group of stores, or for a specific purpose. Some people prefer to have separate credit accounts, such as a petrol credit card, a credit card at a departmental store, etc.

5. Premium cards:

Premium cards such as Platinum or Gold Cards are charge or credit cards that offer additional benefits such as travel upgrades, special insurance or exclusive booking for sports or other entertainments, etc. Generally, premium cards require a substantial income and an excellent credit history, offer a higher credit limit, and may charge higher fees.

6. Affinity credit cards:

Affinity credit cards are associated with specific organizations and offered to people affiliated with those organizations. Generally, an affinity credit card is co-sponsored by the organization it is associated with, and the organization receives a percentage of the sales or profits generated by the card. People who use them generally do so to help support an organization or for the cause they care about.

7. Secured cards:

Secured cards are credit cards guaranteed by a bank account or deposit made by the applicant. The credit limit is based on the amount of deposit and may be the same amount or larger. Secured credit cards are useful to establish or improve a credit record, particularly, if someone has never had credit or has a poor credit history.

8. Smart cards:

Smart cards are also known as Stored-value. They look like credit cards but are actually prepaid cards. A stored-value card has a set value which decreases as the card is used. When the card value is depleted, the customer needs to buy another card.

Smart cards are more flexible because they contain an integrated microship that can be programmed to provide information codes as well as financial information. The prepaid value of a smart card decreases as the customer use the card but can be increased by paying for additional value. Many colleges issue smart cards that give students access to food services, vending, photocopying, laundry, telephone and other purchases as well as access to the library, laboratories and other secured areas on campus.

9. Debit cards:

Debit cards look like credit cards and can be used in many places where a credit card is used. The difference between a credit card and a debit card is that a debit card accesses the money in the customer's bank account to pay for purchases. The payment amount is transferred from the customer's account to the merchant's account the same day. An advantage of a debit card is that the customer can not spend money they do not have, because the customer is not buying on credit. The customer is paying with funds in his bank account. A disadvantage is that debit cards are not subject to many of the consumer legal rights that apply to credit cards regarding returns, resolution of errors, fraud or other issues.

10. ATM Cards:

ATM cards are used to get cash and complete other transactions at a bank machine or automated teller machine (ATM). ATM cards are increasingly being used as debit cards as well. Like all debit cards, the money for these purchases is transferred out of the customer's account within that day's business cycle.

14.4 ADVANTAGES OF CREDIT CARDS

The benefits of the credit card can be grouped as follows:

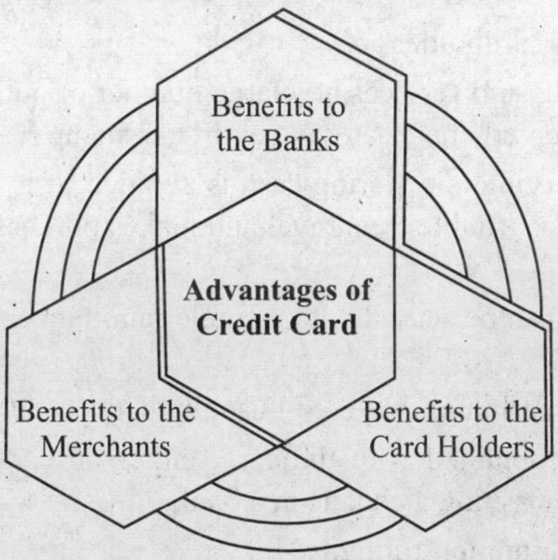

14.4.1 Benefits to the Bank

A credit card is an integral part of bank's major services these days. The credit card provides the following advantages to the Bank:

(*i*) The system provides an opportunity to the bank to attract new potential customers.

(*ii*) To get new customers the bank has to employ special trained staff. This gives the bank an opportunity to find the latent talent from among existing staff that would have been otherwise wasted.

(*iii*) The more important function of a credit card, however, is simply to yield direct profit for the bank. There is scope and potential for better profitability out of income/commission earned from the traders' turnover.

(*iv*) This also provides additional customer services to the existing clients. It enhances the customer satisfaction.

(*v*) More use by the card holders and consequently increased turnover improves national business growth and consequently the growth of banking habits in general.

(*vi*) Better network of card holders and increased use of cards means higher popularity and image for the banks.

(*vii*) Savings of expense on cash holdings i.e., stationery, printing and manpower to handle clearing transactions will considerably be reduced.

(*viii*) It increases customer- base of the bank.

(*ix*) It brings into bank's fold high net worth customers by introducing various types of credit cards like Gold card, Executive card.

(*x*) It brings in new customers from various merchants outlet which accepts credit card against sale of their goods/services.

(*xi*) It creates a brand name and popular image for the bank.

(*xii*) Large scale uses of credit cards and shops etc., accepting them help to increase deposit base of the bank.

(*xiii*) It increases interest income of the bank when card users avail of loan facility to settle the bills.

(*xiv*) It minimises credit risk of the bank as most of the card holders availing of credit facility must have been financially screened by the bank.

(*xv*) This may increase the chances of relationship banking and thereby retaining the customers.

14.4.2 Benefits to the Cardholder:

The principal benefits to a cardholder are:

(*i*) He can purchase goods and services at a large number of outlets without cash or cheque. The card is useful in emergency, can save embarrassment.

(*ii*) The risk factor of carrying and storing cash is avoided. It is convenient for him to carry a credit card and he has trouble free travel and makes purchases without carrying cash or cheques.

(*iii*) A month's purchases can be settled with a single remittance, thus tending to reduce bank and handling charges.

(*iv*) The cardholder has a period of free credit usually between 30-50 days of purchase.

(*v*) Cash can usually be obtained with the card, either on card account or by using it as identification when encashing a cheque at a bank.

(*vi*) Availing credit with minimum formality.

(*vii*) The credit card saves trouble and paper work to traveling businessmen.

(*viii*) The card holder has the option of taking extended credit up to a pre-arranged limit without reference to anyone, in addition to an initial credit and interest free period. Further, revolving credit becomes automatically available as the outstanding balance is reduced.

(*ix*) It also induces a sense of financial discipline in a card holder by allowing him to analyse the statement of expenses incurred which are supplied by card organisations. Cash expenses are often without record and can therefore, result in unplanned spending.

(*x*) It provides a proof of spending through banking channels to strengthen his position in case of disputes with sellers.

(*xi*) It also gives him exposures to banking operations since systematic accounting for spending and payments are routed through banking channels.

(*xii*) He has the convenience for making a single payment for the purchases made during the month rather than many payments by various means.

(*xiii*) It also allows customer to delegate spending power to add on members (with additional cards).

(*xiv*) It also extends additional facilities like free insurance coverage, discount on purchases, free travel booking.

(*xv*) Credit card is considered as a status symbol.

(*xvi*) It provides preferential rates on hotel stay etc., depending upon the arrangement of the card issuing bank/ agency.

Thus, the credit card is a pivotal instrument to the card holder for his convenience, social image and for financial credibility.

14.4.3 Benefits to the Merchant Establishments:

The principal benefits of a credit card to the retailer are:

(*i*) This will carry prestigious weight to the outlets.

(*ii*) Increase in sales because of increased purchasing power of the cardholder due to unbilled credit available to the card holder.

(*iii*) The retailers gain from the impulse buying and 'trading up' the tendency to buy the bigger or better article. This argument has little appeal to service establishments but much to sellers of goods.

(*iv*) He can offer credit without the botheration of cost or book-keeping and bad debts.

(*v*) Credit card ensures timely and certainty of payments.

(*vi*) Suppliers/Sellers no longer have to send reminders of outstanding debts.

(*vii*) Systematic accounting since sales receipts are routed through banking channels.

(*viii*) Advertising and promotional support on national scale.

(*ix*) Development of prestigious clientele base.

(*x*) Avoids all the cost and security problems involved in handling cash.

(*xi*) Less need for merchant establishments to provide customers with extended credit facilities which are likely to be costly burdens on them.

(*xii*) The losses through bad debts are reduced and additional liquidity is achieved.

(*xiii*) As customers are well educated and understanding. Hence there are less customer problems.

14.5 LIMITATIONS OF CREDIT CARDS

The following are the common disadvantages of the credit card:

(*i*) Only a few outlets accept the card. It is the duty of the bank to setup or seek many outlets to service the customers in order to ease out the difficulties.

(*ii*) Some credit card transactions take longer time than cash transactions because of various formalities.

(*iii*) The customer tends to overspend out of immense happiness.

(*iv*) Discounts and rebates can rarely be obtained.

(*v*) The card holder is responsible for charges due to loss or theft of the card and the bank may not be a party for loss due to fraud or collusion of staff etc.

(*vi*) Customers may be denied cash discount for payment through card.

(*vii*) It might lead to spending habits and cardholders may end up in big debts.

It should however be clearly told that the benefits of credit cards far outweigh its disadvantages. But acceptability of a product mainly comes from its usefulness. It will become more popular in India if a large number of service providers and merchant establishments accept payment through credit cards.

The credit and debit cards issued by the scheduled banks at the end of march 2013 can be seen in the following Table:

Credit and Debit Cards Issued by Scheduled Commercial Banks

(As at end-March) (in million)

Sr. No.	*Bank group*	*Outstanding Number of Credit Cards*		*Outstanding Number of Debit Cards*	
		2012	*2013*	*2012*	*2013*
1		2	3	4	5
I.	**Public sector banks**	**3.1**	**3.5**	**214.6**	**260.6**
	1.1 Nationalised banks*	0.8	0.9	97.7	118.6
	1.2 SBI Group	2.2	2.6	112.0	136.4
II.	**Private sector banks**	**9.7**	**11.1**	**60.0**	**67.3**
	2.1 Old private sector banks	0.04	0.04	13.9	15.4
	2.2 New private sector banks	9.6	11.1	46.0	51.9
III.	**Foreign banks**	**4.9**	**5.0**	**3.8**	**3.3**
IV.	**All SCBs (I + II + III)**	**17.7**	**19.5**	**278.4**	**331.2**

Notes: 1. * Excluding IDBI Bank Ltd.

2. Figures may not add up to the total due to rounding off.

From the able table it can be understood that credit card usage is increased rapidly and there is great scope for the banks in this segment.

14.6 FARMERS' CREDIT CARD

Kissan Credit Cards Scheme (KCC Scheme): Union Finance Minister in his budget speech for the year 1998-99 had desired that the banks should issue Kissan Credit Cards to farmers on the basis of their land holdings so that the farmers may use for ready purchase of agricultural inputs such as seeds, fertilizers, pesticides, etc. and draw cash for their production needs NABARD was asked to formulate a model scheme in this regard for uniform adoption by banks.

Accordingly, NABARD has since formulated a model Kisan Credit Card Scheme in consultation with major banks. The Scheme has been recommended to banks for adoption. The salient features of the scheme are as under:

(*i*) Kisan Credit Card Scheme aims at adequate and timely support from the banking system to the farmers for their cultivation needs including purchase of inputs in a flexible and cost effective manner. The scheme is to be implemented by commercial banks, RRBs and Co-operative banks.

(*ii*) The scheme would primarily cater to the short term requirements of the farmers. Under the scheme banks may provide the Kisan Credit Card to farmers who are eligible for production credit of ₹ 5,000/- and above. The credit extended under the KCC Scheme would be in the nature of a revolving cash credit and provide for any number of drawals and repayments within the limit.

(*iii*) While fixing the limit, the bank may take into account the entire production credit requirements of the farmer for the full year including the credit requirements of the farmer for the ancillary activities related to crop production such as maintenance of agricultural machinery/implements, electricity charges, etc.

(*iv*) The Credit Card should normally be valid for 3 years subject to an annual review. The credit limit under the card will be fixed on the basis of the operational land holding, cropping pattern and scales of finance as recommended by the District Level Technical Committee (DLTC)/State Level Technical Committee (SLTC).

(*v*) Banks may apply the same rates of interest as are applicable to crop loans and the security/ margin norms, etc. should be in conformity with the instructions issued by RBI/NABARD from time to time.

(*vi*) The KCC facility being in the nature of cash credit accommodation for agricultural purposes, the prudential norms as applicable to such facilities would apply to KCC accounts.

Repayment: The amount drawn or utilised against the card should be repaid to the bank by the farmers within 12 months of drawal of the money.

Kisan Credit Card Scheme: State-wise Progress

(As at end-March 2013)

(Amount in ₹ billion and Number of cards issued in 'OOO)

Sr. No.	*State/UT*	*Co-operative Bank*		*Regional Rural Banks*		*Commercial Banks**		*Total*	
		Cards issued	*Amount sanctioned*	*Cards issued*	*Amount sanctioned*	*Cards issued*	*Amount sanctioned*	*Cards issued*	*Amount sanctioned*
1	2	3	4	5	6	7	8	9	10
	Northem region	**328**	**28.2**	**167**	**31.9**	**1,090**	**239.3**	**1,586**	**299.4**
1.	Haryana	15	1.2	39	6.2	146	41.1	200	48.5
2.	Himachal Pradesh	16	2.5	7	1.4	35	5.3	57	9.2
3.	Jammu & Kashmir	2	0.1	4	0.3	218	10.3	225	10.7
4.	New Delhi**	–	–	–	–	70	3.8	70	3.8
5.	Punjab	17	1.6	21	7.2	244	101.87	282	110.7
6.	Rajasthan	278	22.8	96	16.7	375	75.6	749	115.0
7.	Chandigarh**	–	–	–	–	2	1.5	2	1.5
	North-eastern region	**17**	**1.1**	**116**	**3.4**	**192**	**8.9**	**325**	**13.5**
8.	Assam	5	0.9	84	2.7	133	6.1	221	9.6
9.	Arunachal Pradesh*	–	–	–	–	4	0.2	4	0.2
10.	Meghalaya*	3	0.1	5	0.2	14	0.6	22	1.0
11.	Mizoram*	–	–	3	0.2	4	0.2	7	0.4
12.	Manipur*	–	–	1	–	5	0.4	6	0.4
13.	Nagaland*	–	–	–	–	8	0.4	9	0.4
14.	Tripura*	9	0.1	23	0.3	21	0.9	53	1.2
15.	Sikkim**	1	–	–	–	3	0.2	3	0.2
	Western region	**409**	**21.4**	**115**	**7.9**	**975**	**148.6**	**1,499**	**178.0**
16.	Gujarat	159	6.3	34	3.1	229	46.5	422	55.8
17.	Maharashtra	250	15.1	81	4.9	741	101.5	1,072	121.4
18.	Goa*	–	–	–	–	4	0.6	4	0.7
19.	Daman and Diu***	–	–	–	–	–	–	–	–
20.	Dadra and Nagar Haveli**	–	–	–	–	–	–	–	–

	Central region	**1,050**	**39.7**	**689**	**41.8**	**1,401**	**193.5**	**3,140**	**275.1**
21.	Uttar Pradesh	338	9.4	551	30.6	918	114.1	2,027	154.0
22.	Uttarakhand	33	2.6	8	0.8	63	10.3	106	13.7
23.	Madhya Pradesh	278	21.0	75	8.0	372	63.2	725	92.1
24.	Chhattisgarh	179	6.8	55	2.5	48	6.0	282	15.3
	Southern region	**472**	**18.5**	**466**	**22.8**	**3,340**	**348.3**	**4,278**	**389.5**
25.	Karnataka	101	3.7	68	6.9	391	72.0	560	82.6
26.	Kerala	104	6.3	69	4.7	193	33.9	366	44.9
27.	Andhra Pradesh**	126	3.1	234	8.0	1,963	141.4	2,325	152.5
28.	Tamil Nadu	142	5.3	94	3.1	773	98.4	1,008	106.9
29.	Lakshadweep**	–	–	–	–	–	–	–	–
30.	Puducherry*	–	–	–	–	18	2.6	18	2.7
	Eastern region	**413**	**10.2**	**494**	**24.8**	**1,246**	**72.2**	**2,154**	**107.3**
31.	Odisha	213	6.3	45	4.9	231	10.0	488	21.2
32.	West Bengal	166	3.1	120	13.3	433	22.9	719	39.3
33.	Andaman and Nicobar Islands**	1	0.1	–	–	1	–	1	0.1
34.	Bihar	16	0.5	242	4.8	356	31.8	615	37.1
35.	Jharkhand**	17	0.2	88	1.9	226	7.4	331	9.6
	Total	**2,691**	**119.2**	**2,048**	**132.6**	**8,243**	**1,010.9**	**12,982**	**1,262.8**

– : Nil/Negligibly.

: StCB functions as Central Financing Agency.

@ : No Co-operative Banks in these UTs.

$: No RRB in these States/UTs.

** : Data under reconciliation.

* : Data pertaining to Commercial Banks includes 'term loan' limits also.

Source: NABARD/Returns from Commercial Banks.

REVIEW QUESTIONS

Short Answer Questions

1. What is credit Card?
2. Write short notes on:
   (*a*) Credit card
   (*b*) Debit card
   (*c*) ATM card
3. Explain briefly the following:
   (*a*) Charge Card
   (*b*) General-purpose credit cards
   (*c*) Limited-purpose credit cards
   (*d*) Premium cards
   (*e*) Secured cards
   (*f*) Smart cards

Essay Type Questions

1. Explain the mechanism of credit card operations.
2. Explain the different types of credit card available today?
3. Explain the advantages of credit cards.
4. What are the limitations of Credit cards?
5. Write a note on Kissan Credit Cards Scheme.
6. Write a detailed note on debit card and how is it different from ATM card?

CHAPTER 15

Merchant Banking

Merchant banking services strengthen the economic development of a country as they acts as sources of funds and information for corporate entities. For the rapid growth of the economy, the role of merchant banking services is indispensable. These financial institutions also act as advisory bodies to help corporations rightly get involved in various financial activities. They act as financial intermediaries. They manage and underwrite new issues, undertake syndication of credit, advice corporate clients on fund raising. Bankers act as intermediaries for transfer of capital from those who own it to those who use it.

Merchant Bankers provide assistance to the corporate houses for setting up industries. While banks assist industrial development by providing term loans and guarantees for setting up units and working capital, merchant bankers play a different role by assisting industrial houses in the very formation of the unit and their horizontal and vertical expansion. The steps involved in the formation of a company, setting up the plant, meeting unforeseen situation – legal and other provisions, rising of capital, etc., require expert assistance in various fields. Merchant bankers assist in this process of co-ordinating various opportunities and financial options.

These services do not come under the control of RBI, but are regulated by Securities and Exchange Board of India (SEBI). However, banks are forming subsidiaries to undertake merchant banking activity and RBI may be interested in verifying the books of banks' subsidiaries.

Merchant banking activity was formally initiated into the Indian capital Markets when Grind lays bank received the license from reserve bank in 1967. Grind lays started with management of capital issues, recognized the needs of emerging class of entrepreneurs for diverse financial services ranging from production planning and system design to market research. Even it provides management consulting services to meet the requirements of small and medium sector rather than large sector. Citibank Setup its merchant banking division in 1970. The various tasks performed by this divisions namely assisting new entrepreneur, evaluating new projects, raising funds through borrowing and issuing equity.

Indian banks Started banking Services as a part of multiple services they offer to their clients from 1972. State bank of India started the merchant banking division in 1972. SBI was the first Indian Bank to set up a merchant banking subsidiary, followed by Canara bank. Commercial banks and foreign development finance institutions have organized them through formation divisions, nationalized banks have formed subsidiaries companies and share brokers and consultancies constituted themselves into public limited companies or registered themselves as private limited companies. Some merchant banking outfits have entered into collaboration with merchant bankers abroad with several branches. Today, a number of banks have set up subsidiaries or separate departments for this business.

15.1 DEFINITION OF MERCHANT BANKERS

The concept of merchant banking is wide. In UK merchant bankers and investment bankers are the same and in U.S. merchant bank is considered as investment bank which is equipped enough to handle the requirements of multinational corporations.

In the Indian context, merchant banking is understood to be non-fund based and non-banking services. Merchant bankers are neither merchants nor bankers. Rule 2(e) of SEBI (merchant bankers) Rules 1992, defines who a merchant banker is "merchant banker means any person who is engaged in the business of issue management either by making arrangements regarding selling, buying or subscribing to securities as manager-consultant, advisor or rendering corporate advisory services in relation to such issue management".

The Notification of the Ministry of Finance defines merchant banker as "Any person who is engaging in the business of issue management either by making arrangements regarding selling, buying or subscribing to securities as manager, consultant, advisor or rendering corporate advisory services to such issue management'

15.1.1 Definitions of Financial Experts on Merchant Banks:

1. Cox.D. defines Merchant banks as "the financial Institutions providing specialist services which generally include the acceptance of bills of exchange, corporate finance, portfolio management, underwriting and other banking services".
2. Skully defines Merchant banks as "a financial institution conducting money market activities and lending, underwriting and financial advice, and investment services whose organization is characterized by a high proportion of professional staff able to able to approach problems in an innovative manner and to make and implement decisions rapidly."

15.2 REASONS FOR THE GROWTH OF MERCHANT BANKING IN INDIA

The role of merchant bankers is indispensable in these days. The reasons for the growth of merchant bankers in India include the following:

1. Growing complexity in the nature of corporate entities.
2. Growing complexity in rules and procedures of the government.
3. Growing industrialization and increase of technologically advanced industries.
4. Need for encouragement of small and medium industrialists, who require specialist services.
5. Need to develop backward areas and states which require different criteria.
6. Due to globalization and liberalization the markets expands to a greater level.
7. Increasing competition and pressure in cost reduction and effective uses of resources..
8. Exploring the possibility of joint ventures abroad and foreign market.
9. Increased technology in stock market and emergence of new products/methods.
10. Large size and number of units to be dealt with- it increases the prospective scope for the banks and thus necessitates the special focus on merchant banking services.

15.3 OBJECTIVES OF MERCHANT BANKING

The merchant banking operations are manifold and are very essential and they are established to achieve the following objectives:

(1) To assist in the capital formation in the economy.

(2) To create secondary market for bills and facilitate discounting or re-discounting of bills.

(3) To assist in foreign exchange dealings with in the ambit of relevant laws and regulations.

(4) To provide guidance to business communities on different aspects including the beginning startup activities. It includes, assisting in managing and advising, underwriting, providing assistance for securities, etc.

(5) To promote the venture capital technology funds and provide services to them.

(6) To assist in project formulation and development.

(7) To assist in modernization and diversification of business units and there by accelerate the activities in the economy.

(8) To assist in mobilizing resources by the business enterprises.

15.4 FEATURES OF MERCHANT BANKERS

Based on the above definitions the main features of merchant banking are as follows:

(*i*) Merchant Banker engages in the business of issue management

(*ii*) The services include the arrangements regarding selling, buying or subscribing to securities

(*iii*) Merchant Banker acts as a manager, consultant, advisor in the process of selling, buying, subscribing to securities and Rendering corporate advisory services in relation to such issue management

(*iv*) Merchant banking is the financial intermediation that matches the entities that need capital and those that have capital for investment.

(*v*) Merchant Banker provides specialist services which generally include the acceptance of bills of exchange, corporate finance, portfolio management, underwriting and other banking services

(*vi*) Merchant Banker mainly engaging in money market activities and lending, underwriting and financial advice, and investment services.

(*vii*) Merchant banking is skill based activities and involves serving every financial need of every client.

(*viii*) High proportion of decision makers as a percentage of total staff.

(*ix*) Possess the basic feature of quick decision process and Intense contact with the environment.

(*x*) The merchant bankers generally have the loose organizational structure.

(*xi*) Mainly concentrates on short and medium term engagements.

(*xii*) The merchant banks have emphasis on fee and commission income.

(*xiii*) The merchant banker posses the special feature of innovative operations instead of repetitive operations.

(*xiv*) They provide special and sophisticated services on a national and international level. Merchant bankers generally follow low rate of profit distribution and having high liquidity ratio.

(*xv*) The organization structure of merchant bankers in India have the special nature of formation, that is they are established on any one of the following forms:

(*a*) Institutional base

(*b*) Banker base

(*c*) Private base and

(*d*) Broker base

15.5 DIFFERENCE BETWEEN MERCHANT BANKING AND COMMERCIAL BANKING

The Clause (*c*) of section 5 of BR Act of 1949, the main business of a bank is to 'accept, for the purpose of lending or investment, of the deposits of money from the public, repayable on demand or otherwise and withdrawable by cheques, drafts, orders or otherwise'.The Sub-section of (1) of section 6 deals with the permissible business. Clause (*d*) of this section enables a banking company to internal underwriting support and to manage any issue. It reads "the effecting, insuring, guaranteeing, underwriting, participating in managing and carrying out of any issue, public or private of state, municipal or other loans or shares, stock, debentures or debenture stock of any company, corporation or association and the lending of money for the purpose of any such issue".

Based on our earlier discussions we could identify the differences between commercial banking and merchant banking as follows:

1. Commercial banks are catering to the needs of the common man whereas the merchant banks cater to the needs of corporate firms.
2. Any person can open a bank account in the commercial bank whereas it cannot be done in the merchant bank.
3. Merchant banks provide assistance in raising capital in the form of equity, preference shares, and syndicated loan working capital instruments. Whereas, commercial banks provide financial assistance in the form of term loan and working capital.
4. Merchant banks do not accept deposits. But, the commercial banks as their primary nature of business accept deposits both demand and time deposits.
5. Merchant bank deals with equities whereas the commercial bank deals with debt related finance which includes the activities like credit proposals, loan sanctions, etc.
6. The merchant bank is exposed to the market so it is more exposed to risk as compared to commercial banks.
7. Merchant bank is related to the primary market whereas the commercial markets are more into secondary markets.
8. Merchant banking activities are capital restructuring, underwriting, portfolio management, etc. whereas the commercial banks play the role of financers.
9. The activities of merchant banks have a direct impact on the growth and liquidity of money markets.
10. Merchant Bank is management oriented whereas the commercial banks are asset oriented.
11. The commercial banks generally avoid risks and on the other hand the merchant banks are willing to take the risks.

As such, a bank can undertake merchant banking business, but a merchant bank can not undertake banking business.

15.6 TYPES OF MERCHANT BANKING ORGANIZATIONS

According to the 1992 guidelines, merchant bankers were classified into one of four categories:

1. Management
2. Consulting
3. Advising
4. Underwriting.

The merchant banking organizations exist in the country are classified in to four categories as follows:

Types of Merchant Banking Organizations in India

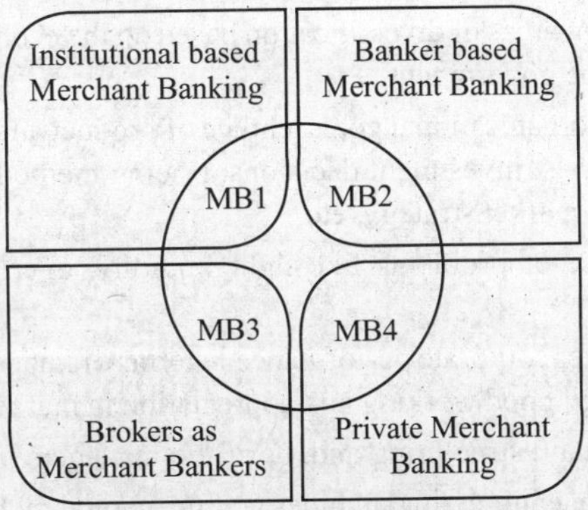

MB-1: Institutional based merchant banking organizations operate as subsidiaries of private financial institutions or those recognized by the state or central governments.

MB-2: Banker based organizations are those that operate as divisions or subsidiaries of the nationalized commercial banks or the foreign banks functioning in the country.

MB-3: The third type of merchant bankers consists of qualified brokers who provide skilled merchant banking services like portfolio management.

MB-4: The third type of merchant bankers include the private merchant banking organizations work as sole proprietorships, private limited, public limited or partnership companies.

According to the 1992 guidelines, merchant bankers were classified into one of four categories: management, consulting, advising or underwriting.

15.7 FUNCTIONS OF MERCHANT BANKERS

The merchant bankers provide assistance to corporate houses on the following lines.

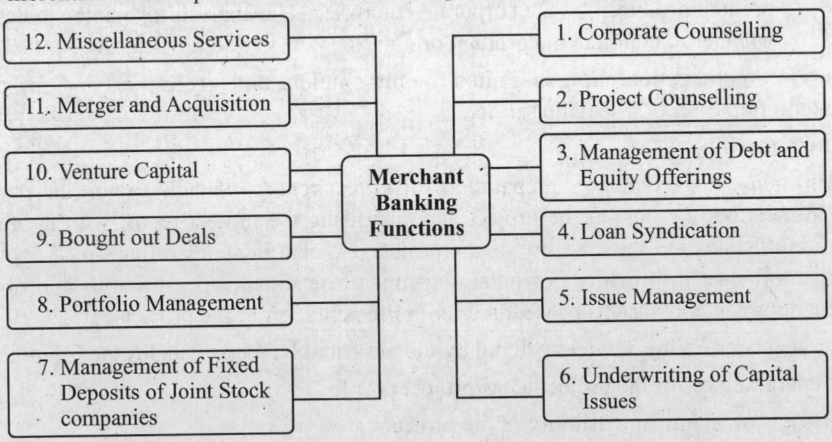

Let us discuss some of these important benefits offered by the merchant bankers.

1. Corporate Counselling:

Under corporate counselling the merchant bankers perform the activities to ensure effective running of a corporate enterprise through efficient management of finance. Merchant banking institutions provide guidance to the clients on organizational goals, choice of product and market survey, forecasting a product, cost analysis, investment decisions, pricing methods, capital management and expenditure control, market strategy and the like.

The merchant banking services in this regard provides many services including the following:

(*a*) Providing guidance in areas of diversification based on the economic and licensing policies and regulations of the government.

(*b*) Guidance on setting organisational goals, choice of product and market survey, forecasting a product, cost analysis, investment decisions, pricing methods, capital management and expenditure control, market strategy, etc.

(*c*) Identifying the cause of problems like tight liquidity, over/under capacity utilization, product mix, etc.

(*d*) Advice to ensure better corporate performance in terms of image building among investors, steady growth through good working and appreciation in market value of its equity shares.

(*e*) Counselling on capital restructuring and, portfolio management.

(*f*) Full range of financial engineering includes venture capital, public issue management, and loan syndication, working capital, fixed deposit, lease financing, acceptance credit, etc.

(*g*) Commissioning of diagnostic studies.

(*h*) Assessment of the revival prospects and planning for rehabilitation through modernization and diversification and revamping of the financial and organizational structure.

(*i*) Arranging for the approval of the financial institutions/banks for schemes of rehabilitation involves financial relief, etc.

(*j*) Providing assistance in getting soft loans from financial institutions for capital expenditure, and the requisite credit facilities from the bank.

(*k*) Merchant bankers also provide corporate counselling services including:

(*i*) Area of diversification considering the government's licensing and economic policies.

(*ii*) Market analysis for growth, present and future demand, and profitability of each product produced by the corporate enterprise. The analysis also helps to determine whether to continue the product or not.

However corporate counselling is limited to only opinions and suggestions and any detailed analysis would form part of a specific service.

2. Project Counselling:

Project counselling comprises preparation of project reports, deciding upon the pattern of financing to meet out the cost of the project and appraising the project report with the financial institutions and banks and the viability of the projects. It also includes filling up of application forms with significant information for obtaining funds from financial institutions and obtaining government approval and various procedures for implementation of the projects, etc.

The project counselling services offered by the merchant bankers includes the following:

(*a*) General review of the project ideas/project profile

(*b*) Review of technical feasibility of the projects

(*c*) Where the company has already prepared a project report, the merchant banker would review the same and advice on the viability of the project and scrutinises the same from financial angle.

(*d*) Merchant Banking assists in introducing/selecting and appointing outside technical consultancy organizations, if considered necessary, for preparation of a detailed project report, market survey report, feasibility study, etc.

(*e*) Assist to obtain letter of intent/industrial licence.

(*f*) Obtain permission if required, of joint controller of imports and exports for import of capital goods.

(*g*) Market survey required for the project finalisation.

(*h*) Advice including obtaining government consents for implementation of projects. Assist corporate houses for incorporation and obtain certificate of commencement of business.

(*i*) Advice on procedural aspects of project implementation- or effective implementation of the project, the merchant banker would advise/guide the company the steps to be taken with regard to procedural matters viz., obtaining consents of the government agencies such as Ministry of Industry, SEBI, Reserve Bank of India, etc.

3. Management of Debt and Equity Offerings:

This is the major function of the merchant banker. Merchant banker assists the companies in raising funds from the market. The main areas of work in this regard can be seen in the following chart:

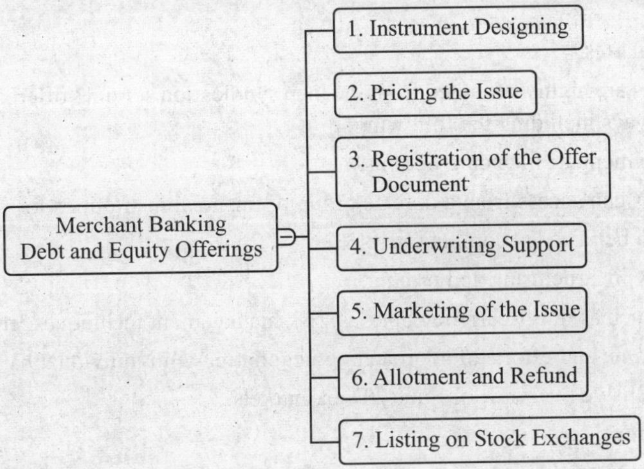

4. Loan Syndication:

Merchant banker helps the clients to get loan for the project. For this, they provide various services towards syndication of loans. The services may be either loan sought for long term fixed capital or of working capital funds. Merchant bankers help in drawing a financial plan setting out the means of financing the project to conform to the requirements of financial institutions/ banks, government agencies as also stock exchange authorities after studying/finalising the project assistance in preparing detailed applications for term loans from financial institutions/banks.

Loan syndication is an assistance provided by merchant bankers to get mainly term loans for projects. Such loans may be obtained from a single development finance institution or a syndicate or consortium. Merchant bankers help corporate clients to raise syndicated loans from banks and other financial institutions.

Merchant banker makes arrangements for loans to their clients. This involves many stages. First the merchant banker analyzes the pattern of the clients' cash flows, based on which the terms of borrowing can be determined. The detailed project report and term loan applications would thereafter be submitted to financial institutions/banks to secure their participation in term loans and necessary follow-up action would be initiated. Then the banker prepares a detailed loan memorandum. It is circulated to various banks and financial institutions and they are invited to participate in the syndicate.

It includes the following steps:

(1) Estimating the total cost of the project to be undertaken.

(2) Drawing up a financing plan for the total project cost which conforms to the requirements of the promoters and their collaborators, financial institutions and banks, government agencies and underwriters.

(3) Preparing loan application for financial assistance from term lenders/financial institutions/banks, and monitoring their progress, including pre-sanction negotiations.

(4) Arrange consortium meetings.

(5) Prepare necessary documents and execution of necessary documents, registration of charges, etc.

(6) Arrange Syndication of normal loans\Euro-currency Loans/guarantees whenever required. (Euro currency loans are foreign currency loans raised outside the country)

(7) The banks then negotiate the terms of lending on the basis of witch the final allocation is done.

Benefits to Corporates:

The corporates are highly benefited from the loan syndication services offered by the merchant bankers in many ways including the following:

(*a*) Complete menu of financing options.

(*b*) Borrowers can access from a diverse group of financial institutions for funding.

(*c*) Funds can be raised at competitive price.

(*d*) Flexibility in structuring and pricing.

(*e*) Options such as multi-currency options, risk management techniques, etc.

(*f*) Save the time and efforts of approaching/negotiating with individual banks for sanction.

(*g*) Comprehensive overview of Equity/Debt markets.

5. Issue Management:

Issue management means management of issues involves marketing of corporate securities such as equity shares, preference shares and debentures by offering them to public. Merchant banks act as an intermediary to transfer capital from those who own it to those who need it. After taking action as per SEBI guidelines, the merchant banker organizes a meeting with company representatives and advertising agents to finalize arrangements relating to date of opening and closing of issue, registration of prospectus, launching publicity campaign and fixing date of board meeting to approve and sign prospectus and pass the necessary resolutions. Pricing of issues is done by the companies in consultant with the merchant bankers. The merchant Bankers provide the following services under issue management:

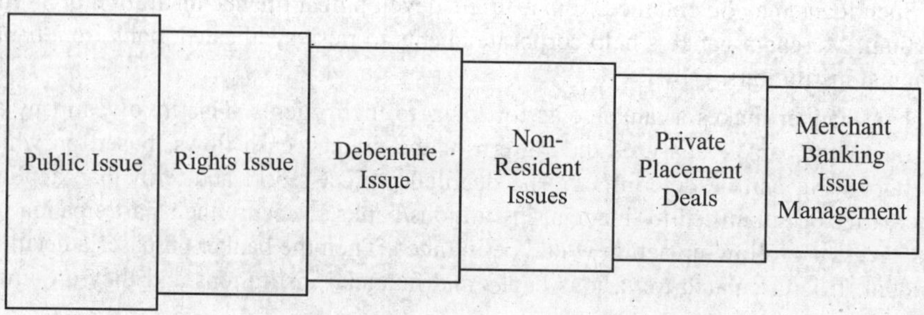

***(a)* Public Issue:** The public issue services of merchant bankers include the following:

(*i*) Advising the company on planning and timing of the issue.

(*ii*) Obtaining the consent of the SEBI including their approval for reservation of shares for non-residents (on repatriation basis) employees and business associates.

(*iii*) Making necessary arrangements for underwriting the issue by financial institutions, banks and/or brokers.

(*iv*) Selection and appointment of a principal broker, brokers and bankers to the issue.

(*v*) Selection and appointment of an issue house and fixing their remuneration.

(*vi*) Selection and appointment of advertising consultants/agencies for organising the necessary publicity campaign including press & brokers/investors' conferences at important centres.

(*vii*) Preparing the draft prospectus, where necessary, 'having it approved by solicitors.

(*viii*) Obtaining the clearance of financial institutions, bankers, other underwriters and stock exchanges for the draft prospectus.

(*ix*) Arranging for designing & printing of draft prospectus as well as despatch of the final prospectus.

(*x*) Filing a copy of the prospectus along with the other necessary documents under section 60 of the Companies Act, with the Registrar of Companies.

(*xi*) Making an application to stock exchanges(s) to have the shares listed and comply with all the listing requirements.

(*xii*) Obtaining written consents from auditors, solicitors and advocates bankers to the company, bankers and brokers to the issue, etc. to act in their respective capacities.

(*xii*) Obtaining permission from Reserve Bank of India for offering shares to non-residents and opening foreign currency collection accounts at our overseas branches.

(*xiv*) Monitoring the progress and furnishing information to the company on the response to the issue.

***(b)* Rights Issue:** The right issue services of merchant bankers include the following:

(*i*) Advising the company on planning and timing of the issue.

(*ii*) Obtaining consent of the SEBI.

(*iii*) Assisting in underwriting/making stand by arrangement with financial institutions, banks brokers.

(*iv*) Drafting and finalising the letter of offer and getting the same approved by the stock exchanges wherever the shares are listed.

(*v*) Selection and appointment of principal broker, broker and banker to the issue.

(*vi*) Selection and appointment of an issue house and advertising consultant/agency.

(*vii*) Designing, printing and mailing of letters of offers, application forms, etc.

(*viii*) Where the shares are held by non-residents of Indian Nationality/origin, assisting the company in obtaining necessary permission from Reserve Bank of India where required.

***(c)* Debenture Issue:** The debenture issue services of merchant bankers include the following:

(*i*) Computation of amount of debentures that can be raised as per the prevailing government guidelines.

(*ii*) All other services mentioned above for public and right issues as applicable.

***(d)* Advisors to Non-Resident Issues:** Merchant bankers provide the following services regarding non-resident issues:

(*i*) Obtaining approval of the Securities and Exchange Board of India (SEBI) for reservation of a part of the issue for non-residents of Indian Nationality/origin.

(*ii*) Obtaining permission from the Reserve Bank of India for offering shares/debentures to non-residents and for opening Foreign Currency Collection Accounts at overseas branches, if applicable.

(*iii*) Advising the strategy of marketing the issue amongst non- residents.

(*iv*) Arranging investors' conferences and publicity campaigns abroad.

(*v*) Arranging collection of application moneys at overseas branches and monitoring the day-to-day progress of the issue.

(*e*) Private Placement: When the issuing company sells securities directly to the investors, especially institutional investors, it takes the form of private placement. In this case, no prospectus is issued, since it is presumed that the investors have sufficient knowledge and experience and are capable of evaluating the risks of the investment. Private placement covers shares,preference shares and debentures. The role of the financial intermediary, such as the merchant bankers and lead managers, assures great significance in private placement. They involve themselves in the task of preparing an offer memorandum and negotiating with investors.

6. Underwriting of Capital Issues:

The companies for raising capital in the stock markets can engage a merchant banker to implement and underwrite the process. The merchant bank determines the number of stocks to be issued, the price at which the stock to be issued, and the timing of the release of this new stock. The merchant banker performs all the work required regarding the compliance with concerned authorities, and also responsible for marketing the new stock. They ensure the minimum subscription. In the event of shortage of public subscription, they under take such shortage and relieve the firms. For large stock issues, two or more merchant banks may work together, with one being the lead underwriter.

7. Management of Fixed Deposits of Joint Stock Companies:

The services of merchant bankers regarding the management of fixed deposits include the following:

(*i*) Computation of amount that a company can raise by way of deposits from public and deposits/loans from shareholders.

(*ii*) Advising the company on terms and conditions for acceptance of fixed deposits and the rate of interest to be paid thereon keeping in view the prevailing conditions in capital and money markets.

(*iii*) Drafting of an advertisement to be issued inviting deposits from public.

(*iv*) Filing a copy of the advertisement with the Registrar of companies for registration.

(*v*) Arranging for issue of advertisement in newspapers as required under the Companies Act.

(*vi*) Drafting of application form and arranging printing there of.

(*vii*) Arranging for collection of deposits at various branches of the Bank.

(*viii*) Submitting periodical statements to the company.

(*ix*) Arranging the company for payment of interest warrants.

(*x*) Assisting the company in observing all the rules and regulations in this connection.

(*xi*) Maintaining of records/registers for the purpose.

8. Portfolio Management:

Portfolio refers to investment in different kinds of securities such as shares, debenture issued by different companies. It is a combination of assets but a carefully combined asset structure. Portfolio management refers to maintaining proper combination of securities in a manner that they give maximum return to the investors. Investors aim at safety, liquidity and profitability of his investment but they may not know how to choose the appropriate combination of securities. Merchant bankers help their investors in deciding such combination of the securities. They conduct regular market and economic surveys. The services of merchant bankers under Portfolio Management include the following:

(*i*) Advise on right mix of securities for maximum returns with minimum risk. Merchant banker helps the investor in matters pertaining to investment decisions. Taxation and inflation are taken in to account while advising on investment in different securities.

(*ii*) Undertake to sell/buy securities on authorisation. The merchant banker also undertakes the function of buying and selling of securities on behalf of their client companies. Investments are done in such a way that it ensures maximum returns and minimum risks.

9. Bought out Deals:

Under the scheme, a portion of equity to be offered to the investing public is taken up in the first instance by the merchant banker. At an appropriate later time these shares are placed with the public at a price which will fetch reasonable and adequate return to them.

A bought-out deal is a deal in which the company sells its shares to an agent or a merchant banker. This merchant banker then offloads or sells the shares at an appropriate time. Bought-out Deals is beneficial to firms and promoters. The main benefits include the following:

(*a*) Easy and quick sale of securities: Bought-out deals offer a mechanism for easy and speedier sale of securities at lower costs relating to the issue. The advantage of the bought deal for the issuer is that they do not have to worry about financing risk.

(*b*) Bought-out deals offer flexibility for promoters to set a realistic price and convince the sponsor about the same.

10. Venture Capital:

Funding an emerging high risk, hi-tech project based purely on Research and Development efforts is termed as venture capital financing. It is a long term financial arrangement and oriented towards capital gains. It is a source of financing for hi-tech industries which use new technology to produce new products.

The services of merchant bankers includes the provision of long term start up funds for high risk ventures promoted by unknown technocrats/entrepreneurs, which suffer from capital deficiencies but have a high profit potential. And the venture capital supports the early stages of a company's life cycle.

11. Merger and Acquisition:

The merchant banker provide service on negotiating acquisitions and mergers by offering expert valuation regarding the quantum and the nature of considerations, and other related matters. The service of the merchant bankers in this regard includes the following:

1. Analyzing and identifying the areas of corporate strength and weakness to help in formulating guidelines and directions for future growth.
2. Conducting exploratory studies to locate overseas markets, foreign collaborations and prospective joint venture associates.
3. Obtaining approvals from shareholders, depositors, creditors, government, and other regulatory authorities.
4. Monitoring the implementation of merger and amalgamation schemes.
5. Identifying organizations which fulfill the requirements for the merger and acquisition.
6. Advice on acquisition plans after careful examination of financial statements, Memorandum and Articles of Associations, legal aspects of Companies Act and other basic documents.

12. Miscellaneous Services:

These services include other services such as:

(*a*) Leasing

(*b*) Counselling to SSI and Sick industrial units

(*c*) Stock broking, for both institutional and retail investors

(*d*) Distribution of financial products

(*e*) Dealing in currency derivatives

(*f*) Insurance broking

(*g*) Asset management

(*h*) Underwriting

(*i*) Investment research

(*j*) Portfolio management services

(*k*) Commodities broking

(*l*) Forex advisory services

(*m*) Advisory services for joint ventures

(*n*) Strategic services related to Merger & Acqusitions.

15.8 MERCHANT BANKING IN INDIA-SEBI GUIDELINES ON MERCHANT BANKING

The Securities and Exchange Board of India -SEBI is the statutory body that supervises India's capital market. This agency has established specific guidelines for merchant bankers, or those involved in buying, selling or managing corporate securities, with the goal of increasing investor protections and encouraging new investment.

Registration of Merchant bankers with SEBI

It is mandatory for a merchant banker to register with the SEBI. Without holding a certificate of registration granted by the Securities and Exchange Board of India, no person can act as a merchant banker in India.

(*a*) Only a body corporate other than a non-banking financial company shall be eligible to get registration as merchant banker.

(*b*) The applicant should not carry on any business other than those connected with the Securities market.

(*c*) All applicants for Merchant Bankers should have qualification in Finance, law or Business Management.

(*d*) The applicant should have infrastructure like office space, equipment, manpower, etc.

(*e*) The applicant must have at least two employees with prior experience in merchant banking.

(*f*) Any associate company, group company, subsidiary or interconnected company of the applicant should not have been a registered merchant banker.

(*g*) The applicant should not have been involved in any securities scam or proved guilt for any offence.

The merchant bankers should register with SEBI according to the categories shown in the following Chart:

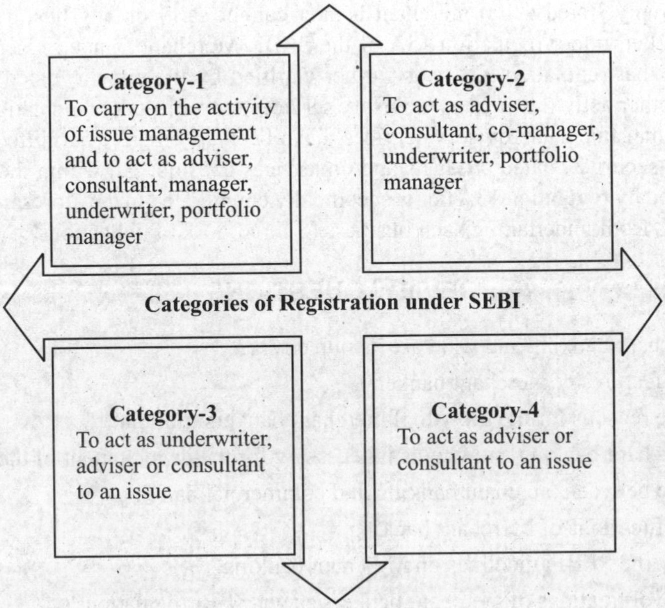

Merchant Banking activities are now being controlled by SEBI because it pertains to Capital market function. Accordingly SEBI licence is required to undertake merchant banking activity. Banks cannot act as Merchant Bankers now. They can carry on such activity only through a subsidiary. And as per the regulations of SEBI the merchant bankers have the following legal obligations:

1. The merchant bankers should maintain proper books of accounts and have to submit half yearly/annual financial statements to the SEBI within the time specified.
2. The merchant bankers can associate only with others who are registered under SEBI.
3. Merchant bankers should act only on authentic official information and not enter into any transactions on the basis of rumors or on unpublished information available to them in the course of their professional assignment.
4. They are subject to the inspection by SEBI and they have to submit all of their records when required for.

Merchant banking facilities provides various benefits to the business houses. It also provides the bankers additional income by way of fees, commission and brokerage. It makes available a large float of funds and provides better corporate image to the bankers. The expertise and advice on the lines of Merchant Banking need to be extended to small scale industries. It is also essential to try to develop 'cultivators Market' on par with the capital market. There is also a further need for trained personnel to handle new challenges in the field of innovative banking in this country.

Note: SEBI has recently stated that a merchant banker cannot carry on any business other than in the securities market. In June 2010 Barclays Securities (India) Pvt. Ltd. ("BSIPL"), a merchant banker registered under the SEBI (Merchant Bankers) Regulations, 1992, had filed with SEBI a request for 'No Action Letter' under the SEBI (Informal Guidance) Scheme 2003 in relation to its proposed referral business. Under the proposed referral business BSIPL would refer its clients to other service providers for non-security related products/ services. The other service providers are in the nature of investment banking firms and/or intermediaries who may assist clients to invest in corporate deposits or property consultants who can advise clients on purchasing or selling real estate assets, etc.

SEBI in its reply stated that a merchant banker cannot carry on any business other than in the securities market, under regulation 13A of the SEBI (Merchant Bankers) Regulations, 1992. SEBI also stated that regulation 13A was further clarified by the circular dated June 05, 1998, whereby certain other activities such as 'advisory services for projects', 'syndication of rupee term loans', 'international financial advisory services' have been specifically permitted. Since referral activities for non-security related products and/or services does not fall within the purview of the activities permitted by regulation 13A nor is specifically enumerated in the aforesaid circular, SEBI disallowed BSIPL from undertaking such business.(Source: SEBI Publications).

REVIEW QUESTIONS

1. Define merchant banking and what are its objectives?
2. Explain the features of merchant bankers.
3. What are the reasons for the growth of merchant bankers in India?
4. What is merchant banking and why is it necessary for the development of the economy?
5. Differentiate between merchant banking and commercial banking.
6. Explain the functions of Merchant banking.
7. Write briefly the SEBI guidelines on Merchant banking.
8. What are the obligations of merchant bankers as per SEBI regulations?

16 CHAPTER Factoring Service

In an economy where competition is tough, it is natural for the weaker units, small scale and medium scale sectors to be left behind. This has been the matter of concern for bankers, creditors, government and society in general. Delay in payments of sales bills leads to inadequate tie-up of working capital which results in industrial sickness. Despite several measures taken by banks like inventory related finance against pledge of goods like loans and cash credits and receivables related finance *i.e.*, discounting bills of exchange, supply bills finance or overdraft against book debts, the problems continued. In this context the policymakers thought of helping the small and medium scale sectors to recover their dues from buyers of its goods more quickly by establishing "Factoring Services" as an alternative.

The term factor has its origin in the Latin word 'Facere' meaning 'to make or do' *i.e.*, to get things done. During the 15th and 16th centuries, Factors were appointed by manufacturers in England, France and Spain to arrange for the sale and distribution of their goods and to collect the proceeds thereof. Factors never received title, but were responsible for the safe keeping of the goods as well as the proceeds of sale.

During the 19th and 20th centuries, the manufacturers retained their distribution function, but transferred the financing, credit and collection functions to the Factor. A 'Factor' is an agent who finances the seller through the purchase of accounts receivables. Though this form was prevalent earlier through travelling merchants, it became significant during 16th century in UK, France and Spain.

16.1 FACTORING: CONCEPTUAL FRAMEWORK

Factoring service, which is perceived as complimentary to bank finance, enables the availability of much needed working capital finance for the small and medium scale industries especially those that have good quality receivables but may not be in a position to obtain enough bank finance due to lack of collateral or credit profile. By having a continuous business relationship with the factoring companies, small traders, industries and exporters get the advantage of improving the cash flow and liquidity of their business as also the facility of availing ancillary services like sales ledger accounting, collection of receivables, credit protection etc. Factoring helps them to free their resources and have a one stop arrangement for various business needs enabling smooth running of their business.

"Factoring" is a new financial service that is developed in India in the last decade. It is not just a single service, rather a portfolio of complimentary financial services available to clients *i.e.*, sellers. The sellers are free to avail of any combination of services offered by the factoring organizations according to their individual requirements.

Factoring is a mechanism under which a financial organization purchases the accounts receivable and makes cash payment to the suppliers immediately, the consideration being the factorage for the services rendered and the risk assumed by the Factor.

The credit sales can be done in anyone of the following ways:

1. Open Accounting sales
2. Through Acceptance of Bills
3. Through Letters of Credit (LC)

Based on the method of credit sales the factoring service is provided. It can be either domestic or foreign factoring. Generally, Factoring involves provision of specialised services relating to credit investigation, sales ledger management, purchase and collection of debts, credit protection as well as provisions of finance against receivables and risk bearing. In factoring, receivables are generally sold to a financial Institution who charges commission and bears the credit risks associated with the accounts receivables purchased by it. In India banks are not permitted by RBI to directly involve themselves in Factoring Services. Hence, the 'Factors' in India are subsidiaries of few commercial banks like SBI, Canara Bank.

16.2 DEFINITION OF FACTORING

The International Institute for the Unification of Private Law in 1988 defined "Factoring means an arrangement between a Factor and his Client which includes at least two of the following services to be provided by the Factor: (1) Finance, (2) Maintenance of Accounts, (3) Collection of Debts and (4) Protection against Credit Risks". Simply, it is the conversion of credit sales into cash.

In brief, Factoring is a "continuing arrangement" between a financial institution (the factor) and a business concern (the client) selling goods or services to trade customers (the customer) whereby the factor purchases the client's accounts receivables/book debts either with or without recourse to the client and in relation there to controls the credit extended to the customers and administers the sales ledger. Factoring is a financial option for the management of receivables.

In factoring, a factor buys the accounts receivable of a company (Client) and pays generally up to 80% of the amount immediately on agreement. Factoring company pays the remaining amount (Balance 20%-finance cost-operating cost) to the client when the customer pays the debt. Collection of debt from the customer is done either by the factor or the client depending upon the type of factoring. The account receivable in factoring can either be for a product or service. Factoring services are offered for the sale of both goods and services.

16.3 FEATURES OF FACTORING SERVICE

The factoring services generally have the following features:

(*a*) Factor offers the facilities of Instant Cash, Follow up and Speedy Collection, MIS Services, Sales Ledger Administration, Credit Protection, and Advisory Services.

(*b*) Large credit / grace period

(*c*) Factoring is an ideal financial solution for new firms without strong financial resources. This is because credit worthiness is evaluated based on the financial strength of the customer (debtor). Hence these companies can leverage on the financial strength of their customers.

(*d*) Bad debts may or may not be considered for factoring.

(*e*) Credit rating is not mandatory. But the factoring companies usually carry out credit risk analysis before entering into the agreement.

(*f*) Factoring is a method of off balance sheet financing.

(*g*) The Cost of factoring is calculated by adding finance cost with operating cost. Factoring cost vary according to the transaction volume, financial strength of the customer, etc.

(*h*) For delayed payments beyond the approved credit period, penal charge is charged

(*i*) The main functions of factoring include provision of finance, collection of debts, absorption of risk of bad debts in certain cases, sales ledger management, etc.

16.4 MECHANISM OF FACTORING

The mechanism of factoring can be explained with the following diagram

MECHANISM OF FACTORING

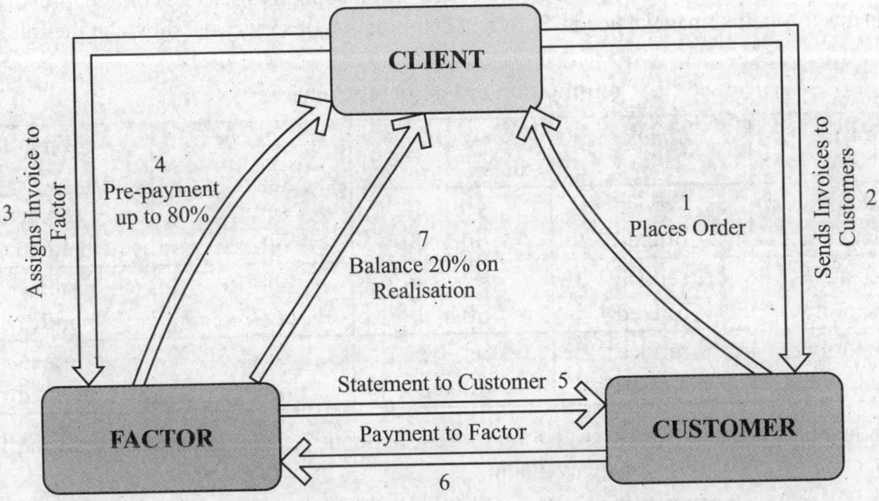

The mechanism of Factoring shown in figure is explained below:

1. Firstly, the Customer places an order with the Client (It may be noted that the client is the seller and customer is the buyer of goods or services).
2. The Client despatches the goods or services to the Customer on credit on open account basis and then sends the corresponding invoices to the Customer directly.
3. Then the Client enters into Factoring arrangement with the Factor. The pre-payment limit, service charges, discount charges and other terms and conditions of the arrangement are agreed upon. The Client assigns invoices to the factor. The original as well as copies of invoices sent to Customer, contain a printed Notice of Assignment addressed to the customer, directing the Customer to make all payments to the Factor.
4. The drawing power is calculated taking into account the prescribed margin (usually around 20%). The prepayment limit is generally around 80%-85% of the eligible debt. The factor retains some percentage of payment for the clearance of payment form the customers. And this retention amount will be released at the end after the complete payment by the customers. The Client is now free to draw any amount up to the drawing power. For the Client to draw money, the Factor issues a cheque favouring the Client's Bank A/c. Realisation are handled by the Factor directly under advice to the client. Outstation cheques are also collected/discounted by the Factor.
5. Periodical statements and reports are furnished to the Client and the Customer.
6. The Customer makes payment on due dates. If monthly instalments are not paid within the due date, follow-up letters are sent.
7. When the payment is cleared by the Customer to Factor, a notice is sent by the Factor to the Client. This is followed by the release of retention margin held by the Factor to the Client.

For rendering the services of collection and maintenance of sales Ledgers, the service charges usually vary on the invoice value, depending on the volume of operations. This service charge is collected at the time of purchase of invoices by the Factor. For making an immediate part payment to the Client, the Factor collects discount charges from the Client. The discount charges are comparable to bank interest rates at these charges are collected monthly.

16.5 FACTORING –COMBINATION OF SERVICES

Factoring has three key elements and the Client has the option to select a combination of these components to suit his financial needs. Different combination of services is shown in the following Table:

Combination of Factoring Services

Service	*Finance*	*Sales Ledger Administration*	*Credit Protection*	*Confidentiality*
Full Factoring	service offered	service offered	service offered	customer notified
Recourse Factoring	service offered	service offered	service not offered	customer notified
Maturity Factoring	service not offered	service offered	service offered	customer notified

(*i*) In Full Factoring which is also known as 'Without Recourse Factoring', all the three components of services are available.

(*ii*) In Recourse Factoring the Customer-risk(risk of default) is borne by the Client.

(*iii*) In Maturity Factoring, Factor makes available funds only at the end of the credit period after collection of sum from customer.

(*iv*) The column 'Confidentiality' in the above table indicates whether the customer *i.e.*, the buyer is notified of the Factoring arrangement or not.

16.6 FACTORING AND BILL DISCOUNTING

Factoring is in some respects similar to bills in the views that both these services provide short term finance. Also both of them discount receivables which the clients would have otherwise received from the buyer at the end of the credit period. But, these differ in many important aspects. Let us see the differences between factoring and bills discounting hereunder:

Bills Discounting *vs.* Factoring

Sl. No.	*Bills Discounting*	*Factoring*
	1. Nature of Accommodation	
1.	It is Purely a financial accommodation. That is, it facilitates only financing.	It provides a package of services including financing. That is, in addition to financing other services such as follow up and collection of invoices, sales ledger administration, etc. Thus, factoring is both financial and service greement in nature.
	2. Mode of Accommodation	
2.	It is an advances against bills.	It is a purchase of debt assignment.

	3. Volume of Finance	
3.	It is individual transaction oriented and the amount of finance extended is usually a lesser amount.	It is whole turnover oriented and the amount of finance is bulk in nature.
	4. Payment of Charges	
4.	In bills discounting the charges are recovered upfront *i.e.*, in advance, and this increase the total effective cost.	In factoring no such upfront / advance recovery of charges.
	5. Nature of Procedures	
5.	The procedures to be followed in bills discounting is difficult and the finance is not instant.	The procedure to be followed in bills discounting is easy and the finance in many cases are instant and in some cases in a very few days.
	6. Position in Balance Sheet	
6.	It is of the nature of "In Balance sheet Financing".	It is of the nature of "Off Balance Sheet Financing". That is , Factoring is not a loan. It is the purchase of a company's accounts receivables at a discount. As a result, advances made to the company from a factor are not classified as a liability on the balance sheet. The financial goal to keep debt to a minimum is the therefore maintained.
	7. Grace Period	
7.	In bills discounting the grace period is maximum 3 Days.	In factoring the grace period is liberal and to the maximum of 75 days in general.
	8. Scope for minimizing Interest Cost	
8.	In bills discounting entire bill amount is to be drawn on the date of discount. There is no scope for minimizing interest cost.	In factoring amount can be drawn as and when required. Finance charge is levied on daily products at monthly intervals. Only on actual drawings. Hence, there is scope for minimizing interest cost.
	9. Responsibility of the Client	
9.	Under bills discounting it is always offered with Recourse to the clients. That is the responsibility for bad debts is always with the clients.	Factoring can be either with Recourse or without Recourse to the client.
	10. Documents to be Submitted	
10.	Under bills discounting, the original documents like RR, and Bill of Lading, etc. are to be submitted.	Under factoring, only the copies of the documents like RR, and Bill of Lading, etc. are to be submitted.

16.7 TYPES OF FACTORING

The different types of Factoring are can be seen in the following chart:

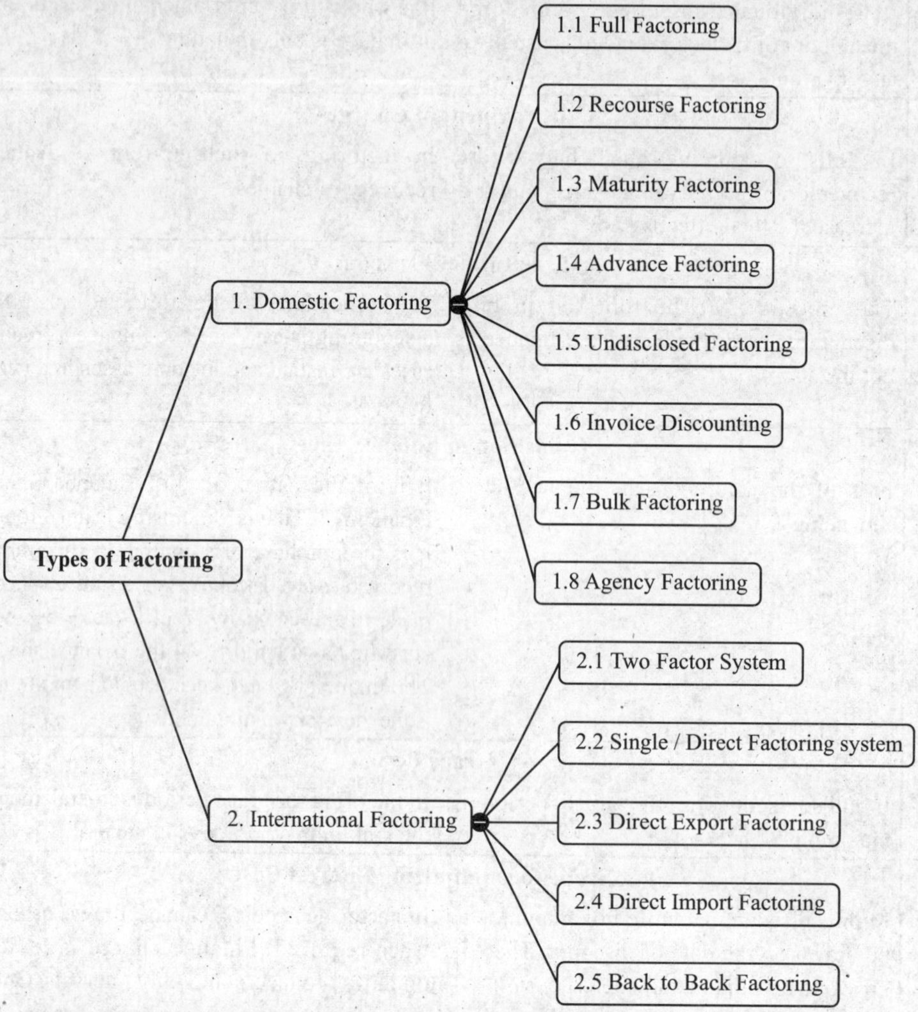

Let us see the meaning of these types of factoring here under:

16.7.1 Domestic Factoring

Different types of Domestic Factoring are as follows:

1. Full Factoring

This is also known as "without-Recourse Factoring". It is the most comprehensive type of facility offering all types of services namely finance, sales ledger administration, collection, debt protection and customer information.

2. Recourse Factoring

The Factoring provides all types of facilities except debt protection. This type of service is offered in India. As discussed earlier, under Recourse Factoring, the client's liability to Factor is not discharged until the customer pays in full. That is, if the customer fails to pay the amount on the due date, the factor will recover the amount from the client.

3. Maturity Factoring

It is also known as "Collection Factoring". Under this arrangement, except providing finance, all other basic characteristics of Factoring are present. The payment is effected to the client at the end of collection period or the day of collecting accounts whichever is earlier.

4. Advance Factoring

This could be with are without recourse. Under this arrangement, the Factor provides advance at an agreed rate of interest to the client on uncollected and non-due receivables. This is only a pre-payment and not an advance.

5. Undisclosed Factoring

Under this, the customer is not notified about the arrangement between the client and the Factor. Hence the buyer is unaware of factoring arrangement, the debt collection is organised by the client who makes payment of each invoice to the Factor, if advance payment had been received earlier.

6. Invoice Discounting

In this arrangement, the only facility provided by the Factor is finance. In this method the client is a reputed company who would like to deal with its customers directly, including collection, and keep this Factoring arrangement confidential. The client collects payments from customer and hands it over to Factor. The risk involved in invoice discounting is much higher than in any other methods. The Factors has liberty to convert the facility by notifying all the clients to protect his interest. This service is becoming quite popular in Europe and nearly one third of Factoring business comprises of this facility.

7. Bulk Factoring

It is a modified version of Invoice discounting wherein notification of assignment of debts is given to the customers. However, the client is subject to full recourse and he carries out his own administration and collection.

8. Agency Factoring

Under this arrangement, the facilities of finance and protection against bad debts are provided by the Factor, whereas the sales ledger administration and collection of debts are carried out by the client.

16.7.2 International Factoring

Traditionally international trade is based on Letters of Credit. When the exporter knows the importer well with repetitive transactions, he may be willing to export on 'Open Account' basis. On open account the exporter ships the goods without letter of credit or advance payment. Hence, it is credit risky for exporter. If credit is extended (say 90 days usance), the exporter will be quite reluctant as he encounters a credit risk and hence invariably insists on L/C. In advanced countries bankers do not make much of a distinction between fund-based and non-fund based facilities and hence if they have to open L/C's it may be at the cost of a reduced overdraft or bills limit for the importer.

The system of L/C's operates on the "Doctrine of Strict Compliance" which means the Letter of Credit opening bank will pay money to the exporter only when all the conditions listed in the Letter of Credit document are satisfied by the exporter/shipper of goods. In many cases, the documents fail to pass the grade which means the exporter has simply lost the security available to him under the L/C. Further, nowadays, goods move very fast and hence if documents are held up in banks for processing, it causes delay and inconvenience to the importer.

In the light of the above, international trade has slowly started moving from cash to credit, and from L/C's to open account sales. International Factoring is a service which helps the exporter and importer to trade on open account terms.

Types of International Factoring

The following are the important types f International Factoring. The client can choose any type of international factoring depending upon exporter - client needs and his price bearing capacity.

1. Two Factor System

This is the most common system of international factoring and involves four parties *i.e.*, Exporter, Importer, Export Factor in exporter's country and Import Factor in Importer's country.

The functions of the Export Factor are:

(*a*) Assessment of the financial strength of the exporter

(*b*) Prepayment to the exporter

(*c*) Follow-up with the Import Factor

(*d*) Sharing of commission with the import Factor

The functions of the Import Factor are:

(*a*) Maintaining the books of the exporter in respect of sales to the debtors in his country.

(*b*) Collection of debts from the importer and remitting the proceeds to the exporter's Factor.

(*c*) Providing credit protection in case of financial inability on the part of any of the debtors.

2. Single / Direct Factoring System

In this system, a special agreement is signed between two Factoring companies for single Factoring. Whereas in Two Factor System, credit is provided by import Factor and pre-payment, book keeping and collection responsibilities remain with export Factor. For this system to be effective there should be strong co-ordination and co-operation between two Factoring companies. Pricing is lower when compared to Two Factor System.

3. Direct Export Factoring

Here only one Factoring company is involved *i.e.*, export Factor, which provides all services including finance to the exporter.

4. Direct Import Factoring

Under this system, the seller chooses to work directly with Factor of the importing country. The Factoring agreement is executed between the exporter and the import Factor. The import Factor is responsible for sales ledger administration, collection of debts and providing bad debt protection up to the agreed level of risk cover.

5. Back to Back Factoring

It is a much specialised form of International Factoring, used when suppliers are selling large volumes to a few debtors for which it is difficult to cover the credit risk in International Factoring. In this case, International Factor can sign a domestic Factoring agreement with the debtor whereby it will be getting the receivables as security for the credit risk taken in favour of Export Factor.

16.8 BENEFITS OF FACTORING SERVICE

Factoring service provides various benefits to business community, especially small and medium firms and also to the banks as well. They are given here under:

16.8.1 Benefits to the Clients

1. The client or seller can convert accounts receivables into cash without bothering about sales ledger administration even repayment in some cases.
2. Factoring ensures a definite pattern of cash inflows.

3. Continuous Factoring virtually eliminates the need for the credit department. That is why receivable financing through Factoring is gaining popularity as useful source of financing short term fund requirements of business enterprises because of the inherent advantage of flexibility it affords to the borrowing firm. The seller firm may continue to get finance on its receivables on a more or less automatic basis. If its sales expand or contract, it can vary the financing proportionately.
4. Unlike an unsecured loan, compensating balances are not required in this case. Another advantage consists of relieving the borrowing firm of substantial credit and collection costs and further to certain extent from a considerable part of cash management.
5. The customer is relieved of maintaining record relating to credit sales customers A/c, reminders to debtors, initiating recovery measures, etc. This saves substantial administration expenditure.
6. In export sales, difficulties of credit assessment and debt collection are more pronounced. Availing of Professional factoring services is more advantageous
7. Under factoring arrangement, regular cash inflow at periodical intervals is assured. This helps, short-term fund flow and availing of discounts from suppliers.
8. Factoring as a professional approach in collection of debts inculcates discipline in cash management among customers.
9. Firms engaged in a highly seasonal business may submit the peak loan of receivables to the Factor for credit review and approval as a cheaper alternative to expanding its own credit department.
10. Finally, when credit is necessary and cannot be obtained elsewhere either because of tight money conditions or poor financial position, the Factoring of receivables will be more appropriate.

16.8.2 Benefits to the Banks

The following are the advantages of Factoring service to the banks:

1. Factoring provides the banks an integrated receivables management.
2. Factoring improves the service efficiency of the banks through closer follow up of credit sales.
3. Factoring provides increasing cash flow and liquidity to the banks.
4. Factoring improves the quality of the advances made by the banks by reducing the turnover of receivables and by increasing operating cycles.
5. Factoring enhances the profits through cash discounts on purchase.
6. Factoring safeguards as insurance against non-performing assets of the banks. In this, all proceeds of factored bills are credited to bank, hence bank account will not become non-performing assets for shortage of credits.

16.9 LIMITATIONS OF FACTORING

Factoring service suffers from the following limitations:

1. **Factoring is a high risk prone area:** It may possibly result in over dependence on Factoring, mismanagement, over trading or even dishonesty on the clients part.
2. **Factoring as a costly source of financing:** The cost of financing being higher than the normal lending rate, Factoring is an expensive way of financing.

16.10 FACTORING IN INDIA

Factoring is a new financial concept in India. In keeping pace with the growing need of credit, the necessity to develop more and more asset based financing agencies has become imperative. Especially for SSI units which have serious liquidity problems on account of non-payment from public sector undertakings. Factoring services provide good relief in such cases. There is greater potential for factoring in SSI sector alone. SBI Factors, a subsidiary of State Bank of India, is one of the leading factoring companies in India with an asset base of ₹ 1908.00 crore as on March 31, 2008. It is the first factoring company to be set up in India. SBI Factors and GT.F together command more than 80 per cent of the factoring market, amounting to ₹ 34,000 crore. The total asset size of the merged entity(The merger between SBI Factors and Global Trade Finance (GTF)) would be around ₹ 5,000 crore and this would go up to ₹ 7,000 crore by Financial Year 2009.

Suggestions of C.S. Kalayana Sundaram Committee Jan 28, 1988

1. The committee recommended the introduction of factoring services in India to complement the services provided by banks. Export Factoring can also be launched.
2. Factors should cover wide range of industries embracing all sectors of economy.
3. The cost of funds should not be more than 13.5% per annum. Factors will have to charge the price for services at a rate not higher than banks. The price for administrative services may not exceed 2.5 to 3% of debt services.
4. Factoring agencies may be promoted on zonal basis. One each for North, South, East and West (For South, Canana Bank has sponsored Can Bank Factors Ltd. while in the Western Zone SBI Factors Ltd. has been set up).
5. Banks have considerable experience in financing and collection of receivables. Besides, they have access to credit information regarding both sellers and buyers. An additional advantage is the large network of branches. At present only two Factoring subsidiaries of State Bank of India and Canara Bank are functioning namely SBI Factors Ltd. and Can Bank Factors Ltd. covering west and south zones. They are also permitted to operate in other zones as the Punjab National Bank and Allahabad Bank have not come forward to set up subsidiaries for North and East Zones.
6. The committee has recommended that the government may enact a suitable legislation for the levy of penal interest for delayed payment from the debtors beyond specified period. It has also recommended that the government should exempt assignment of factored debts from stamp duty.

Factoring in India and Role of Reserve Bank

Government of India enacted the Factoring Act, 2011 to bring in the much needed legal framework for the factoring business in the country. It has provided definitions for the terms factoring, factor, receivables and assignment. The Act also specifies that any entity conducting factoring business would need to be registered with RBI as NBFCs; while exempting banks, government companies and corporations established under an Act of Parliament, from the requirement of registration with RBI for conducting factoring business. The Act, thus, gave clarity to the activity of assignment of receivables and also granted exemption from stamp duty on documents executed for the purpose of assignment of receivables in favour of Factors thereby making the business more viable. The Act also envisages that all transactions of assignment of receivables shall be registered with the Central Registry established under the SARFAESI Act, 2002 to reduce the possibility of frauds and for strengthening the due diligence process for the clients.

The Act has given powers to the Reserve Bank to stipulate conditions for 'principal business' of a Factor as also powers to give directions and collect information from factors. Subsequent to the passing of the Act, the Reserve Bank has created a separate category of NBFCs, *viz*; NBFC-Factors and issued directions for their regulation. The prudential norms as applicable to NBFCs engaged in lending business, has also been extended to the NBFC-Factors. Further, bank finance to factoring companies and the factoring business conducted by banks are also regulated by the RBI. (*Source:* RBI Publications)

Factoring service so far not picked up in India due to various deficiencies including high cost service charges, documentation difficulties, legal lacuna, etc.

REVIEW QUESTIONS

Short Answer Questions

1. What is meant by factoring?
2. Define factoring and what are the features of factoring?
3. What are the functions of factoring?
4. Write short notes on:
   (*a*) Full Factoring
   (*b*) Recourse Factoring
   (*c*) Maturity Factoring
   (*d*) Advance Factoring
   (*e*) Undisclosed Factoring
   (*f*) Invoice Discounting
   (*g*) Bulk Factoring
   (*h*) Agency Factoring
5. Write a short note on Two Factor System.

Essay Type Questions

1. Explain the meaning and features of factoring.
2. Explain the mechanism of factoring operations.
3. Write a detailed note on different combinations of factoring services.
4. Differentiate between factoring and bills discounting.
6. Explain the types of factoring service offered for domestic customers.
7. What are the different types of international factoring? Explain.
8. Explain the various benefits of factoring service.
9. Write a note on the factoring service in India.

17 CHAPTER Mutual Funds

Today, there are different investment opportunities available to investors. Mutual funds are one among them. Like all other investments, mutual funds also not free of risks. The investors should compare the risks and expected yields after adjustment of tax on various instruments while taking investment decisions. The investors may seek advice from experts and consultants including agents and distributors of mutual funds schemes while making investment decisions. But, while investing in mutual funds such difficulties are reduced considerably.

Mutual Funds are agencies which pool together the investors' funds and invest them in diversified securities, thus reducing risks. The funds are managed by experts known as portfolio managers and are constituted as a trust. In a simpler term, Mutual Funds are holders of vast pools of money mostly collected from retail investors like individual savers. In one respect they are similar to a bank that is intermediaries between savers and users of capital. They are usually permitted to invest in Financial Assets and not in physical asset like gold and real estate.

17.1 MEANING OF MUTUAL FUND

A Mutual Fund is formed by the coming together of a number of investors who hand over their surplus funds to a professional organisation to manage it through investments in capital market.

Definition: Mutual fund can be defined as "the mechanism for pooling the resources by issuing units to the investors and investing funds in securities in accordance with objectives as disclosed in offer document". Since, the investments made in securities are spread across different industries and sectors, the risk is greatly reduced. Diversification reduces the risk because all stocks may not move in the same direction in the same proportion at the same time.

Mutual fund issues units to the investors in accordance with quantum of money invested by them. Investors of mutual funds are known as unit holders. The profits or losses are shared by the investors in proportion to their investments. That is, the Mutual Fund is basically a risk reducing tool. Risk reduction is achieved by diversification of the portfolio. Diversification means that a Mutual Fund invests in a large number of shares and financial instruments thereby lowering the overall risk. Further the fund managers' investment decisions are based on the basis of intensive research and are backed by informed judgment and experience.

17.2 CONCEPT OF OPERATION OF MUTUAL FUNDS

The basic concept of operation of mutual funds can be explained as follows:

Basic Operation of Mutual Funds
Basics of Mutual Funds

Mutual Fund Organisation

↓

Many investors with common financial objectives pool their money

↓

Investors, on a proportionate basis, get mutual fund units for the sum contributed to the pool

↓

The money collected from investors is invested into shares, debentures and other securities by the fund manager

↓

The fund manager realizes gains or losses, and collects dividend or interest income

↓

Any capital gains or losses from such investments are passed on to the investors in proportion of the number of units held by them

Although Mutual Fund units are quoted on the market, a Mutual Fund unit is not same as a share. Each unit of a Mutual Fund represents a portion of the total corpus it manages under a scheme. The mutual funds normally come out with a number of schemes with different investment objectives which are launched from time to time

For example, a mutual fund may float a scheme for collecting ₹50 crore for investment in equity shares. Here the total corpus/quantity of the scheme is ₹50 crore. The corpus may be divided into five crore units of ₹10 each. Hence the unit value of Fund is ₹10 each. The value of shares in which the investment has been made may have been doubled. If so, the market value of unit may also rise. Further, a Mutual Fund distributes everything that it earns to the investors. Expenses relating to the fund, however are charged to the fund. To sum up, a Mutual Fund collects money from investors and invests it for them. The fund however has to disclose the full details of the investment scheme in advance to the investors. The entire income/profit are distributed to the investors in proportion to their investments. Expenses for managing the fund (Subject to a maximum limit as prescribed by SEBI) are charged to the fund.

17.3 ORGANISATION OF MUTUAL FUND

Mutual funds in India are established in the form of a trust by a sponsor to raise money by trustees through the sale of units to the public. Mutual fund organisation consists of the following entities:

1. Sponsor
2. Mutual Fund Trust
3. Asset Management Company(AMC)

4. Custodian
5. Transfer Agent

It can be explained with the help of the following diagram:

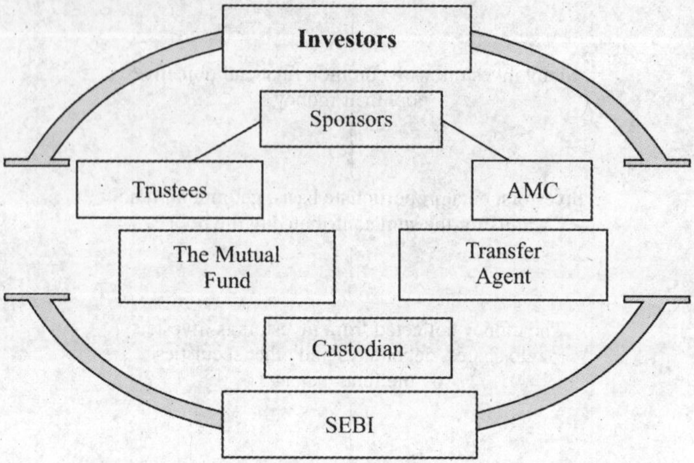

A mutual fund is set up in the form of a trust, which has sponsor, trustees, asset management company (AMC), custodian and transfer agent. Here the investors are the holders of mutual fund units. And regarding SEBI, its primary aim is to protect the interest of the mutual fund investors. SEBI has formulated several policies for better functioning and controls the mutual funds. SEBI issued guidelines pertaining to the mutual funds. All mutual funds, private sector and public sector are regulated by the guidelines of the SEBI. The Asset Management Company managing the funds has to be approved by the SEBI. Let us see about the other important entities of Mutual funds.

17.3.1 Sponsor

Sponsor for the mutual fund could be a company registered under the companies Act. 1956. The company can be in the form of either a public limited or a private limited company. Two or more companies can join together to sponsor a mutual fund. In simple, the Sponsor is the company which set up the mutual fund. To promote a mutual fund, the Sponsor has to meet criteria laid down by SEBI. These criteria broadly deal with sufficient net worth, and past track record in terms of fair dealings and integrity. Only those who qualify in terms of these criteria are permitted by SEBI to set up a mutual fund.

Actually the sponsors take all the basic steps in the establishment of mutual fund trust. They appoint the fund managers or the asset management company. And after obtaining permission from the SEBI, the role of sponsor will be over and the trust will deal with SEBI there after.

17.3.2 Mutual Fund Trust

The trust is established by a sponsor or more than one sponsor who is like promoter of a company. The trustees of the mutual fund hold its property for the benefit of the unit holders. Sponsors created the Mutual Fund Trust under the Indian Trust Act, 1882. The Trust performs the following essential functions:

1. Planning and formulating new schemes for the mutual fund established.
2. Getting the approval of SEBI for the schemes formulated.
3. Designing and implementing the marketing plans for public subscription more efficiently.
4. Monitoring the AMC and ensure that the AMC complies with all the guidelines. And report periodically the progress to the unit holders of the mutual fund.

5. Ensuring that the investments made by AMC are according to prescribed guidelines.
6. Ensuring that the securities are safely kept in custody with the approved Custodian.
7. Ensuring that the returns on the investments are properly accounted and maintained.
8. Issuing the annual report to the unit holders or members of the fund.

In general, the trustees are vested with the general power of superintendence and direction over AMC. They monitor the performance and compliance of SEBI Regulations by the mutual fund. The Trustees are an important link in the working of a mutual fund. Trustees are people with long experience who have earned a name for themselves for financial integrity and excellence in their fields. It is the responsibility of the Trustees to see that the AMC always acts in the best interest of the investors.

17.3.3 Asset Management Company

Asset Management Company (AMC) approved by SEBI manages the funds by making investments in various types of securities. They are the Fund Managers and manage the various schemes of mutual funds. The planning, marketing and collection of funds of the schemes are the responsibility of the mutual fund trust, where as, the investment of the pooled funds is the responsibility of the AMC.

It makes appropriate investment decisions and invest either directly in the primary market or through brokers in the secondary market. It is the duty of the AMC to maintain proper accounts and give necessary information regarding investments and fund management operations to the trustees. The AMC employs a large number of professionals for investments and research and for investor and agent servicing. The AMC also comes out with new schemes periodically. It plays a key role in the running of a mutual fund and it operates under the supervision and guidance of the Trustees.

17.3.4 Custodian

Custodian, who is registered with SEBI, holds the securities of various schemes of the fund in its custody. The AMC decide and makes investments. But the custodians have the responsibility of the custody of investments made. It is their duty to do all checking and verify the securities. They also deal with transfer of shares, settlements etc and act as transfer agents by performing the functions of transfer, exchange, redemption, receipt of dividends, maintenance of detailed records of transactions etc.

SEBI Regulations require that at least two thirds of the directors of trustee company or board of trustees must be independent i.e. they should not be associated with the sponsors. Also, 50% of the directors of AMC must be independent. All mutual funds are required to be registered with SEBI before they launch any scheme.

17.3.5 Transfer Agents

Under mutual funds the mutual fund investors do a number of transactions on any given day. They may buy, sell or switch units. They could request for a bank address change or an address change. Each such request is a transaction by itself. Mutual fund houses have to maintain records of each such transaction. A mutual fund may not want to invest in these processes nor would have the skilled expertise to handle these huge transactions on a professional basis.

Hence, they may outsource this work to an agency which can handle these requests from investors on a regular basis. The transfer agents help them in this process. The transfer agent maintains these records on behalf of the mutual fund house, through its offices across the country.

Custodians also can act as transfer agents by performing the functions of transfer, exchange, redemption, receipt of dividends, maintenance of detailed records of transactions etc.

17.4 TYPES OF MUTUAL FUND SCHEMES

A Mutual Fund is free to design its schemes (subject to SEBI regulations) to suit the needs of various group of investors in terms of nature of investments, dividend distribution, capital appreciation and liquidity etc. The broad classifications of the mutual fund schemes can be seen in the following chart:

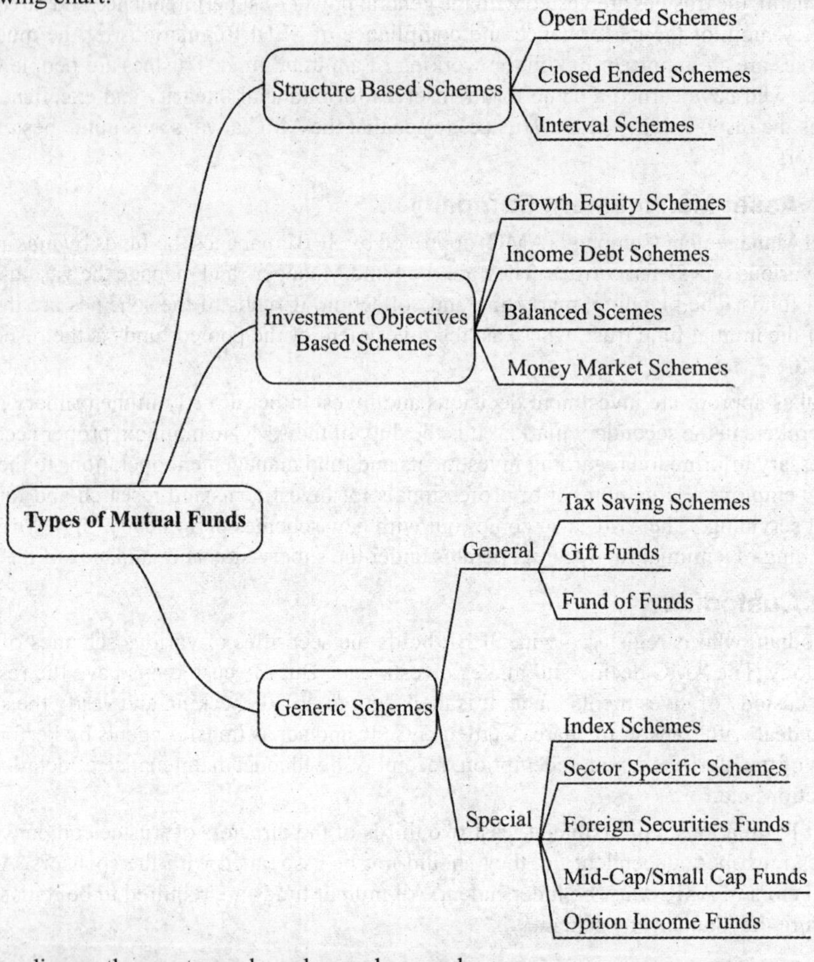

Let us discuss the most popular schemes here under:

17.4.1 Classifications on the basis of the structure of the funds

The funds can be classified on the basis of structure as follows:

17.4.1.1 Open Ended Schemes

An open ended scheme is a scheme in which an investor can buy and sell units on a daily basis, wherein the scheme has perpetual existence, and a flexible ever changing corpus. That is, the open-ended fund or scheme is one that is available for subscription and repurchase on a continuous basis. These schemes do not have a fixed maturity period. The key feature of open-end schemes is liquidity.

In simple terms, investors are free to buy and sell any number of units at any point of time, at prices announced by the Fund. In other words, an open-ended fund issues new units every time an investor puts in his money. Similarly when the units are repurchased by the Fund the units are retired to the extent they are repurchased. Hence the value of the Fund keeps on changing on day to day basis. The prices, that is, the buying and selling price of the unit are linked to the Net Asset Value of the units. Investors can conveniently buy and sell units at NAV related prices which are declared on a daily basis.

Features of Open Ended Funds

The following are the important features of open ended funds.

1. **Regular Investment Plan:** Some Open Ended Funds offer a Regular Investment Plan wherein a fixed amount can be invested every month subject to a minimum of ₹1,000 and in multiples of ₹100 thereafter. The investor in such a case gives 12 post dated cheques dated first of every month . The amount so invested is converted into units at the day's sale price. The same is added to the unit balance of the unit holder. Certain class of investors who go in for recurring monthly deposit schemes can avail this plan to maximise returns with easy liquidity.
2. **Regular Withdrawal Plan:** Conversely, the Open Ended Fund also offers Regular Withdrawal Plan wherein a fixed amount can be withdrawn every month subject to a minimum of ₹500, for a minimum period of 12 months. The amount so withdrawn by sale is converted at NAV of the 15th / 30th working day of every month and the same is subtracted from the unit balance of the unit holder. Investors wanting monthly income to manage their affairs can withdraw every month with easy liquidity. Certain Open Ended Fund offer the option of Dividend Reinvestment Plan, in which any dividend, if declared is automatically reinvested and adequate number of units based on the day's sale price are credited to the unit holders account.
3. **Instant Liquidity:** As the units can be sold on any working day at the repurchase price, the investor is offered instant liquidity all through the year. Instant liquidity means, the fund operates like a bank account wherein the investor is able to get cash across the counter for the units sold.
4. **Free Entry:** There is free entry and exit of investors in an Open Ended Fund. The investor can join in and come out from the fund as and when he desires. Often he enters when the NAV is at a low price and comes out when the NAV is quoted at a higher rate thereby making cash profits.

17.4.1.2 Close Ended Schemes

A close-ended fund or scheme means that it has a predetermined maturity period e.g. 5-7 years. The fund is open for subscription only during a specified period at the time of launch of the scheme. Thus, the Close Ended Schemes have a fixed corpus and operates for a fixed duration, at the end of which the entire corpus is disinvested and, proceeds distributed to the various unit holders in proportion to their holdings. After final distribution, the scheme ceases to exist. Thus close-ended fund has a fixed number of units or shares like a company.

Investors can invest in the scheme at the time of the initial public issue and thereafter they can buy or sell the units of the scheme on the stock exchanges where the units are listed. That is, these units or shares are traded on stock exchange where they are listed. Their stock market price may be more or less over their NAV depending upon supply and demand for the units. In order to provide an exit route to the investors, some close-ended funds give an option of selling back the units to the mutual fund through periodic repurchase at NAV related prices. SEBI Regulations stipulate that at least one of the two exit routes is provided to the investor i.e. either repurchase facility or through listing on stock exchanges. These mutual funds schemes disclose NAV generally on weekly basis.

17.4.1.3 Interval/Hybrid Schemes

The Interval schemes are called as hybrid schemes because, these types of schemes combine the features of both open-ended and closed-ended schemes. They may be traded on the stock exchange or may be open for sale or redemption during pre-determined intervals at NAV based prices.

17.4.2 Classifications on the basis of Investment Objectives

The mutual funds can be classified on the basis of investment objectives as follows:

1. Growth Schemes
2. Income Schemes
3. Balanced Schemes
4. Money Market Schemes

1. Growth / Equity Oriented Schemes: Growth schemes are also called as Equity Oriented Schemes. A pure growth scheme aims at generating long term capital appreciation for the investors by investing a substantial portion of the corpus (*i.e.*, funds collected) in high growth equity shares or other equity related instruments of corporate bodies. Although declaration of dividend is not prohibited, the principal objective remains capital appreciation.

The aim of growth funds is to provide capital appreciation over the medium to long- term. Such schemes normally invest a major part of their corpus in equities. Such funds have comparatively high risks. These schemes provide different options to the investors like dividend option, capital appreciation, *etc.* and the investors may choose an option depending on their preferences. The investors must indicate the option in the application form. The mutual funds also allow the investors to change the options at a later date. Growth schemes are good for investors having a long-term outlook seeking appreciation over a period of time.

2. Income / Debt Oriented Schemes: A Pure Income Scheme aims at generating and distributing regular income (yearly / half yearly etc.) to the investors by investing a substantial portion of the corpus in high income yielding, fixed income instruments, such as debentures, bonds. Declaration of regular dividends is the main objective in such schemes.

The aim of income funds is to provide regular and steady income to investors. Such schemes generally invest in fixed income securities such as bonds, corporate debentures, Government securities and money market instruments. Such funds are less risky compared to equity schemes. These funds are not affected because of fluctuations in equity markets. However, opportunities of capital appreciation are also limited in such funds. The NAVs of such funds are affected because of change in interest rates in the country. If the interest rates fall, NAVs of such funds are likely to increase in the short run and vice versa. However, long term investors may not bother about these fluctuations.

3. Balanced Schemes: A Balanced Scheme is one which aims at both, distributing regular income and also end-scheme capital appreciation to the investors by balancing the investments of the corpus between the high growth equity shares and also the fixed income earning debt securities of the companies.

The aim of balanced funds is to provide both growth and regular income as such schemes invest both in equities and fixed income securities in the proportion indicated in their offer documents. These are appropriate for investors looking for moderate growth. They generally invest 40-60% in equity and debt instruments. These funds are also affected because of fluctuations in share prices in the stock markets. However, NAVs of such funds are likely to be less volatile compared to pure equity funds.

4. Money Market Schemes: Money market schemes are also called as liquid funds.These funds are also income funds and their aim is to provide easy liquidity, preservation of capital and moderate income. These schemes invest exclusively in safer short-term instruments such as treasury bills, certificates of deposit, commercial paper and inter-bank call money, government securities, etc. Returns on these schemes fluctuate much less compared to other funds. These funds are appropriate for corporate and individual investors as a means to park their surplus funds for short periods.

17.4.3 Generic Type Schemes

The generic type schemes include the General and Special schemes. They are as follows:

17.4.3.1 General Schemes

The generic schemes of mutual funds are as follows:

1. **Tax Savings Schemes:** Tax savings schemes are basically growth schemes which also offer tax rebates to the investors under the Income Tax Laws. Currently, the provisions for deductions are covered under section 80C of the Income Tax Act 1961.
2. **Gift Fund:** The Gift funds invest exclusively in government securities. Government securities have no default risk. NAVs of these schemes also fluctuate due to change in interest rates and other economic factors as is the case with income or debt oriented schemes.
3. **Fund of Funds:** A scheme that invests primarily in other schemes of the same mutual fund or other mutual funds is known as a Fund of Funds scheme. A Fund of Funds scheme enables the investors to achieve greater diversification through one scheme. It provide investors with an added advantage of diversifying into different mutual fund schemes with even a small amount of investment, which further helps in diversification of risks across a greater universe. That is, the mutual funds that do not invest in financial or physical assets, but do invest in other mutual fund schemes offered by different AMCs, are known as Fund of Funds. Fund of Funds maintain a portfolio comprising of units of other mutual fund schemes, just like conventional mutual funds maintain a portfolio comprising of equity/debt/money market instruments or non financial assets.. However, the expenses of Fund of Funds are quite high on account of compounding expenses of investments into different mutual fund schemes.

17.4.3.2 Special Schemes

1. **Index Schemes:** Index Funds replicate the portfolio of a particular index such as the BSE Sensitive index, NSE 50 index (Nifty), etc. These schemes invest in the securities in the same weightage comprising of an index. NAVs of such schemes would rise or fall in accordance with the rise or fall in the index, though not exactly by the same percentage due to some factors known as "tracking error" in technical terms. Necessary disclosures in this regard are made in the offer document of the mutual fund scheme.
2. **Sector Specific Schemes:** These are the schemes invest in the securities of only those sectors or industries as specified in the offer documents. e.g. Software, Fast Moving Consumer Goods (FMCG), Petroleum stocks, etc. The returns in these funds are dependent on the performance of the respective sectors. While these funds may give higher returns, they are more risky compared to diversified funds.
3. The other types of schemes under this category includes, Foreign security Schemes, Small-cap equity Schemes, Option Income schemes etc

17.5 REGULATION OF MUTUAL FUNDS IN INDIA

In India the concept of mutual funds was first introduced by Unit Trust of India in 1963. In the year 1992, Securities and exchange Board of India (SEBI) Act was passed. The objectives of

SEBI are – to protect the interest of investors in securities and to promote the development of and to regulate the securities market. In early 1990s, Government allowed public sector banks and institutions to set up mutual funds. A mutual fund is required to be registered with Securities and Exchange Board of India (SEBI) which regulates securities markets before it can collect funds from the public. Many banks have set up subsidiaries for starting mutual fund business. Some important bankers include, SBI, Canara Bank, Bank of India, Punjab National Bank *etc.*,

As far as mutual funds are concerned, SEBI formulates policies and regulates the mutual funds to protect the interest of the investors. SEBI notified regulations for the mutual funds in 1993. Thereafter, mutual funds sponsored by private sector entities were allowed to enter the capital market. The regulations were fully revised in 1996 and have been amended thereafter from time to time. SEBI has also issued guidelines to the mutual funds from time to time to protect the interests of investors.

All mutual funds whether promoted by public sector or private sector entities including those promoted by foreign entities are governed by the same set of Regulations. There is no distinction in regulatory requirements for these mutual funds and all are subject to monitoring and inspections by SEBI. The risks associated with the schemes launched by the mutual funds sponsored by these entities are of similar type.

17.5.1 SEBI (Mutual Funds) Regulations-The rights of investors under SEBI (MF) Regulations, 1993:

A. Investor servicing

(*a*) Certificates: An investor under a close ended scheme is entitled to receive the unit certificates on allotment within a period of 10 weeks from the date of closure of subscription lists. In case of an open ended Mutual Fund schemes this period is 6 weeks from the date of closure of the initial offer.

(*b*) Transfer of Units: An investor is entitled to get the unit certificates transferred within a period of 30 days from the date of lodgement of the certificates along with the relevant transfer forms.

(*c*) Refund : If the total collections of the funds by a Mutual Fund is less than the statutory minimum (Closed ended funds : ₹ 20 crore, open ended funds : ₹ 50 crore or 60% of the targeted amounts whichever is higher) the applicants are entitled to receive the entire application monies as refund within a period of 6 weeks from the date of closure of subscription lists. If the refund is delayed beyond this period, the applicants are entitled to receive, along with the application money, interest at the rate of 15% p.a. for the period of delay.

B. Disclosures

(*a*) An investor under a Mutual Fund scheme is entitled to receive information about the Net Asset Value at intervals not exceeding 3 months in case of open ended schemes and one month in the case of closed ended schemes. This information would be published in atleast two daily newspapers.

(*b*) Every Mutual Fund is under an obligation to its investors to publish the audited annual report and unaudited half yearly report, through prominent newspapers in respect of each of its schemes, within 6 months and 3 months respectively of the date of closure of accounts.

17.6 NET ASSET VALUE OF A MUTUAL FUND SCHEME

The performance of a particular scheme of a mutual fund is denoted by Net Asset Value (NAV). Mutual funds invest the money collected from the investors in securities markets. In simple words, Net Asset Value is the market value of the securities held by the scheme. Since market value of securities changes every day, NAV of a scheme also varies on day to day basis. The NAV per unit is the market value of securities of a scheme divided by the total number of units of the scheme on any particular date. For example, if the market value of securities of a mutual fund scheme is ₹ 200 lakhs and the mutual fund has issued 10 lakhs units of ₹ 10 each to the investors, then the NAV per unit of the fund is ₹20. NAV is required to be disclosed by the mutual funds on a regular basis - daily or weekly - depending on the type of scheme.

The net asset value of a Mutual Fund scheme is basically the per unit market value of all the assets of the scheme. It can be explained with the help of the following example.

Scheme name	:	XYZ
Scheme size	:	₹ 50,00,00,000 (Rupees fifty crore)
Face value of units	:	₹ 10/-
No. of units	:	5,00,00,000
Investments	:	In shares
Market value of Shares	:	₹ 75,00,00,000/- (Rupees seventy five crore).

$$\text{NAV} = \frac{\text{Market value of investments}}{\text{No. of units}}$$

$$= \frac{75,00,00,000}{5,00,00,000}$$

$$= ₹\,15$$

Thus each unit of ₹ 10/- is now worth ₹ 15/-.

17.7 ADVANTAGES OF MUTUAL FUNDS

The Mutual Fund concept is based upon the rationalistic choice of investment portfolio. Minimisation of risks, maximisation of yield and liquidity are the objectives of investment. Individual investors have to make strenuous efforts to achieve a rational choice of securities for minimising risks and maximising yield. The task becomes difficult for the individual investors who are not so well informed, whereas a Mutual Fund possesses the resources and expertise to make the right choice for him. The individual investors may have problems of dealing with a large number of companies, and making the right choice of securities for overall portfolio whereas, by investing in Mutual Funds, he gets the benefit of maximum return, minimum risk and capital appreciation, thus benefiting from the choices of portfolio made by the Mutual Fund intermediary.

The following are the advantages of Mutual funds

1. Better market rates and lower rates of brokerage

The pooling of funds from a large number of investors ensures that a total corpus of a Mutual Fund is very large. Due to the large funds, Mutual Funds are normally able to buy cheaper and sell dearer than individual investors. This is because of better market rates and lower rates of brokerage.

2. Optimum diversification is possible

In Mutual Funds, optimum diversification is possible because of large funds. Whereas an individual investor cannot hold more than a few companies shares because of limited funds, a Mutual Fund invests in a large number of shares to reduce risk. In simple terms a mutual fund follows the saying "don't put all the eggs in one basket". This reduces the risk for the investor.

3. Maintains a large Research Team

Due to the large funds available, a Mutual Fund is able to maintain a large research team. The research team consists of experts who constantly analyse various economic and sector specific factors affecting various industries and companies and accordingly take informed decisions on subscriptions to new issues and purchases / sales on the stock exchanges.

4. Increase the overall Return on Investment

Mutual Funds help to increase the overall return on investment to the small investors. The returns are higher than bank deposits. The investment has the same benefits as investment in equity and debentures *i.e.*, capital appreciation and regular income.

5. Greater Accessibility

The Mutual Funds have greater accessibility to investors through the branch network of banks. They have the financial muscle to move the stock market due to large funds at their disposal.

6. Direct Access

Mutual Funds have direct access to big investment opportunities through private placement and disinvestments methods.

7. Risk Diversification

Mutual Funds have the capacity for risk diversification geographically and industry groupwise.

8. Limited expenses

In Mutual Funds, only the expenses relating to the schemes as permitted by SEBI guidelines are charged to the respective schemes. Hence, unnecessary expenditure cannot be charged to Fund Account.

9. Small Investors can also Participate

A small Investment of as low as ₹1,000 in the mutual fund makes a person as an investor in a large company through Fund investment.

10. Tax Benefits

Mutual Funds (Equity Investment related Schemes) are totally exempt from tax on its all income. Mutual Funds do not deduct tax at source on dividends payable to the Unit holders. Central Government, may, however, make changes in the regulations through the Union Budgets.

The investments made by a Mutual Fund are thus based on thorough research and latest information. As this research requires a large number of analysts, a library, various databases and visit to companies, it involves a lot of effort, time and expenditure. It is not possible for individual investors to share this kind of time, effort or money. This is where a Mutual Fund becomes useful for investors.

11. Liquidity

Mutual funds by its large Fund base, provides liquidity to capital market – both for Equity segment and Debt segment. It thereby develops capital market and ultimately the economy of the country.

12. Transparency

Funds provide investors with updated information pertaining to the markets and the schemes. All material facts are disclosed to investors as required by the regulator.

13. Flexibility

Investors also benefit from the convenience and flexibility offered by Mutual Funds. Investors can switch their holdings from a debt scheme to an equity scheme and vice-versa. Option of systematic (at regular intervals) investment and withdrawal is also offered to the investors in most open-end schemes.

14. Mobilisation of Savings

It helps to mobilise savings of small investors scattered around the country and channelise the funds for the growth of industry and economy through their capital market activity.

15. Increase in Shareholder Value

Mutual Funds mostly put their money in corporate financial instruments like shares, debentures etc. When they actively deal in these instruments, the liquidity of those scrips improve. Further, due to demand for those instruments, their market value picks up. This value addition to the shares ultimately increases shareholder value of the companies' investors.

17.8 RISKS INVOLVED IN MUTUAL FUNDS

Just like any other investments, mutual fund investments also carry certain risk. The risk in a particular scheme of a mutual fund is basically a function of two factors:

(1) The Nature of the scheme and Market risk.

(2) Investment expertise of the Asset Management Company (AMC).

As all of us know shares are more risky than debentures.Thus a scheme which invests mainly in shares (a pure growth scheme), is more risky than a scheme which invest partly in shares (Balanced Scheme), which in turn is more risky than a scheme which invests mainly in debentures (Income Scheme).

The question now is why should one invest in a growth scheme which carries more risk? The answer is that risk and return go hand in hand. If one wants more returns he has to take more risks. These risks may be a general decline in prices of output, increase in tax rate, unfavourable government policy, economic downturn and recessionary conditions, increase in raw materials cost, interest rate, wages etc., Such factors will affect the prices of the shares in general. These general risks associated with investments in shares are termed as "Market Risk". It may be noted that the risk of investment in shares is reduced by investing in the shares of selected number of stable and growing industries. Thus market risk can be minimised but cannot be completely eliminated even by good investment management team. However, company specific risk, known as unsystematic risk can be eliminated through proper selection of shares.

The second aspect of investment expertise is more relevant for investment in shares. As we know, some people lose money and some make money in shares. Most of us attribute this to "luck" or "chance". Well, it is not as simple as that: while "luck" or "chance" do have a role to play, what is more important is the investment expertise of these people and their quick action. Similarly, the investment expertise of various Mutual Funds is different and so will be the returns which they offer to the investors.

In the present day world, the fortunes of many companies are fast changing due to globalisation of market, changes in technology, changing consumer preferences, government economic and political policies etc. These affect the companies' value, sales, profit and public perception of the companies. An immediate reaction to these changes are reflected in the value of shares and hence, having implications on the value of investors money. A Mutual Fund, by constantly shuffling its portfolio of investments according to market perception, is in a position to manage the funds better. Again the retail investors may not be in a position to own high value stock due to their limited resources. Thousands of such investors going through Mutual Funds will be able to have a stake even in such stocks.

The trends in transaction on stock exchanges by mutual funds during the last decade can be seen in the following Table:

Indian Scene

Trends in Transactions on Stock Exchnaged by Mutual Funds (since January 2000)

Period	*Debt Equity*	*Gross Purchases (₹ Crores)*	*Gross Slaes (₹ Crores)*	*Net Investment (₹ Crores)*
April 2008-Mar 2009	Equity	144068	137085	6983
	Debt	327744	245942	818003
April 2007-Mar 2008	Equity	217578	201274	16306
	Debt	298605	224816	73790
April 2006-Mar 2007	Equity	135948.16	126885.82	9062.34
	Debt	153733.05	101189.59	52543.46
April 2005-Mar 2006	Equity	100435.90	86133.70	14302.20
	Debt	109804.91	73003.67	36801.24
April 2004-Mar 2005	Equity	45045.25	44597.23	448.02
	Debt	62186.46	45199.17	16987.29
April 2003-Mar 2004	Equity	36663.58	35355.67	1307.91
	Debt	63169.93	40469.18	22700.75
April 2002-Mar 2003	Equity	14520.89	16587.59	–2066.70
	Debt	4663.83	34059.41	12604.42
April 2001-Mar 2002	Equity	12098.11	15893.99	–3795.88
	Debt	33583.64	22624.42	10959.22
April 2000-Mar 2001	Equity	11375.78	20142.76	–2766.98
	Debt	13512.17	8488.68	5023.49
Jan 2000-Mar 2000	Equity	11070.54	11492.19	–421.65
	Debt	2764.72	1864.29	900.43

Source: SEBI Publications

REVIEW QUESTIONS

Short Answer Questions

1. What is mutual fund?
2. What is meant by sector specific mutual funds?
3. Write short notes on:
   (*a*) Open Ended Schemes
   (*b*) Close Ended Schemes
   (*c*) Growth Schemes
   (*d*) Income Schemes
   (*e*) Balanced Schemes
   (*f*) Money Market Schemes
   (*g*) Tax Savings Schemes
   (*h*) Fund of Funds
   (*i*) Gift Fund
   (*j*) Index Schemes
4. Differentiate between open-ended schemes and closed ended schemes.

Essay Type Questions

1. Write a note on the basic operation of mutual funds.
2. Explain the organization structure of mutual funds.
3. Explain the different classifications of mutual funds.
4. Explain the following:
   (*a*) Structure based schemes of mutual funds
   (*b*) Investment objectives based schemes of mutual funds.
5. Explain the special types of mutual funds.
6. Write a detailed note on the regulation mutual funds in India.
7. Explain the Net Asset Value of Mutual fund scheme with example.
8. What are the advantages of mutual funds? Explain.
9. Explain the risks involved in mutual funds.

CHAPTER 18 Accounts of Non-Residents

Usually residents in India maintain bank accounts within the country. These residents may be individuals, institutions, corporate bodies, Government Departments, Business Firms etc. However, as per Reserve Bank notifications issued under Foreign Exchange Regulation Act (FERA) 1973, Non-Resident Indians, can also maintain accounts with banks in India. These accounts are normally SB Accounts and different types of Term Deposit accounts. In order that a bank is eligible to maintain these accounts it should be authorised to do so by Reserve Bank of India.

In this chapter, two categories of accounts are discussed. They are:

1. Accounts of Non-Residents
2. Foreign Currency Accounts of Residents

Before going in to the details of these accounts, we shall see the necessary background for these accounts in India.

18.1 FOREIGN EXCHANGE MANAGEMENT ACT 1999 (FEMA 1999)

Until May 2000, all foreign exchange operations in India were governed by the provisions of FERA 1973. However in the year 2000, Parliament had passed a new legislation, known as Foreign Exchange Management Act 1999 to govern the operations relating to foreign exchange transactions. As the new Act had been passed, the previous FERA 1973 was repealed. The new Act, FEMA 1999 came into being from June 1, 2000. Thus all foreign exchange operations including maintaining of non–resident accounts by banks are governed by the provisions of the new Act. Reserve Bank of India (RBI) is mainly empowered with authority under the Act (Central Govt. has also powers under the Act) to regulate foreign exchange operations. As such rules and regulations relating to non resident accounts are issued by RBI.

18.2 NON-RESIDENT INDIAN (NRI)

A Non Resident Indian (NRI) is a person resident outside India, who is a citizen of India or is a person of Indian origin.

NRI: NRIs are those individuals who reside outside India for the purpose of employment, business activities, vocation etc or who have not stayed in India for a period exceeding 182 days in a financial year. They should however be Indian nationals.

(a) Persons of Indian Origin (PIO): A Person of Indian Origin (PIO) for this purpose is defined in Regulation 2 of FEMA Notification ibid as a citizen of any country other than Bangladesh or Pakistan, if (a) he at any time held Indian passport; or (b) he or either of his parents or any of his grandparents was a citizen of India by virtue of the Constitution of India or the Citizenship Act, 1955 (57 of 1955); or (c) the person is a spouse of an Indian citizen or a person referred to in sub-clause (a) or (b).

In simple, People of Indian origin means people who are originally from India but settled in course of time in other countries and acquired the citizenship of foreign country like, the Tamils living in Malaysia, SriLanka or Gujarati speaking people living in UK, Kenya etc.

(b) Overseas Corporate Bodies (OCB): OCBs are institutions, corporates, trusts etc registered outside India but importantly such bodies should be owned to a minimum of 60 per cent by NRIs / PIOs. If the body is a Trust or so, then a minimum of 60 per cent of beneficial interest of the body should go to NRIs / PIOs.

(c) Non-Residents (NRs): When the term NR is merely used, it refers to persons neither of foreign nationals who are neither Indian citizen nor of Indian origin, e.g. pure Americans like Bill Clinton or a British subject like Tony Blair.

18.3 NON-RESIDENT ACCOUNTS

The NRI accounts are broadly classified in to three categories as given in the following diagram:

- Types of NRI Accounts
  1. Non-Resident Ordinary Account (NRO Account)
  2. Non-Resident (External) Rupee Account (NRE Account)
  3. Foreign Currency Non-Resident (Bank) Account-FCNR (B) Account

18.3.1. Non-Resident Ordinary Rupee Account (NRO Account)

Non-resident ordinary accounts can be opened either by money received from abroad in foreign exchange or out of rupees earned in India. When an Indian resident goes abroad for job / employment his local account will automatically be designated into a non resident ordinary account by bank. For this the bank should be advised of his / her departure outside India for job. This account can be maintained jointly with residents. Funds held in the account can normally be utilised only in India. Repatriation (the right to take the money outside India is known as 'Repatriation Right') of money outside India is normally not allowed. However with the introduction of current account convertibility, Reserve Bank permitted remittances even out of NRO accounts.

Any person resident outside India may open NRO account with an authorised dealer or an authorised bank for the purpose of putting through bona fide transaction in rupees. Opening of accounts by individual/ entities of Pakistan and entities of Bangladesh require prior approval of Reserve Bank of India.

Features of NRO Account:

The NRO account has the following features:

1. NRO accounts may be opened and maintained in the form of current, savings, recurring or fixed deposit accounts.
   (a) **Savings Account** - Normally maintained for crediting legitimate dues /earnings / income such as dividends, interest etc. Banks are free to determine the interest rates.
   (b) **Term Deposits** - Banks are free to determine the interest rates. Interest rates offered by banks on NRO deposits cannot be higher than those offered by them on comparable domestic rupee deposits.
2. Account should be denominated in Indian Rupees.

3. Permissible credits to NRO account are transfers from rupee accounts of non-resident banks, remittances received in permitted currency from outside India through normal banking channels, permitted currency tendered by account holder during his temporary visit to India, legitimate dues in India of the account holder like current income like rent, dividend, pension, interest, etc., sale proceeds of assets including immovable property acquired out of rupee/ foreign currency funds or by way of legacy/ inheritance.
4. Eligible debits such as all local payments in rupees including payments for investments as specified by the Reserve Bank and remittance outside India of current income like rent, dividend, pension, interest, etc., net of applicable taxes, of the account holder.
5. NRI/PIO may remit from the balances held in NRO account an amount not exceeding USD one million per financial year, subject to payment of applicable taxes.
6. The limit of USD 1 million per financial year includes sale proceeds of immovable properties held by NRIs/ PIOs.
7. Other than current income and the limit of USD 1 Mn per financial year applicable to NRIs/ PIOs, balances in NRO accounts cannot be repatriated without the prior approval of RBI.
8. The accounts may be held jointly with residents and/or with non-resident Indian.
9. The NRO account holder may opt for nomination facility.
10. NRO (current/savings) account can also be opened by a foreign national of non-Indian origin visiting India, with funds remitted from outside India through banking channel or by sale of foreign exchange brought by him to India. The details of this facility are given in the FAQs on "Accounts opened by Foreign Nationals and Foreign Tourists" available on the RBI website.
11. Loans to non-resident account holders and to third parties may be granted in Rupees by Authorized Dealer / bank against the security of fixed deposits subject to certain terms and conditions.

18.3.2. Non-Resident (External) Rupee Account (NRE Account)

These are again rupee accounts. The NRE account can be opened only with money received from abroad and not from local rupee sources. There can be joint holder to the account but not with residents. The joint account holder should also be a non resident. The funds held in the account can be freely repatriated outside India without limit and without any approval from RBI. Since the account is maintained in rupee, for repatriation purpose the Rupee will be converted into the desired foreign currency at the prevailing rate of exchange. Interest earned on the account is free from income tax. The account can be maintained as savings bank account, fixed deposit, recurring deposit etc. However fixed deposit account should be for a minimum period of one year and for a maximum period of 3 years.

Features of NRE Account:

The NRE Account has the following features:

1. NRE account may be in the form of savings, current, recurring or fixed deposit accounts (with maturity of minimum one year). Such accounts can be opened only by the NRI (as defined under Regulation 2(vi) of Notification No. FEMA 5/2000-RB dated May 3, 2000) himself and not through the holder of the power of attorney.
2. NRIs may be permitted to open NRE account with their resident close relatives (relative as defined in Section 6 of the Companies Act, 1956) on 'former or survivor 'basis. The resident close relative shall be eligible to operate the account as a Power of Attorney holder in accordance with the extant instructions during the life time of the NRI/PIO account holder.

3. Account will be maintained in Indian Rupees.
4. Balances held in the NRE account are freely repatriable.
5. Accrued interest income and balances held in NRE accounts are exempt from Income tax and Wealth tax, respectively.
6. Authorised dealers/authorised banks may at their discretion/commercial judgement allow for a period of not more than two weeks, overdrawings in NRE savings bank accounts, up to a limit of ₹ 50,000 subject to the condition that such overdrawings together with the interest payable thereon are cleared/repaid within a period of two weeks, out of inward remittances through normal banking channels or by transfer of funds from other NRE/FCNR accounts.
7. Savings – Banks are free to determine the interest rates.
8. Term deposits – Banks are free to determine the interest rates of term deposits of maturity of one year and above. Interest rates offered by banks on NRE deposits cannot be higher than those offered by them on comparable domestic rupee deposits.
9. Permissible credits to NRE account are inward remittance to India in permitted currency, proceeds of account payee cheques, demand drafts / bankers' cheques, issued against encashment of foreign currency, where the instruments issued to the NRE account holder are supported by encashment certificate issued by AD Category-I / Category-II, transfers from other NRE / FCNR accounts, sale proceeds of FDI investments, interest accruing on the funds held in such accounts, interest on Government securities/dividends on units of mutual funds purchased by debit to the NRE/FCNR(B) account of the holder, certain types of refunds, etc.
10. Eligible debits are local disbursements, transfer to other NRE/FCNR accounts of person eligible to open such accounts, remittance outside India, investments in shares/securities/commercial paper of an Indian company, etc.
11. Loans can be extended against security of funds held in NRE Account either to the depositors or third parties without any ceiling subject to usual margin requirements.
12. NRE accounts can be operated through power of attorney in favour of residents for the limited purpose of withdrawal of local payments or remittances through normal banking channels to the account holder himself.

Differences between NRE and NRO Accounts:

The basic differences between NRE and NRO Accounts are given below:

1. **Repatriation:** NRE account is freely repatriable (Principal and interest earned) while the NRO account has restricted repatriability i.e permitted remittance is allowed.
2. **Tax Treatment:** NRE account is Tax free in India. But, the interest earned in NRO account and credit balances are subject to income tax, wealth tax and gift tax.

18.3.3. Foreign Currency Non Resident (Bank) Account – FCNR (B) Account

FCNR Accounts are Term Deposit Accounts. They can be maintained in four important currencies viz. US Dollar, Pound Sterling, Japanese Yen. Presently it can be maintained in the new European Currency "Euro" also. They can be maintained for period ranging from one year to 3 years. They are paid back in the same currencies and are repatriable. These accounts are now known as FCNR (B) Accounts. 'B' stands for Banks. Since the account is maintained in foreign currency and paid back in the same currency, there is no conversion of currency takes place when balance is repatriated outside India. However if the account holder decides to convert the balance into rupees at maturity, the conversion takes place at exchange rate ruling at the time of conversion. In case rupee value is fallen (say \$ 1 = ₹ 50.00 when account is opened and \$ 1 = 57.00 when account is matured) at the time of conversion, account holder will gain an extra 7 rupees per dollar for the principal as well as for interest since both are paid in currency of deposit. Interest earned on the account is tax exempted.

Features of FCNR(B) Account:

The FCNR(B) Account has the following features:

1. NRIs are eligible to open and maintain these accounts.
2. FCNR (B) accounts are only in the form of term deposits of 1 to 5 years.
3. All debits/credits permissible in respect of NRE accounts, including credit of sale proceeds of FDI investments, are permissible in FCNR (B) accounts also.
4. Account can be held in any freely convertible currency.
5. Loans can be extended against security of funds held in FCNR (B) deposit either to the depositors or third parties without any ceiling subject to usual margin requirements.
6. The interest rates are stipulated by the Department of Banking Operations and Development, Reserve Bank of India. With effect from March 1, 2014, in respect of FCNR (B) deposits of maturities, 1 year to less than 3 years, interest shall be paid within the ceiling rate of LIBOR/ SWAP rates plus 200 basis points for the respective currency/ corresponding maturity. For FCNR(B) deposits with maturity of 3-5 years interest shall be paid within the ceiling rate of LIBOR/ SWAP rates plus 300 basis points. On floating rate deposits, interest shall be paid within the ceiling of SWAP rates for the respective currency/ maturity plus 200 bps/ 300 bps, as the case may be. For floating rate deposits, the interest reset period shall be six months.
7. When an account holder becomes a person resident in India, deposits may be allowed to continue till maturity at the contracted rate of interest, if so desired by him.
8. Terms and conditions as applicable to NRE accounts in respect of joint accounts, repatriation of funds, opening account during temporary visit, operation by power of attorney, loans/ overdrafts against security of funds held in accounts, shall apply mutatis mutandis to FCNR (B). NRI can open joint account with a resident close relative (relative as defined in Section 6 of the Companies Act, 1956) on former or survivor basis. The resident close relative will be eligible to operate the account as a Power of Attorney holder in accordance with extant instructions during the life time of the NRI/PIO account holder.

18.4. FOREIGN CURRENCY ACCOUNTS OF RESIDENTS

Usually residents (those living in India) are required to maintain their bank accounts in India in rupee only. However, in respect of certain categories of residents Reserve Bank has permitted to maintain foreign currency accounts. These are Resident Foreign Currency accounts (RFC Accounts). The types of such accounts include the following:

18.4.1. RFC Accounts

RFC Accounts are accounts of resident individuals, who had come back to India after being abroad as NRIs for sometime. It is natural that when an NRI/PIO comes back to India for settlement he may bring with him the foreign exchange earned by him while abroad. Similarly he may sell his foreign assets like securities, property etc. at the time of return to India. The Returning Indian/PIO may use such foreign exchange to open the RFC accounts. It is a rule when an NRI/PIO returns to India for permanent settlement i.e. when he/she has no intention to go back abroad, their existing NRE/FCNR accounts should be converted into resident accounts. As such, funds held in NRE/ FCNR accounts, on return to India, can be utilised to open RFC accounts.

These accounts can be maintained in any foreign currency of the choice of depositors. No permission from Reserve Bank is necessary for maintaining this account. The funds in this account can be used by the account holders practically for all purposes. To illustrate, the account holder can use the RFC balance again to acquire some asset abroad while being in India, open fresh bank account outside India, spend the money for his travel / business purposes, he can gift it to any one in the world, use it for educational purposes of his relations etc. In fact the depositor can decide about the purpose of use of such funds without the permission of RBI.

Features of RFC Accounts:

The RFC Accounts have the following features:

1. A person resident in India may open, hold and maintain with an authorised dealer in India a Resident Foreign Currency (RFC) Account.
2. Proceeds of assets held outside India at the time of return can be credited to RFC account.
3. The funds in RFC accounts are free from all restrictions regarding utilisation of foreign currency balances including any restriction on investment in any form outside India.
4. RFC accounts can be maintained in the form of current or savings or term deposit accounts, where the account holder is an individual and in the form of current or term deposits in all other cases. RFC accounts are permitted to be held jointly with a resident close relative(s) as defined in the Companies Act, 1956 as joint holder (s) in their RFC bank account on 'former or survivor basis'. However, such resident Indian close relative, now being made eligible to become joint account holder shall not be eligible to operate the account during the life time of the resident account holder.

18.4.2. Exchange Earners Foreign Currency Accounts (EEFC Accounts)

These accounts can be maintained by residents who happen to receive money from abroad in foreign currency. They can be individuals or corporates like Exporters. However, normally EEFC accounts are opened by exporters out of sale proceeds of exports. One important different of this account from RFC account is that EEFC account can be opened only out of foreign exchange earned.

Funds held in EEFC Accounts can be used by the depositors for personal and business purposes as approved by RBI from time to time. Exporters can maintain this account only in the form of current account without any interest. The main advantage of resident foreign currency account is that depositor can use the funds for personal and business purposes without buying foreign currency from banks at the ongoing market rate.

The above type of foreign currency accounts cannot be maintained by all banks. Only those Commercial Banks, (also few co-operative banks) which have obtained licence from Reserve Bank under Foreign Exchange Management Act (FEMA), 1999 are permitted to open and operate these accounts. Such banks are known as authorised dealers or authorised person in Foreign Exchange.

REVIEW QUESTIONS

1. Write a brief note on FEMA.
2. Explain the main types of NR Accounts.
3. What are the features of Non-Resident Ordinary Rupee Account?
4. Explain the concept and features of Non-Resident (External) Rupee Account.
5. Discuss briefly the main features of Foreign Currency Non Resident (Bank) Account.
6. What are the foreign currency accounts available for residents?
7. Write a short note on Exchange Earners Foreign Currency Accounts.
8. Explain NR accounts and their importance.

19 CHAPTER Customer Service and Ombudsman Scheme in Banking Sector

"Customer is the most important visitor in our premises. He is not dependent on us. We are dependent on him. He is not an interruption on our work. He is the purpose of it. He is not an outsider on our business. He is a part of it. We are not doing him a favour by serving him. He is doing us a favour by giving us an opportunity to do so" – so said the Father of the Nation, Mahatma Gandhi long ago.

The Gandhian concept of customer accepted by banks exhibit their customer orientation. Transition of banks from class banking to mass banking and thrust upon profitability in recent period has led them towards customer orientation. Now it is their duty to accept the principle of customer as "King" in service industry in the present era of cut-throat competition. With the advancement of science and technology, our world has reduced to a global village. Thus, change is, both inevitable and desirable. In such a situation, customer orientation has become the key word for competitive success.

19.1 CUSTOMER ORIENTATION

Banks cannot exist without customers. The banks' operation is invested to serve customers and not vice versa. A customer looks for certain values like product, quality, reliability, superior service, state of the art technology, low cost, a premium image, etc.; while purchasing anything. In service sector like bank, customer service should not only a critical function, but a way of life also. Banks can be said as being customer oriented if its various organisational activities like organizational restructuring, staffing, co-ordination are geared to fulfils customers' needs. So, total customer satisfaction should be the focal point. That alone serves the banks' objective of maximization of profit. It is obvious that a bank cannot think of making profit without customers.

Customer orientation comprises two factors—customers' need analysis and banks' effort to fulfill those needs up to the level of their satisfaction. At present customer satisfaction may be called a complicated mix of hardware (technology, product, price, quality) and software (attitude, responsiveness, deliverance and communications). In fact customer satisfaction is currently changed into 'Customer Delight'. The aim is to provide such services at Customer's door step so that he gets delighted by the service and not merely satisfied of it. Look, how competition brings about sea-change in the attitude of bankers to customers.

Customer belongs to two categories, the existing or present customer and new customer including potential customer *i.e.*, children and new class of entrepreneurs. Now banks have two jobs to perform:

1. Retaining the old customers, and
2. Attracting new customers

But finding a new customer is costlier and time consuming business than retaining on old one. In spite of maintaining the old customer, attracting new customer for banks to increase its business. In the fast changing market scenario, old concepts have shattered and new concepts are taking their places. Now, a sale is viewed as the beginning rather than the end of a company's interaction with the customer. The marketing takes off the moment customer declines a product. Because, this is the time of SWOT (Strength, Weakness, Opportunity and Threat) analysis. A rejection by the customer provides for the idea to analyse the staff themselves and strengthen them to meet the customer challenges. With the increase in variety and volume of business and growth of bank branches over the decades customer service has declined in many aspects; at the same time, customer expectations have gone up.

The working group on customer service was first headed by R.K. Talwar, the then Chairman of SBI. The study was pioneering survey on customer service by banks. It has made a number of recommendations to improve service by banks. Most of the recommendations of the working group have been implemented after approval by RBI. The RBI also set up another committee on Customer Service headed by Mr.Goiporia, the then Chairman of SBI. This Committee made important recommendations for improving customers service by the staff of banks.

The banks have also setup committees, carried out surveys, etc. to continually assess the level of customer service in the banks and enhance its quality. The customer service is considerably enhanced by the quality and job knowledge of bank personnel. Inexperienced and ill-informed staff tends to postpone decision-making, and their decisions when taken, often turnout to be unsound.

When we talk of customer service in banks, one may expect the following types of service from banks and its staff.

(*i*) A gentle behaviour of staff.
(*ii*) A positive attitude and willingness to serve customers.
(*iii*) Providing quick service.
(*iv*) Avoiding unnecessary talk within the bank staff.
(*v*) Providing requisite information to customer and guiding members of public.
(*vi*) Manning their desk continuously and not leaving their counters unattended.
(*vii*) Exchange good notes for soiled / torn notes without any charges.
(*viii*) Providing the requisite denomination of notes when drawing money from banks.
(*ix*) Providing only good notes while withdrawing money.
(*x*) Accepting soiled and slightly torn notes while depositing money.
(*xi*) Not getting angry while replying customers.
(*xii*) Having patience and proper guidance to loan seekers particularly that of borrowers.
(*xiii*) Staff possessing sufficient knowledge on all matters of banking to guide customers correctly.
(*xiv*) Making rules and regulations simple and understandable.
(*xv*) Making small loan documents and procedure simple and fast moving.
(*xvi*) Banks educating public/customers through brochures, weekly meetings, etc., on banking services.
(*xvii*) Avoiding delays.
(*xviii*) Starting counters in time and extending service right upto closing time.

19.2 BASIC ASPECTS OF CUSTOMER SERVICE

To enhance the customer service the following aspects may be considered. (Many of the points are already under implementation by banks). They can be classified under the following categories

(1) Deposit Accounts
(2) Remittances

(3) Collections
(4) Loans and Advances
(5) Discipline and Attitudes
(6) Complaints

Let us discuss these items one by one in detail

19.2.1 Deposit Accounts

(*a*) Introduction of Accounts

All Deposit accounts should be properly introduced. Passport and postal identification cards are deemed to be adequate identification. In terms of RBI instructions every accountholder is required to produce two passport size recent photographs to the bank for opening any type of account with a bank. Similarly, as per Income-Tax Regulations a depositor desirous of opening a Fixed Deposit account in excess of ₹50,000 needs to furnish his/her Income-Tax Permanent Account Number (PAN).

(*b*) Transfer of Accounts

The instruction of a customer for transfer of his deposit account from one branch to another should be carried out immediately on receipt of and in accordance with his instructions. It should be ensured that along with the balance in the account, the relative papers, such as, the account opening form, specimen signature cards, standing instructions, stop payment instructions, etc. are also simultaneously transferred. After effecting the transfer the customer should be informed of such transfer at his last and new address. On receipt of instructions of the transfer from the transferor branch, the account should be opened as per instructions of the transferer branch and this should be intimated to the customer. No charges should be collected for transfer of accounts.

(*c*) Pass Books / Statements of Accounts

Pass Books and Statement of Accounts should be written accurately, neatly and legibly. Statements of Accounts to Current AccountHolders should be sent within 5 days from the due date. These due dates should be marked in the relative ledger folios and statements of accounts should be prepared sufficiently early to be sent to the customers on due dates. Entries in Pass Books should be done then and there and Pass Books should be returned to the customers without making them wait long.

(*d*) Standing Instructions

Standing instructions refer to an authority given by the customer to the bank to debit his accounts periodically for certain specified purposes like payment of rent , telephone bills, electricity charges, etc., Standing Instructions are accepted on all types of Accounts and they should be carried out on the due dates without fail.

Whenever, the Standing Instructions could not be carried out for any reason, the Account-holder should be intimated in time so that the least inconvenience and damage is caused to him. Whenever any complaint is received of non-compliance of the instructions given by the customer in time and the consequential loss or damage to the customer, appropriate action will be initiated against the employees responsible of such lapse.

(*e*) Advices of Credits and Debits Made to Accounts

Credits and Debits made to the Accounts of customers including those on account of outstation cheques/bills realised, should be intimated to the customers by Post / Local delivery on the date of debit / credit or latest by the next day. Cheques and Bills returned unpaid should be despatched along with the debit advices by the local delivery or by Registered Post on the Day on which the debit is made or latest by the next day. The debit / credit advices and cheques/bills returned unpaid should not be detained at the branches in anticipation of the customers calling on the branch for collecting them.

(*f*) Timely Issue of Due Date Notices for Term Deposits

Due Date Notices should be sent to all-Term Deposit Accountholders, atleast 15 days before the date of maturity of the Deposit. Due Date Notices need not be sent in cases where the Depositors have given specific instructions not to send such Notices. Due Date Notices should not be handed over to neighbours of the depositors or any third party.

(*g*) Safe Custody of Deposit Receipts

Customers may keep their Term Deposit Receipts in safe custody with the bank free of charge.

(*h*) Teller System

Under this system Tellers will pay against cheques drawn on Savings Bank as well as Current accounts upto certain amount. It is usually up to a maximum amount fixed per payment in an account, per day. In branches where the average payments handled by the Teller is less than 100 per day, Tellers will also accept cash receipts up to certain limit and hand over the relative counter foils to the customers after signing the challans.

(*i*) Cash Payment after Normal Banking Hours.

To meet the urgent requirements of customers, in exceptional circumstances, personal cheques for reasonable amounts presented by the drawer himself, may be paid even after the normal banking hours, but within the working hours.

(*j*) Any Branch Transactions.

Many banks are now providing deposits and withdrawals facility through any of the branches although the account is maintained in a particular branch. This type of operation is usually restricted in metropolitan cities. Few banks like Indian Overseas Bank have introduced this type of facility.

19.2.2 Remittances Service

(*a*) Issue of Demand Drafts

Demand Drafts should be issued to any person who applies for it, irrespective of whether he has an account with the Bank or not. Banks will cash more than the amount fixed under Income-Tax Regulations. The banks levy a charge for issue of every Demand Draft.

(*b*) Payment of Demand Drafts

Payment of Demand Drafts should not be refused for the only reason that the relative remittance advice has not been received. If necessary, the paying branch should contact the issuing branch over telephone and seek confirmation of issue of the Demand Draft.

(*c*) Issue of Duplicate Demand Drafts

On receipt of request for issue of a duplicate DD, the issuing branch should send a communication about the loss of the DD, to the drawee branch. Immediately on receipt of such communication, the drawee branch should go through its records to ascertain whether the said DD has been paid or not, and should inform the position to the issuing branch, by return of post. If not paid, the drawee branch should note to exercise caution.

(*d*) Beneficiary's Full Address in Telegraphic Transfers

The address as well as the name of the beneficiary should be communicated in the TT message so that the receiving branch will be in a position to contact the beneficiary immediately on receipt of the message.

(*e*) Payment of Telegraphic Transfers under Reserve

At the discretion of branch Managers, Telegraphic Transfers may be credited under reserve, to the account of a beneficiary of standing, even if the message or check signal is mutilated in transit.

Wherever, warranted, a suitable general indemnity should be obtained from the beneficiaries of such Telegraphic Transfers.

***(f)* Payment of Interest on Delayed Credit of Mail Transfers**

The normal transit period for a Mail Transfer to be credited to the beneficiary's account is 7 days (10 days for Mail Transfers to and from branches in the North Eastern Region and Sikkim). In cases where the Mail Transfer advice reaches the destination branch after 7 /10 days, as the case may be, branches should pay interest on the proceeds of the Mail Transfer, for the delayed period, at the rate of 2% over the Savings Bank rate, irrespective of whether the mail Transfer is meant for Current / Savings Bank / Term Deposit / Borrowal account and also whether the delay occurs in postal transit / due to misplacement, etc.

19.2.3 Collections Service

(a) With a view to provide this service promptly with out any complaints, it should be ensured that:

(*i*) instructions in respect of the collection, including the date on which the bills is to be returned if unpaid, are given correctly, clearly and completely by the branch sending the bills / cheques

(*ii*) the proceeds of the cheques /bills collected are despatched on the day of realisation

(*iii*) intimation of all bills are sent on the day they are received, and in case of local parties, the hand delivery

(*iv*) proper follow up measures are initiated, whenever proceeds of the bills / cheques are not received in time

(*v*) the collecting branch / bank is contacted immediately through letter / telegram / telephone when a report of loss of the instrument sent for collection is received , and there is no let up in the follow up.

(*vi*) instructions of drawers of bill for collection of overdue interest, collection of 'C' form, etc, are carried out meticulously and unpaid bills are returned to the drawers as per their instructions.

***(b)* Service Branches:** With a view to avoiding delays and to quickening the process of collection of outstation cheques, Service Branches may be set up in important places. Branches should send all the cheques / instruments drawn on these places to Service Branches only for collection.

The facility of immediate credit is afforded in respect of Dividend Warrants, interest Warrants, Refund Orders and Demand Drafts as well, if the customer so desires.The Service Charges for immediate credit of cheques will be as applicable for collection of cheques plus charges applicable for Registered post. On cheques which are afforded immediate credit but returned unpaid, interest at the stipulated rate will be charged from the date of return of the cheque to the date of reimbursement of the amount to the Bank.

***(c)* Payment of Interest on Delayed Collection of Outstation Cheques:** Branches will pay interest over the Savings Bank rate on the amounts of outstation cheques / instruments sent for collection, if the proceeds are not realised / credited to the customers' account, or the unpaid instruments are not returned to the customers, within the periods specified. Where the proceeds of collection instruments are credited to cash credit, overdraft or loan accounts, the interest payable will he at the minimum lending rate stipulated by the Reserve Bank of India from time to time.

No interest will be paid on instruments lost in transit. Branches should pay interest on delayed collections, as a matter of routine at the time of crediting the customers' accounts with the proceeds of the cheques / instruments realised. The period of delay has to be arrived at taking into account the date of lodgement of the cheque /instrument by the customer and not from the date of entry in the Bills Register.

In cases where the delay has been at the collecting Bank's side, branches should pay interest to the customer for the period of delay and lodge a claim with the collecting bank for reimbursement.

19.2.4 Loans and Advances

Common Guidelines for Priority Sector Advances

(*a*) Applications Forms: In areas covered by special schemes like the Integrated Rural Development Programme, the concerned Project Authorities Rural Development Agencies and District Industries Centres, will identify the borrowers and forward to the Bank applications received for loans. In other areas, the Bank staff will help the applicants filling in the application forms.

The Branch Manager should have a dialogue with the applicant for the loan and during the course of the conversation should try to get as much information as is necessary for the purpose of processing the application.

(*b*) Repayment Schedule: Repayment instalments should be fixed invariably not in relation to the size of the loan or on the basis of willingness of the applicant, but strictly in relation to the applicant's paying capacity realistically assessed by the bank. The Repayment Programme should take into account the sustenance requirements, surplus generating capacity, the break-even point, the life of the asset, etc., and should not be fixed in an ashoc manner.

(*c*) Disposal of Applications: All loan applications under the Integrated Rural Development Programme and other Programme for the weaker sections of society should be disposed within 15 days from the date of receipt. Whenever, any loan application is rejected, reasons for the rejection should be advised to the applicant.

19.2.5 Discipline and Attitudes

(*a*) Staff Members of all Categories will ensure that:

(*i*) They are at their respective desks sufficiently in advances to begin work exactly at the commencement of the working hours

(*ii*) They devote entirely to the Bank's work during working hours

(*iii*) They are at their desks during working hours except when they go out on Bank work

(*b*) Staff Meetings: To review the level of customers satisfaction at the branch and to have a frank and free exchange of views on the working of the branch, each branch should hold a staff Meeting atleast once a month, participated by all members of staff.

(*c*) 'MAY I HELP YOU' Counters: 'May I Help You' counters should be set up in all branches excepting those categorised as 'small', to guide the customers.

19.2.6 Complaints

(*a*) Complaints / Suggestions of Customers: A complaint / Suggestion Box is to be provided at a prominent place in each branch. Near the box, blank slips serially numbered should be made available which should also provide for the name and address of the customers and details of complaint or suggestion. Complaints received through the Customer Service Centres also must be attended to quickly. Reply to any complaint received from customers should be sent within 7 days from the date of receipt. In cases where reply could not be sent within such time, an interim acknowledgement stating the reason for the delay as well as the probable time when a suitable reply may be expected, should be sent.

(*b*) Customers Service Committees: Each branch should set up a joint Customer Service Committee comprising the Branch Manager and representatives of Officers and Award staff. The Committee should meet atleast once a month to study the complaints / suggestions; causes of delay and other difficulties members; and evolve ways and means of improving customer service. The committee should also examine the complaints / suggestions received by the Branch during the month and discuss the action taken / to be taken. At periodic intervals, select customers from a section of the clientele of the branch should also be invited to participate in the meeting.

19.2.7 Other Services

(*a*) Nomination Facility: All banks have been directed by RBI to provide nomination facilities in respect of personal accounts like SB Accounts. This facility should be incorporated in the opening form itself. This facility should be extended even without asking for, by the customer. In the unfortunate event of death of the customer, the bank will be obliged to pay the outstanding balance in the account by the nominee of the accountholder. This quickens the pace of settlement of funds after the death of the account holder without involving any hassles. The nomination facility is also available for deposits made with registered NBFCs.

(*b*) Exchange of Soiled Notes/Torn Notes: Many times we come across badly soiled currency notes or torn notes. What shall we do with these currency notes? As per RBI instructions all branches of public sector banks must accept soiled notes and torn notes (not exceeding two pieces and subject to certain other conditions) for exchange against good currency notes without any charges. The RBI from time to time issues advertisement in this regard for the knowledge of public. These notes can also be given along with good notes while depositing money into the accounts. It should, however, be made clear that a soiled or torn note should not be a forged note.

(*c*) Mutilated Currency Notes: Supposing we happened to have mutilated currency notes with more than two pieces or the note is cut through a number panel on the currency note. Can we get value against such currency notes? Yes, it is possible to get value meaning good notes against such mutilated notes. The RBI has prepared guidelines known as "RBI Note Refund Rules" for paying value against mutilated notes.

Public sector and Private Sector Bank branches having currency chests have been directed to accept the mutilated notes and give good notes in exchange subject to fulfilment of certain conditions. We must remember that mutilated notes should properly be pasted on the back side with a special brown paper and submitted to the bank. If a bank does not accept such notes one can write to the RBI.

19.3 KNOW YOUR CUSTOMER (KYC) POLICY

Of late unscrupulous persons seem to be using the banks as a medium for transferring illegal money and even legal source of money for terrorist activities. This will definitely bring the banking system into disrepute. With a view to avoid banks being caught unaware in transferring money for or on behalf of undesirable persons, RBI has advised all banks to ensure that new accounts are opened only after proper introduction with photographs and full address of the accountholders. The banks should further ensure that transfer or remittance of funds and other banking operations should be conducted only on behalf of their customers and banking transactions should not be undertaken on behalf of unknown or undesirable persons. This policy of clear identification of persons with proper introduction, full address , PAN number, etc. before entertaining banking transactions with such persons is known as KYC policy.

Banking operations are susceptible to the risks of money laundering and terrorist financing. In order to arrest money laundering, where banks are mostly used in the process, it is imperative that they know their customers well. On combating financing of terrorism, RBI has specified certain standards based on which the banks have to formulate a policy on identification and acceptance of customers to have a business relationship with them. The branches of the banks are required to prepare and maintain documentation on their customer relationships and transactions to meet the provisions of the Prevention of Money Laundering Act and other laws and regulations.

In this regard, RBI has issued the KYC guidelines under Section 35 (A) of the Banking Regulation Act, 1949 and any contravention of the same will attract penalties under the relevant provisions of the Act. Thus, the Bank has to be fully compliant with the provisions of the KYC procedures.

The due diligence expected under KYC involves going into the purpose and reasons for opening an account, anticipated turnover in the account, sources of wealth (net worth) of the person opening the account and sources of funds flowing into the account. Thus, KYC policy enables banks to know/understand their customers and their financial dealings to be able to serve them better and prudently manage the risks of Money Laundering and Financing of Terrorism.

19.3.1 Definition of Customer

For the purpose of KYC policy, a 'Customer' may be defined as:

(*i*) a person or entity that maintains an account and/or has a business relationship with the bank;

(*ii*) one on whose behalf the account is maintained (*i.e.* the beneficial owner)

(*iii*) beneficiaries of transactions conducted by professional intermediaries, such as Stock

(*iv*) Brokers, Chartered Accountants, Solicitors, etc. as permitted under the law

(*v*) any person or entity connected with a financial transaction which can pose significant reputational or other risks to the bank, say, a wire transfer or issue of a high value demand draft as a single transaction.

19.3.2 Objectives of Know Your Customer

The objective of KYC guidelines is to prevent banks from being used, intentionally or unintentionally, by criminal elements for money laundering activities. KYC procedures also enable banks to know/understand their customers and their financial dealings better which in turn help them manage their risks prudently. The Basic objectives of this policy includes:

1. To establish the identity of the client. This means identifying the customer and verifying his/her identity by using reliable, independent source documents, data or information.
   - For individuals, Bank will obtain identification data to verify the identity of the customer, his address/location and also his recent photograph. This will be done for the joint holders and mandate holders, as well.
   - For non-individuals, Bank will obtain identification data to :

     (*a*) verify the legal status of the legal person/entity

     (*b*) verify identity of the authorised signatories and

     (*c*) verify identity of the beneficial owners/controllers of the account.
2. To ensure that sufficient information is obtained on the nature of employment/business that the customer does/expects to undertake and the purpose of the account.

19.3.3 Key Elements of KYC Policy

Banks should frame their KYC policies incorporating the following four key elements:

(*a*) Customer Acceptance Policy

Banks should develop a clear Customer Acceptance Policy laying down explicit criteria for acceptance of customers. The Customer Acceptance Policy must ensure that explicit guidelines issued by RBI on aspects of customer relationship in the bank.

(*b*) Customer Identification Procedures

The policy approved by the Board of banks should clearly spell out the Customer Identification Procedure to be carried out at different stages i.e. while establishing a banking relationship; carrying out a financial transaction or when the bank has a doubt about the authenticity/veracity or the adequacy of the previously obtained customer identification data.

Customer identification means identifying the customer and verifying his/her identity by using reliable, independent source documents, data or information. Banks need to obtain sufficient information necessary to establish, to their satisfaction, the identity of each new customer, whether regular or occasional, and the purpose of the intended nature of banking relationship.

(*c*) Monitoring of Transactions

Ongoing monitoring is an essential element of effective KYC procedures. Banks can effectively control and reduce their risk only if they have an understanding of the normal and reasonable activity of the customer so that they have the means of identifying transactions that fall outside the regular pattern of activity. However, the extent of monitoring will depend on the risk sensitivity of the account.

Banks should pay special attention to all complex, unusually large transactions and all unusual patterns which have no apparent economic or visible lawful purpose. The bank may prescribe threshold limits for a particular category of accounts and pay particular attention to the transactions which exceed these limits.

(*d*) Risk Management

The Board of Directors of the bank should ensure that an effective KYC programme is put in place by establishing appropriate procedures and ensuring their effective implementation. It should cover proper management oversight, systems and controls, segregation of duties, training and other related matters. Responsibility should be explicitly allocated within the bank for ensuring that the bank's policies and procedures are implemented effectively.

Banks may, in consultation with their boards, devise procedures for creating Risk Profiles of their existing and new customers and apply various Anti Money Laundering measures keeping in view the risks involved in a transaction, account or banking/business relationship.

19.3.4 KYC Policy and Customer Education

Implementation of KYC procedures requires banks to demand certain information from a customer which may be of personal nature or which has hitherto never been called for. This can sometimes lead to a lot of questioning by the customer as to the motive and purpose of collecting such information. There is, therefore, a need for banks to prepare specific literature/ pamphlets, etc. so as to educate the customer of the objectives of the KYC program. The front desk staff needs to be specially trained to handle such situations while dealing with customers.

19.3.5 KYC Policy and Introduction of New Technologies – Credit Cards/ Debit Cards / Smart Cards/Gift Cards

Banks should pay special attention to any money laundering threats that may arise from new or developing technologies including internet banking that might favour anonymity, and take measures, if needed, to prevent their use in money laundering schemes. Banks should ensure that appropriate KYC procedures are duly applied before issuing the cards to the customers. It is also desirable that agents are also subjected to KYC measures.

19.3.6 Existing Customer

Banks were advised to apply the KYC norms to all the existing customers in a time bound manner. While the revised guidelines will apply to all new customers, banks should apply the same to the existing customers on the basis of materiality and risk. However, transactions in existing accounts should be continuously monitored.

19.3.7 Customer Identification Procedures

The customer identification procedures under KYC Policy can be seen from the following Table (Source: RBI Publications):

Customer Identification Procedure

Features to be verified and documents that may be obtained from customers

Features	*Documents*
Accounts of individuals	
– Legal name and any other names used.	(*i*) Passport (*ii*) PAN card (*iii*) Voter's identify card (*iv*) Driving licence (*v*) Identity card (subject to the bank's satisfaction) (*vi*) Letter from a recognized public authority or public servant verifying the identity and residence of the customer to the satisfaction of bank.
– Correct permanent address	(*i*) Telephone bill (*ii*) Bank account statement (*iii*) Letter from any recognized public authority (*iv*) Electricity bill (*v*) Ration card (*vi*) Letter from employer (subject to satisfaction of the bank) (anyone document which provides customer information to the satisfaction of the bank will suffice)
Accounts of companies – Name of the company – Principal place of business – Mailing address of the company – Telephone/Fax Number	(*i*) Certificate of incorporation and memorandum and Articles of Association (*ii*) Resolution of the Board of Directors to open an account and identification of those who have authority to operate the account (*iii*) Power of Attorney granted to its managers, officers or employees to transact business on its behalf (*iv*) Copy of PAN allotment letter (*v*) Copy of the telephone bill.
Accounts of Partnership Firms – Legal name – Address – Names of all partners and their addresses – Telephone numbers of the firm and partners.	(*i*) Registration certificate, if registered (*ii*) Partnership deed (*iii*) Power of Attorney granted to a partner or an employee of the firm to transact business on its behalf (*iv*) Any officially valid document identifying the partners and the persons holding the Power of Attorney and their addresses (*v*) Telephone in the name of firm/partners.
Accounts of trusts & foundations – Names of trustees, settlers, beneficiaries and signatories – Names and addresses of the founder, the managers/directors and the beneficiaries – Telephone/fax numbers	(*i*) Certificate of registration, if registered (*ii*) Power of Attorney granted to transact business on its behalf (*iii*) Any officially valid document to identify the trustees, settlors, beneficiaries and those holding Power of Attorney, founders/managers/directors and their addresses. (*iv*) Resolution of the managing body of the foundation/association (*v*) Telephone bill.

Source: RBI Notifications

19.4 BANKING OMBUDSMAN SCHEME

During 2009-10, focused attention was paid to customer service in the banking sector by sensitising banks to render an efficient customer service. Reserve Bank has taken a number of steps to disseminate instructions/guidelines relating to customer service and grievance redressal by banks through the multilingual website by placing all customers related notifications and press releases in a specific page titled 'For Common Person'. Customers of commercial banks can also approach the Reserve Bank with their grievances and queries through 'Contact Us' mode of the website. A complaint form for lodging complaints with the Banking Ombudsman has also been made functional.

Making banks more customer-friendly has been high on the agenda of the Reserve Bank. Accordingly, a number of steps have been taken towards enhancing financial literacy and strengthening channels of information dissemination relating to banking services to customers. A full-fledged Customer Service Department was set up in 2006 by the Reserve Bank to enhance the pace and quality of provision of customer services, while providing customers a forum for redressal of their grievances.

The Banking Ombudsman Scheme enables an expeditious and inexpensive forum to bank customers for resolution of complaints relating to certain services rendered by banks. The Banking Ombudsman Scheme introduced by RBI in 1995. There after many norms were issued by RBI and the important one was issued in 2006.

Banking Ombudsman is a quasi judicial authority (the Banking Ombudsman— is a senior official appointed by the Reserve Bank of India) to redress customer complaints against deficiency in certain banking services. The Banking Ombudsman Scheme functioning under India's Banking Ombudsman Scheme 2006, and the authority was created pursuant to the a decision by the Government of India to enable resolution of complaints of customers of banks relating to certain services rendered by the banks.

The Banking Ombudsman provides speedy solutions to the grievances faced by the customers from various banks. It addresses grievances by way of its legal framework and redressal is done accordingly. It is set up specifically for handling grievances related to banking services and related matters under its purview. As on date, fifteen Banking Ombudsmen have been appointed with their offices located mostly in state capitals. All Scheduled Commercial Banks, Regional Rural Banks and Scheduled Primary Co-operative Banks are covered under the Scheme.

19.4.1 Scope of Complaints

The customer can lodge complaint to Banking Ombudsman on the following deficiency in banking services (including internet banking):

(*i*) Non-payment or inordinate delay in the payment or collection of cheques, drafts, bills, etc.

(*ii*) Non-acceptance, without sufficient cause, of small denomination notes tendered for any purpose, and for charging of commission for this service

(*iii*) Non-acceptance, without sufficient cause, of coins tendered and for charging of commission for this service

(*iv*) Non-payment or delay in payment of inward remittances

(*v*) Failure to issue or delay in issue, of drafts, pay orders or bankers' cheques

(*vi*) Non-adherence to prescribed working hours

(*vii*) Failure to honour guarantee or letter of credit commitments;

(*viii*) Failure to provide or delay in providing a banking facility

(*ix*) Delays, non-credit of proceeds to parties' accounts, non-payment of deposit, etc.

(*x*) Refusal to open deposit accounts without any valid reason for refusal (*xi*) Levying of charges without adequate prior notice to the customer

(*xii*) Refusal to accept or delay in accepting payment towards taxes, as required by Reserve Bank/Government

(*xiii*) Forced closure of deposit accounts without due notice or without sufficient reason

(*xiv*) Refusal to close or delay in closing the accounts

(*xv*) Non-adherence to the fair practices code as adopted by the bank

(*xvi*) Any other matter relating to the violation of the directives issued by the Reserve Bank in relation to banking or other services.

A customer can also lodge a complaint on the following grounds of deficiency in service with respect to loans and advances:

(*a*) non-observance of Reserve Bank Directives on interest rates

(*b*) delays in sanction, disbursement or non-observance of prescribed time schedule for disposal of loan applications

(*c*) non-acceptance of application for loans without furnishing valid reasons to the applicant

(*d*) non-adherence to the provisions of the fair practices code for lenders as adopted by the bank or Code of Bank's Commitment to Customers, as the case may be

(*e*) non-observance of any other direction or instruction of the Reserve Bank as may be specified by the Reserve Bank for this purpose from time to time

(*f*) The Banking Ombudsman may also deal with such other matter as may be specified by the Reserve Bank from time to time

The customer can file a complaint before the Banking Ombudsman if the reply is not received from the bank within a period of one month after the bank concerned has received his/her representation, or the bank rejects the complaint, or if the complainant is not satisfied with the reply given by the bank.

19.4.2 Present Scenario

Bank group-wise classification of complaints received by OBOs is indicated in the following: Table:

Bank group-wise classification

Bank Group	*No of Complaints Received During*		
	2010-11	*2011-12*	*2012-13*
Nationalized Banks	20417	22326	21609
	(29%)	(31%)	(31%)
SBI & Associates	22307	25848	23134
	(31%)	(35%)	(33%)
Private Sector Banks	17122	15090	15653
	(24%)	(21%)	(22%)
Foreign Banks	7081	5068	4859
	(10%)	(7%)	(7%)
RRBs / Scheduled Primary Urban Co-op. Banks	1130	1439	1489
	(2%)	(2%)	(2%)
Others	3217	3118	3797
	(4%)	(4%)	(5%)
Total	71274	72889	70541

There are 27 grounds of complaints against deficiency in banking services specified under Clause 8 of BOS 2006 for which complaints can be lodged with the OBO. Complaints received under these grounds are broadly categorized into major heads indicated in the Table below:

Category-wise distribution of complaints			
Complaint Category	*No of complaints received*		
	2010-11	*2011-12*	*2012-13*
Deposit accounts	1727	8713	3913
	(2%)	(12%)	(6%)
Remittances	4216	3928	2664
	(6%)	(5%)	(4%)
Card Related (ATM / Debit / Credit Card)	17116	14492	17867
	(24%)	(21%)	(25%)
Loans and advances	4564	6016	5996
	(6%)	(8%)	(9%)
Levy of Charges without prior notice	4149	3806	3817
	(6%)	(5%)	(5%)
Pension Payments	5927	5944	5740
	(8%)	(8%)	(8%)
Failure to meet commitments / Non observance of fair practices code / BCSBI Codes	16,302	18365	18130
	(23%)	(25%)	(26%)
DSAs and recovery agents	1722	459	351
	(2%)	(1%)	(0.8%)
Notes and coins	146	165	56
	(0.2%)	(0.2)	(0.2%)
Others	7201	7327	8635
	(10%)	(10%)	(12%)
Out of Subject	8204	3674	3372
	(11%)	(5%)	(5%)
Total	71,274	72889	70541

The table below indicates a comparative position of disposal of complaints by OBOs. During the year 2012-13, OBOs handled 75183 complaints. This, comprised of 4642 complaints brought forward from the previous year and 70541 fresh complaints received during the year under review. Of these, 69704 complaints (93%) were disposed of during the year 2012-13.

Comparative position of disposal of complaints by OBOs			
Number of complaints	*Year*		
	2010-11	*2011-12*	*2012-13*
Received during the year	71274	72889	70541
Brought forward from previous year	5364	4618	4642
Handled during the year	76,638	77507	75183
Disposed of during the year	72,020	72865	69704
Rate of Disposal (%)	94%	94%	93%
Carried forward to the next year	4618	4642	5479

Source: RBI Publications

According to the Annual Report of Banking Ombudsman Scheme, increased awareness and easy accessibility of the offices of Banking Ombudsmen contributed to the increase in number of complaints received by Banking Ombudsmen. The reasons for larger number of complaints from the rural and semi urban areas were increased penetration of banking, increased awareness and increased expectations of customers in these areas.

Banking Ombudsmen, also brought about greater awareness in rural and semi urban areas through their personal visits as part of the Reserve Bank's outreach activities, media coverage of these visits and advertisements.

REVIEW QUESTIONS

1. Write a detailed note on customer orientation in banking sector.
2. What are the basic aspects to be considered for customer service? Explain.
3. Explain KYC policy. Why is it important?
4. What are the objectives of KYC policy?
5. What are the key elements of KYC policy?
6. Write a note on KYC policy and Customer Education.
7. Write a note on customer identification procedures as laid down by RBI.
8. Explain the Banking Ombudsman Scheme and state its importance.
9. What are the different types of complaints covered under Banking Ombudsman Scheme.

CHAPTER 20

Recent Trends in Indian Banking

Indian Banking System developed enormously in this decade. Commercial Banks extend financial assistance or the credit facilities in many ways. Although all-Credit facilities are basically a loan, different methods of financing are adopted depending upon the period of finance, purpose of finance, Quantum of balance, etc. Some of these methods of financing introduced in the Indian banking in the recent period have been explained below. Similarly, the repayment of loan is also arranged in specific ways to suit customers/borrowers requirements. Few such methods of repayment have also been explained in this chapter.

20.1 TYPES OF FINANCING

The following are the types of financing:

1. Take out Financing
2. Revolving Credit Facilities
3. Ever Greening Of Loan
4. Syndicated Loan
5. Bridge Loan
6. Consortium Finance
7. Preferred Financing
8. Non-Fund Based Business

Let us discuss these items one by one.

20.1.1 Take-out Financing

Banks usually lend for short-term. It is because their source of funds for financing comes form deposits which are usually for a maximum period of 3 to 5 years. However, presently banks are encouraged to provide finance for long-term projects like infrastructure industry. Hence when a bank, say, lend for 10 years against a 4 years deposit, there is a problem of continuing the loan after 4 years. It is possible that the bank will continue to get deposits every year. Yet, the fact today is a 10 year loan has been made based on a 4 year deposit which is a risky affair. In such a situation, few banks will come together and under an agreement each one of them will take up the loan portfolio in turn, for a fixed period of time till the loan matures. For example, if Bank A has provided a 10 year loan, with an arrangement with Bank B and Bank C whereby, after the end of the 4th year, Bank B will finance the loan for next 3 years and Bank C will finance the loan during the last 3 years. Illustratively, the financial arrangement works as follows:

Bank	Period of Loan Financing
A	0 to 4 years
B	5th, 6th and 7th year
C	8th, 9th and 10th year

Bank B and C have done take out financing. This system of financing takes care of banks' asset-liability mismatch. Long-term projects can be financed by Commercial Banks and funds can be ensured for nationally important projects like infrastructure industries.

20.1.2 Revolving Credit Facility

Under a Revolving Credit Facility a bank fixes up a credit limit to a borrower for certain period, say ₹10 crore for 3 years period. The borrower will get a maximum credit facility of ₹10 crore at any point of time once the loan is repaid. The borrower's facility automatically gets renewed up to ₹10 crore during the 3 year period any number of times. In other words, the credit facility revolves around with a maximum of ₹10 crore outstanding at any point of time over a 3 years period. In principle, under a Revolving Facility there is no formal repayment period. The borrower is allowed to draw, repay and again draw throughout the loan period.

20.1.3 Evergreening of Loan

Sometimes a bank provides a second finance facility to a borrower to help him to pay back the original loan. Why should a bank do it when the bank's exposure to the customer remains same? It is because when a borrower defaults on payment of interest/principal to the bank as per prudential norms, the loan account will become an NPA and the bank has to make provisions. To avoid such an unpleasant situation and to show a rosy picture of bank's loan portfolio, sometimes banks do resort to evergreening. RBI does not permit this type of replacement credit.

20.1.4 Syndicated Loan

It is a loan facility provided to a single borrower by a group of banks. As the loan is extended by a group of lenders, the size of syndicated loan is normally large and a single lender/ banker may not have been in a position to extend such a facility. It could also be that a single lender may not like to have such a large exposure (credit risk) to a single borrower. Syndicated loans are arranged to finance projects needing large sums of money where the credit risk is also high. These loans are for financing medium to long term requirements. Since, the bankers involved in providing such loan facility are many, usually co-ordination work is done by a 'lead manager' who acts as an intermediary between the lenders and the borrower. One interesting point in syndicated loan arrangement is that the borrower indicates his requirement of loan sum and the prospective lenders have to offer as to what extent they are prepared to extend the facility. Also under this arrangement one bank in the syndicate acts as an agent for collecting interest and other payments from borrower and distributes to other banks.

20.1.5 BRIDGE LOAN

Bridge loan is a short-term temporary loan extended by financial institutions to help the borrower to meet the immediate expenditure pending disposal of requests for long term funds or regular loans. For example, when a borrower's application for project finance is pending for final sanction, the bank may extend a bridge loan to the borrower to meet urgent expenses. Usually, a bridge loan gets repaid out of the main loan when sanctioned. During 1980's corporates used to avail of bridge loans from banks against the expected subscription on public issue of debentures, equity, etc., Here, the bridge loan is not against any main loan arrangement but against anticipated cash flow. Again, if an individual is negotiating the sale of his asset, say a house, a bridge loan may be extended by a bank to meet the seller's immediate cash requirements. The loan will be paid off when the borrower realises his sale proceeds.

Bridge loan is relatively risky for the bankers when repayment depends upon an external factor not under the control of lenders.

20.1.6 Consortium Finance

Under consortium finance a large credit facility may be jointly arranged by a combination of several banks. Usually, one of the banks in the group will act as the leader for the credit. The consortium leader will extend a larger share of the credit as compared to other banks in the consortium. The word consortium here refers to 'a combination of many banks who have agreed to extend the credit facility'. The share of credit agreed to be extended will be decided by the banks in the beginning. The borrower need not deal separately with all the banks in the group. Usually, he deals with the consortium leader who takes care of other banks' credit.

In India till two years back, as per RBI guidelines, large credit facility, say ₹10 crore and above, should be granted only under consortium arrangement. The reason for such a condition is that a single bank should not have large credit exposure to a single borrower. RBI has recently liberalised the norms and banks are permitted to fix their own norms for lending. A bank is however not permitted to extend credit beyond 25 per cent of its net owned funds or 25 per cent of borrower's net owned funds (whichever is lower) to a single borrower. This norm is known as single exposure limit. This limit is intended to be lowered to 15 per cent gradually to conform to international standard. As a first step, this limit is being reduced to 20 per cent from April 2000.

20.1.7 Preferred Financing

In the highly competitive world of banking today, banks are reaching out to customers, particularly high networth or wealthy customers. One area of lucrative finance for bankers is consumer finance, more particularly car finance. A preferred financier is a lender or a bank, who provides large consumer loans like car loan under an arrangement with the car manufacturer. Because of the tie-up, the manufacturer agrees to provide some concession in the car price and some additional facilities in the car. This the manufacturer makes available for two reasons.

(*a*) One, purchase price is assured and

(*b*) Second it gives some push for the demand of that car.

Preferred Financier also benefits. He gets wealthy customers. Default in the consumer finance sector is minimum, because most of the customers have regular income. And loans are provided against hypothecation of car, which has a resale value. In the event of default, it can be sold and value realised. The preferred financier sending his officials to the Dealer's Showroom provides all information about the loan facility and gets all documentation done at the showroom itself for the loan. The customer also gains in some ways. Comparatively reduced rate of interest for loan, getting finance documentations done at the dealer's showroom itself, benefit from some gift scheme, etc.,

20.1.8 Guarantee Services / Non-fund Based Business

Non-fund based business is not a credit facility or a financial assistance. However, the banks make sizeable income out of non-fund based business, mainly from guarantee services. This has explained below.

Banks offer 'Guarantee Services' to valued customers. Guarantee service refers to a legal undertaking by the bank to pay a certain sum of money to a third-party or a creditor in the event of the bank's client/customer fails to fulfil his part of obligation. The obligation may be to pay some money or to perform certain duties like a contract job. The guarantee from bank enhances the certainty of performance or payment.

Usually, banks issue guarantees on behalf of their customers in favour of Government Departments like Customs authority saying if the customer does not perform under a contract or does not pay the required sum, the bank will pay the money or damages. This function of issuing a guarantee is done for certain amount of fees. Hence, it is called fee-based services of banks. You will understand, under a guarantee a bank does not provide any credit facility to the customer. Hence, this type of services by banks are called non-fund based business. Other examples are issue of Travellers' Cheques, Demand Drafts, remittance facilities, arrangement of foreign currency loans, etc.

20.2 REPAYMENT METHODS

Types of Repayment System include the following:

1. Bullet Payment System
2. Balloon Payment System

20.2.1 Bullet Payment System

Under this method of borrowing and lending, the borrower will not be required to pay back the loan and interest payments periodically like every 6 months or so. The full loan amount together with interest payments will be made at a single time on maturity of loan. This system of lending is rare in India as there are no regular cash flows for the bank. This method of payment is adopted in term loans.

20.2.2 Balloon Payment System

Under this system, the repayment of a term-loan facility will be so arranged that the instalment value will be smaller in the beginning and as the repayment progresses towards maturity value of instalments will be larger and larger. In other words, under Balloon Payment System, the borrower's repayments are higher at end and smaller in the beginning. This type of arrangement will be helpful to borrower who expect smaller returns in the beginning and higher returns later out of his investments. You will notice that bullet and Balloon payments systems refer to repayment of term loans. These methods are not common in Indian Banking.

Now let us see some of the new developments in the bank related business / service.

20.3 VENTURE CAPITAL

A 'venture' is a new risky business. 'Venture Capital', therefore refers to providing start-up capital to a new and risky business operations.

Every new business operation is risky. Then what distinguishes venture capital business operations from other business operations? In Venture Capital business:

(*a*) the promoters may be new technocrats, who have not proved their business acumen or expertise so far; and

(*b*) the idea of new product is yet to be tested in the market.

Hence, the venture capitalist (one who provides finance for venture capital business) takes a bigger risk in financing the production of a new product by persons who have not proven their business capabilities so far. It can be said that venture capital is the Equity investment in young private companies. The venture capitalist may be financial institutions, banks, investment companies or even wealthy individuals. The venture capitalist is prepared to back an untried business operations in exchange for a share of future expected profits. The venture capitalists usually provides capital in stages depending upon growth of business operations and not at one stroke. If the business succeeds the venture capitalist makes big profit from a share in profit and form value appreciation of investment in Equity Shares.

In USA it started in a big way in 1980s. Even the US Government provided cheap loans to investment companies to encourage them to relend the money to deserving new entrepreneurs. There are many success stories of venture capital assisted business operations. However failures of Venture Capital business are more than success stories.

In India Venture Capital business idea caught the minds of financial institutions only in 1990s. The government allows banks tax concession for venture capital business operations. However this business started only in a small scale in India so far. The reason mainly is the reluctance of banks to provide funds for untested and doubtful business operations. However, new software engineers have started in a big way with venture capital assistance. In India, SEBI have laid down rules and regulations for venture capital business.

As per RBI guidelines banks providing finance to venture capital business can treat such advances as priority sector loans. The Technology Development and Information Company of India Ltd., Risk Capital and Technology Finance Corporation, SBI Capital Market, Canbank Financial services and Credit Capital Finance Corporation are already financing high risk, new ventures under Venture Capital Financing Schemes.

20.4 BANKNET

The collecting, processing and distribution of information is vital to business growth of banks. Computerisation takes care of only the processing. The gathering and distribution on use of telephone, mail, telegraph and telex which leads to delay and high cost due to handling at several stages. Hence a common communications network called 'Banknet' operated by banks and financial institutions on a co-operative basis within the country is being set up. The Banknet can be put to several uses. Some of the illustrative areas are given here under:

(*i*) Transfer of funds from one place to another distant place or bank.

(*ii*) Exchange of statistical information among banks.

(*iii*) Foreign exchange business operations.

(*iv*) Inter-Bank applications, like settlement of funds between banks.

The transfer of funds includes that customer can draw cash against their deposit at any branch of the bank as envisaged under 'on-line banking' and can also deposit cash at any branch for credit to an account at some other branch. Advance can be allowed at one branch against deposit at some other branch. This concept is known as 'Banking Anywhere'. (For more details please see the chapter 'Banking and Technology' in this book)

20.5 DEPOSIT INSURANCE SCHEME

To protect the interests of the depositors, the Deposit Insurance Corporation of India was established by an Act of Parliament in 1962. It provides insurance cover on deposits held with the commercial, and co-operative banks and the scheme of deposit insurance was introduced with effect from 1st Jan 1962. In 1978, the credit guarantee corporation of India was merged with the deposit insurance corporation and the corporation has been renamed as **'Deposit Insurance and Credit Guarantee Corporation'** with effect from 15th July 1978. The corporation provides protection to small depositors by insurance and provides guarantee to the banks for loans extended to small borrowers.

20.5.1 Coverage

All commercial banks including branches of foreign banks functioning in India, local area banks and regional rural banks are insured by the DICGC. Cooperative Banks: All State, Central and Primary Cooperative Banks, also called urban cooperative banks, are covered under the Deposit Insurance System. At present all co-operative banks other than those from the States of Meghalaya, and the Union Territories of Chandigarh, Lakshadweep and Dadra and Nagar Haveli are covered under the deposit insurance system of DICGC. Primary cooperative societies are not insured by the DICGC. (*Source*: RBI Publications).

20.5.2 Types of Deposits Covered

In the event of a bank failure, DICGC protects bank deposits that are payable in India. The DICGC insures all deposits such as savings, fixed, current, recurring, etc. except the following types of deposits:

(*i*) Deposits of foreign Governments

(*ii*) Deposits of Central/State Governments

(*iii*) Interbank deposits

(*iv*) Deposits of the State Land Development Banks with the State Co-operative Bank

(*v*) Any amount due on account of any deposit received outside India

(*vi*) Any amount, which has been specifically exempted by the corporation with the previous approval of Reserve Bank of India

Presently deposits with banks upto ₹1,00,000 per account is guaranteed for repayment by the Corporation.

20.6 GOLD DEPOSIT SCHEME

The Government of India has proposed a new Gold Deposit Scheme in its Budget for 1999-2000. The purpose of the Scheme was to mobilise idle gold lying with people / institutions like temple in India and utilise the same for productive purposes through the banking system. As per the scheme announced in September/October 1999 selected commercial banks are permitted to accept gold deposits from individuals, trusts and companies in the form of gold coin, jewellery, ornaments, gold bars, etc. The banks after ascertaining their gold content through the process of assaying will issue interest bearing gold bonds or pass books to the depositors. The depositors at the maturity of the bond will get back same quantity of gold or its equivalent value in rupees. Interest amount will be paid separately and it is exempted from income tax. Gold value is exempted from Wealth Tax. One of the purposes of the scheme is to reduce the import of gold from abroad. In 1998-99 India imported 540 tonnes of gold through official channels. Non-Resident Indians are also permitted to bring with them 10 kgs of gold subject to certain conditions when they come to India.

This scheme which was first launched in Nov 1999 at the initiation of the then union finance minister Yashwant Sinha in the budget 1999-2000 did not gel well with the public at large and was thus withdrawn within a few years of its launch.

The scheme has been re-launched and is available only at select SBI branches. Currently only 50 branches across the country have been nominated to accept these deposits of which four are in Maharashtra. Only two branches in Mumbai have been nominated for the purpose, namely, Mumbai Main Branch and Shivaji Park Branch. The bank is also setting up a separate branch at the gold hub of Mumbai - Zaveri Bazaar to manage these deposits.(*Source*: Economic Times: March 21, 2009)

20.6.1 Features

(*a*) During the investment tenure, the deposited gold will earn an interest, which is currently tagged as 1% (3 years), 1.25% (4 years) and 1.5% (5 years). The investment shall be locked-in for one year.

(*b*) Premature withdrawal, after the lock-in period but before the maturity, shall attract a penal interest of 0.5% if withdrawn within 3 years and 0.25% thereafter.

(*c*) However, unlike the regular deposits, interest here is calculated in grams and not in rupees. Thus, an investment of 500 grams of gold for three years shall earn 5 grams of gold as interest per annum, compounded annually. At the end of the maturity term, the interest so earned shall be converted into rupee equivalent of gold then and paid to the investor.

(*d*) For the principal investment, investor will have an option to claim back pure gold (0.999 purity) or cash equivalent of gold as on that day. The scheme is also attractive from tax perspective as the interest earned as well as tax on any capital gains arising from rise in price of gold after maturity is exempt from tax. Gold so deposited has also been exempted from wealth tax.

(*e*) The gold so deposited with the bank shall be checked for purity and melted at the Government of India mint. A certificate of purity will then be issued by the Government, which can be used by the investor to claim back the gold after the maturity period.

20.7 CORE BANKING SYSTEMS

The last decade witnessed a sea change in the way banking services are made available to customers. The implementation of Core Banking Systems has proven to be a big boon in providing anywhere access to banking services and the treatment of a customer as that of a bank and not as a constituent of a specific branch. With the interlinking of ATMs, the customer has been further transformed into constituent of the financial sector rather than a bank. Alongside, the banking sector has made significant efforts to identify security gaps in an IT enabled scenario and have addressed them effectively as well.

20.8 BANCASSURANCE

Bancassurance services have evolved in different parts of the world according to the nature of deregulation and other national or regional factors in place. "Bancassurance" – a term coined by combining the two words bank and insurance (in French) – connotes distribution of insurance products through banking channels. Bancassurance encompasses terms such as 'Allfinanz' (in German), 'Integrated Financial Services' and 'Assure banking'. Banks, with their geographical spread and penetration in terms of customer reach of all segments, have emerged as viable sources for the distribution of insurance products.

Bancassurance, is basically selling insurance products and services by leveraging the vast customer base of a bank and fulfill the banking and insurance needs of the customers at the same time.

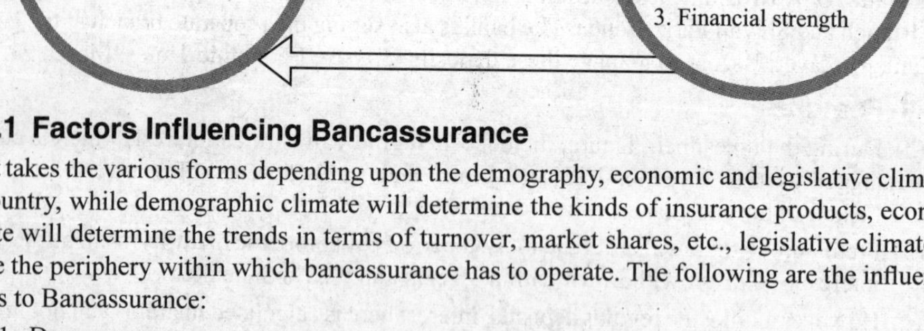

20.8.1 Factors Influencing Bancassurance

It takes the various forms depending upon the demography, economic and legislative climate of the country, while demographic climate will determine the kinds of insurance products, economic climate will determine the trends in terms of turnover, market shares, etc., legislative climate will decide the periphery within which bancassurance has to operate. The following are the influencing factors to Bancassurance:

1. Democracy
2. Economic factors
3. Consumer awareness
4. Legal Environment
5. Organizational Brand and Positioning

20.8.2 Bancassurance in India

Bancassurance as a means of distribution of insurance products is already in force. Banks are selling Insurance directly to their vast customers as a value addition to their products. Banks distribute accidental, personal and mortgage linked insurance products like fire, motor or cattle insurance to their customers. Banks can straightaway employ their existing sources and means in terms of database and face-to face contact to market insurance products to generate some income for themselves.

Banks have expertise on the financial needs, saving patterns and life stages of the customers they serve. Banks also have much lower distribution costs than insurance companies and thus are the fastest emerging distribution channel. For insurers, tying up with banks provides extensive geographical spread and countrywide customer access; it is the logical route for insurers to take. In India there is greater scope for Bancassurance due to the following special features of Banking and customers:

1. Banks are major players in the Indian Financial system
2. Large Structure and network of banking sector with effective regulations
3. Consumer awareness and their banking habits.

20.8.3 Benefits of Bancassurance

The following are the general benefits of Bancassurance:

For banks – it is a means of product diversification and a source of additional fee income.

For Insurance companies: it is a tool for increasing their market penetration and premium turnover.

For customer: it is a boon in terms of reduced price, high quality product and delivery at door steps.

In India there is greater scope for Bancassurance.

For the topics ATM, Phone Banking and Internet Banking, please see the next Chapter 20, 'Banking and Technology' in this book.

20.9 PAYMENT SYSTEMS IN INDIA

The central bank of any country is usually the driving force in the development of national payment systems. The Reserve Bank of India as the Central Bank of India has been playing this developmental role and has taken several initiatives for Safe, Secure, Sound, Efficient, Accessible and Authorised payment systems in the country.

The Board for Regulation and Supervision of Payment and Settlement Systems (BPSS), a sub-committee of the Central Board of the Reserve Bank of India is the highest policy making body on payment systems in the country. The BPSS is empowered for authorising, prescribing policies and setting standards for regulating and supervising all the payment and settlement systems in the country. The Department of Payment and Settlement Systems of the Reserve Bank of India serves as the Secretariat to the Board and executes its directions.

In India, the payment and settlement systems are regulated by the Payment and Settlement Systems Act, 2007 (PSS Act) which was legislated in December 2007. The PSS Act as well as the Payment and Settlement System Regulations, 2008 framed thereunder came into effect from August 12, 2008. In terms of Section 4 of the PSS Act, no person other than the Reserve Bank of India (RBI) can commence or operate a payment system in India unless authorised by RBI. Reserve Bank has since authorised payment system operators of pre-paid payment instruments, card schemes, cross-border in-bound money transfers, Automated Teller Machine (ATM) networks and centralised clearing arrangements.

Payment Systems

The Reserve Bank has taken many initiatives towards introducing and upgrading safe and efficient modes of payment systems in the country to meet the requirements of the public at large. The dominant features of large geographic spread of the country and the vast network of branches of the Indian banking system require the logistics of collection and delivery of paper instruments. These aspects of the banking structure in the country have always been kept in mind while developing the payment systems. The payment systems can be classified as under:

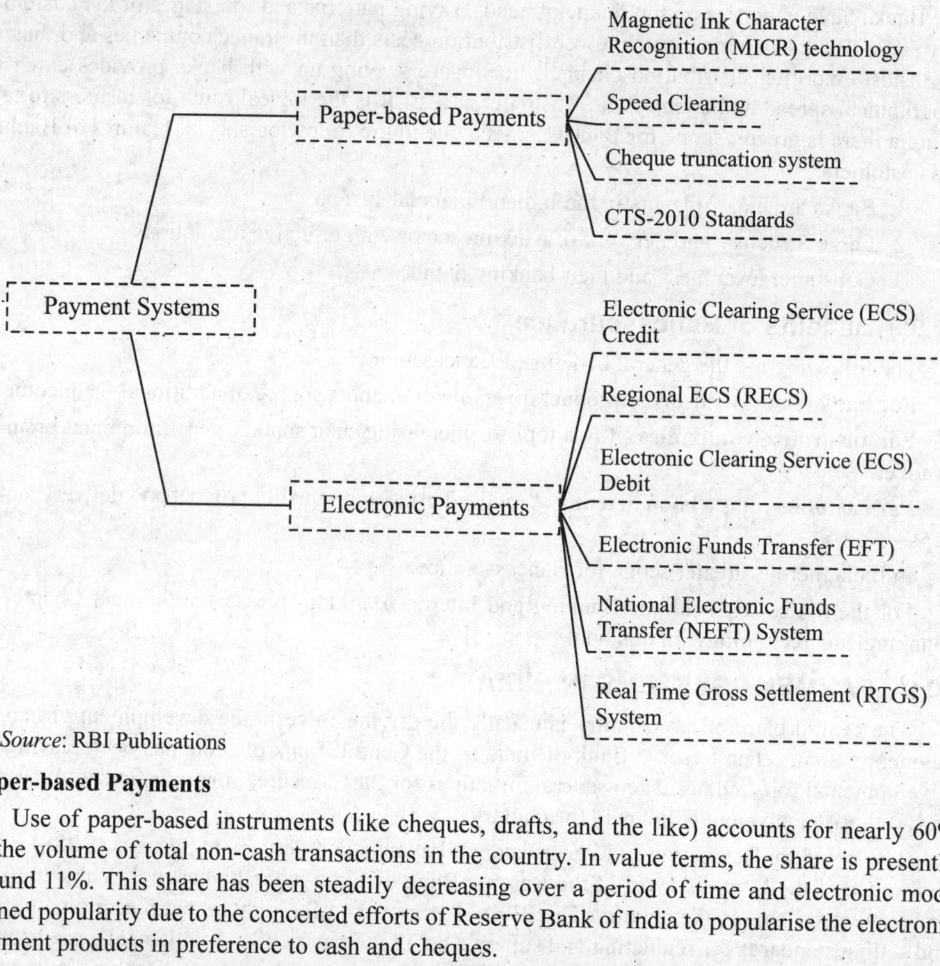

Source: RBI Publications

Paper-based Payments

Use of paper-based instruments (like cheques, drafts, and the like) accounts for nearly 60% of the volume of total non-cash transactions in the country. In value terms, the share is presently around 11%. This share has been steadily decreasing over a period of time and electronic mode gained popularity due to the concerted efforts of Reserve Bank of India to popularise the electronic payment products in preference to cash and cheques.

Since paper based payments occupy an important place in the country, Reserve Bank had introduced Magnetic Ink Character Recognition (MICR) technology for speeding up and bringing in efficiency in processing of cheques.

Later, a separate High Value Clearing was introduced for clearing cheques of value Rupees one lakh and above. This clearing was available at select large centres in the country (since discontinued). Recent developments in paper-based instruments include launch of Speed Clearing (for local clearance of outstation cheques drawn on core-banking enabled branches of banks), introduction of cheque truncation system (to restrict physical movement of cheques and enable use of images for payment processing), framing CTS-2010 Standards (for enhancing the security features on cheque forms) and the like.

While the overall thrust is to reduce the use of paper for transactions, given the fact that it would take some time to completely move to the electronic mode, the intention is to reduce the movement of paper – both for local and outstation clearance of cheques.

Electronic Payments

The initiatives taken by RBI in the mid-eighties and early-nineties focused on technology-based solutions for the improvement of the payment and settlement system infrastructure, coupled with the introduction of new payment products by taking advantage of the technological advancements in banks. The continued increase in the volume of cheques added pressure on the existing set up, thus necessitating a cost-effective alternative system. (the detailed discussion on electronic payment system, is given in the next Chapter 21-Banking and Technology).

Electronic Clearing Service (ECS) Credit

The Bank introduced the ECS (Credit) scheme during the 1990s to handle bulk and repetitive payment requirements (like salary, interest, dividend payments) of corporates and other institutions. ECS (Credit) facilitates customer accounts to be credited on the specified value date and is presently available at all major cities in the country.

During September 2008, the Bank launched a new service known as National Electronic Clearing Service (NECS), at National Clearing Cell (NCC), Mumbai. NECS (Credit) facilitates multiple credits to beneficiary accounts with destination branches across the country against a single debit of the account of the sponsor bank. The system has a pan-India characteristic and leverages on Core Banking Solutions (CBS) of member banks, facilitating all CBS Bank branches to participate in the system, irrespective of their location across the country.

Regional ECS (RECS)

Next to NECS, RECS has been launched during the year 2009.RECS, a miniature of the NECS is confined to the bank branches within the jurisdiction of a Regional office of RBI. Under the system, the sponsor bank will upload the validated data through the Secured Web Server of RBI containing credit/debit instructions to the customers of CBS enabled bank branches spread across the Jurisdiction of the Regional Office of RBI. The RECS centre will process the data, arrive at the settlement, generate destination bank-wise data/reports and make available the data/reports through secured web-server to facilitate the destination bank branches to afford credit/debit to the accounts of beneficiaries by leveraging the CBS technology put in place by the bank. Presently RECS is available in Ahmedabad, Bengaluru, Chennai and Kolkata

Electronic Clearing Service (ECS) Debit

The ECS (Debit) Scheme was introduced by RBI to provide a faster method of effecting periodic and repetitive collections of utility companies. ECS (Debit) facilitates consumers / subscribers of utility companies to make routine and repetitive payments by 'mandating' bank branches to debit their accounts and pass on the money to the companies. This tremendously minimises use of paper instruments apart from improving process efficiency and customer satisfaction. There is no limit as to the minimum or maximum amount of payment. This is also available across major cities in the country.

Electronic Funds Transfer (EFT)

This retail funds transfer system introduced in the late 1990s enabled an accountholder of a bank to electronically transfer funds to another account holder with any other participating bank. Available across 15 major centers in the country, this system is no longer available for use by the general public, for whose benefit a feature-rich and more efficient system is now in place, which is the National Electronic Funds Transfer (NEFT) system.

National Electronic Funds Transfer (NEFT) System

In November 2005, a more secure system was introduced for facilitating one-to-one funds transfer requirements of individuals / corporates. Available across a longer time window, the NEFT system provides for batch settlements at hourly intervals, thus enabling near real-time transfer of funds. Certain other unique features, *viz*., accepting cash for originating transactions, initiating transfer requests without any minimum or maximum amount limitations, facilitating one-way transfers to Nepal, receiving confirmation of the date / time of credit to the account of the beneficiaries, etc., are available in the system.

Real Time Gross Settlement (RTGS) System

RTGS is a funds transfer systems where transfer of money takes place from one bank to another on a "real time" and on "gross" basis. Settlement in "real time" means payment transaction is not subjected to any waiting period. "Gross settlement" means the transaction is settled on one to one basis without bunching or netting with any other transaction. Once processed, payments are final and irrevocable. This was introduced in in 2004 and settles all inter-bank payments and customer transactions above ₹ 2 lakh.

Clearing Corporation of India Limited (CCIL)

CCIL was set up in April 2001 by banks, financial institutions and primary dealers, to function as an industry service organization for clearing and settlement of trades in money market, government securities and foreign exchange markets.

The Clearing Corporation plays the crucial role of a Central Counter Party (CCP) in the government securities, USD –INR forex exchange (both spot and forward segments) and Collaterised Borrowing and Lending Obligation (CBLO) markets. CCIL plays the role of a central counterparty whereby, the contract between buyer and seller gets replaced by two new contracts - between CCIL and each of the two parties. This process is known as 'Novation'. Through novation, the counterparty credit risk between the buyer and seller is eliminated with CCIL subsuming all counterparty and credit risks. In order to minimize the these risks, that it exposes itself to, CCIL follows specific risk management practices which are as per international best practices.In addition to the guaranteed settlement, CCIL also provides non guaranteed settlement services for National Financial Switch (Interbank ATM transactions) and for rupee derivatives such as Interest Rate Swaps.

CCIL is also providing a reporting platform and acts as a repository for Over the Counter (OTC) products.

Other Payment Systems

Pre-paid Payment Systems

Pre-paid instruments are payment instruments that facilitate purchase of goods and services against the value stored on these instruments. The value stored on such instruments represents the value paid for by the holders by cash, by debit to a bank account, or by credit card. The pre-paid payment instruments can be issued in the form of smart cards, magnetic stripe cards, internet accounts, internet wallets, mobile accounts, mobile wallets, paper vouchers, etc.

Subsequent to the notification of the PSS Act, policy guidelines for issuance and operation of prepaid instruments in India were issued in the public interest to regulate the issue of prepaid payment instruments in the country.

The use of pre-paid payment instruments for cross border transactions has not been permitted, except for the payment instruments approved under Foreign Exchange Management Act,1999 (FEMA).

Mobile Banking System

Mobile phones as a medium for providing banking services have been attaining increased importance. Reserve Bank brought out a set of operating guidelines on mobile banking for banks in October 2008, according to which only banks which are licensed and supervised in India and have a physical presence in India are permitted to offier mobile banking after obtaining necessary permission from Reserve Bank. The guidelines focus on systems for security and inter bank transfer arrangements through Reserve Bank's authorised systems. On the technology front the objective is to enable the development of inter-operable standards so as to facilitate funds transfer from one account to any other account in the same or any other bank on a real time basis irrespective of the mobile network a customer has subscribed to.

ATMs / Point of Sale (POS) Terminals / Online Transactions

Presently, there are over 61,000 ATMs in India. Savings Bank customers can withdraw cash from any bank terminal up to 5 times in a month without being charged for the same. To address the customer service issues arising out of failed ATM transactions where the customer's account gets debited without actual disbursal of cash, the Reserve Bank has mandated re-crediting of such failed transactions within 12 working day and mandated compensation for delays beyond the stipulated period. Furthermore, a standardised template has been prescribed for displaying at all ATM locations to facilitate lodging of complaints by customers.

There are over five lakh POS terminals in the country, which enable customers to make payments for purchases of goods and services by means of credit/debit cards. To facilitate customer convenience the Bank has also permitted cash withdrawal using debit cards issued by the banks at PoS terminals.

The PoS for accepting card payments also include online payment gateways. This facility is used for enabling online payments for goods and services. The online payment are enabled through own payment gateways or third party service providers clled intermediaries. In payment transactions involving intermediaries, these intermediaries act as the initial recipient of payments and distribute the payment to merchants. In such transactions, the customers are exposed to the uncertainty of payment as most merchants treat the payments as final on receipt from the intermediaries. In this regard safeguard the interests of customers and to ensure that the payments made by them using Electronic/Online Payment modes are duly accounted for by intermediaries receiving such payments, directions were issued in November 2009. Directions require that the funds received from customers for such transactions need to be maintained in an internal account of a bank and the intermediary should not have access to the same.

Further, to reduce the risks arising out of the use of credit/debit cards over internet/IVR (technically referred to as card not present (CNP) transactions), Reserve Bank mandated that all CNP transactions should be additionally authenticated based on information not available on the card and an online alert should be sent to the cardholders for such transactions.

National Payments Corporation of India

The Reserve Bank encouraged the setting up of National Payments Corporation of India (NPCI) to act as an umbrella organization for operating various Retail Payment Systems (RPS) in India. NPCI became functional in early 2009. NPCI has taken over National Financial Switch (NFS) from Institute for Development and Research in Banking Technology (IDRBT). NPCI is expected to bring greater efficiency by way of uniformity and standardization in retail payments and expanding and extending the reach of both existing and innovative payment products for greater customer convenience.

Oversight of Payment and Settlement Systems

Oversight of the payment and settlement systems is a central bank function whereby the objectives of safety and efficiency are promoted by monitoring existing and planned systems, assessing them against these objectives and, where necessary, inducing change. By overseeing payment and settlement systems, central banks help to maintain systemic stability and reduce systemic risk, and to maintain public confidence in payment and settlement systems.

The Payment and Settlement Systems Act, 2007 and the Payment and Settlement Systems Regulations, 2008 framed thereunder, provide the necessary statutory backing to the Reserve Bank of India for undertaking the Oversight function over the payment and settlement systems in the country.

REVIEW QUESTIONS

Short Answer Questions

1. Write a short note on:
   (*a*) Take out Financing
   (*b*) Revolving Credit Facilities
   (*c*) Ever Greening of Loan
   (*d*) Syndicated Loan
   (*e*) Bridge Loan
   (*f*) Consortium Finance
   (*g*) Preferred Financing
   (*h*) Non-Fund Based Business
2. What is venture capital?
3. Write a note on Bank Net?
4. What is core banking system?

Essay Type Questions

1. Explain the following repayment methods in detail:
   (*a*) Bullet Payment System
   (*b*) Balloon Payment System
2. Explain Deposit Insurance Scheme.
3. Write a note on and Gold Deposit Scheme. What are its features?
4. Explain in detail the Bancassurance services.
5. Explain the concept and features of Bancassurance services. What are its benefits?
6. Discuss in detail on the payment systems in India.

21

CHAPTER

Banking and Technology

The rapid development of technology has created an extraordinary effort upon our economy in general. It has particularly profound impact in expanding the scope and utility of financial products over the last decade. Information technology has made possible the creation, valuation and exchange of financial products on global basis.

The revolution in technology disseminates in every walk of life and the banking sector is no exception. As the banking sector is undergoing a paradigm shift in its role and functions as a result of increased competition and growing consumer awareness, application of IT in banking has become important to face the challenges of tough competition from other players through better customer service with efficiency. With the expansion of and easy access to the digital communication across the country at an affordable cost, the customers' expectation, for efficient services in banking, has gained momentum. Commercial Banks have road maps of technology applications in banking in various areas through recommendations of number of committees appointed by RBI such as Working Group to consider feasibility of introducing MICR / OCR, Technology for cheques processing, Rangarajan Committee, Committee on Communication networks in Banks, Committee of Payment System, Cheques Clearing, Committee on Electronic Fund Transfer and Electronic Payments, etc,.

What is really quite extraordinary is that there is no sign that this process of acceleration in financial technology is approaching an end. We are moving at an exceptionally rapid pace, fueled not only by the enhanced mathematical applications produced by our ever rising computing capabilities but also by our expanding telecommunications capabilities and the associated substantial broadening of our markets.

Since the economy is growing and with the advent of technology, the banks are being expected to deliver services to the maximum effective, safer and convenient manner. The driving forces of modern banking can be seen in the following diagram:

Driving Forces of Modern Banking

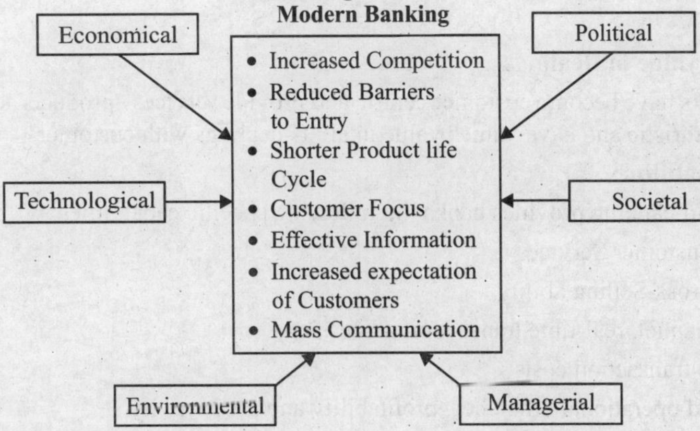

21.1 IMPORTANCE OF TECHNOLOGY IN BANKING INDUSTRY

All the new financial products that have been created in recent years contribute economic value by unbundling risks and reallocating them in a highly calibrated manner. The rising share of finance in the business output of India and other countries is a measure of the economic value added by the ability of these new instruments and techniques to enhance the process of wealth creation. The importance of Technology in banking industry can be seen as follows:

1. Opens New Avenues of Market opportunities

Technology has opened up new markets, new products, new services and efficient delivery channels for the banking industry. Online electronics banking, mobile banking and internet banking are just a few examples.

2. Provides Ability to deal with the Challenges

Information Technology has also provided banking industry with the ability to deal with the challenges the new economy poses. Information technology has been the cornerstone of recent financial sector reforms aimed at increasing the speed and reliability of financial operations and of initiatives to strengthen the banking sector.

3. Increase the volume of Financial Activities

The IT revolution has set the stage for unprecedented increase in financial activity across the globe. The progress of technology and the development of world wide networks have significantly reduced the cost of global funds transfer.

4. Helps I meeting customers growing demands and expectations

It is information technology which enables banks in meeting such high expectations of the customers who are more demanding and are also more techno-savy compared to their counterparts of the yester years. They demand instant, anytime and anywhere banking facilities.

5. Maintenance of Accounts and Information

IT has been providing solutions to banks to take care of their accounting and back office requirements. This has, however, now given way to large scale usage in services aimed at the customer of the banks. IT also facilitates the introduction of new delivery channels–in the form of Automated Teller Machines, Net Banking, Mobile Banking and the like.

6. Increased Network

With advancement of information techonology, banks are increasingly interconnecting their computer systems not only across branches in a city but also to other geographic locations with high-speed network infrastructure, and setting up local area and wide area networks and connecting them to the Internet. As a result, information systems and networks are now exposed to a growing number.

7. Creates Time value in Dealings

With IT, banks have become customer centric and provide services / products across a range of channels to be futuristic and have "time" value in all its dealings with customers.

8. Enhanced capabilities

Technology in banking provides banks the following specific capabilities:

(*a*) Better Customer Service

(*b*) Better Cross-Selling ability

(*c*) Multi-channel, real-time transaction processing

(*d*) Minimal transaction costs

(*e*) Increased operational efficiency, profitability and productivity

(*f*) Efficient NPA and Risk Management
(*g*) Improved management / accountability
(*h*) Improved financial analyses capabilities
(*i*) New avenues in delivery channels

21.2 DELIVERY CHANNELS OF BANKING SECTOR

Banks strategise on products, pricing, and margins, but those efforts ultimately rely on the effective delivery of products and services to the customer. Until recently, banks rarely viewed delivery as one cohesive strategic requirement, seeing it as a collection of disparate services at best. At the same time, consumers have been spoiled by the superior delivery of services from providers outside the financial industry. Retailers are leading the way in marketing, selling, and delivering products to consumers much more effectively across integrated channels. Consumers are pressuring financial services institutions to improve the way they deliver their products as well.

They have, over a long time, been using electronic and telecommunication networks for delivering a wide range of value added products and services. The delivery channels include direct dial – up connections, private networks, public networks etc and the devices include telephone, Personal Computers including the Automated Teller Machines, etc. With the popularity of PCs, easy access to Internet and World Wide Web (WWW), Internet is increasingly used by banks as a channel for receiving instructions and delivering their products and services to their customers.

Banks have been in the forefront of harnessing technology to improve their products, services and efficiency. The continuous development in technology has opened avenues for different channels of delivery to the banking industry. They include the following:

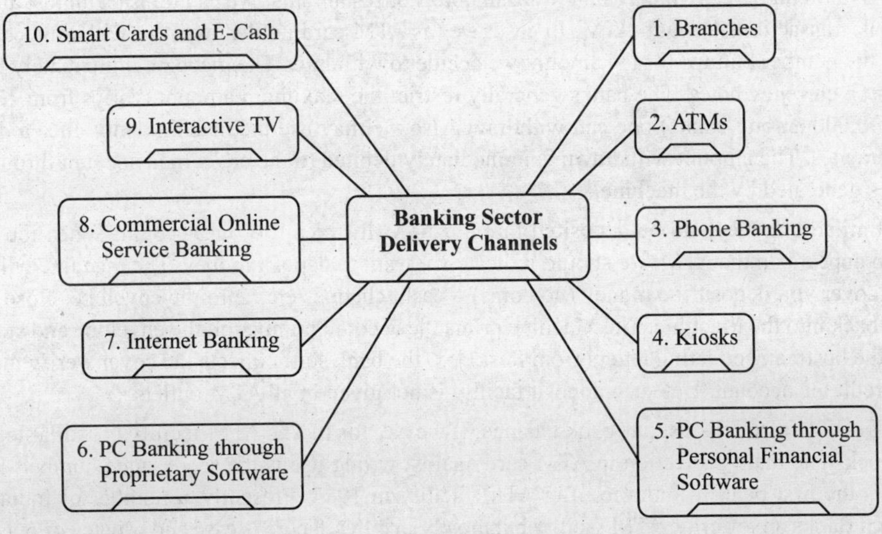

21.2.1 Branches

Many customers continue to follow to this traditional banking delivery channel. Only a few banks nationwide have rid themselves of bricks and mortar *i.e.*, the traditional banking system of operations.

21.2.2 ATM

Automated Teller Machines have evolved as the primary delivery channel for cash withdrawals. The evolutionary trend from cash economy to cheque economy and onwards to plastic card economy is witnessed in the introduction of ATMs. ATM or Automated Teller Machine outwardly appears like a human weighing machine kept in Railway Platforms. The ATMs released banks from the constraints of time and geographical location. They presented banks with a more economical substitute for brick and mortar branches. The revolution brought about by this technology was longer banking hours which extended beyond office hours.

These days, ATMs are securedly placed inside the walls of bank's premises. While a weighing Machine measures the weight of a person in kilograms, the ATM measures the bank balance of a person in rupees. In the weighing machine we insert a coin and we get a card telling our weight and fortune. In ATM we insert a plastic card and we get brand new currency notes and our bank balance. Can we all get such currency notes from ATM? Is it a Lottery? Let us see how ATM works.

ATM is a computerised telecommunications device that provides the customers of a bank with access to financial transactions in a public place without the need for a cashier. The current and Savings Bank Accountholders of a bank having certain minimum balance (say ₹1000 in SB A/Cs or ₹5000 in Current A/Cs) are issued with an ATM card. It is a plastic card having magnetic strip with the Account number of the person. When the card is inserted in the ATM, the machine's sensing equipment identifies the account holder and asks for his identification code number. Every accountholder is given a separate code number through computers and it is not known even to bank staff. This code number is like the secret code number available in telephone connection for use of STD facility. When the number is asked by the ATM (it comes on the ATM screen), the card holder identifies himself/herself by pressing relevant number buttons on the machine. The machine verifies the account number on the ATM card with secret code number stored in the ATM. When the numbers tally, the machine shows in the screen as to what he wants? This is done through a Menu Screen, like a Menu Card in hotels or restaurants. We can transact almost all types of bank transactions through ATM. In case, we (as ATM card holder) want to withdraw cash, we press the number buttons for the amount we decide to withdraw. The machine immediately throws out fresh currency notes. The banks generally restrict the maximum amount (varies from ₹20,000 to ₹100,000 among banks) one can withdraw. Also we may use the machine only once a day for withdrawals. The amount withdrawn is immediately debited to the concerned account through the entries generated by the machine.

Similarly, money can be deposited through ATM for credit to our account. When the Menu screen appears on the ATM, we should indicate we want to deposit money. The machine will flash out a cover you deposit the money (no coins) – cash, cheques etc., into the envelope, close it and put it back into the Machine. The Machine prints the account number on the envelope and stores it. Like the postman collecting letters from Post Box, the bank staff collects the cover, verify the cash and credit the account. But such deposit facility is not given in all ATM outlets.

The ATM also tells us, our bank balance, if we ask for it. The ATM facility is available round the clock. The main protection in ATM card against wrong use is the secret code number. HSBC bank is the first bank in India to offer ATM facility in 1987. Presently, a number of Indian and Foreign Banks are offering ATM facility but mostly in cities. There is ease and privacy of operation through self service.

In ATMs, the customer is identified by inserting a plastic ATM card with a magnetic stripe that contains a unique card number and some security information. Authentication is provided by the customer entering a personal identification number (PIN). Using an ATM, customers can access their bank accounts in order to make cash withdrawals and check their account balances. They are continuously being enhanced with foreign language, touch-screen, advanced transaction, video conferencing, and related capabilities. This channel is likely to continue to be an important one for most banks.

Automated Teller Machines or 24 hours Tellers are electronic terminals that let us do banking operations almost any time. To withdraw cash, make deposits, or transfer funds between accounts, we need to generally insert an ATM card/debit cards and enter our personal identification number (PIN). Some ATMs impose a surcharge, or usage fee, on consumers who are not members of their institution or on transactions at remote locations. In addition to cash dispensing ATMs may have many services/facilities such as:

- Account information
- Cash Deposit
- Regular bills payment
- Purchase of Re-load Vouchers for Mobiles
- Mini / Short Statement
- Loan account enquiry, etc.

The details of ATMs of scheduled commercial banks are given in the following Table:

ATMs of Scheduled Commercial Banks

(As at end-March 2013)

Sr. No.	*Bank group*	*On-site ATMs*	*Off-site ATMs*	*Total number of ATMs*
1	2	3	4	5
I	**Public sector banks**	**40,241**	**29,411**	**69,652**
	1.1 Nationalised banks*	20,658	14,701	35,359
	1.2 SBI Group	18,708	13,883	32,591
II	**Private sector banks**	**15,236**	**27,865**	**43,101**
	2.1 Old private sector banks	4,054	3,512	7,566
	2.2 New private sector banks	11,182	24,353	35,535
III	**Foreign banks**	**283**	**978**	**1,261**
IV	**All SCBs (I + II + III)**	**55,760**	**58,254**	**1,14,014**

ATMs have many advantages, some of which are given below:

(*i*) In ATM one can draw cash round the clock (for 24 hours a day) and no employee interface is required.

(*ii*) ATM provides customer not having credit card facilities an alternative for obtaining cash when required.

(*iii*) It eliminates the need for the customers to travel to the branch at which his accounts are maintained if the machines are conveniently located and networked.

(*iv*) Automatic and instantaneous accounting is possible.

(*v*) When labour cost is high the technology provides a cost effective solution.

(*vi*) Customers can deposit cash/instruments and leave instructions for the requirements of statement of accounts, transfer, etc.

(*vii*) As transactions are handled through software, without cash or instruments scope for frauds, robberies and misappropriation is reduced.

21.2.3 Phone Banking

Phone Banking is yet another banking service offered by banks. Under this system, like in ATM card, a secret code number is provided to each account holder. A customer wanting to know his bank balance or any other information relating to his bank account should dial up a particular phone number indicated by the bank. When the number is dialed, a recorded voice will ask us to identify ourself with our account number and code number. If the numbers are tallied, we will get all the information we want to know about our account. Presently many foreign banks provide this service. We cannot draw cash or deposit cash through phone banking. It is basically an information service. With low set up costs for banks, phone banking is another delivery channel that's taken hold recently.

Telecommunication companies and call centers now offer sophisticated voice response and video telephone services which increase functionality for bankers who prefer to contact their banks from home. It includes Mobile banking and Interactive Voice Response (IVR)

(*a*) Interactive Voice Response (IVR): IVR is a software application that accepts a combination of voice telephone input and touch-tone keypad selection and provides appropriate responses in the form of voice. It is the first step in Telephone Banking. It is suitable for transaction volume in salary payment days for balance inquiry and it is integrated with ATM system.

(*b*) Mobile banking: As banks search for new delivery channels for their products and services, mobile banking has come to the forefront as one of the leading options. Mobile banking is a term used for performing balance checks, account transactions, payments, etc. via a mobile device such as a mobile phone. SMS banking can be defined as a banking transaction conducted using a mobile phone via an SMS application. SMS stands for short message services.

Introduction for SMS has taken place due to competition among banking institutions as well as non- financial institutions.

Mobile phones as a delivery channel for extending banking services have off-late been attaining greater significance. The rapid growth in users and wider coverage of mobile phone networks have made this channel an important platform for extending banking services to customers. With the rapid growth in the number of mobile phone subscribers in India (about 261 million as at the end of March 2008 and growing at about 8 million a month), banks have been exploring the feasibility of using mobile phones as an alternative channel of delivery of banking services.

Some banks have started offering information based services like balance enquiry, stop payment instruction of cheques, transactions enquiry, location of the nearest ATM/branch, etc. Acceptance of transfer of funds instruction for credit to beneficiaries of same/or another bank in favour of pre-registered beneficiaries have also commenced in a few banks. In order to ensure a level playing field and considering that the technology is relatively new, Reserve Bank has brought out a set of operating guidelines for adoption by banks.

The volume and number of mobile banking transactions are given in the following picture:

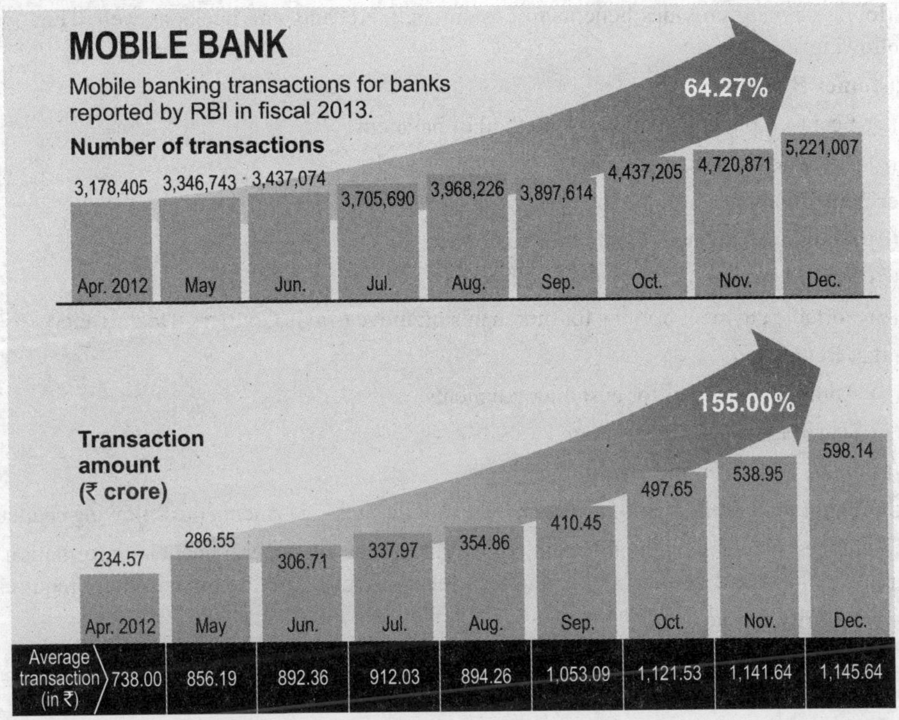

Source: RBI Research

From the above picture, it can be seen that the use of mobile banking service is growing up steadily over the period.

Reasons for the application of mobile banking: The main reasons for the growing use of mobile banking include the following:

(*i*) The growing population of mobile phone users in the country can be taken as a good indicator, which will also affect mobile phone application for banking purpose.

(*ii*) Introduction of new technologies.

(*iii*) Mobile phone can act as a new platform to inform others regarding information dissemination.

(*iv*) Internet/online servers support it.

(*v*) It is flexible.

(*vi*) For customers, mobile banking offers improved and convenient access to their account balances and transactions.

(*vii*) For banks, it offers a way to strengthen existing customer relationships and expand into more-profitable areas, such as payment and trading revenue.

(*viii*) For others in remote locations with bad roads and/or inaccessible landlines, it substitutes for travel to the local branch, access to personal accounts and the marketplace, and an easier way of doing business overall.

(*ix*) Control costs, removal of cost duplication.

(*x*) Cater to increasing online channel customers.

(*xi*) Personalise customer interactions

(*xii*) Unparalleled convenience and proactive customer service.

Benefits of Mobile Banking

Mobile banking provides benefits to customers, merchants and banks as well. They include the following:

1. Customer Benefits

(*a*) Secure, Convenient and easy method of payment

(*b*) Anywhere anytime payment

2. Merchant Benefits

(*a*) Additional payment method for customers

(*b*) Small payment amounts can be accepted

(*c*) Portable payment options for merchants on move (Taxis,Couriers, Doctors etc.)

3. Banks, Benefits

(*a*) Additional channel for customer payments

(*b*) Use of existing Infrastructure

(*c*) Value added service to customers

Challenges to mobile banking system: The mobile banking is facing the following challenges:

The biggest challenge in mobile banking is protecting a customer's financial information over the air and on handheld devices. For example, a secure mobile banking infrastructure requires:

(1) Security for the handheld device

(2) Security for the application running on the device

(3) Authentication of the device with the service provider before initiating a transaction

(4) ID/password authentication of the customer

(5) Encryption of the data being transmitted over the air

(6) Encryption of the data that will be stored in the device for later review by the customer. It is a complex process.

(7) Customer Education.

21.2.4 Kiosks

Video kiosks give customers a direct connection to the most appropriate service agents. Although currently most do not link directlyto a customer's records, this functionality is expected in the near future. At that time, banking kiosks will become enhanced ATMs.

21.2.5 PC Banking through Personal Financial Software

The software such as Quicken, Microsoft Money, Managing Your Money, and related programmes are a familiar delivery channel to many customers. These personal financial software companies offer direct links to many large banks. Some banks reject this delivery channel because they believe customers will transfer their loyalty to the software company, not the bank.

21.2.6 PC BANKING THROUGH PROPRIETARY SOFTWARE

PC banking or dial-up banking is a form of online banking that enables customers to execute bank transactions from a PC via a modem. In most PC banking ventures, the bank offers the customer a proprietary financial software programme that allows the customer to perform financial transactions from his or her home computer. The customer then dials into the bank with his or her modem, downloads data, and runs the programmes that are resident on the customer's computer.

Currently, many banks offer PC banking systems that allow customers to obtain account balances and credit card statements, pay bills, and transfer funds between accounts. Bank's proprietary software system are generally considered more secure than "open" systems. Their primary drawback is that they require the bank and/or its technology provider to issue and maintain the software program and its upgrades.

21.2.7 Internet Banking

Internet banking, sometimes called online banking, is an outgrowth of PC banking. Internet banking uses the Internet as the delivery channel by which to conduct banking activity, for example, transferring funds, paying bills, viewing checking and savings account balances, paying mortgages, and purchasing financial instruments and certificates of deposit. An Internet banking customer accesses his or her accounts from a browser— software that runs Internet banking programs resident on the bank's World Wide Web server, not on the user's PC. Internet bank is defined as the banking system that provides account balances and some transactional capabilities to retail customers over the World Wide Web. Internet banks are also known as virtual, cyber, net, interactive, or web banks.

All we need is Internet connectivity–Anywhere. And we will also need to sign-up for Registration. We can download the application form and submit it to our branch after completing it and we will shortly receive our User-Id and Password. We can change our username and password. Internet banking is simple, fast and convenient–anytime anywhere and always open. We can now check our account balances, view our account, request for cheque book, drafts, Bankers cheques, stop cheque payment and issue standing instructions. We can also transfer funds to our other accounts at the Branch, request for third party transfers, invest and renew Term Deposits. (For further details please see the part 20.3. of this chapter)

21.2.8 Commercial Online Service Banking

Online services are becoming an increasingly important delivery channel for some banks. Some computer users prefer commercial online services because they find them easier to use and because they think they are more secure than direct internet connections.

21.2.9 Interactive TV

TV banking is currently being sampled in various test markets. Interactive TV market is primarily pay-per-view services. Some analysts believe it will grow to compete with the Internet (both for functionality and market share). If interactive TV takes off with added functionality, TV banking is likely to be an important delivery channel.

21.2.10 Smart Cards and E-Cash

Smart cards: Smart cards opened a new system of money age *i.e.*, the e-money. These cards are fitted with microprocessors and enable quick transfer of money. The extensive use of these smart cards has made traveling easy and safe.

Electronic cash is also called as digital cash. It is a technology that uses varied electronic methods to execute financial transactions. The technology is classified into two types:

(*a*) Online form – conducting transactions through the Internet

(*b*) Offline form – the usage of the digitally encoded smart cards, like the ATM cards

Banking services based on Information and Communication Technologies

Let us discuss some important aspects of banking services based on Information and communication technologies:

21.3 Internet Banking

Internet banking is the part of electronic banking. Internet banking refers to systems that enable bank customers to access accounts and general information on bank products and services through a personal computer (PC) or other intelligent device. Internet banking products and services can include wholesale products for corporate customers as well as retail products for consumers. Ultimately, the products and services obtained through Internet banking may mirror products and services offered through other bank delivery channels.

21.3.1 Growth in Internet Banking

The factors influencing the growth of internet banking include the following:

1. **Cost effectiveness:** The cost of transactions through internet delivery channels is considerably cheaper to that of the traditional methods of service. Hence, it is cost effective and thus, banks can provide services at the competitive pricing.
2. **Intensity of Competition:** The competitive pressure is the main driving force behind increasing use of Internet banking technology. Banks see Internet banking as a way to keep existing customers and attract new ones to the bank.
3. **Scope of Increase in Revenue:** with the advent of internet banking, the banks find it as a good avenue of raising additional revenue by attracting and increasing the customer base and there by the volume of transactions.
4. **Geographical Reach:** Internet banking provides the opportunity for expanding customer contact through increased geographical reach and lower cost delivery channels.
5. **Brand Equity:** Relationship building is a strategic priority for most of the banks. Internet banking technology and products can provide a means for the banks to develop and maintain an ongoing relationship with their customers by offering easy access to a broad array of products and services. By capitalising on brand identification and by providing a broad array of financial services, banks hope to build customer loyalty, cross-sell, and enhance repeat business.

21.3.2 Types of Internet Banking

The internet banking services are provided on the following basis:

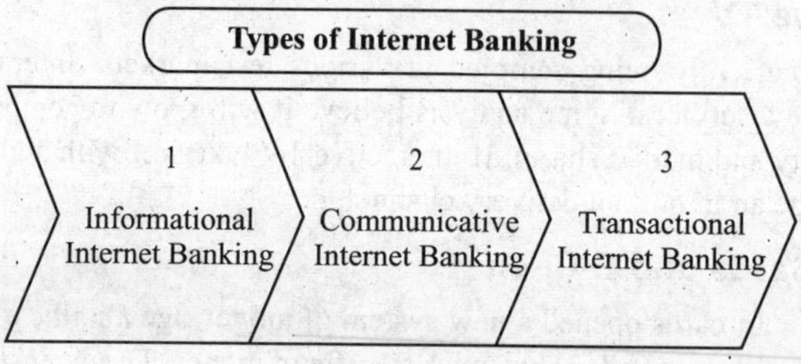

1. Informational Internet Banking

This is the first level of Internet banking. As such, the banks having marketing information about the bank's products and services provide information on a stand-alone server. Here, the risk is relatively low, as informational systems typically have no path between the server and the bank's internal network. This level of Internet banking can be provided by the bank or outsourced.

2. Communicative Internet Banking

This is the second level of internet banking. This type of Internet banking system allows some interaction between the bank's systems and the customer. The interaction may be limited to electronic mail, account inquiry, loan applications, or static file updates (name and address changes). Because these servers may have a path to the bank's internal networks, the risk is higher with this configuration than with informational systems. Appropriate controls need to be in place to prevent, monitor, and alert management of any unauthorised attempt to access the bank's internal networks and computer systems.

3. Transactional Internet Banking:

This is the fully functional type of internet banking. Typically, this level of internet banking allows customers to execute transactions. Since a path typically exists between the server and the bank's or outsourcer's internal network, this is the highest risk architecture and must have the strongest controls. Customer transactions can include accessing accounts, paying bills, transferring funds, etc.

21.3.3 Services of Internet Banking

The internet banking provides both wholesale and retail banking services. The following are the services being provided under whole sale and retail basis:

(*a*) Whole sale services

(*i*) Cash management

(*ii*) Automated clearinghouse transactions

(*iii*) Bill presentment and payment.

(*b*) Retail services

(*i*) Balance inquiry

(*ii*) Funds transfer

(*iii*) Downloading transaction information

(*iv*) Loan applications

(*v*) Investment activity

21.4 E-BANKING

E banking is the service provided by the modern banking institutions through electronic channels and customers can access the data without any time and geographical limitations. Let us see the details of e-banking here under.

21.4.1 Meaning of e-banking

e Banking -E-bank is the electronic bank that provides the financial service for the individual client by means of Internet. The terms, personal computer (PC) banking, internet banking, virtual banking, online banking, home banking, remote electronic banking, and phone banking, etc., refer to one form or another of electronic banking. PC banking and internet or online banking are the most frequently used names. It should be noted, that the terms used to describe the various types of electronic banking are often used interchangeably. E-banking is defined as the automated delivery of new and traditional banking products and services directly to customers through electronic, interactive communication channels. E-banking includes the systems that enable financial institution customers, individuals or businesses, to access accounts, transact business, or obtain information on financial products and services through a public or private network, including the Internet. Customers access e-banking services using an intelligent electronic device, such as a personal computer (PC), personal digital assistant (PDA), automated teller machine (ATM), Kiosk, or Touch Tone telephone.

PC banking and Internet or online banking are the most frequently used designations. It should be noted, however, that the terms used to describe the various types of electronic banking are often used interchangeably. E-banking systems can vary significantly in their configuration depending on a number of factors. Financial institutions should choose their e-banking system configuration, including outsourcing relationships, based on the basic factors influencing its effectiveness. Through a combination of internal and outsourced solutions, management has many alternatives when determining the overall system configuration for the various components of an e-banking system.

Electronic banking is a form of banking where funds are transferred through an exchange of electronic signals between financial institutions, rather than an exchange of cash, checks, or other negotiable instruments. The ownership of funds and transfers of funds between financial institutions are recorded on computer systems connected by telephone lines. Customer identification is by access code, such as a password or Personal Identification Number instead of a signature on a check or other physical document.

21.4.2 E-Banking Structure

E-banking systems differ in their structure depending on the following factors:

E-Banking- Simplified Structure

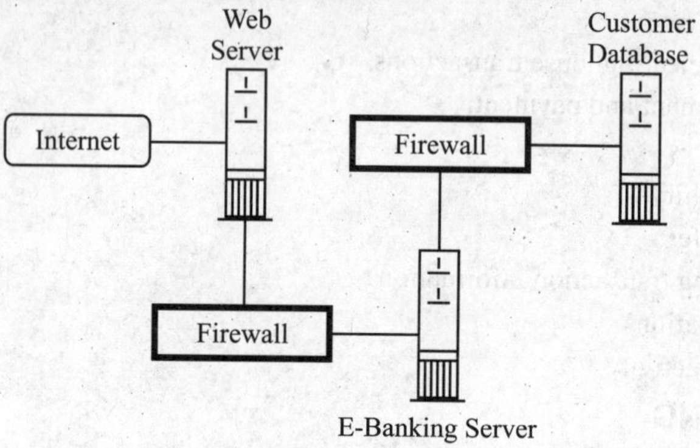

(*a*) The objectives of banks for e-banking.

(*b*) The technological expertise required and the relevant capacity of the banks in affording such technology.

(*c*) The level of Operations – It is based on the scope and complexity of equipment, systems, and planned activities of the banking institutions.

Hardware –The hardware requirements include:

(*i*) Servers

(*ii*) Storage device and database

(*iii*) Communication channels and lines

(*iv*) Gateways and remotely located devices (*e.g.*, thin clients or Internet appliances) serving as interfaces between users and computers.

(*d*) The software requirements and the limit that the bank can afford – including upgradation in future.

Software –The software requirements include:

(*i*) Operating systems

(*ii*) Firewalls

(*iii*) Database management systems

(*iv*) Security application program.

(*e*) Technology for security –This is based on the internal control requirements. It includes the authentication of customers such as passwords, etc.

(*d*) Training required to administer at the institutional level and the resultant cost elements

21.4.3 Components of E-Banking

E-banking systems rely on a number of common components or processes. The following are the potential components and processes required for a common E- banking structure:

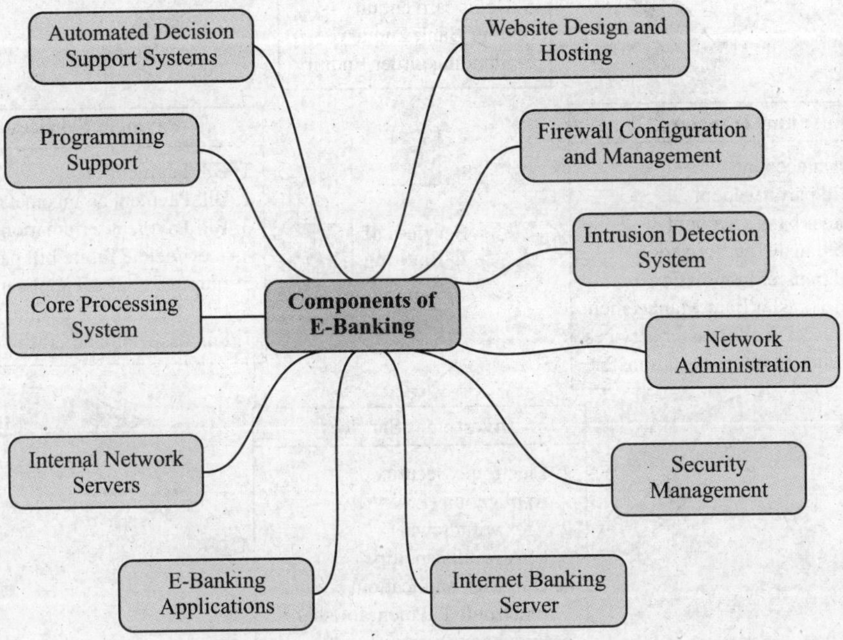

All of these components have to work together to deliver e-banking services. The banks have many options when determining the overall e-banking system. There is scope for outsourcing also.

21.4.4 E-Banking- Service Requirements

In addition to traditional banking products and services, financial institutions provide a variety of services under e- banking. For effective delivery of e- banking services the following additional services are required:

1. **Weblinking-** a word or image in the bank's webpage that contains some coding that takes the viewers of the website to the different parts of the same website or to another website by a few clicking of the mouse.
2. **Hosting of Websites-** It includes the arrangements for the maintaining of the electronic files that make up the website.
3. **Identification and Authentication** – This includes the identification of the customers and authorizing them for e-banking activities using Passwords and personal identification numbers (PINs) etc. These are the central elements of e-banking services.
4. **Payments for e-banking services-** It is very important requirement. The mode of electronic payments for the services offered by the banks.

21.4.5 E-Banking Services

The modern day banks provide the following e-banking services:

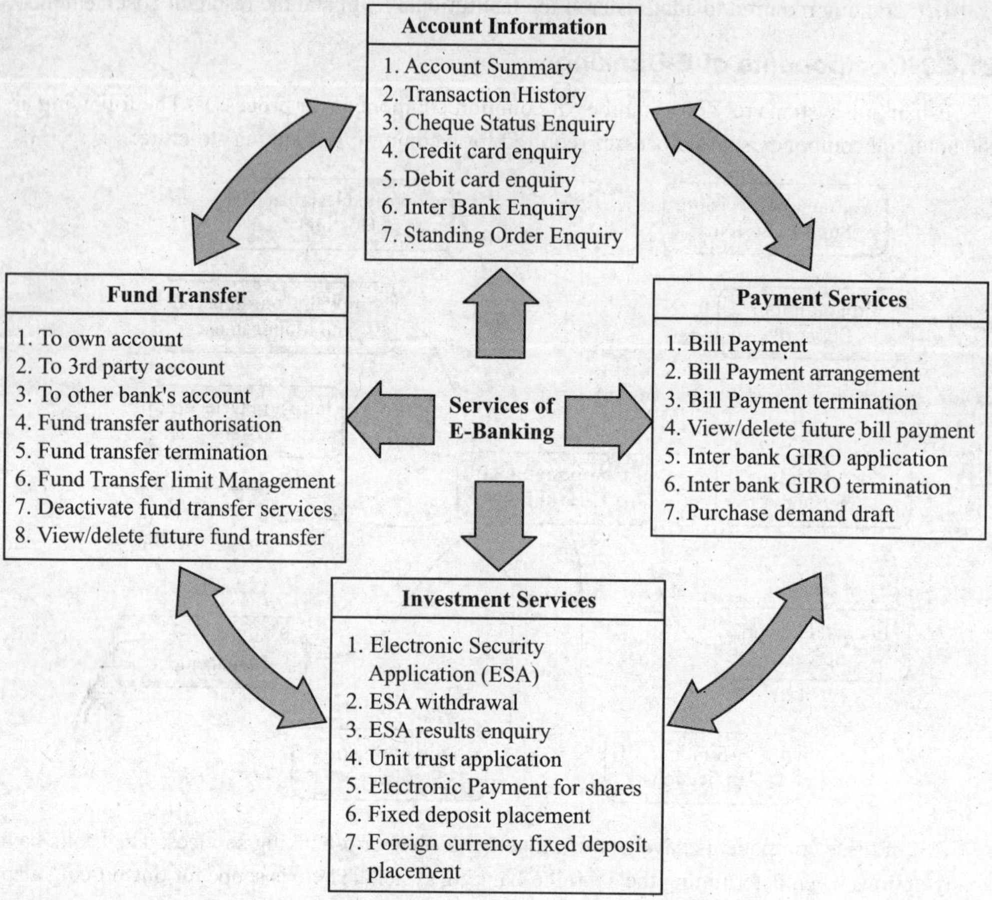

21.4.6 Advantages of E-Banking

The following are the important benefits of e-banking:

1. Account Information

Real time balance information and summary of day's transaction can be obtained.

2. Fund Transfers

We can manage our Supply-Chain network, effectively by using our online fund transfer mechanism. We can effect fund transfer on a real time basis across the bank locations.

3. Request

We can make a banking request online.

4. Account Information

The complete database that the bank has about our company is available to us at our terminal. It provides us:

(*i*) Current balance in our account on real-time basis.

(*ii*) Day's transactions in the account.

(*iii*) Details of cash credit limit, drawing power, amount utilised, etc.

5. Downloading of account statements

Account statements can be downloaded as an excel or text file. The statements can be integrated with our ERP system for auto-reconciliation.

6. Fund Transfers

Manage our Supply-Chain network, effectively by using our online fund transfer mechanism. We can effect fund transfer on a real time basis across the bank locations. The product facilitates:

(*a*) One-to-one fund transfer between two linked accounts.

(*b*) Bulk fund transfer: In bulk fund transfers, we upload a flat file containing payment/ collection information. Our systems take care of processing the entire file and once the file is processed we can integrate the processed file to our ERP for auto reconciliation.

7. Effect payments.

With a Power of Attorney from our dealers, we can link the dealer's accounts to our account in order to have an online fund transfer, saving us time and money involved with cheque collection systems. Alternatively, the dealer can credit our account through this channel. Similarly, we could also effect vendor and other payments online.

8. Customers Request Online

Customers can also submit the following requests online: Registration for account statements by e-mail daily /weekly /fortnightly /monthly basis.

(*i*) Stop payment of cheque

(*ii*) Cheque book replenishment

(*iii*) Demand Draft/Pay-order

(*iv*) Opening of fixed deposit account

(*v*) Opening of Letter of credit

9. Cost effective

The company/customer does not have to spend anything extra to avail such facilities. All it requires is internet connectivity. The product enables the company to proactively manage its cash flows, ease reconciliation efforts as all the MIS is available at the click of the mouse.

10. Integration with ERP

Customer can Integrate the System with his Own ERP: The customer can download the account statements either as a text file or as an excel file. The bank can help him in integrating the account statements and bulk payment files with his ERP system. The Bank may charge a nominal fee depending upon the nature of work involved.

11. Bill Payment

Internet has thus ushered the concept of any time and anywhere banking. To the individual the difficult task of visiting several places to settle his service bills like telephone, water, electricity, etc., can be overcome through the electronic Bill Payment service provided by the bank. He can pay his regular monthly bills (telephone, electricity, mobile phone, insurance, etc.) right from his desktop. No more missed deadlines, no more loss of interest. He can schedule his bills in advance, and thus avoid missing the bill deadlines as well as earn extra interest on his money.

12. The Electronic Shopping Mall:

The customer can also make his shopping payment through the Bank's secure website—so that he can shop online without any security worries, as the bank can provide online real time shopping mall services through partner shopping sites.

13. Effecting Personal Investments

The bank's website can also allow the customer to invest in shares and other financial products. Electronic banking also brings the customer the same convenience while investing in Mutual funds — Hassle free and Paperless Investing. He can invest in mutual funds without the hassles of filling application forms or any other paperwork. He needs to provide no signatures or proof of identity for investing. Once he places a request for investing in a particular fund, there are no manual processes involved. His bank funds are automatically debited or credited while simultaneously crediting or debiting his unit holdings.

14. Trading in shares:

(*i*) **Cash Trading.** This is a delivery based trading system, which is generally done with the intention of taking delivery of shares or monies.

(*ii*) **Margin Trading**. Customer can also do an intra-settlement trading normally up to 4 times his available funds, wherein he can take long buy / short sell positions in stocks with the intention of squaring off the position within the same settlement cycle.

(*iii*) **Spot Trading.** When looking at an immediate liquidity option, 'Cash on Spot' may work the best for him. On selling shares through "cash on spot", money is credited to his bank A/c the same evening and not on the exchange payout date. This money can then be withdrawn from any of the Bank's ATMs.

(*iv*) The customer can also trade directly at the recognised stock exchanges of the country through his bank.

15. Trade in Derivatives

Trading in derivatives includes futures and options. Futures- Through electronic banking the customer can also trade in index and stock futures on the approved stock exchange.

16. Initial Public Offers Online

The customer could also invest in initial public offers online without going through the hassles of filling any application form/ paperwork.

There can be no end to the variety of services that can be provided through the electronic channel by banks and financial institutions. Every Institution is trying constantly to innovate and offer new products to the customer. The benefit to the customer on account of the internet is that he is able to know at a time the types of facilities being provided by different Institutions and he is able to make the best choice suited for his needs.

17. Other benefits to customers

The e-banking provides some other benefits also. They are:

(*i*) Convenience
(*ii*) Speed of concluding transactions
(*iii*) Safety - banking from own home
(*iv*) Economy - banking without visiting our bank
(*v*) Cheaper service fees
(*vi*) Seamless Integration with existing environment
(*vii*) Highly Scaleable
(*viii*) Easy Customization
(*ix*) Lower Costs of both Installation and Maintenance
(*x*) Platform Independence
(*xi*) Round-the-Clock and Cross-Border Availability
(*xii*) Remote Authorisation

18. Benefit to Banks

The e- banking system provides the following benefits to the bankers:

(*i*) Larger customer coverage
(*ii*) Reduced cost of operation
(*iii*) Promoting the products and services internationally
(*iv*) Increasing customer satisfaction and providing a personalized relationship with customers

19. Benefits to Small and Medium Enterprises

The e- banking system provides the following benefits to the small and medium enterprises

(*i*) To run business effectively
(*ii*) Lower cost than traditional financial management mechanisms

21.4.7 Limitations of E-Banking

The e- banking system has certain limitations which can be solved in due course. They include the following:

(*i*) It needs customer skills in dealing with computers and browsers. It is difficult for elders and who do not have computer operations.
(*ii*) Change of site will cause confusion and delay
(*iii*) Security risk.

21.5 ELECTRONIC BANKING IN INDIA

With the development of technology the expectation of consumers from banking industry is growing. They want instant transfer of funds and their settlements. Indian banking industry under the effective directions and supervision of RBI serve this end more efficiently. The main services in this regard are given in the following diagram:

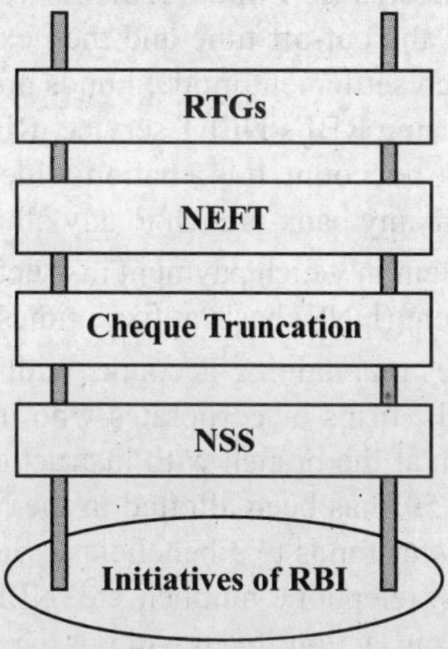

Let us discuss about the popular systems of e –banking in India, here under:

21.5.1 RTGS -Electronic Payment System

RTGS -Electronic Payment system initiated by RBI is **Real Time Gross Settlement**. RTGS is a funds transfer system where transfer of money takes place from one bank to another on a real time basis. This is the fastest mode of funds transfer available in India through banking channel. RTGS is an electronic payment system in which payment instructions between banks are processed and settled individually and continuously, on a real time basis, throughout the day.

This is the fastest possible money transfer system through the banking channel. Settlement in 'real time' means payment transaction is not subjected to any waiting period. The transactions are settled as soon as they are processed. 'Gross settlement' means the transaction is settled on one to one basis without bunching with any other transaction. The RTGS system facilitates transfer of funds from accounts in one bank to another on a "real time" and on "gross settlement" basis.

The RTGS system is the fastest possible inter bank money transfer facility available through secure banking channels in India. The main benefit of the RTGS is that the banks and their customers can avail of this facility and make instantaneous transfer of funds to beneficiary's account at other bank at a nominal cost. Similarly, the customers of the bank can also get instant transfer of funds to their accounts with certainty. It includes the following:

(*i*) **Real Time Payment Settlement:** Payments made on real-time and transaction by transaction basis.

(*ii*) **Gross Settlement:** Continuous settlement without netting

(*iii*) **Lower Risk**

(*a*) No Credit Risk: Payments settled instantly, no end of day procedures

(*b*) Reduced Systemic Risk- Intraday Finality

Benefits of RTGS: RTGS provides the following benefits:

(*i*) **Predictability of Cash Flows:** Clients know when their accounts debited or credited

(*ii*) **Increased efficiency:** Lower transaction costs and STP results in fewer errors, quicker processing

(*iii*) **Economic Factors**: Fast, secure and irrevocable settlement of major business and financial market transactions. It is robust, modernized payments system.

21.5.2 NEFT -National Electronic Funds Transfer

NEFT stands for **'National Electronic Funds Transfer'** and the funds transfer takes place within the same day if it is within the cut-off time and the next working day if it is beyond the cut-off time prescribed. It is a Batch settlement mode. Funds are transferred to the credit account with the other participating Bank using RBI's NEFT service. RBI acts as the service provider and transfers the credit to the other bank's account. It is a nation-wide system that facilitates individuals to electronically transfer funds from any bank branch to any other bank branch in the country.

It is an electronic payment system in which payment instructions between banks are processed and settled on deferred net settlement (DNS) basis at fixed times during the day.

Individuals, firms or corporates maintaining accounts with a bank branch can transfer funds using NEFT. Even such individuals, firms or corporates who do not have a bank account (walk in customers) can also deposit cash at the branch with instructions to transfer funds using NEFT. A separate Transaction Code (No. 50) has been allotted in the NEFT system to facilitate walk-in customers to deposit cash and transfer funds to a beneficiary. Such customers have to furnish full details including complete address, telephone number, etc. NEFT, thus, facilitates originators or remitters to initiate funds transfer transactions even without the need for having a bank account.

For being part of the NEFT funds transfer network a bank branch has to be NEFT-enabled. As at end-November 2009 as many as 62,000 branches / offices of 94 banks in the country (out of around 75,000 bank branches) are NEFT-enabled. Steps are being taken to further widen the coverage both in terms of banks and branches.(source: RBI Publications)

RTGS *vs* NEFT

The RTGS and NEFT systems are differ in some aspects. They include the following:

1. The main difference between NEFT and RTGS is that the NEFT works on net settlement basis and RTGS works on gross settlement basis.

2. No minimum limit and any small amount can be sent with NEFT. Where as the under RTGS the minimum amount is ₹ 1 lack or more.
3. For the maximum amount of remittance, there is some limit for retail internet banking but no maximum limit for corporate internet banking.
4. The time taken under NEFT usually 24 hrs, where as RTGS is the fastest payment method and usually the amount credited to payee account in real time

Information required for RTGS and NEFT Payment

For making payments under RTGS and NIFT, the Remitter has to provide the following details:

1. Amount to be remitted.
2. Account number which is to be debited.
3. Name of the beneficiary bank.
4. Name of the beneficiary.
5. Account number of the beneficiary.
6. Remarks or description, if any.
7. The IFSC code of the beneficiary branch. -IFSC stands for Indian Financial System Code. In the Structured Financial Messaging System (SFMS), the IFSC is being used as the addressing code in user-to-user message transmission. The Payment System Applications such as RTGS and NEFT developed by the Reserve Bank of India, use these codes. The code consists of 11 Characters - First 4 characters represent the entity; Fifth position has been defaulted with a '0' (Zero) for future use; and the Last 6 character denotes the branch identity. IFSC is being identified by the RBI as the code to be used for various payment system projects within the country.

21.5.3 Cheque Truncation

Truncation is the process of stopping the flow of the physical cheque issued by a drawer to the drawee branch. The physical instrument will be truncated at some point en-route to the drawee branch and an electronic image of the cheque would be sent to the drawee branch along with the relevant information like the MICR fields, date of presentation, presenting banks, etc. Thus with the implementation of cheque truncation, the need to move the physical instruments across branches would not be required, except in exceptional circumstances. This would effectively reduce the time required for payment of cheques, the associated cost of transit and delay in processing, etc., thus speeding up the process of collection or realisation of the cheques.

Importance of Cheque Truncation in India:

(*i*) Cheque Truncation speeds up collection of cheques and therefore enhances customer service, reduces the scope for clearing related frauds, minimizes cost of collection of cheques, reduces reconciliation problems, eliminates logistics problems, etc.

(*ii*) With the other major product offering in the form of RTGS, the Reserve Bank created the capability to enable interabank payments online real time and facilitate corporate customer payments.

(*iii*) The other product, National Electronic Funds Transfer, is an electronic credit transfer system. However, to wish away cheques is simply not possible and that is the reason why the Bank decided to focus on improving the efficiency of the Cheque Clearing Cycle. Cheque Truncation is the alternative. Moreover contrary to perceptions, Cheque Truncation is a more secure system than the current exchange of physical documents in which the cheque moves from one point to another, thus, not only creating delays but inconvenience to the customer in case the instrument is lost in transit or manipulated during the clearing cycle.

(*iv*) In addition to operational efficiency, Cheque Truncation has several benefits to the banks and customers which includes introduction of new products, re-engineering the total receipts and payments mechanism of the customers, human resource rationalisation, cost effectiveness, etc.,

(*v*) Cheque Truncation thus is an important efficiency enhancement initiative in the Payments Systems area, undertaken by RBI.(Source RBI Publications)

21.5.4 NSS- National Settlement System

National Settlement System is a system established by Reserve Bank of India through which the clearing houses/clearing organisations can settle the net position of the participating banks at the national level.

21.5.5 SFMS -Structured Financial Messaging System

The SFMS system provides a solution for financial message communication across the Indian Financial Network. The system enables exchange of messages in a highly secured environment. A message structure in SFMS (Structured Financial Messaging Solution) has been developed to take care of all kinds of Financial Transactions involved in Indian Banking System.

SFMS (it is at National level) is like a SWIFT(it is used at international level) messaging System which would serve as a safe, secure communication carrier of intra and inter bank messages in fixed message format, to improve efficiency and speed in fund transfer. All the Branches selected for implementation of SFMS will be provided with Corporate Mail. SFMS will be operational on all days except Sundays and on common holidays across all-States of India.

21.5.6 SWIFT-Receiving Payments from outside India

For transfer with in the country, we use EFT, RTGS and NEFT. If we want to receive a foreign payment from banks abroad (in US Dollars or Euro or the other) then we have to provide the sender in foreign country SWIFT/BIC code of the bank in India where we have account. Usually this is commonly called International Wire Transfer or TT.

While sending money to India from abroad the speed and efficiency of transfer are more important. The **Society for Worldwide Interbank Financial Telecommunication (SWIFT)** supplies secure messaging services. Each financial institution has a Swift code which is commonly used to identify the banks involved in an international wire transfer. The banks in India have their respective SWIFT codes through which the money can be remitted to India safely and quickly. Provides reliable, fast tele-communication facilities for exchange of financial messages all over the world between Banks and FIs

21.6 COMPUTERISATION OF BANK BRANCHES

The reforms in the 1990s, which led to expansion, consolidation and liberalisation of the banking and financial sector in India, brought in many changes and challenges. A number of private and foreign players entered the Indian market with superior technologies that helped them service their customers efficiently through multiple channels such as ATMs and online banking. Indian banks on the other hand have been using IT more out of compulsion and primarily for transaction processing. They now need to adopt IT to reposition banks into the integrated financial services market.

The need for providing improved customer service, reducing transaction costs and increasing productivity, shall be the main drivers for Banking sector to adopt IT. These considerations are particularly important for public sector banks in India, who are facing immense competition from private and foreign banks. IT can help them move from the present scenario where they are working as isolated islands to providing a centralised banking experience. There is a need today for IT and the financial community to corne together and develop customised IT solution to make the Indian Banking sector globally competitive.

IT adoption in the banking sector will provide real time availability of transaction processing through multiple channels. It would enhance a bank's ability to cross sell products, ensure better management and security and safety of funds and increase efficiency through integration of systems across various locations. It would also ensure efficient management of Non Performing Assets (NPAs), minimise transaction costs, enhance ability to conduct in-depth financial analysis and gather business intelligence. Enhanced use of IT would also encourage the use of Internet to provide access for online bill payments, funds transfers and e- statements in addition to encouraging wireless mobile banking and e-commerce.

With growing competition faced by foreign banks and financial institutions, the public sector banks in co-operation with the Indian IT industry would need to equip themselves for the next phase of introducing the benefits of IT to their customers by providing a centralised banking solution.

21.6.1 Opportunity for Indian Banking Sector in Branch Computerisation

The Opportunities for Indian Banking Sector in Branch Computerization include the following:

(*i*) IT Networking

(*ii*) System Integration and Management

(*iii*) Customer Relationship Management (CRM) Applications

(*iv*) Back Office processing and Call Centres

(*v*) Data warehousing/ Data mining

(*vi*) Mobile and e-banking.

21.6.2 Computerisation of Banks in India

E-commerce and e-banking are the buzz words in the global commercial activities today. E-banking or Electronic banking refers to conducting banking activities with the help of Information Technology (IT) and Computers.

Computerisation of banking functions in India was resisted by labour unions for fear of loss of job opportunities. Secondly, computerisation needs IT savvy personnel which require intensive technical training. Thirdly, computerisation needs heavy capital outlay for purchase of machines. Fourthly, to have effective computerisation of banks a large number of bank branches situated in rural areas need to be connected. Telecommunication facility at rural areas is slow to reach. For the reasons mentioned above, computerisation made a slow entry in Indian banks.

Rangarajan Committee: In the early 1980s, a high level committee was formed under the chairmanship of Dr. Rangarajan , the then Governor of Reserve Bank of India to suggest measures for phased introduction of computers and mechanisation of banking activities in India. However, the focus of computerisation at that time was on customer service in banks. Accordingly during 1985 - 89 two models of branch automation were developed for implementation in banks. They were (*a*) front office mechanisation, and (*b*) back office automation. In the front office mechanisation front desk operations were computerised leaving back office activities carried under manual system.

In the back office automation, back office operations like maintenance of General Ledger accounts, etc. were computerised while front office work was done manually. Under both the systems, customers were given regular and timely statement of accounts without any errors. Having achieved the basic objective of introducing elements of automation in banks, the second committee constituted in 1988 under the chairmanship of same Dr. Rangarajan drew up a detailed plan for computerisation of banks in India. Accordingly automation, *i.e*, use of machines like computers, use of IT, etc., were extended to other areas of banking activities like funds transfer, Automated Teller Machines (ATM), transmission of messages through electronic mail system, etc.

Other committees: In 1987 the Committees on Communication Network for Banks and SWIFT implementation (1987) was formed under the chairmanship of Shri. TNA Iyer. It is followed by the appointment of the 'Committee on Technology Issues relating to Payments System, Cheque Clearing and Securities System in the Banking Industry' in 1994 under the chairmanship of Shri W.S. Saraf. In 1995 the Committee on proposing Electronics Funds Transfer and Electronics Payments was appointed under the chairmanship of Smt K. S. Shere. Many other committees were appointed by RBI for the continuous development of technology in banking sector.

21.6.3 Present Position of Computerisation of Banks in India

Based on the suggestions made by Rangarajan Committee, banks started initiating measures to computerise their various operations. Public Sector Banks (PSU banks) started identifying important / large branches for full branch computerisation. Banks which had fully computerised some of their branches started interconnecting their computerised branches using leased telephoned lines or through satellite system. This enabled banks to have a better centralised control over branches besides ensuring comprehensive service to their customers. In the third stage, banks started providing for sizeable funds for computerisation of their operations. It was necessitated due to financial sector reforms initiated in the early 90s through Narasimham Committee recommendations. Further globalisation and liberalisation measures introduced during 1990s allowed setting up of new private sector banks and free entry of foreign banks into India. This brought in a different and new operating environment to banks.

The deregulation of interest rate regime, phased reduction in Cash Reserve Ratio / Statutory Liquidity Ratio, introduction of universal banking system, permission to start new banks in the private sector, etc., by Reserve Bank of India encouraged competition among banks. These measures had pushed the Indian banks to go for state-of-art IT and services and products like" anywhere banking", "telebanking", etc. Simultaneously, the importance of effective Management Information System (MIS) for control of operations, maintenance of data base, good customer relationship was felt. Accordingly banks presently cover performance monitoring, decision making, control of branches, administrative matters, submission of statutory returns to RBI, inter branch transactions, reconciliation of outstanding entries in various accounts, funds transfer, credit related information, investment management, treasury operations through money market, forex market, securities market, employees personal data and scores of other operations with the use of IT and computers. Yet the level of computerisation may differ from banks to banks. The process is fast picking up even at rural branch level.

REVIEW QUESTIONS

Short Answer Questions

1. What are the driving forces of modern banking?
2. What is Phone Banking?
3. What is Mobile banking?
4. What are the benefits of mobile banking?
5. Write a short note on Smart cards and e-cash.
6. What is e- banking?

7. What are the components of e- banking?
8. What are the limitations of e-banking?
9. Explain RTGS and NEFT.
10. Explain the concept and use of SWIFT.

Essay Type Questions

1. Explain the importance of technology in banking sector.
2. Write a detailed note on the delivery channels of modern banking industry.
3. Explain ATM in detail.
4. What is internet banking? Explain its types along with its services.
5. Explain the meaning of e-banking along with its structure.
6. Explain the various services of e-banking in detail.
7. Write a detailed note on the advantages of e-banking.
8. Explain Cheque Truncation and its importance.
9. Write a note on the computerization of Bank branches in India.

ANNEXURE - I

BANKING SECTOR REFORMS
SECOND NARASIMHAM COMMITTEE REPORT
(Major Recommendations)

The Committee on Banking Sector Reforms with Mr. M.Narasimham as Chairman, popularly known as the second one by the same Chairman on the same/related subject, was constituted on December 26, 1997 to review the record of financial sector reforms of the Narasimham Committee on Financial system (1991), and to suggest remedial measures for strengthening the banking system covering areas of banking policy, institutional structure, supervisory system, legislative and technological changes. The major recommendations of the Committee are summarised below.

A. Strengthening the Banking System

To strengthen the banking system, the Committee recommended an increase in the minimum capital adequacy ratio (CRAR) to 10 percent by 2002. Besides, the entire portfolio of Government securities should be marked to market in three years. Also, a 5 percent weightage is to be assigned for Government and other approved securities to hedge against market risk. Net NPAs have to be brought down to below 5 percent by 2000 and to 3 percent by 2000 and 2002, respectively and net NPAs to 3 percent and 0 percent respectively. The Committee proposed asset Reconstruction Company (ARC) to tide over the backlog of NPAs. In case of prudential norms relating to income recognition, the present norm of 180 days should be brought down to 90 days in a phased manner by 2002. As regards asset classification, an asset may be classified as 'doubtful' if it is in substandard category for 18 months in the first instance and eventually for 12 months and 'loss' if it has been so identified but not written off. These norms which should be regarded as the minimum, may be brought into force in a phased manner.

B. Systems and Methods in Banks

To bring about efficiency in banks, the Committee recommended a number of measures. These include, revision of operational manual and its regular updation, simplification of documentation systems, in production of computer audit, and evolving of filtering mechanism to reduce concentration of exposures in lending and drawing geographical/industry/sectoral exposure norms with Board's concurrence. Besides, the Committee has suggested induction of one more whole time director in nationalised banks in view of changing environment. As outsourcing of services would improve productivity. It suggested the same may be introduced in the fields of building maintenance, cleaning security despatch of mail, computer-related work, etc. subject to relevant Laws.

The Committee suggested a reduction in the minimum stipulated holding of the Government/ Reserve Bank in the equity of nationalised banks/State Bank of India to 33 percent.

In regard to tenure of a Chief Executive of a bank, the Committee indicated a minimum period of three years but the reasonable length of tenure should be not less than five years.

C. Structural Issues

The Committee recommended that after the convergence of activities between Development Financial Institutions DFIs and banks over a period of time, they should get converted into banks, resulting in the existence of only two intermediaries, *viz.*, banks and nonbanks. While mergers between strong financial institutions would make sense, the weak banks in the system will have to be given a revival package subject to a set of criteria.

The licensing of new private sector banks needs a review for their enhancement, while foreign banks will have to be encouraged to extent their operations on certain norms.

All appointments of chairmen, managing directors and executive directors of public sector banks and financial institutions, should be determined by an Appointments Board. The Committee felt the urgent need to raise the competency levels in public sector banks by resorting to a lateral induction of talented personnel. It also felt that the remuneration structure should be flexible and market driven.

The Committee recommended the corporatisation of IDBI. It also desired that the minimum net worth of NBFCs should at the same time to be raised to ₹ 2 crore progressively. For purposes of registration with the Reserve Bank, however, the minimum limit for networth has been doubled to ₹ 50 lakh. Besides, no deposit insurance corporation for NBFCs was proposed.

The Committee proposed prudential and regulatory standards besides new capital norms for Urban Co-operative Banks (UCBs).

D. Integration of Financial Markets

The Committee recommended that banks and primary dealers alone should be allowed in the inter-bank call and notice money markets. Non-Bank Financial Institutions would get access to other forms of instruments in money market like bill rediscounting, CPs Treasury Bills, etc. It also suggested opening the Treasury Bill Market Foreign Institutional Investors for broadening its base.

E. Rural and Small Industrial Credit

The Committee proposed review and strengthening of the operation of Rural Financial Institutions (RFIs) is terms of appraisal, supervision and follow up, loan recovery strategies and development of bank-client relationships in view of higher NPAs in public sector banks due to directed lending. In regard to capital adequacy requirements, RRBs and co-operative banks should reach a minimum of 8 percent capital to risk-weighted assets ratio over a period of 5 years. It also proposed that all regulatory and supervisory functions over rural credit institutions should rest with the Board for Financial Regulation and Supervision (BFRS).

F. Regulation and Supervision

The Committee made a suggestion that the 'Basle Core Principles of Effective bank Supervision' should be regarded as the minimum to be attained. It should be made obligatory for banks to take into account risk weights for market risks to facilitates soundness and stability of the system.

For effective conduct of monetary policy by the Reserve bank, delineation of supervision/regulation from monetary policy is required implying that the Executive associated with monetary authority should not be in the Supervisory Board, to avoid weakening of monetary policy of banking regulation and supervision. The process of separating BFS from the Reserve Bank would need to be initiated and supervise the activities of banks, financial institutions and NBFCs, a new agency in the name of BFR would have to be formed,. With a view to achieving in integrated system of supervision over the financial system, the Committee recommended bringing Urban Co-operative Banks within the amibit of the BFS.

G. Legal and Legislative Framework

The Committee recommended the amendment to RBI Act and Banking Regulations Act with regard to the formation of BFRS. It also gives more autonomy and powers to public sector banks (Nationalisation Act). As wide ranging changes in the legal framework affecting the working of the financial sector are sought by the Committee, an Expert Committee could be constituted comprising representatives from the Ministry of Law, banking Division, Ministry of Finance, the Reserve bank of India and some outside experts.

Source: RBI Annual Report.

Financial Markets-Reform Measures

Since the early 1990s, various measures were initiated in all segments of financial markets aimed at improving depth and liquidity in the markets. The reforms also emphasised on improving the transparency and efficiency of the markets. The key reform measures undertaken in different market segments are briefly presented below.

Money Market

A ceiling of 10 percent on call money rates imposed by the Indian banks Association was withdrawn in 1989.

Initially, the participation in the call market was gradually widened by including non-banks, such as, financial institutions, non-banking finance companies, primary/satellite dealers, mutual funds, corporates (Through primary/dealers), etc. The process of transformation of call money market of a pure inter-bank market commenced effective May 2001.

The 182-day treasury bills were introduced effective November 1986, followed subsequently by phasing out of on-tap treasury bills, introduction of auctioning system in 91-day treasury bills since January 1993, and introduction of 14-day and 364-day treasury bills. The system of *ad hoc* treasury bills (with a fixed 4.6 percent interest rate since July 1974) which were issued by the Central Government to the Reserve Bank, was abolished effective April, 1997. Currently only the 91-day and 364-day treasury bills exist.

The Discount and Finance House of India (DFHI) was set up in April 1988, and was allowed to participate in the call/notice money market both as borrower and lender commencing from July, 1988.

Several new financial instruments were introduced, such as inter-bank participation certificated (1988), certificates deposit (June 1989), commercial paper (January 1990) and repose (December, 1992).

Derivative products like forward rate agreements and interest rate swaps were introduced in July 1999 to enable banks, FIs and PDs to hedge interest rate risks.

A full-fledged Liquidity Adjustment Facility was introduced on June 5, 200 with a view to modulating short-term liquidity under diverse market conditions.

With a view to adopting the sound risk management procedures and eliminating country-party risk, the Clearing Corporation of India Ltd, was set up on February 15, 2002. The CCIL, acts as a central counter-party to all trades involving foreign exchange, government securities and other debt instruments routed through it and guarantees their settlement.

The segments refinance facility for banks is gradually being phased out.

Government Securities Market

New auction-based instruments were introduced with varying maturities such as 364-day, 182 day, 91-day and 14-day treasury bills and the zero coupon bond. The auction system was also introduced for Government of India dated securities. An innovative feature of 'part payment' was added to the auction of Government of India dated securities.

In the long-term segment, Floating Rate bonds (FRBs) benchmarked to the 364-day treasury bills yields and a 10 year loan with embedded call and put options exercisable on or after 5 years from the date of issue were introduced.

A system of Primary Dealers (PDs) was made operational in March 1996.

Foreign Institutional Investors (FIIs) were allowed to set up 100 percent debt funds to invest in Government (Central and State) dated securities in both primary and secondary markets.

The system of automatic monetisation of budget deficit through *ad hoc* treasury bills which hampered the development of the market was phased out over a period of three years from 1993-94 to 1996-97 and was replaced by the system of Ways and Means Advances (WMA) with effect from April 1, 1997.

The Delivery-*versus*-payment system (DvP) was introduced in 1995 for the settlement of transactions in Government securities. A screen-based trade reporting system with the use of VSAT communication network complemented by a centralised Subsidiary General Ledger (SGL) accounting system was put in place.

The Negotiated Dealing System (NDS) (Phase I) was operationalised in February 2002 to enable on-line electronic bidding facility in the primary auctions of Central/State Government securities, OMO/LAF auctions, screen-based electronic dealing and reporting of transactions in money market instruments, including repo and to facilitate information on trades with minimal time lag.

Since timely flow of information is a critical factor in evolving the efficient price discovery mechanism, improvements were brought in transparency of operations and data dissemination.

A practice of pre-annoucing a calender of treasury bills and government securities auctions to the market was introduced.

Retail trading in Government securities at select stock exchanges commenced in January 2003.

Foreign Exchange Market.

The current account was gradually made convertible leading to the acceptance of obligations under Article VII of the IMF. The exchange rate, which was pegged to a basket of currencies, was made market-determined in a phased manner. Several transactions in the capital account were also gradually liberalised over the years.

In line with the liberal policy environment of the 1990s, the Forign Exchange Regulation Act, 1973 (FERA) was replaced by the foreign Exchange Management Act (FEMA) in 1999.

Capital Market

With the repeal of the Capital Issues (Control) Act, 1947, companies were given freedom to price their issues. The book-building process in the new issue of capital was introduced with a view to further strengthen the price discovery process.

In the secondary market, the floor-based open outcry trading system was replaced by electronic trading system in all the stock exchanges.

The account period settlement system was replaced by rolling settlement, thus, reducing the scope for speculation. The rolling settlement cycle was shortened from T + 5 to T + 3 with effect from April 1, 2002. This process was enabled by a shift to electronic book entry transfer system through depository mechanism.

The Indian companies were allowed to raise funds from abroad, through American/Global Depository Receipts (ADRs/GDRs), foreign currency convertible bonds (FCCBs) and external commercial borrowing (ECBs). The Reserve bank allowed two-way fungibility of ADRs/GDRs in February 2002,

Foreign institutional investors (FIIs) were allowed to participate in the capital market. For strengthening the process of information flows from the listed companies, several measures were introduced: (*i*) While sufficient disclosures are mandatory for the companies at the stage of public issue, the listed companies are also required under the listing agreement to make disclosures on a continuing basis; (*ii*) for ensuring quick flow of information to the public, the decision pertaining to dividend, bonus and right announcements or any material event are now required to be disclosed to the public within 15 minutes of the conclusion of the board meeting in which the decisions are taken; (*iii*) the accounting practices were streamlined with norms introduced for segment reporting, related party transactions and consolidated balance sheets.

Insider trading was made a criminal offence. The regulations governing substantial acquisition of shares and takeovers of companies were also introduced aimed at protecting the interests of minority shareholders by making the takeover process more transparent.

For providing market participants instruments for hedging and risk management, several types of derivative products on equities were introduced. Non-transparent products like 'badla' were banned.

Source: RBI Report on Currency and Finance

ANNEXURE - II

INDIAN BANKS' ASSOCIATION (IBA)

IBA is an Association of Commercial banks. Foreign banks operating in India are also members of this Association. It is an advisory service organisation for the Commercial banks. It takes care of the interest of banking industry and serves as a forum for exchange of views among bankers. Its main activities include the following:

1. Promoting banking culture, encouraging academic achievement in banking related matters;
2. Exchange of ideas and views on systems, procedures, operations and administration of banks in India;
3. Help evolve common ideas and thinking on major banking policies and problems;
4. Collection and interpretation of banking data for improved performance of banks;
5. Negotiating with labour union of banks on wage settlement, service conditions, customer service, etc.
6. Encouraging sports and cultural activities among bank employees;
7. Organising meetings and seminars and releasing publicity measures to project the good of banks;
8. Conduct examination and award diplomas in banking related subjects;
9. Co-ordinate with RBI on behalf of banks;
10. Advising members of public through advertisements about new banking facilities, customer service, proposed labour strike, bank closure, etc.

Normally, one of the Chairmen of a Commercial bank is elected as the Chairman of IBA. The secretariat of IBA is situated in Mumbai and the expenses of its secretariat are met through member-banks' subscriptions, examination fees, etc. It also brings out a monthly journal known as "The Indian Institute of Bankers".

ANNEXURE - III

LIST OF PUBLIC SECTOR BANKS, PRIVATE SECTOR BANKS AND FOREIGN BANKS

(As at end-March 2010)

Sr. No.	*Name of the Bank*	*Sr. No.*	*Name of the Bank*
	Nationalised Banks		**Private Sector Banks**
1.	Allahabad Bank		*Old Private Sector Banks*
2.	Andhra Bank	1.	Bank of Rajasthan Ltd.
3.	Bank of Baroda	2.	Catholic Syrian Bank Ltd.
4.	Bank of India	3.	City Union Bank Ltd.
5.	Bank of Maharashtra	4.	Dhanalakshmi Bank Ltd.
6.	Canara Bank	5.	Federal Bank Ltd.
7.	Central Bank of India	6.	ING Vysya Bank Ltd.
8.	Corporation Bank	7.	Jammu & Kashmir Bank Ltd.
9.	Dena Bank	8.	Karnataka Bank Ltd.
10.	IDBI Bank Ltd.	9.	Karur Vysya Bank Ltd.
11.	Indian Bank	10.	Lakshmi Vilas Bank Ltd.
12.	Indian Overseas Bank	11.	Nainital Bank Ltd.
13.	Orriental Bank of Commerce	12.	Ratnakar Bank Ltd.
14.	Punjab & Sind Bank	13.	SBI Commercial & International Bank Ltd.
15.	Punjab National Bank		
16.	Syndicate Bank	14.	South Indian Bank Ltd.
17.	UCO Bank	15.	Tamilnad Mercantile Bank Ltd.
18.	Union Bank of India		**New Private Sector Banks**
19.	United Bank of India	16.	Axis Bank Ltd.
20.	Vijaya Bank	17.	Development Credit Bank Ltd.
	State Bank Group	18.	HDFC Bank Ltd.
21.	State Bank of Bikaner & Jaipur	19.	ICICI Bank Ltd.
22.	State Bank of Hyderabad	20.	IndusInd Bank Ltd.
23.	State Bank of India	21.	Kotak Mahindra Bank Ltd.
24.	State Bank of Mysore	22.	Yes Bank Ltd.
25.	State Bank of Patiala		
26.	State Bank of Travancore		

Sr. No.	*Name of the Bank*
	Foreign Banks
1.	AB Bank Ltd.
2.	Abu Dhabi Commercial Bank Ltd.
3.	American Express Banking Corp.
4.	Antwerp Diamond Bank NV
5.	BNP Paribas
6.	Bank of America N.T. & S.A.
7.	Bank of Bahrain & Kuwait B.S.C.
8.	Bank of Ceylon
9.	Bank of Nova Scotia
10.	Barclays Bank PLC
11.	Chinatrust Commercial Bank
12.	Citibank N.A.
13.	Commonwealth Bank of Australia
14.	Credit Agricole Corporate and Investment
15.	Deutshi Bank (Asia)
16.	Development Bank of Singapore Ltd.
17.	FirstRand Bank
18.	HSBC Ltd.
19.	JPMorgan Chase Bank
20.	JSC VTB Bank
21.	Krung Tnai Bank Public Co. Ltd.
22.	Mashrec Bank PSC
23.	Mizuho Corporate Bank Ltd.
24.	Oman International Bank S.A.O.G.
25.	Shinhan Bank
26.	Societe Generale
27.	Sonali Bank
28.	Standard Chartered Bank
29.	State Bank of Mauritius Ltd.
30.	The Bank of Tokyo-Mitsubushi UFJ. Ltd.
31.	The Royal Bank of Scotland N.V
32.	UBS AG

Excluding IDBI the total number of Public Sector Commercial Banks = 19 + 6 = 26

Source: RBI Publications.

MODEL QUESTION PAPERS

Question Paper - 1

PART - A

Choose the best answer for each of the following from the given alternatives

1. Number of subsidiaries of S.B.I. is
(*a*) 10 (*b*) 8 (*c*) 7 (*d*) 9

2. Most idle asset from the bankers point of view is
(*a*) B/R (*b*) investment (*c*) premises (*d*) cash

3. Merchant banking concept was first introduced by
(*a*) SBI (*b*) RBI (*c*) Co-op. bank (*d*) none

4. Main focus of mutual funds advertising during February and March is on
(*a*) capital association (*b*) tax benefit (*c*) liquidity (*d*) safety

5. Which of the following is not a Quantitative weapons of credit control
(*a*) bankrupt (*b*) open market operation
(*c*) variable reserve ratio (*d*) direct action

6. RBI is governed by the
(*a*) Banking Company Regulation Act (*b*) RBI Act 1934
(*c*) Central Finance Act (*d*) none

7. Money market deals with
(*a*) short term fund (*b*) long term fund
(*c*) medium term fund (*d*) bills

8. Main reason for the popularity of London money market is the existence of
(*a*) acceptance house (*b*) discount house
(*c*) acceptance & discount house (*d*) none

9. The bank which provides mainly to the requirements of the farmers in village is
(*a*) Regional Rural Bank (*b*) Co.op. Banks
(*c*) SBI (*d*) RBI

10. SBI was established on the recommendations of the
(*a*) All India Rural Credit Survey (*b*) Rural Credit and Investment Committee
(*c*) Finance Committee–Govt. of India (*d*) none

PART - B

11. (*a*) State the advantages of Unit banking.

Or

(*b*) List out the limitations of credit creation by commercial banks.

12. (*a*) What is merchant banking ? What are the services offered by it ?

Or

(*b*) Explain any four important steps taken by commercial banks to improve the customer services in banks.

13. (*a*) Discuss the role of RBI as bankers bank.

Or

(*b*) What is open market operation ? How does it controls credit ?

14. (*a*) What are the features of American money market ?

Or

(*b*) Explain the drawbacks of Indian money market.

15. (*a*) State the reasons for the failure of Regional Rural Banks in India.

Or

(*b*) Discuss the role of Co-op banks in the provision of rural credit.

PART - C

16. (*a*) Explain the role of commercial banks in economic development of a country.

Or

(*b*) Explain the process of credit creation by banks with suitable examples.

17. (*a*) What are the objectives of nationalisation of commercial banks in India ? How far these objectives have been achieved by them ?

Or

(*b*) Trace out the recent trends in Indian banking and explain it.

18. (*a*) Discuss the different selective credit control methods adopted by central bank.

Or

(*b*) Discuss the roll of RBI as a government bank.

19. (*a*) What are the features of Indian money market ? Can it be called a developed one ?

Or

(*b*) Compare British money market with American money market.

20. (*a*) Bringout clearly the roll of SBI in the development of small scale industries.

Or

(*b*) Explain the roll of RBI in the rural development of India.

MODEL QUESTION PAPERS

Question Paper - 2

PART - A

Choose the best answer for each of the following from the given alternatives

1. Unit banking system is popular in:
(*a*) Great Britain (*b*) America (*c*) India (*d*) Pakistan

2. Primary deposit is otherwise known as:
(*a*) Cash deposit (*b*) Created deposit (*c*) Fixed deposit (*d*) Current deposit

3. At present India has _______ nationalised banks:
(*a*) 20 (*b*) 21 (*c*) 19 (*d*) 22

4. Among the banks given below, which one is a private sector bank ?
(*a*) Dena Bank (*b*) Canara Bank
(*c*) City Union bank (*d*) Central Bank of India

5. The Central Banking institution of India is:
(*a*) Central Bank of India (*b*) Reserve Bank of India
(*c*) State Bank of India (*d*) Union Bank of India

6. The prevailing bank rate in India is:
(*a*) 10% (*b*) 11% (*c*) 12% (*d*) none of the above

7. The leader of the Indian money market is:
(*a*) Government of India (*b*) Ministry of Finance
(*c*) Indian Bank Association (*d*) Reserve Bank of India

8. The other name for American money market is:
(*a*) Washington Money Market (*b*) California Money Market
(*c*) Federal Reserve System (*d*) Newyork Money Market

9. The Head Office of the State Bank of India is located at
(*a*) New Delhi (*b*) Calcutta
(*c*) Bombay (*d*) Madras

10. The number of Regional Rural Banks operating in Tamil Nadu is:
(*a*) three (*b*) four (*c*) five (*d*) two

PART - B

11. (*a*) What is branch banking ? What are its advantages.

Or

(*b*) Draw a balance sheet of a commercial bank, briefly explain the various items appearing in the balance sheet.

12. (*a*) Explain the concept of merchant banking.

Or

(*b*) Explain the concept of mutual.

13. (*a*) What are qualitative credit control methods ?

Or

(*b*) How the Reserve Bank of India exercises control over banks ?

14. (*a*) What are the salient features of the London money market ?

Or

(*b*) What are the salient features of the New York money market ?

15. (*a*) Critically analyse the functioning of Regional Rural Banks.

Or

(*b*) Critically analyse the functioning of commercial banks in rural finance.

PART - C

16. (*a*) Explain the function of commercial banks.

Or

(*b*) Explain the process of credit creation by banks.

17. (*a*) 'Nationalisation of commercial banks is a success' - Elaborate.

Or

(*b*) 'Nationalisation of commercial banks is a failure' Elaborate.

18. (*a*) Explain the function of central bank.

Or

(*b*) How the quantitative methods control the volume of credit ?

19. (*a*) Explain the composition of the Indian money market.

Or

(*b*) Explain the deficiencies of the Indian money market.

20. (*a*) 'State Bank of India is instrumental for economic growth' - Explain.

Or

(*b*) What is the place of co-operative banks in the Indian banking system ?

MODEL QUESTION PAPERS

Question Paper - 3

PART - A

Choose the correct answer to each of the following from the given alternatives

1. Commercial banks in India are governed by the
(*a*) Banking Regulation Act (*b*) Reserve Bank of India Act
(*c*) Regional Rural Banks Act (*d*) Negotiable Instruments Act

2. The primary function of a commercial bank is
(*a*) lending (*b*) providing subsidiary services
(*c*) accepting deposits (*d*) accepting deposits and lending

3. The first private sector bank set up in India after the implementation of financial sector reforms is
(*a*) Bank of Madura (*b*) The IDBI Bank
(*c*) The American Express Bank (*d*) The UTI Bank

4. Factoring includes
(*a*) management of fixed assets (*b*) management of man power
(*c*) cash management (*d*) management of receivables

5. The Governor of the RBI is
(*a*) Dr. Manmohan Singh (*b*) Mr. M. Gopalakrishnan
(*c*) Dr. C. Rangarajan (*d*) Mr. D.R. Mehta

6. One rupee currency notes of India is issued by
(*a*) The Ministry of Finance, Government of India
(*b*) The Reserve Bank of India
(*c*) The state bank of India
(*d*) Concerned State Government

7. Treasury bills are
(*a*) instruments used in the money market (*b*) instruments used in the capital market
(*c*) securities issued by banks (*d*) liabilities of moneylenders

8. The leader of the London Money Market is
(*a*) Barclays Bank
(*b*) Bank of Credit and Commerce International Ltd.
(*c*) House of Commons
(*d*) Bank of England

9. The share capital of the State Bank of India is contributed by
(*a*) the Government of India (*b*) the Reserve Bank of India
(*c*) the public (*d*) the Government of India and the public

10. Interest rates given by banks on deposits is determined by
(*a*) the market forces (*b*) the RBI
(*c*) the Indian Banks Association (*d*) the individual banks

PART - B

11. (*a*) What are the various factors that determined that cash balance of a bank ?

Or

(*b*) What are the functions of a commercial bank ?

12. (*a*) What are the services rendered by a merchant banker ?

Or

(*b*) State the advantages of investing funds in a mutual fund.

13. (*a*) What are the assumptions of the bank rate policy ?

Or

(*b*) How does the RBI control credit ?

14. (*a*) What are the deficiencies of the Indian Money Market ?

Or

(*b*) What is the composition of the London money Market ?

15. (*a*) What are the differences between a commercial bank and a Regional Rural Bank ?

Or

(*b*) What are the functions of NABARD ?

PART - C

16. (*a*) Explain the main items of the assets appearing in the Balance Sheet of a Commercial bank.

Or

(*b*) Explain the role of commercial banks in the economic development of a nation.

17. (*a*) Explain the objectives of bank nationalisation.

Or

(*b*) Explain the importance of better customer service in banks.

18. (*a*) Explain the function of central bank.

Or

(*b*) Explain the role of a central bank in a developing economy.

19. (*a*) Discuss the features of a developed money market.

Or

(*b*) Explain the structure of the Indian money Market.

20. (*a*) Explain the sources of rural financing.

Or

(*b*) Explain the role of co-operative banks in rural credit.

MODEL QUESTION PAPERS

Question Paper - 4

Answers all the questions

PART - A

Choose the best answer for each of the following from the given alternatives

1. A primary deposit is created when a bank:
   (*a*) Lends money to the public (*b*) Lends money to the Government
   (*c*) Accepts money from the public (*d*) Invests money on shares.
2. The most liquid asset from the banker's point of view is:
   (*a*) Cash (*b*) Bills receivable (*c*) Investments (*d*) Gold
3. A document which facilitates a farmer to purchase his requirements on credit is
   (*a*) Letter of credit (*b*) Credit card (*c*) Gold card (*d*) Green card
4. In India, the major 14 banks were nationalised in the year:
   (*a*) 1967 (*b*) 1969 (*c*) 1971 (*d*) 1980
5. Which one of the following is a quantitative weapon of credit control ?
   (*a*) Variable reserve ratio (*b*) Direction action
   (*c*) Regulation of consumer credit (*d*) Moral Suasion
6. The loans provided by the Reserve Bank of India to the Government are called:
   (*a*) Call loans (*b*) Government loans
   (*c*) Ways and means advances (*d*) Treasury loans.
7. The major institution of the Indian money market is:
   (*a*) Commercial banks (*b*) Reserve Bank of India
   (*c*) Co-operative banks (*d*) Non-banking financial companies
8. The market where loans are given extremely for a short period not exceeding 7 days is called:
   (*a*) Money Market (*b*) Collateral loan market
   (*c*) Call money market (*d*) Acceptance Market
9. The State bank of India was established by nationalising the:
   (*a*) Presidency Banks (*b*) Bank of Jaipur
   (*c*) Bank of Indore (*d*) Imperial Bank of India
10. The rural banks were established mainly to give credit to:
    (*a*) Small farmers (*b*) Small farmers and artisans
    (*c*) Big farmers (*d*) Small and medium farmers

PART - B

11. (*a*) State the demerits of branch banking.

Or

(*b*) What factors determine the investment policy of a commercial bank ?

12. (*a*) Discuss any four recent steps taken by commercial banks to improve the customer service in banks.

Or

(*b*) What is a mutual fund ? What are its benefits ?

13. (*a*) How does a central bank act as Banker's bank ?

Or

(*b*) Explain the different methods of issuing currency notes. Which method is followed by the Reserve bank of India ?

14. (*a*) Bring out any four monetary instruments recently introduced in India.

Or

(*b*) What are the constituents of the Indian Money Market ?

15. (*a*) Analyse the special problems faced by the co-operative banks in providing agricultural credit.

Or

(*b*) "Commercial banks are reluctant to enter into rural areas" Discuss.

PART - C

16. (*a*) Explain the process of multiple expansion of bank credit with suitable illustrations.

Or

(*b*) Discuss the role of commercial banks in the economic development of a country.

17. (*a*) Discuss the recent trends in bank lending.

Or

(*b*) What is Merchant banking ? Examine the services rendered by a merchant bank.

18. (*a*) How does a central bank control the flow of credit ?

Or

(*b*) Discuss the role of the Reserve bank of India in controlling and regulating the commercial banks in India.

19. (*a*) What are the deficiencies of the Indian Money Market ? Suggest measures to overcome them.

Or

(*b*) Compare British Money Market with that of the American Money Market.

20. (*a*) Evaluate the role of the Regional Rural banks in the provision of rural credit.

Or

(*b*) Define a small scale unit. Explain the role of the State Bank of India in the promotion of small scale industries in India.

MODEL QUESTION PAPERS

Question Paper - 5

PART - A

Choose the best answer for each of the following from the given alternatives

1. In India Monopoly of Note issue is in the hands of
(*a*) Central bank of India (*b*) State Bank of India
(*c*) Reserve bank of India (*d*) None of the above

2. Unit banking system is famous in
(*a*) England (*b*) United States of America
(*c*) Germany (*d*) India

3. Nationalisation of 14 Commercial Banks took place in
(*a*) 1959 (*b*) 1969 (*c*) 1979 (*d*) 1989

4. Investment banking and portfolio management is done by
(*a*) Mutual Fund (*b*) Merchant Banking (*c*) SEBI (*d*) None of the above

5. Reserve Bank of India was started as a bank owned by
(*a*) Private individuals (*b*) Central Government
(*c*) Central and State Govenments (*d*) None of the above

6. Rationing of credit is a
(*a*) Quantitative credit control method (*b*) Selective credit control method
(*c*) Direct credit control method (*d*) None of the above

7. Money market means
(*a*) A place where money is dealt with
(*b*) Occasional markets to transact money business
(*c*) Market in which short-term funds are borrowed and lent.
(*d*) None of the above

8. The leader of the Indian money market is
(*a*) Unit Trust of India (*b*) State bank of India
(*c*) Stock Exchange (*d*) None of the above

9. State Bank of India was formed by the Nationalisation of
(*a*) Imperial Bank of India (*b*) Palai Central Bank
(*c*) National Bank of India (*d*) None of the above

10. Regional Rural Banks are started to bring about
(*a*) Speedy rural development (*b*) Agricultural revolution
(*c*) Industrial revolution (*d*) None of the above

PART - B

11. (*a*) Bring out the merits and defects of Unit Banking.

Or

(*b*) Write a short note on evolution of Indian Banking System.

12. (*a*) What do you mean by a 'Mutual Fund' ? What are its main functions ?

Or

(*b*) Write a brief note on Merchant Banking.

13. (*a*) Analyse the need for Central Bank in a country.

Or

(*b*) Describe any two methods of note issue.

14. (*a*) Why is Indian money market termed as an undeveloped one ?

Or

(*b*) Mention the importance of developed money market.

15. (*a*) Examine the role of Regional Rural Banks in Rural Development.

Or

(*b*) Write a brief note on Co-operative Banks and rural credit.

PART - C

16. (*a*) Describe the various functions performed by a modern Commercial bank.

Or

(*b*) Describe credit creation by Commercial Banks.

17. (*a*) Comment on the recent trends in commercial Banking in India.

Or

(*b*) Detail the force which forced the government to nationalise 14 Commercial Banks in india.

18. (*a*) Critically examine the role of RBI in regulating and controlling credit.

Or

(*b*) Briefly describe the functions of a Central Bank.

19. (*a*) What are the characteristics of a developed money market ?

Or

(*b*) Compare British money market with American money market.

20. (*a*) Write briefly about State Bank and rural credit.

Or

(*b*) Analyse the role of State Bank of India in Indian Economy.

MODEL QUESTION PAPERS

Question Paper - 6

PART - A

Choose the best answer for each of the following from the given alternatives

1. Which of the following bank is the Central Bank of our country ?

(*a*) Central Bank of India (*b*) State Bank of India
(*c*) Reserve Bank of India (*d*) None of the above

2. Branch banking system was first followed by the following country:

(*a*) England (*b*) America (*c*) India (*d*) None of the above

3. In 1969 the following number of Commercial Banks were Nationalised:

(*a*) 6 (*b*) 12 (*c*) 14 (*d*) 20

4. Credit cards are issued by the following institution:

(*a*) Reserve Bank of India (*b*) Government of India
(*c*) Commercial Banks (*d*) None of the above

5. Credit control function is done by the following bank:

(*a*) Industrial Development Bank of India (*b*) Reserve Bank of India
(*c*) State Bank of India (*d*) None of the above

6. Which of the folowing methods is not a quantitative credit control method ?

(*a*) Open Market operation (*b*) Bank Rate
(*c*) Variation of Cash Reserve Ratio (*d*) Direct action

7. Which of the following is not a part of the organised Money Market ?

(*a*) Bill Market (*b*) Acceptance Houses
(*c*) Money lenders (*d*) Discount Houses

8. London money Market is a

(*a*) Underdeveloped Money Market (*b*) Developing Money market
(*c*) Developed Money Market (*d*) None of the above

9. Before nationalisation, State Bank of India was names as the following:

(*a*) Indian National Bank (*b*) Imperial Bank of India
(*c*) Presidency Bank (*d*) None of the above

10. Which of the following Bank is the leader of the Indian Money Market ?

(*a*) State Bank of India (*b*) Indian Bank
(*c*) Industrial Development Bank (*d*) Reserve Bank of India

PART - B

11. (*a*) Define a Branch banking. What are its merits ?

Or

(*b*) Briefly explain the evoluation of Commercial Banking in India.

12. (*a*) Explain how the assets are listed in the Balance Sheet of a Commercial Bank.

Or

(*b*) What is Merchant Banking ? What are the services rendered by a Merchant Banker ?

13. (*a*) Explain any four methods of qualitative credit control methods of R.B.I. ?

Or

(*b*) Explain the function of note issuing by the R.B.I.

14. (*a*) Make a comparison of Indian money Market with that of American Money Market.

Or

(*b*) Explain how the Indian Money Market is constituted.

15. (*a*) What role is played by Commercial Banks in rural finance ?

Or

(*b*) What are Regional rural banks ? What are its objectives ?

PART - C

16. (*a*) Explain the process of credit creation by Commercial Banks.

Or

(*b*) What are the functions of modern Commercial Banks ?

17. (*a*) Explain the following:

(*i*) Mutual Fund (*ii*) Credit Cards (*iii*) Customer Service

Or

(*b*) What are the causes for the Nationalisation of Commercial banks in India ?

18. (*a*) Briefly explain the role of R.B.I. in regulating and controlling the Commercial Banks in the country ?

Or

(*b*) What are the quantitative methods of credit control adopted by the R.B.I. ?

19. (*a*) What are the defects of Indian Money Market ?

Or

(*b*) Compare and contrast the Indian Money Market and London Money Market.

20. (*a*) Explain the role played by the State bank of India in the banking field.

Or

(*b*) What is the importance of co-operative banks in the Indian Banking System ? Explain the various types of co-operative banks.

MODEL QUESTION PAPERS

Question Paper - 7

Answer all the Questions

PART - A

Choose the Correct Answer

1. The secondary reserve of a commercial bank is ___________

(*a*) Money (*b*) Money at call and short notice (*c*) Bills

2. The most perfect liquid asset of a bank is ___________

(*a*) Bank balance (*b*) Cash (*c*) Shortterm investments

3. Nationalisation of banks increases ___________

(*a*) Bank expansion (*b*) Deposit mobilisation (*c*) All the above

4. Service area approach is a ___________

(*a*) Credit plan (*b*) Avoid implication of credit (*c*) All the above

5. Present bank rate in India is ___________

(*a*) 10% (*b*) 12% (*c*) 11.5%

6. Quantitative credit control weapons are applicable to ___________

(*a*) All trade transactions (*b*) Only selected transactions

(*c*) All the above

7. NABARD was stated in ___________

(*a*) 1st July 1982 (*b*) 1st July 1980 (*c*) 1st July 1976

8. Two tier system of credit extended by Co-operative banks to ___________ period.

(*a*) ST, MT and LT (*b*) LT only (*c*) MT and LT.

9. Important component of money market is ___________

(*a*) RBI (*b*) Bill market (*c*) Regulated market

10. Money market mutual funds was marked in ___________

(*a*) 1990 (*b*) 1989 (*c*) 1992

PART - B

11. (*a*) What are the merits of unit banking ?

Or

(*b*) Who can influence bank liquidity ?

12. (*a*) State the limitations of credit creation.

Or

(*b*) State the factors which have influenced deposit growth in India.

13. (*a*) What are the limitations of selective credit control system ?

Or

(*b*) What are the differences between commercial bank and central bank of a country ?

14. (*a*) What is Money Market ?

Or

(*b*) What are the steps taken by RBI to improve the Indian Bill Market ?

15. (*a*) Explain the role of SBI in rural credit.

Or

(*b*) State the need for institutional Finance in India.

PART - C

16. (*a*) State the merits of Branch Banking system.

Or

(*b*) Describe the main items of a bank's assets.

17. (*a*) Explain the concept of diversification in banking.

Or

(*b*) Explain the role of RBI in regulating banks.

18. (*a*) Explain the Reserve Ratio as one of the weapons of credit control measures adopted by RBI.

Or

(*b*) Explain the theory of open market operation as a weapon for controlling credit.

19. (*a*) Explain the components of money market.

Or

(*b*) Describe the new instruments introduced in the Indian money market.

20. (*a*) Explain the Multi-Agency approach in Rural Finance.

Or

(*b*) What are the causes for the slow growth of Co-operative PACBs ?

PART - D

21. (*a*) Describe the components of credit planning.

Or

(*b*) Discuss the functions of RBI.

22. (*a*) Discuss the features and weaknesses of Indian Money Market.

Or

(*b*) What are the weaknesses of RRBs and give your suggestions for improvement ?